International and Cultural Psychology

Series Editor

Anthony J. Marsella, Alpharetta, GA, USA

This book series explores problems and challenges to mental health, psychosocial wellbeing, human growth and development, and human welfare that are emerging from our contemporary global context. It advances psychological knowledge regarding the nature and consequences of the many social, cultural, economic, political, and environmental events and forces that affect individuals and communities throughout the world.

The series covers areas like therapy, assessment, organizational psychology, community psychology, gender, child development, and specific disorders. In addition, it addresses major global challenges such as poverty, peace, urbanization, modernization, refugees, and migration. The series acknowledges the multidisciplinary, multisectoral, and multicultural nature of the global context of our lives, and publishes books that reflect this reality. Publish your next book in this series! Send your manuscript to Series Editor: Anthony J. Marsella, marsella@hawaii.edu.

More information about this series at http://www.springer.com/series/6089

Grant J. Rich • Neeta A. Ramkumar
Editors

Psychology in Oceania and the Caribbean

Springer

Editors
Grant J. Rich
Walden University
Juneau, AK, USA

Neeta A. Ramkumar
Psychology Across Borders
Austin, TX, USA

ISSN 1571-5507 ISSN 2197-7984 (electronic)
International and Cultural Psychology
ISBN 978-3-030-87762-0 ISBN 978-3-030-87763-7 (eBook)
https://doi.org/10.1007/978-3-030-87763-7

This Springer imprint is published by the registered company Springer Nature Switzerland AG
The registered company address is: Gewerbestrasse 11, 6330 Cham, Switzerland

To our parents

Mom and Dad, together you taught me both the value of the science of modernity and the value of honoring our ancestors, family, and heritage. My gratitude for showing me the significance of both looking back as well as looking forward, while never forgetting the present.

– Grant J. Rich

Mom and Dad, you taught me to live in new homelands, as our ancestors before us. Together you showed me how to honor our traditions and roots while navigating change and embracing new cultures. Thank you for the gift of raising me across and between worlds.

– Neeta A. Ramkumar

And to the descendants of all peoples whose ancestors have been colonized, exploited, and displaced across the lands and seas of the Earth. May we honor their histories and celebrate their resilience and strengths.

Foreword

One definition of psychology is the study of behavior and mental processes. What this broad definition makes clear is the fact that psychology applies in every cultural and national context, as well as in every area of human endeavor. Although behaviors may be very different in different parts of the world, people everywhere are concerned with promoting psychological well-being and reducing psychological distress. However, psychological research has been concentrated on populations in Western industrialized countries, especially the United States (Arnett, 2008), and even within these countries, on populations of European descent (e.g., Arnett, 2008; Guthrie, 2004).

In addition to the limited base of psychological knowledge on people of color, culture is often absent in the interpretation of psychological findings (Brady et al., 2018). As Brady et al. (2018, p. 11412) observed:

> Building interpretive power requires understanding how culture, experience, and context shape both researchers' and subjects' perspectives, experiences, and behaviors. It requires understanding that people are products of their cultural environments just as their thoughts, attitudes, and behaviors shape and reinforce these environments (5). Rather than regarding differences as problematic or dismissing them as noise, psychologists with interpretive power view differences as generative and work to understand their causal influences.

Without interpretive power related to culture, psychology cannot contribute in the ways that it can and should in different contexts, and this is a concern that psychologists need to address. Finally, there is a limited knowledge on psychology and its role in several parts of the world, especially in countries in Africa, the Caribbean, and the South Pacific. Thus, this book is timely because it provides information on psychology in countries where psychological science and practice are nascent or still very young, and equally importantly, the chapters acknowledge the role of culture.

To highlight the importance of this book, let me provide an example of the gap that this book is addressing. As a school psychologist, one psychological construct that I am very interested in is learning, and in April of 2021, I participated in a panel discussing findings on the construct of growth mindset from the Programme for International Student Assessment (PISA) 2018 data collection conducted by the

Organisation for Economic Co-operation and Development. Growth mindset (Dweck, 2016) is an extremely popular construct related to learning outcomes in the United States, and PISA chose to ask about this construct in the 2018 data collection. In preparing for my presentation, I looked up the 79 countries that were included in the PISA study (Gouëdard, 2021), and perhaps not surprisingly, the majority of the countries included in this book were not included in the PISA study.

The PISA report indicated that the percentage of individuals who endorsed a growth mindset differed across countries:

> Overall, a majority of students present a growth mindset in PISA: in 53 countries and economies more than 50% of students disagreed with a fixed mindset statement. However, some countries lag behind: in 25 countries and economies, more than 50% of students agreed with a fixed mindset statement. The contrasting landscape of growth mindset in PISA makes the case that every student can develop a growth mindset. When a group of students (for instance, girls vs boys, disadvantaged vs advantaged, immigrant vs non-immigrant) is less likely to exhibit growth mindset, this should raise questions as to whether they benefitted from adequate resources and learning environment. (Gouëdard, 2021, p. 17)

Additionally, although growth mindset was positively associated with PISA academic outcomes, growth mindset was less strongly associated with achievement in East Asian countries than in the other parts of the world. Similarly, growth mindset was significantly associated with educational expectations in 37 countries, but also not associated with educational expectations in 37 other countries. Gouëdard (2021) cautioned against drawing causal conclusions from the correlational data that is included in the report. However, these data also speak to the importance of national and cultural contexts and why these are important in psychology. What works in one context does not necessarily work in another, and the fundamental premise of the PISA report—that growth mindset should be cultivated in all students—is one that is premature in the absence of further research.

Although based in the United States, I am a native of Trinidad and Tobago who has worked on bringing psychology back to that country and I have collaborated with colleagues in many parts of the world, including New Zealand and Fiji. Thus, I am delighted to learn from psychologists based in countries in which psychology is still relatively new. Our discipline has been an important one for some time, and I would argue that it has taken on more importance in the context of the Covid-19 pandemic. Psychology has implications for health and mental health and education and work and diversity and discrimination among many other things. Thus, psychology has implications for hope and future possibilities on individuals and social groups and, ultimately, societies. It is my belief that all of us—those in the countries represented in the chapters in this book and those who live elsewhere—will benefit from the documentation of psychology in these contexts heretofore underserved by our discipline.

Graduate School of Education
University of California, Berkeley
Berkeley, CA, USA

Frank C. Worrell
frankc@berkeley.edu

References

Arnett, J. J. (2008). The neglected 95%. Why American psychology needs to become less American. *American Psychologist, 63*, 602–614. https://doi.org/10.1037/0003-066X.63.7.602

Brady, L. M., Fryberg, S. A., & Shoda, Y. (2018). Expanding the interpretive power of psychological science by attending to culture. *Proceedings of the National Academy of Sciences, 115*(45), 11406–11413. https://doi.org/10.1073/pnas.1803526115

Dweck, C. S. (2016). *Mindset–The new psychology of success: How we can learn to fulfil our potential* (Updated ed.). Ballantine Books.

Gouëdard, P. (2021). *Sky's the limit: Growth mindset, students and schools in Pisa.* Organisation for Economic Co-operation and Development. https://www.oecd.org/pisa/growth-mindset.pdf

Guthrie, R. V. (2004). *Even the rat was white: A historical view of psychology* (2nd ed.). Upper Saddle Rive, NJ: Pearson.

Preface: Psychology in Oceania and the Caribbean: An Overview Chapter

Introduction

Sun and Sand. Surf and Turf. Rest and Relaxation. A Tropical Paradise. Many psychologists are likely to conjure up such images of palm-fringed shores when first thinking of life in Oceania and the Caribbean, the geographic foci of this book. In fact, perhaps gentle reader, you have enjoyed such a vacation, sabbatical, or winter escape from academic responsibilities in one of these island nations. Yet just how realistic are such visions? Is everyday life in such places as idyllic and carefree as imagined?

There is a relative paucity of research concerning the realities of life in the Caribbean and Oceania from a psychological perspective. With about one million psychologists in the world, psychology is growing more quickly outside the mainland United States and Western Europe than within it (Zoma & Gielen, 2015). Our world is globalizing, yet our psychology, and our psychologists, too often represent dominant culture male perspectives with research based on what has justly been termed WEIRD (Western, Educated, Industrialized, Rich, and Democratic) populations (Henrich, 2020), neglecting whole peoples, cultures, and continents, let alone the islanders of the archipelagos of the book. This volume offers a corrective to the dominant paradigm through the knowledge and experiences of top-notch psychologists and mental health professionals in the Caribbean and Oceania and their colleagues.

The reader will observe diverse, rich cultural traditions, resilient communities, and abundant economic opportunities in many island nations. On the flip side, these regions also reflect the challenges of modernity, including poverty, crime, ethnic tensions, migration, and disparities in health and education. Many countries featured in this book face high treatment gaps across all psychological disorders due to the scarcity of mental health resources and inequalities in accessing them. Psychologists and mental health professionals with interests in life in such nations will find this book to be a must-read, as will other readers seeking to deepen their cultural and international understandings.

When first conceptualizing and proposing this book project we did receive some puzzled looks by persons who wondered what the two regions—so widely geographically dispersed—could share beyond paradisical imaginations, and why they should be presented in one volume together. Careful readers will note that several common themes emerge both within and between Oceania and the Caribbean. The historic transit of peoples across the Caribbean and Pacific are records of cross-cultural contact, dark narratives of slavery and blackbirding, and accelerated change. For instance, many chapters describe behavioral health-care systems that reflect challenges shared by island communities: small populations, postcolonial societies fraught with political tension as new national and cultural identities emerge, and economies tested by the relative remoteness of some islands. Moreover, while responding to natural disasters may not be a typical competency of mainland psychologists, the psychosocial strain associated with climate change is profound in island regions. With few exceptions, the majority of island populations and infrastructure are located near coastal areas or on flood plains. As such the social, economic, and psychological impact due to natural disasters is among the world's highest in island nations.

In this chapter, the authors first aim to offer capsule descriptions of the Caribbean and then Oceania, highlighting some key geographic, demographic, historical, and sociocultural points, recognizing that even if readers have visited or indeed reside in one nation/island, that they may be less familiar with other regions. The last part of this chapter orients the reader to the structure of the subsequent chapters on psychology in the Caribbean and Oceania. The authors of this chapter suspect that upon completing this chapter, and indeed the book, the reader will see points of connection between the situation of the Pacific Islands and the Caribbean in the early twenty-first century. We also hope that leveraging lessons learned can stimulate thinking on one's own topic of interest and perhaps invite evidence-based adaptation and modification of existing practices or lead to creative insights and innovations for indigenous psychologies. Now, to work!

The Caribbean

In brief, one may describe the Caribbean as that region of the world that includes the Caribbean Sea, with its 700 islands, as well as surrounding coasts. Within the region, several methods of categorizing the Caribbean exist. One approach divides the Caribbean into the Greater Antilles in the north, with the Lesser Antilles and the Leeward Antilles to the south and to the east. If one includes the Lucayan Archipelago, together that would comprise the classic West Indies, though technically the Bahamas and Turks and Caicos (which comprise the Lucayan Archipelago) are not located in the Caribbean Sea. It should also be noted that a number of continental nations do have Caribbean coastlines, including islands. These nations include Belize, Colombia, Costa Rica, French Guiana, Guatemala, Guyana, Honduras, Nicaragua, Panama, Mexico, Suriname, the USA, and Venezuela. In addition, a number of scholars will include Belize in Central America, as well as Suriname and Guyana in South America, as part of the Caribbean, as even though these nations are physically located in Central and South America, they share much in common culturally with the island Caribbean nations. Indeed, this book features chapters on Belize, Guyana, and Suriname, viewing these nations as part of the Caribbean.

The Greater Antilles includes independent nations such as Haiti, the Dominican Republic, Jamaica, and Cuba, as well as those with connections to colonial powers such as Puerto Rico and the Cayman Islands. There are full chapters on each of these countries, save the Cayman Islands, representing the Greater Antilles in this book. The Lesser Antilles include the Leeward Islands, the Windward Islands, and the Leeward Antilles. The Leeward islands include the US (e.g., St. Croix and St. Thomas) and British Virgin Islands, Anguilla, Antigua and Barbuda, St. Martin, Saba, Sint Eustatius, Saint Barthélemy, St. Kitts and Nevis, Montserrat, and Guadeloupe. Representing the Leeward Islands is a chapter on St. Kitts and Nevis. The Windward Islands include Trinidad and Tobago, as well as Barbados, Dominica, Grenada, Martinique, St. Lucia, St. Vincent, and the Grenadines. This book contains chapters focused on Barbados and on Trinidad and Tobago. The Leeward Antilles include the three ABC islands, Aruba, Curaçao, and Bonaire, for which the book editors could not obtain a chapter by publication time.

Another method of analyzing, categorizing, and at least partially understanding the Caribbean is by dividing up the regions by historical, colonial groupings. One could note that the following categorization has both historical import and implications for the islands/nations/regions as they exist in the early twenty-first century. Thus, one could list the regions as follows: British West Indies/Anglophone Caribbean, Dutch West Indies, French West Indies, Spanish West Indies, Danish West Indies, Portuguese West Indies, Swedish West Indies, and Courlander West Indies. The present-day Caribbean nations represented in the book from this perspective are as follows: British West Indies/Anglophone Caribbean (e.g., Barbados, Belize, Guyana, Jamaica, St. Kitts and Nevis, and Trinidad and Tobago), the Dutch West Indies (e.g., Suriname), the French West Indies (e.g., Haiti, and briefly Tobago and St. Kitts), and the Spanish West Indies (e.g., Dominican Republic, Puerto Rico, and Cuba). Notably, many of these nations felt the influence of more than one colonial power; for instance, until 1655 Jamaica was under Spanish control, and Haiti was first under Spanish then French control prior to its independence (Higman, 2011; Knight, 2011; Rogozinski, 2000).

Finally, one notes yet another way to categorize the Caribbean would be via membership in CARICOM (the "Caribbean Community), an organization, founded in 1973, of 15 states/dependencies that aims at economic growth policy and cooperation, as well as peaceful foreign relations among members. Its full members are Antigua and Barbuda Barbados, the Bahamas, Belize, Dominica, Grenada, Guyana, Haiti, Jamaica, Montserrat, St. Kitts and Nevis, St. Lucia, St. Vincent and the Grenadines, Suriname, and Trinidad and Tobago. Of these 15 nations, eight are represented in the present book (Higman, 2011; Knight, 2011; Rogozinski, 2000).

The Caribbean in total is tremendously diverse. For instance, statistically overall, the most common official languages are Spanish, French, and English, though Haitian Kreyòl, Dutch, and Papiamento are also official languages in some nations. Almost all the Caribbean nations/islands feature at least one form of Creole, often with inflection from the related colonial language. In addition, many other dialects and languages are spoken, such as indigenous languages, as well as Chinese, African, and Indian (e.g., Hindi) languages from more recent arrivals (Higman, 2011; Knight, 2011; Rogozinski, 2000). Religious belief and practice vary widely as well, though Christianity in its many forms (e.g., Catholic and Protestant) is likely practiced by nearly 85% of those in the Caribbean. There is also strong representation from other religions, such as Hinduism, Islam, Judaism, Buddhism, Bahá'í, Rastafarianism, African and African-influenced traditions (e.g., Yoruba, Santería, Brujeria, Vodou, Orisha, Espiritismo, Obeah, Winti, and Candomblé), and indigenous faith traditions (Chevannes, 1997; Glazier, 2001; Métraux, 1959).

Caribbean nations vary widely in terms of wealth and poverty and general economic conditions. To cite a few examples to illustrate this point, among the Caribbean nations/islands with the greatest per capita GDP (PPP) are Puerto Rico ($32,290), St. Kitts and Nevis ($17,435), Trinidad and Tobago ($15,384), and Barbados ($15,191). In the middle are nations such as the Dominican Republic ($7268) and Suriname ($6491). Among the Caribbean nations/islands with the lowest per capita GDP (PPP) are Jamaica ($4664), Belize ($4435), and—usually ranked lowest, even prior to its devastating 2010 earthquake—Haiti ($1940) (GDP Per Capita, 2021).

The populations of the Caribbean nations and islands are also incredibly diverse. To cite a few examples to demonstrate the range, recent population figures estimate Cuba with 11,252,999, Haiti with 10,981,229, and the Dominican Republic with 10,766,998. Considerably smaller are Puerto Rico with 3,508,000, Jamaica with 2,729,000, and Trinidad and Tobago with 1,357,000. Notably, even the nations located on Caribbean Coasts of Central and South America are not large in population: Guyana with 743,700, Suriname with 575,990, and Belize with 419,199. Even smaller populations can be found in other island nations such as Barbados with 283,000, St. Lucia with 172,000, Grenada with 104,000, and Dominica with 71,000. Finally, among the lowest populations are the Cayman Islands with 59,000, St. Kitts and Nevis with 46,000, and Montserrat with 5000 (List of Caribbean Nations by Population, 2021). Compare such nations' sizes with China (1.4 billion) or India (1.3 billion), or even with the mainland United States (with 330 million). Population size of course impacts the type of economies and services nations can provide, including higher education, specialized health care, including behavioral health service training and provision.

Above and beyond the difficulties presented by low population size, the Caribbean also shares a difficult colonial heritage and, in many cases, a postcolonial challenge of finding the best path to a desirable, successful future. At European contact at the time of Columbus, the Caribbean islands were populated by indigenous groups, including Taíno, Arawak, and Carib as well as smaller groups. The Atlantic Slave Trade from the sixteenth to nineteenth century enslaved an estimated 12–13 million Africans and dramatically altered the course of not only Caribbean but also world history (Eltis & Richardson, 2010; Rediker, 2007; Thomas, 2013). After abolition, the so-called labor shortage resulted in colonial contracting, and sometimes coercing, an estimated 500,000 Indians, 250,000 Chinese, and 90,000 others to the Caribbean and Peru in indentured servitude (Roopnarine, 2019). Today's Caribbean populations often include large, and sometimes majority populations of mixed-race origin populations. The legacy of color discrimination and prejudice did not end with apprenticeship or emancipation from slavery and is often reflected in the social, educational, and health disparities witnessed in today's Caribbean.

Furthermore, the Caribbean is prone to many natural disasters, especially hurricanes, but also floods and earthquakes, which can result in not only tragic loss of life and injury but also can devastate food security, homes, and infrastructure. Finally, many but not all Caribbean nations/islands have faced political turmoil, including violence, coups, and war. Thus, despite a range of cultural differences, the Caribbean also shares a number of challenges.

Oceania

The Pacific Ocean comprises over a third of the earth's surface area (165 million square kilometers or 63 million square miles) and 80% of the world's islands (Fischer, 2013). While definitions of Oceania vary, it has been dubbed the "water continent" and, broadly speaking, includes the world's most geographically dispersed landmasses, which include Australasia, Melanesia, Micronesia, and Polynesia. Technically speaking, our book title probably more accurately would mention the Caribbean and the Pacific Islands to describe the scope of this volume, as the Pacific Islands do not include Australia, Indonesia, the Philippines, or Japan. As Matsuda (2006) writes, "the 'Pacific' has been historically reimagined many times: from an ancient Polynesian and early modern Magellanic space of transit, to an Enlightenment theater of sensual paradise, to a strategic grid of labor movements and military "island-hopping," to a capitalist basin, the key to a Pacific Century of emerging wealth and "globalization" at the end of the last millennium" (p. 759–760). Despite conceptualizations that the vastness was a historic barrier to trans-and intra-Pacific interaction, the Pacific World legacy is significant (D'Arcy, 2008).

The South Pacific region spreads across ocean three times the size of Europe, with the total landmass comparable to the area of Denmark. Larger islands such as New Caledonia and Aotearoa New Zealand are more continental, while other island landforms may be coral atolls, coralline, or volcanic. Natural forces play significant roles in shaping Pacific societies such as adaptation due to climatic variation (e.g., rainfall, hurricanes/cyclones). Oceania is geologically active with volcanic eruptions, earthquakes, and *tsunamis* from seismic activity; particular islands in Vanuatu are estimated to have disappeared three or four times in the last 500 years (Matsuda, 2012). There is also historical evidence of submerged land bridges and clans venturing inland as sea levels rose.

The diversity of Pacific island cultures coexists with trans-local interconnected stories and histories defined by exploration, trade, marriages, alliances, warfare in which the winds and waters were actors in historical movements (Matsuda, 2012). In 1831, the French explorer Dumont d'Urville suggested dividing the Pacific into Melanesia, Micronesia, and Polynesia (Campbell, 2011). Although the terms represented constructed racial classifications that have been misused to stereotype dissimilar groups, the peoples of the regions themselves have adopted these designations as parts of their own historical identities (Armitage & Bashford, 2014). Scholars concede the geographical distinctions continue to be useful while acknowledging both differences and considerable overlap between regions. A more recent movement insists that the Pacific Ocean—as a connector of landmasses—also represents a coherent unit of analysis in its own right (D'Arcy, 2008). Anthropologist, Epeli Hau'ofa, envisioned the Pacific as a "Sea of Islands"—not a "vast, empty expanse, nor a series of isolated worlds flung into a faraway ocean, but rather with a crowded world of transits, intersections, and transformed cultures" (Matsuda, 2012, p. 3).

Polynesia includes Hawai'i to the north, Aotearoa New Zealand to the southwest, and Tonga, Samoa, and America Samoa to the west, as well as French Polynesia (e.g., the Marquesas, Society Islands, and Austral Islands), and Easter Island to the East. Recent population estimates range greatly within the region: Aotearoa New Zealand (5.1 million), Hawai'i (1.4 million), American Samoa (56,951), and Samoa (199, 853), with an equally wide range of economies, from GDPs of $58,185 in Hawai'i and $41,791 in Aotearoa New Zealand to GDPs of $11,534 in American Samoa and $4067 in Samoa (Campbell, 2011; GDP Per Capita, 2021; GDP Per Capita of Hawai'i, 2021; Pacific Data Hub, 2020). At the time of publication, chapters representing Tuvalu, Niue, the Cook Islands, the Marquesas, and Easter Island were not available. Representing Polynesia in this book, are chapters on Hawai'i, Aotearoa New Zealand, French Polynesia, and both Samoa and America Samoa.

The largest of the three regions, Polynesia, was more culturally homogenous than either Melanesia or Micronesia pre-European contact (Fischer, 2013), so much so that Captain Cook utilized a Tahitian as interpreter in Aotearoa New Zealand. The related languages often share similar words, for instance, island is *motu* in Tonga, Samoa, the Marquesas, Tahiti, and Aotearoa New Zealand, and *moku* in Hawai'i (Campbell, 2011). Polynesians excelled at food preservation which enabled them to settle islands in the early years, not only to escape hazards of drought or resource depletion, but also because voyaging and exploration was culturally embedded (Fischer, 2013). Traditional Polynesian societies were known for richly complex cultures, political organizations and ancestral genealogies (Matsuda, 2012). They were both ambilineal (mothers' and fathers' lines together) and patrilineal with stratified social classes based on inherited rank and autocratic chiefly rule (Fischer, 2013).

Religion was embedded into everyday life, often an extension of political power and control. Campbell (2011) remarked, "the two key concepts in Polynesian religious life were mana and tapu" (p. 22), with *mana* referring to sacred power that both humans and gods could possess, while *tapu* (tabu/kapu/taboo) refers in part to forbidden elements, but more accurately refers to items/activities that were either sacred or cursed, and operates in part as a method of social control to ensure persons without appropriate permissions/reasons would behave according to societal expected norms (Campbell, 2011). Some scholars have explored evolving, nuanced regional differences between Eastern and Western Polynesia, such as in fishing, land tenure, gardening/cuisine, art, music, canoe design, and social practices such as kava drinking (Fischer, 2013; Campbell, 2011). Of course, anthropologists focusing on a particular historical period, village, or culture will note even more subtle nuances, that such broad generalizations obscure. In the last 200 years, the histories of Polynesia have diverged considerably with the effects of European intrusion (Fischer, 2013).

Melanesia has been and still is characterized by tremendous ethnic, social, and cultural diversity (Fisher, 2013). Today's Melanesia includes Fiji, Vanuatu, New Caledonia, New Guinea, and the Solomon Islands. With the exception of the Solomon Islands, for which a chapter author could not be located by press time, all of these countries are represented in this volume. It is worth noting that Fiji is located on the border of Melanesia and Polynesia, and illustrates how European categories do not always suit the Pacific reality. Colonial agendas continue to be a felt presence today. Indians and other Melanesian islanders were brought to Fiji plantations through blackbirding. New Caledonia is a French territory and a francophone hub of the South Pacific. The landmass of New Guinea is 70% of Pacific Islands' land (Fischer, 2013) and contains Papua New Guinea, an independent nation, and West Papua, which is controlled by Indonesia. Recent population estimates range greatly within the region: from Papua New Guinea (9,122,994) and Fiji (898,402), to New Caledonia (273,674) and Vanuatu (301,295), with an equally wide range of economies, from GDPs of $12,579 in relatively wealthy New Caledonia, to $4881 in Fiji, $2783 in Vanuatu, and $2636 in New Guinea (Campbell, 2011; GDP Per Capita, 2021; Pacific Data Hub, 2020).

Melanesian and Polynesian worlds had divided millennia before and thus developed vastly distinct cultures that did not readily understand each other. Melanesia was known as the "dark islands" for what early colonial explorers and later Polynesian preachers viewed not only as the darker complexions and woolly hair of the people—but the difficulties encountered by their missions from hostile warriors to deadly diseases (Matsuda, 2012). Though unusual for Pacific islanders, Melanesians were not sailors or frequent travelers historically and generally speaking, kept away from feared outsiders, which led to thousands of relatively small communities of neighboring trade networks (Fisher, 2013). Traditional political and social organization has ranged from both matrilinear and patrilinear society, and from smaller clans of dozens to hereditary monarchies/chiefdoms of several hundred, though concentrated and not typically consolidated into the larger units as in Polynesia (Campbell, 2011). Melanesia's multiplicity of cultures is also apparent in the number of languages spoken in the region, with some estimates suggesting about 1300 languages—one fifth of all the world's language—are spoken here, and in Papua New Guinea alone, scholars estimate there are over 800 languages in this nation of about nine million (Campbell, 2011).

Additionally, as Melanesian tribes were more likely to live on larger islands with jungles and mountain valleys, they developed agriculture inland, whereas Polynesians and Micronesians were more reliant on the sea, leading some to distinguish "saltwater people" from "bush people" (Campbell, 2011). Like Polynesia, kava drinking plays a significant cultural role in ceremonial and social life, particularly among men. Another notable aspect of a number of Melanesian cultures is their "Big Man" practices, referring to patronage to persuasive leaders, whose power is achieved through demonstrated individual ability rather than inherited their role (Matsuda, 2012). Demonstrations of leadership included distributing wealth in various forms (depending on the country), such as providing for feasting or resourcing villages. In contrast to Polynesia, Melanesian society was classless and demonstrated rule by consensus (Fisher, 2013) even with the singular authority of local chieftain cultures (Matsuda, 2012).

Micronesia is the least populous of the three regions of the Pacific Islands, with a total of just above one half million persons, divided among the following four archipelagos: the Caroline Islands, the Gilbert Islands, the Mariana Islands, and the Marshall Islands. (NB: These terms are seldom used now, with many contemporary archaeologists and anthropologists dividing the region instead into east, central, and western regions, rather than utilize these colonial terms.) Micronesia features several sovereign nations, including the Federated States of Micronesia (FSM), Republic of Kiribati, Palau, Nauru, Republic of the Marshall Islands, as well as the US Territory of Guam, and the US Commonwealth of the Northern Mariana Islands. This book includes a chapter on the Federated States of Micronesia, including coauthors from several of its islands, including Yap, Chuuk, Pohnpei, and Kosrae. FSM is the most populated nation in Micronesia, with about 102,436 persons, though the US Territory of Guam's population is approximately 178,306 (Pacific Data Hub, 2020; Campbell, 2011; Hezel, 2013). Other recent population estimates range greatly within the region: Kiribati (120,740), Northern Mariana Islands (56,801), and the Marshall Islands (54,516) to Palau (17,957) and Nauru (11,832), with an equally wide range of economies, from GDPs of $37,723 in Guam, and $20,659 in the Northern Mariana Islands, to $10,983 in Nauru, $3585 in the Federated States of Micronesia, and $1670 in Kiribati (Campbell, 2011; GDP Per Capita, 2021; Hezel, 2013; Pacific Data Hub, 2020).

Micronesia is characterized by a multiplicity of seafaring atoll and small island cultures (Matsuda, 2012). Scholars indicate that it has been one of the world's most difficult places to settle as most islands are uninhabitable coral atolls with exposure to extreme weather and isolation (Fisher, 2013). Perhaps most notable is the impressive sea voyaging and utilization of marine resources of Micronesians to thrive without the resources of larger islands. Typically, traditional social organization followed a matrilinear system, with two or three social classes, and a political system that was hierarchical and aristocratic, with council decisions, and inter-lineage alliances (Campbell, 2011). Kava drinking is common, and as in Melanesia, betel nut chewing is also ubiquitous. Given its geographic location, some early European explorers argued whether the region reflected stronger Asian or Polynesian influences, though more modern scholarship appreciates multiple waves of settlers entering Micronesia at different periods (Fisher, 2013). While the geographic proximity to Asia is reflected in pottery style and weaving looms of some communities, Micronesians closely resemble Polynesians in culture, society, and ethnicity albeit with more diversified ancestry and practices.

More recent history and colonial legacies of Micronesia have linked the islands and their economies to military and political contests in the United States, China, Taiwan, Korea, and Vietnam (Matsuda, 2006). Atomic and nuclear testing from the 1940s to the 1990s by the Americans, British, and French caused devastating ecological destruction with severe health consequences to and evacuation of entire peoples, particularly the Bikini Islanders of the Marshall Islands. Located at the intersection of historical cultural and trading zones, the islands of Kiribati have long been the crossroads of wayfinding paths (Matsuda, 2012). Today, Kiribati is a tiny state with fewer than 100,000 citizens spread across archipelagos of low-lying atolls with encompassing waters the size of the continental United States. Kiribati is now predicted to be the first Pacific Island country of the twenty-first century to disappear as oceans rise and has raised the question of resettlement. Matsuda (2012) writes, "Tens of thousands of threatened islanders have begun requesting residency in larger Pacific states line New Zealand. The flats of Oceania may, within the lifetime of living generations carry the marks of submerged homes for islanders in Vanuatu, the Marshall Islands, Tuvalu, Kiribati, and coastal island territories of Papua New Guinea" (p. 14).

Together the diverse islands, nations, and regions of Oceania reflect shared cultural histories and future challenges. Epic voyaging, global trade, invasion, colonialism, war, and mass migration are visible legacies. Much indigenous history passed down through oral traditions has been lost over the course of depopulation and disruption that followed sustained contact with Europeans and continental diseases in the eighteenth and nineteenth centuries (D'Arcy, 2008). While the specifics of the colonial power and process vary, there is no question that postcolonial and neocolonial realities have intensely impacted the region and contributed to sociopolitical upheaval in the last decades (e.g., Campbell, 2011, Kirsch, 2017; Thompson, 2019). Europe, the Americas, and Asia have all crossed and continue to act in these islands with renewed foreign intrusion (Matsuda, 2012). Given the small population sizes of the Pacific Island nations, each nation shares similar concerns with developing and appropriately sustaining environmental resources (e.g., coral ecosystems and their fish stocks) and viable economies including opportunities for training of a behavioral health workforce. In sum, despite a broad range of cultural practices and diversity in traditions, religions, languages, demographics, economies, educational and employment opportunities, and sociopolitical organization, Pacific communities also share a number of challenges.

Conclusion

While there are some specialized books on psychological issues in single nations in the South Pacific (e.g., Fiji; Katz, 1999; Leckie, 2019) and in the Caribbean (e.g., Jamaica; Hickling, 2020), and a handful of broadly construed books about psychology in the Caribbean (e.g., Hickling, 2012; Roopnarine & Chadee, 2015) and Asia/Pacific as a whole (e.g., Minas & Lewis, 2017), psychology in the Caribbean and in Oceania has been neglected despite its diverse, rich history, and its emerging potential for economic growth and development. Books on these archipelago nations are typically written from anthropological, sociological, or economic perspectives, rather than psychological. The current volume aims to fill this gap, by providing a single volume specifically dedicated to psychology in the Caribbean and Oceania, with chapters authored or coauthored by well-known psychologists and behavioral health professionals from the region and their colleagues. Thus, this volume should be valuable not only to professors, researchers, and students in these island nations, seeking a core text or supplement for the introductory and more advanced psychology courses, but also to those outside the regions who seek insight into cultural and international processes and issues. Beyond psychology, mental health professionals and educators from related disciplines (e.g., psychiatry, counseling, social work), and those involved in development projects will find the topics in this book relevant.

Readers will note that the chapters bridge multiple psychology subdisciplines in a cross-cutting manner, including clinical, counseling, developmental, personality, health, and community psychology as well as topics in psychology of gender, research methods, and cross-cultural psychology. Each chapter provides capsule descriptions of the nation/region regarding geography, history, demographics (e.g., languages, ethnic groups, spiritual traditions, literacy rate/education), political system, and economy. Then, chapters proceed to describe the historical context and contemporary status of psychology and behavioral health in that nation/region, including service provision, credentialing and workforce development, and client access to and utilization of services. Authors were also invited to describe the role of traditional healing practices as appropriate. Significantly, we encouraged authors to note any special issues relevant to psychology, such as impacts of climate change/disaster response, political instability, poverty, crime, cultural nuances, religious/ethnic group differences/disparities, and so on. Finally, we asked authors to predict future trends in psychology and to suggest recommendations for future development of psychology research, education, and services in their nation/region.

We hope that you, dear reader, will accept our invitation to read not only the chapters on your region, but will also immerse yourself in the work of your colleagues representing other islands, nations, and regions in this book. There is much to learn from each other. Finally, it must be said, we had tremendous fun exchanging with authors across oceans and seas to produce this special book project, and hope that you will enjoy reading it!

Juneau, AK, USA — Grant J. Rich
Austin, TX, USA — Neeta A. Ramkumar

References

Armitage, D. & Bashford, A. (2014). *Pacific histories: Ocean, land, people.* Basingstoke: Palgrave Macmillan.

Campbell, I. A. (2011). *Worlds apart: A history of the Pacific Islands* (2nd Ed.). Christchurch, Aotearoa New Zealand: University of Canterbury Press.

Chevannes, B. (Ed.). (1997). *Rastafari and other African-Caribbean worldviews.* New Brunswick, NJ: Rutgers University Press.

D'Arcy, P. (2008). *Peoples of the Pacific: The history of Oceania to 1870.* Aldershot, England; Burlington, VT: Ashgate/Variorum.

GDP Per Capita. (2021). Retrieved from https://data.worldbank.org/indicator/NY.GDP.PCAP.CD

GDP Per Capita of Hawai'i. (2021). Retrieved from https://www.opendatanetwork.com/entity/0400000US15/Hawaii/economy.gdp.per_capita_gdp?year=2018

Glazier, S. D. (Ed.). (2001). *Encyclopedia of African and African-American religions.* NY: Routledge.

Eltis, D., & Richardson, D. (2010). *Atlas of the transatlantic slave trade.* New Haven, CT: Yale University Press.

Fischer, S. R. (2002). *A history of the Pacific Islands.* New York: Palgrave, http://www.loc.gov/catdir/toc/hol031/2002072647.html

Henrich, J. (2020). *The WEIRDest people in the world: How the West became psychological peculiar and particularly prosperous.* New York, NY: MacMillan.

Hezel, F. X. (2013). *Making sense of Micronesia.* Manoa, HI: University of Hawai'i Press.

Hickling, F. W. (Ed.). (2012). *Psychology in the Caribbean.* London, England: Jessica Kingsley Publishers.

Hickling, F. W. (2020). *Decolonization of psychiatry in Jamaica.* London, England: Palgrave.

Higman, B. W. (2011). *A concise history of the Caribbean.* Cambridge, UK: Cambridge University Press.

Katz, R. (1999). *The straight path of the spirit: Ancestral wisdom and healing traditions in Fiji.* Rochester, VT: Park Street Press.

Kirch P. V. (2017). *On the roads of winds: An archaeological history of the Pacific Islands before European contact* [Revised Ed.]. Oakland, CA: University of California Press.

Knight, F. W. (2011). *The Caribbean: The genesis of a fragmented nationalism.* New York, NY: Oxford University Press.

Leckie, J. (2019). *Colonizing madness: Asylum and community in Fiji.* Honolulu, Hawai'i: University of Hawai'i Press.

List of Caribbean Nations by Population (2021). Retrieved from https://en.wikipedia.org/wiki/List_of_Caribbean_countries_by_population

Matsuda, M. K. (2006). AHR forum: The Pacific. *The American Historical Review, 111,* 3, 758–780. https://www.jstor.org/stable/10.1086/ahr.111.3.758

Matsuda, M. K. (2012). *Pacific worlds: A history of seas, peoples, and cultures.* Cambridge, England; New York, NY: Cambridge University Press.

Métraux, A. (1959). *Voodoo in Haiti.* New York, NY: Schocken Books.

Minas, H., & Lewis, M. (Eds.). (2017). *Mental health in Asia and the Pacific: Historical and cultural perspectives.* New York, NY: Springer.

Pacific Data Hub. (2020, March 23). Retrieved from stats.pacificdata.org

Rediker, M. (2007). *The slave ship: A human history.* New York, NY: Penguin.

Rogozinski, J. (2000). *A brief history of the Caribbean: From the Arawak and Carib to the present.* New York, NY: Plume.

Roopnarine, J. L., & Chadee, D. (2015). *Caribbean psychology: Indigenous contributions to a global discipline.* Washington, DC: APA.

Roopnarine, L. (2019). European, Javanese, and African and indentured servitude in the Caribbean. *Atlantic History.* https://doi.org/10.1093/obo/9780199730414-0313. Retrieved from: https://www.oxfordbibliographies.com/view/document/obo-9780199730414/obo-9,780,199,730,414–0313.xml

Thomas, H. (2013). *The slave trade: The story of the Atlantic Slave Trade: 1440–1870*. New York, NY: Simon & Schuster.

Thompson, C. (2019). *Sea people: The puzzle of Polynesia.* New York, NY: HarperCollins.

Zoma, M., & Gielen, U. (2015). How many psychologists are there in the world? *International Psychology Bulletin, 19,* 47–50.

We should not be defined by the smallness of our islands, but in the greatness of our oceans.

— Epeli Hauofa

The time will come when, with elation, you will greet yourself arriving at your own door, in your own mirror, and each will smile at the other's welcome.

— Derek Walcott

We are like islands in the sea, separate on the surface but connected in the deep.

— William James

Contents

Author Biographies

Brief Biographies of Editors

Grant J. Rich, PhD Fellow, American Psychological Association, Fellow, Association for Psychological Science, is senior editor of eight books, including “Pathfinders in International Psychology” (2015), “Internationalizing the Teaching of Psychology” (2017), “Human Strengths and Resilience: Developmental, Cross-Cultural, and International Perspectives” (2018), “Teaching Psychology around the World, Volume 4” (2018), “Teaching Psychology around the World, Volume 5” (2020), and “Psychology in Southeast Asia” (2020). Dr. Rich has published over 75 peer-reviewed journal articles/book chapters in journals such as *American Psychologist*, *Humanistic Psychologist*, and *Journal of Positive Psychology*; has published over 100 book reviews; and has presented at over 110 conferences around the globe from the Bahamas, Belize, Haiti, Jamaica, and Suriname to Africa, Asia, Australia, Europe, the Middle East, and North America. He received the President’s Award for Extraordinary Service: APA Division of International Psychology, and was a National Endowment for the Humanities, Institute Fellow (in Mexico, Belize, Guatemala, and Honduras, and in the Tropical Atlantic). He is Senior Contributing Faculty at Walden University and lives in Juneau, Alaska.

Neeta A. Ramkumar (BA Psychology, BA History, University of Texas at Austin; MS Educational Psychology, PhD Counseling Psychology, Texas A&M University) is a licensed psychologist, consultant, and the founder of Psychology Across Borders, PLLC. She is dedicated to facilitating international partnerships that will expand access to mental health care worldwide. She completed her APA accredited clinical psychology internship and postdoctoral fellowship at US Veterans Affairs hospitals and specialized in the treatment of trauma. As a lecturer at the University of the South Pacific, she focused on mental health capacity building and contextualizing psychology training in island nations. She is particularly interested in how telepsychology, distance education, and exchange programs can improve access in the Global South. She consults for various community agencies internationally including firefighters/first responders, medical personnel, disability, law, and education groups and organizations. Her research interests include cross-cultural and indigenous aspects of professional psychology, the role of self-compassion, family and multicultural factors in health outcomes, and a handful of understudied psychosocial issues in populations she works with.

Brief Biography of Foreword Author

Frank C. Worrell, PhD is a Professor in the Graduate School of Education where he also holds an affiliate appointment in the Social and Personality Area in the Department of Psychology. A licensed psychologist and certified school psychologist, his areas of interest include at-risk youth, cultural identities, gifted education/talent development, scale development and validation, teacher effectiveness, time perspective, and the translation of psychological research findings into practice, and his scholarship crosses several subdisciplines of psychology, including cultural, developmental, educational, international, quantitative, school, and social and personality. Author of more than 200 scholarly works, Dr. Worrell is a Fellow of the American Educational Research Association, the American Psychological Association, and the Association for Psychological Science, and a member of the National Academy of Education and the Society for the Study of School Psychology. A former editor of *Review of Educational Research*, he is also the 2021 President-elect of the American Psychological Association.

Part I
Psychology in Oceania

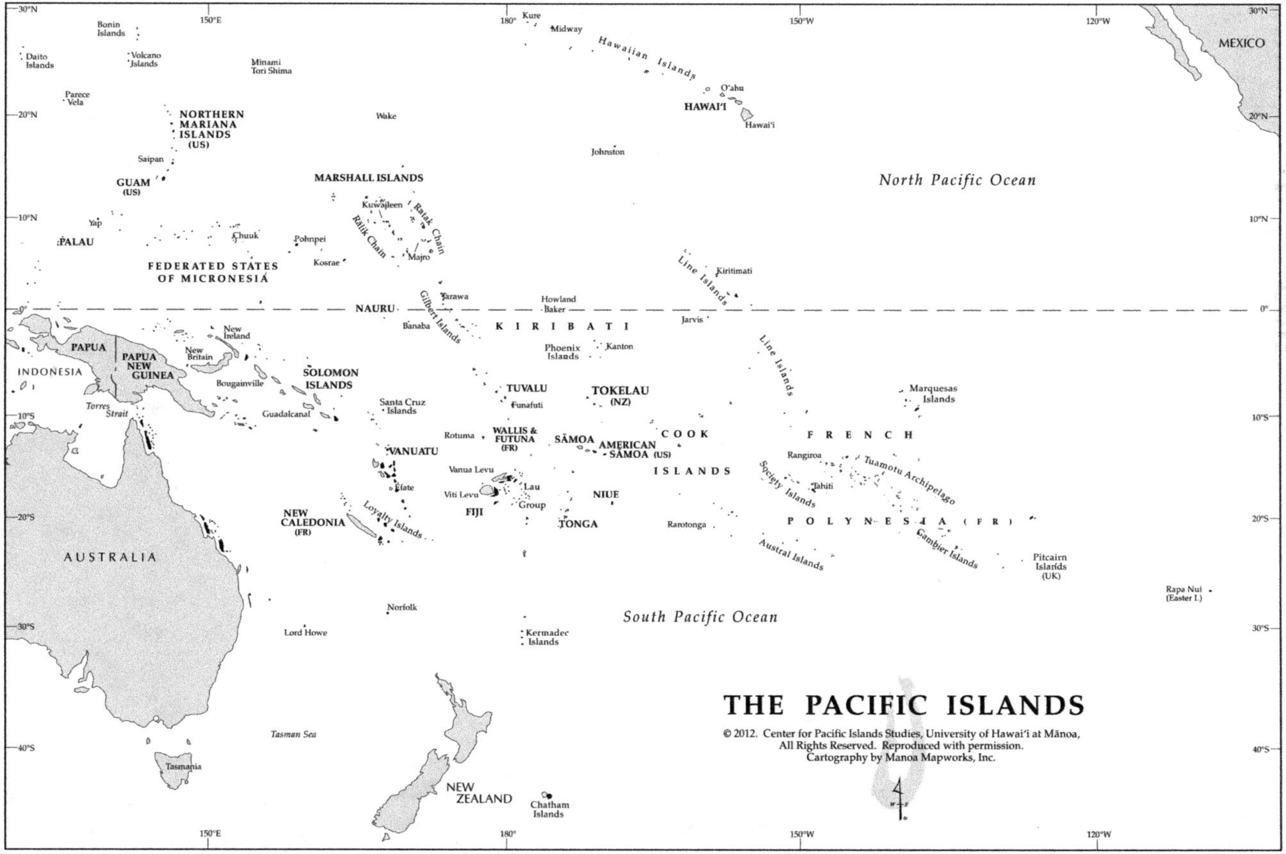
THE PACIFIC ISLANDS
© 2012. Center for Pacific Islands Studies, University of Hawai'i at Mānoa,
All Rights Reserved. Reproduced with permission.
Cartography by Manoa Mapworks, Inc.
North Pacific Ocean
South Pacific Ocean
Tasman Sea
MEXICO
AUSTRALIA
INDONESIA
PAPUA
PAPUA NEW GUINEA
NEW ZEALAND
HAWAI'I
Hawaiian Islands
Kure
Midway
O'ahu
Hawai'i
Johnston
Wake
Minami Tori Shima
Bonin Islands
Volcano Islands
Daito Islands
Parece Vela
NORTHERN MARIANA ISLANDS (US)
Saipan
GUAM (US)
Yap
PALAU
Chuuk
Pohnpei
Kosrae
FEDERATED STATES OF MICRONESIA
MARSHALL ISLANDS
Kwajalein
Ratak Chain
Ralik Chain
Majuro
NAURU
Tarawa
Banaba
Gilbert Islands
KIRIBATI
Howland
Baker
Phoenix Islands
Kanton
Line Islands
Kiritimati
Jarvis
New Ireland
New Britain
Bougainville
SOLOMON ISLANDS
Guadalcanal
Santa Cruz Islands
Torres Strait
TUVALU
Funafuti
TOKELAU (NZ)
WALLIS & FUTUNA (FR)
Rotuma
SĀMOA
AMERICAN SĀMOA (US)
COOK ISLANDS
Rarotonga
NIUE
TONGA
VANUATU
Efate
Vanua Levu
Viti Levu
Lau Group
FIJI
NEW CALEDONIA (FR)
Loyalty Islands
Norfolk
Lord Howe
Kermadec Islands
Chatham Islands
Tasmania
FRENCH POLYNESIA (FR)
Marquesas Islands
Rangiroa
Tuamotu Archipelago
Society Islands
Tahiti
Austral Islands
Gambier Islands
Pitcairn Islands (UK)
Rapa Nui (Easter I.)
30°N
20°N
10°N
0°
10°S
20°S
30°S
40°S
150°E
180°
150°W
120°W

Chapter 1
Psychology in Micronesia

Iain K. B. Twaddle, Francis X. Hezel, Donald H. Rubinstein, James E. H. Arriola, Annette M. David, Holden J. Nena, Camarin G. Meno, Aieleen D. Mauricio, Joyce B. Anefal, Martha A. Thomson, Everlynn J. Temengil, Iris L. Palemar, Hilda Tafledep, Inda L. Maipi, and Victor H. Wasson

Overview of the Micronesian Region

In this chapter, we describe the five US-affiliated Pacific Island (USAPI) jurisdictions in the western Pacific region of Micronesia: the US Territory of Guam, the quasi-independent Commonwealth of the Northern Mariana Islands (CNMI), and the three independent nations of Palau, the Federated States of Micronesia (FSM), and the Republic of the Marshall Islands (RMI) (see Table 1.1). The Federated States of Micronesia includes four states: Yap, Chuuk, Pohnpei, and Kosrae. Although the term "Micronesia" commonly comprises the island nations of Kiribati and Nauru in addition to the USAPI, we exclude these two non-USAPI countries in this chapter, as their long colonial histories under the United Kingdom have shaped

I. K. B. Twaddle (✉)
Division of Social & Behavioral Sciences, University of Guam, Mangilao, Guam, USA
e-mail: psychology@triton.uog.edu

F. X. Hezel
Santa Barbara Parish, Dededo, Guam, USA

D. H. Rubinstein
Micronesian Area Research Center, University of Guam, Mangilao, Guam, USA
e-mail: rubinste@triton.uog.edu

J. E. H. Arriola
Brabu Behavioral Health Services, Saipan, Commonwealth of the Northern Mariana Islands, USA

A. M. David
Guam State Epidemiological Outcomes Workgroup (SEOW), Guam Behavioral Health & Wellness Center, Tamuning, Guam, USA
e-mail: amdavid@guam.net

G. J. Rich, N. A. Ramkumar (eds.), *Psychology in Oceania and the Caribbean*, International and Cultural Psychology,
https://doi.org/10.1007/978-3-030-87763-7_1

Table 1.1 Population, land area, and gross domestic product (GDP) per capita for the five USAPI jurisdictions

USAPI jurisdiction	Population (2020)	Land area (km^2)	GDP per capita (2017/2018)
Guam[a]	168,775	540	$31,848
CNMI[a]	57,559	460	$23,117
Palau[a]	18,094	460	$12,310
FSM[b]	104,650	710	$2408
Yap	11,577	124	$3468
Chuuk	49,509	127	$1436
Pohnpei	36,832	344	$3393
Kosrae	6732	111	$2344
Marshall Islands[a]	59,190	180	$3195

[a]Adapted from Worldometer (2021) (https://www.worldometers.info/), with population figures projected for 2020 and GDP figures projected for 2017.
[b]Adapted from the FSM Statistics Division (2020) (https://www.fsmstatistics.fm/), with population figures projected for 2020 and GDP figures projected for 2018.

their development and contemporary social services along different paths than the USAPI.

Geographically, the region is composed of both "high" volcanic islands and low-lying coral atolls and islands (see Fig. 1.1). Although small in land area, the region is enormous in ocean area. The combined exclusive economic zones (EEZs)

H. J. Nena
RMI Ministry of Health & Human Services, Majuro, Republic of the Marshall Islands
e-mail: hnena@rmihealth.org

C. G. Meno
Division of Social & Behavioral Sciences, University of Guam, Mangilao, Guam, USA

A. D. Mauricio
Pohnpei Behavioral Health & Wellness Program, Pohnpei, Federated States of Micronesia
e-mail: AMauricio@fsmhealth.fm

J. B. Anefal · I. L. Palemar · H. Tafledep
Yap Behavioral Health & Wellness Program, Yap, Federated States of Micronesia
e-mail: janefal@fsmhealth.fm; ipalemar@fsmhealth.fm; htafledep@fsmhealth.fm

M. A. Thomson
Kosrae Behavioral Health & Wellness Program, Kosrae, Federated States of Micronesia
e-mail: mthomson@fsmhealth.fm

E. J. Temengil
Division of Behavioral Health, Palau Ministry of Health, Koror, Palau
e-mail: everlynn.temengil@palauhealth.org

I. L. Maipi
Chuuk Behavioral Health & Wellness Program, Chuuk, Federated States of Micronesia

V. H. Wasson
FSM Behavioral Health & Wellness Program, Department of Health & Social Affairs, Pohnpei, Federated States of Micronesia
e-mail: VWasson@fsmhealth.fm

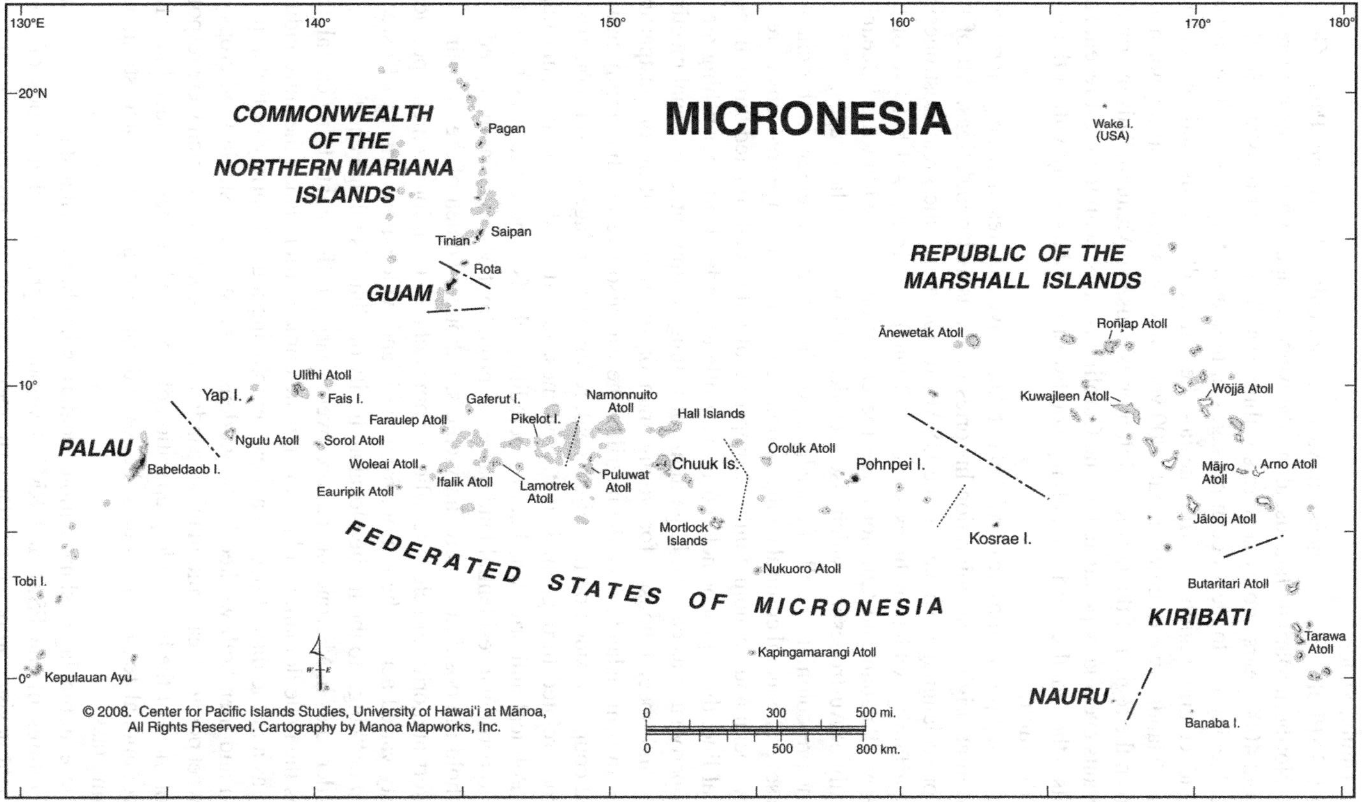

Fig. 1.1 Map of Micronesia. (Reproduced with permission)

of the five island areas total 5.3 million km^2, or about two-thirds the size of the continental United States.

The USAPI all share an ancestral Austronesian cultural heritage. Palau, Guam, and the Northern Mariana Islands, along the western edge of Micronesia, were settled about 4000 years ago by seafarers sailing east directly out of Island Southeast Asia, achieving the longest ocean passages in human history to date. The eastern edge and central region of Micronesia—the Marshall Islands and the central Caroline Islands—were settled about 2000 years ago by seafarers sailing north and west from the region of the northern Solomon Islands and Vanuatu. This later wave of migrants eventually populated all the Caroline Islands, with the most recent settlements—the small coral islands lying southwest of Palau—only within the past half-millennium.

The contemporary mosaic of related but distinctive cultures in this region reflects the different origins and migration histories of the island populations. All of the dozen or so languages spoken in the USAPI region are in the great Austronesian language family, which includes some 1200 languages in all. All but two of the languages (Palauan and Chamorro are the exceptions) are within the "Oceanic" subfamily of Austronesian, which also includes all Polynesian languages.

In the pre-colonial era, all of the island populations under review in this chapter shared several general cultural configurations. Matrilineal lineages or clans were the primary social and economic units. Comprised of individuals related through their maternal line, these groups held customary title to garden land, reef fishing areas, and property such as canoes, large items of fishing equipment, communal meeting houses, and special houses for young men or for menstruating or postpartum women. In some island areas, the matrilineage was also a residential group; newly married couples resided on the wife's land, resulting in village sections comprised of women related through their maternal lines, joined by their in-marrying husbands. Political authority was held by hereditary chiefs, whose title was typically linked to particular residential land parcels. Throughout Micronesia, men predominantly hold the position of hereditary chiefs, although women of the matrilineage may exert authority in selecting who becomes chief. Traditional chiefs' political authority varied across the region, from the island-wide paramountcy of Kosrae's *Tokosra* or "king," to the limited local authority of Chuuk's village chiefs.

Gender roles in Micronesian cultures were sharply differentiated. In general, the sea was the male domain and land the female domain. Men fished the surrounding reef areas and the distant deep-sea areas, employing a great variety of techniques. Women and men both worked in the gardens, harvesting the staple food crops of taro, sweet potato, breadfruit, manioc, pandanus, and coconut. Women were responsible for most of the household preparation of meals, while men provided labor for large communal feasts and rituals, house and canoe construction, and strenuous gardening tasks.

In these archipelagic island nations, seafaring has been a vital skill for survival. Atoll cultures of the FSM and RMI developed sophisticated methods of non-instrument navigation based on star movements, ocean currents, and other natural signs. Their large, single-outrigger sailing canoes were expertly engineered to enable long-distance voyages across thousands of kilometers of open ocean, permitting inter-island trade, access to distant resources, and maintenance of dispersed kin networks.

Although sharing some core cultural features, the island entities have experienced different colonial and postcolonial histories, resulting in a spectrum of modernity across the region. At one extreme is Guam, which in the late 1600s was the first Pacific island to be missionized and colonized, and to suffer from the devastating effects of foreign diseases and forced relocation of its people, resulting in the loss of 90% of the Indigenous population over the first several decades of European impact. Today, Guam is a modern transportation and communication hub, with high-rise hotels, luxury shopping malls, and an international airport handling over 40 flight arrivals daily. At the other extreme are small, isolated coral islands throughout the region, some with populations of only several families, serviced by government ships operating infrequently. Missionization and colonization impacted the islands of Palau, the FSM, and the RMI nearly two centuries later than in Guam and the northern Marianas. After nearly a century of colonization by Spain, Germany, Japan, and the United States, these three island nations achieved independence in the final decades of the twentieth century. They remain linked to the United States by "compacts of free association" (COFA), which provide direct financial assistance, support an array of social services and economic programs, and permit visa-free entry into the United States for their citizens.

The Travails of Social Change in Micronesia

Despite popular Western illusions of Pacific Islands as timeless Edenic spaces, social change has been a dimension of life since the first Austronesian seafarers set foot on uninhabited islands millennia ago. Populations evolved from small bands and boatloads of explorers occupying coastal sites to complex stratified societies numbering in the tens of thousands. Sustainable agricultural and fishing technologies intensified to support growing populations. Occasional inter-village or inter-island warfare resulted in new political relationships, as the defeated side faced either abandoning their land or accepting domination by the victors. Periodic natural disasters—typhoons, tsunamis, earthquakes, droughts—caused localized loss of life and land, with subsequent reordering of social relations and land tenure.

The arrival of foreigners, beginning in the seventeenth century, had profound impacts on island societies. Colonization, missionization, and militarization of the islands resulted in initial episodes of massive depopulation and dislocation, followed by fundamental changes in political authority, economic activity, belief systems, and social relations over the ensuing centuries. Today, viewing social change from the vantage point of elder islanders reflecting on what they have witnessed in their own lifetimes—roughly from the immediate post-WWII years to the present day—we can briefly describe two momentous trends. One is economic modernization and the other is demographic shifts; both have had significant social implications.

Economic modernization has involved a shift away from agrarian work, subsistence gardening and artisanal fishing, to wage labor and increased dependence on money. In mid-twentieth-century Guam and the Northern Mariana Islands, the village was the basic social and economic unit, while in the islands of Palau, FSM, and RMI, the lineage was the primary unit. The increasing role of nuclear households as social and economic units has been accompanied by a loss of the social connective tissue once provided by wider networks and shared resources among village neighbors and lineage mates. This nuclearization of households and loss of wider social roles and supports in lineage economic activities has been linked to the emergence of particular social problems in Micronesia, such as the rising rates of adolescent male suicides in the 1970s (Hezel, 1989; Rubinstein, 2002). The shift away from subsistence gardening and fishing has also eroded traditional roles, perhaps most noticeably for young men, who served as the labor force for village and lineage work in previous generations.

Dependence on wage labor and money has generated growing disparities in wealth and pockets of poverty within the island populations (see Table 1.1). The island populations are increasingly stratified across socioeconomic levels, with sharp differences between rural and urban areas, and between well-educated individuals holding positions of skilled employment, versus unskilled workers and people supporting themselves through subsistence gardening and fishing. Economic modernization has also led to radical shifts in diet and daily activity levels for a growing portion of the island populations, and coupled with the introduction of Western medicine, this has produced a dramatic epidemiological transition from infectious diseases to noncommunicable diseases as the primary causes of morbidity and mortality. Current epidemic levels of diabetes, and some of the highest obesity rates in the world, are stark indicators of this transition.

Demographic shifts over the past 75 years have likewise been significant. In Guam, the Indigenous Chamorro people became a minority in their own island for the first time in 1950, as a large contingent of US military personnel, plus a sizeable influx of skilled Filipino laborers hired to work on the postwar reconstruction of the island, outnumbered the native population. Chamorro out-migration to Hawai‘i, California, and other US states accelerated beginning in the 1960s, and today, Chamorros living in the United States outnumber those living in Guam. A similar pattern holds in the CNMI, where the Indigenous Micronesian population is outnumbered by Asian immigrant workers. Since the 1986 implementation of the COFA treaties between the United States, FSM, and RMI, about one-third of the populations of those island nations have moved to Guam and the United States. Chuukese are now the fastest-growing ethnic group in Guam, and there are growing enclaves of FSM and RMI citizens in Hawai‘i and scattered from Oregon to Arkansas. The anticipated end of COFA direct financial assistance, scheduled for 2023, is accelerating out-migration and putting further economic pressure on FSM and RMI (Palau negotiated a different schedule).

The migration flows and demographic shifts have added layers of social complexity to modern life in the islands and, in some cases, have contributed to specific social problems. The heavy flow of military personnel between Guam and Southeast

Asia during the American War in Vietnam, including numerous Chamorro enlistees, contributed to a severe epidemic of heroin and other drugs in Guam in the 1960s and 1970s. The flood of American Peace Corps Volunteers in Micronesia in the 1960s, and the swelling numbers of Micronesian students attending US colleges in the 1970s, introduced marijuana and other drugs into the islands. Asian garment factories and casino developments in the Northern Mariana Islands, beginning in the 1980s, have been associated with sex trafficking and the introduction of hard drugs. More recently, the flow of Marshall Islanders between home in the RMI and diasporic communities in Arkansas and elsewhere has become a conduit for the importation of methamphetamine and other drugs. As island families and communities evolve into transnational kinship networks, islanders increasingly are navigating multiple cultural worlds. For Micronesian youth envisioning their future, the prospects can be exciting yet also daunting, as they face pathways for both success and failure that previous generations could hardly imagine.

Behavioral Health Problems in Micronesia

The social and cultural changes that have swept across Micronesia in recent decades have been accompanied by a significant rise in behavioral health problems throughout the region. Here, we look at two behavioral health concerns that have impacted Micronesian island societies: suicide and mental illness.

Suicide

Suicide was not unheard of in premodern times, but historical sources suggest that the rates were low—about 6 or 8 per 100,000—and cases were largely confined to mature adults (Purcell, 1987). Recent data compiled over the past six decades, however, point to an explosion of suicide throughout the region. At present, suicide ranks as one of the major psychosocial problems in Micronesia.

In FSM and the Marshalls, suicide rates surged beginning about 1970, and the rates in both places hovered close to 30 per 100,000 over the following years, finally dipping to about 20 in recent years (Hezel, 1989, 2016b; RMI Epidemiological Workgroup, 2018). Palau showed a similar although more gradual increase that peaked at 35 before it also declined in the past decade (Cash, 2013; Palau Ministry of Health, 2021). Guam's increase was also slight until the early 1990s when its annual number doubled (Workman & Rubinstein, 2019). Unlike the other island groups in Micronesia, Guam's suicide rate has not abated in recent years; rather, it has peaked at 24 in the past 5 years (David, 2021). The continuing high incidence of suicide in Guam may be due to the growing numbers of people from FSM (Hezel, 2017). CNMI is the only jurisdiction in the region not to have reached a rate of 20, although it came close during the last 5 years (CNMI CHCC, 2021).

What accounts for the rapid rise in suicide throughout the region since the 1970s? This question has prompted a series of articles on the subject (e.g., Rubinstein, 1987). The cultural patterns of suicide are unmistakable. Hanging is by far the most common method. Suicide is almost always motivated by the disruption of a personal relationship—in some cases with a spouse, but far more often with someone in the victim's own blood family. Rarely is suicide occasioned by failure in school or business, or by despair at lack of personal success (Hezel, 1989). The studies suggest that the increase in suicide might be tied to the rapid change in social organization, especially in the dynamics of family life.

Another characteristic of Micronesian suicide is the very low incidence among women. In Guam, females make up only 15% of cases over the past 20 years (Guam DPHSS, 2021). In the rest of Micronesia, the female share is even lower: less than 10%. In the Marshalls, it is only about 5% (Majuro Hospital, 2021). Some observers have suggested the low rates of female suicide are linked to the low consumption of alcohol among women, but this explanation is unconvincing. Still, the female risk of suicide has recently begun to rise in some places. In the FSM, the female share doubled from 6% in the 1960s and 1970s to 14% in the first 15 years after 2000 (FSM DHSA, 2019) and then more recently soared to 34% (FSM DHSA, 2021).

Suicide might have once represented the choice of a mature adult, but in recent years, an alarmingly high number of suicides occur in the very young age group. In FSM, during the height of the suicide epidemic, half the suicides were aged 20 and younger, although this proportion has dropped to 38% in recent years (Hezel, 2017). The high incidence of suicide among the young, and the declining rates within each older age cohort, inverts the trend found in most developed societies. This suggests that suicide might often be an impulsive response to a troublesome family situation.

Even if suicide rates have shown a recent decline, suicide seems to be a growing problem in more rural and culturally traditional areas. A recent update of the FSM data shows a significant increase in suicides in the outer islands of Yap and Chuuk as well as Pingelap in Pohnpei. This is most striking in Yap, where the number of suicides in the outer islands now exceeds those of the more populous main island (Hezel, 2017).

While the recent rise in suicide rates may have been generated by some of the social changes that have swept the islands over the years, there is also evidence of suicide "contagion" or modeling. Clustering of suicides is a pronounced feature in the region. The death of a prominent political figure in one island triggered a spate of suicides in the months that followed. The same contagion effect is suggested by the clusters of victims occurring in a single village during a short time frame (Rubinstein, 1987).

Although suicide may not be a new phenomenon in the islands, as those stories from the deep past attest, it has become a much more serious challenge in recent times. Responding effectively to that challenge will require that we understand its cultural meaning and the dynamics affecting it.

Mental Illness

Comprehensive data for FSM, Palau, and the Marshall Islands was obtained in a 1990 study that gathered life histories on all those identified by the community as mentally unstable (Hezel & Wylie, 1992). Because of the limited access to psychiatric help and clinical diagnosis, the researchers relied on a community-based definition of serious mental illness (SMI), but one that required that the condition had persisted for more than a year and excluded individuals impaired from birth or those whose mental problems stemmed from physical trauma. Prevalence rates in the islands ranged considerably—from a rate of 3 or 4 per 1000 population (aged 15 years and older) in the Marshalls and the eastern Carolines, to a rate of 8 per 1000 in Yap, and a rate of over 16 per 1000 in Palau. Although Palau's very high rates may fall within the broad range of international studies, they attracted the attention of several researchers who visited the island group during the 1990s (Sullivan et al., 2007). There was no recent data to provide prevalence rates for Guam and the Northern Marianas.

Prevalence of SMI exhibits a strong gender imbalance throughout the islands: in the Marshalls, for every female with mental illness, there are 3.5 males; in Palau, the ratio is 2.3:1, and in FSM, it is 4.4:1 (Hezel & Wylie, 1992). Why do males appear at much higher risk of SMI than females in the islands? Are cultural factors, such as the disproportionate stress placed on males, at play here? Or are the symptoms so attenuated in females that they might not be easily identified?

Alternatively, some researchers have suggested that the preponderance of males among persons with SMI is related to their much greater consumption of alcohol and drugs. Indeed, in the 1990 survey, it was noted that 83% were drinking alcohol and 61% using cannabis before the onset of their illness (Hezel & Wylie, 1992). But there is little hard evidence to support a causal link. Moreover, the correlation raises the question as to whether the use of drugs is cause or effect. While drug use might trigger mental illness, it might also be regarded as an attempt by those suffering from SMI to self-medicate. Other correlations might also be explored in future research. Those with SMI were found to be slightly better educated than average, and they are significantly better traveled: the 1990 study showed that nearly half of those with SMI spent 6 months or longer abroad.

A follow-up study conducted in 2015 offered observations on the course of the disease for those identified as suffering from SMI 25 years earlier (Hezel, 2016a). During this interval, fully half of those with mental illness had died; this is 2.5 times the mortality rate that would have occurred in the general population. Unsurprisingly, then, it appears that mental illness shortens the lifespan of those afflicted with it.

The follow-up survey also showed that of those whose condition stabilized and whose symptoms disappeared in time, many were drug users who had ceased drug use in the course of their illness. This might suggest that drug use was the cause of SMI or that cessation of drug use simply attenuated the symptoms. The follow-up survey also suggested that retaining strong ties with the family appeared to improve the condition of the mentally ill. Indeed, support from the family and community may be one of the most important factors in the treatment for SMI in Micronesia.

Behavioral Health Services in Micronesia

Traditionally, psychological and behavioral problems have been addressed by familial and community support networks, traditional healers, and other Indigenous approaches to helping and healing. Yet recent decades have seen the importation of Western mental health frameworks and practices through government programs, US federal grants, and community-based initiatives. Below we provide a brief overview of the available behavioral health services for the USAPI communities discussed in this chapter.

Each of the five USAPI jurisdictions has a government behavioral health agency or program funded at least in part by block grants from the US Department of Health and Human Services. On paper, the governmental behavioral health services that have been established in Guam, CNMI, Palau, FSM, and RMI are virtually indistinguishable from those of their sister programs throughout the United States. In actuality, behavioral health services provided within this expansive and culturally diverse region are far from conventional and include a range of highly specialized, culturally specific prevention and intervention strategies reflecting the unique geographic characteristics and distinct cultures of each island community.

Guam

As a US Territory and the most populous of the five USAPIs, Guam has the most comprehensive behavioral health services in the region. Its primary psychiatric facility, the Guam Behavioral Health and Wellness Center, is an autonomous government agency that provides inpatient, outpatient, day treatment, community outreach, and residential services through a staff of over 200, including psychiatrists, clinical psychologists, mental health counselors, substance abuse counselors, and social workers. Behavioral health services are also available through various other government agencies including public health, the judicial system, adult and youth correctional facilities, the public schools, and institutions of higher learning, as well as through numerous private clinics, faith-based and nonprofit organizations, and programs for military personnel and veterans. Guam is a single island with a good road system; hence, its behavioral health programs are accessible by car or bus in less than an hour from any village.

Commonwealth of the Northern Mariana Islands

The CNMI's behavioral health services are based in Saipan, where 90% of the population reside, and extend via outreach to Tinian and Rota, the only other inhabited islands within the 14 islands of the Commonwealth. The primary government entity for behavioral health is the Commonwealth Healthcare Corporation's Community

Guidance Center (CGC), which provides mental health and substance abuse services through outpatient, day treatment, and community outreach programs. The Center places a strong emphasis on education and prevention, although comprehensive treatment services are also available. The Center's more than 50 staff include a clinical psychologist and several mental health counselors, substance abuse counselors, and care coordinators. Inpatient and outpatient psychiatric services are provided at Saipan's government-run hospital where several psychiatrists are employed. Residential care for persons with substance use disorders is also available in the community. These services are supplemented by mental health counselors working in the public schools, public safety department, and the prison, as well as through community-based nonprofit organizations and faith-based programs. Several psychologists and psychiatrists also provide mental health treatment through private clinics. In Tinian and Rota, outreach services are provided through a care coordinator assigned to each island's government health center. Treatment services are offered by CGC counselors who fly out from Saipan monthly, as well as by the CGC psychologist and the hospital psychiatrists who are on call, ready to travel to Tinian and Rota when needed.

Palau

The Palau Ministry of Health (MOH) Division of Behavioral Health is based in the state of Koror, the nation's urban center where 70% of Palau's population live. Among the 300 islands of this archipelagic nation, only nine are inhabited. The Division has a mental health unit located in the Belau National Hospital, which provides inpatient and outpatient psychiatric services and an adjacent recovery unit focused on psychosocial rehabilitation. Programs focusing on prevention, behavioral health promotion, and alcohol and drug treatment are located in the community. The Division's 25–35 staff include two psychiatrists, two social workers, and a cadre of nurses and counselors. All services are community based and emphasize outreach, which the staff refer to as "clinics without walls." For example, when working with patients who are not taking their medication consistently, the mental health unit applies the DOT (Directly Observed Therapy) strategy developed for the treatment of tuberculosis. In the DOT approach, mental health nurses seek out patients in their homes, at their workplace, or even in public places, to ensure they take their medication daily. Moreover, to provide access to services for the entire population, the behavioral health staff make quarterly visits to each of Palau's inhabited islands. While the villages in Koror and Babeldaob are connected by causeways and bridges, the behavioral health staff must travel 2–3 hours on MOH boats to reach Kayangel, Peleliu, and Angaur, and by larger ships to reach the Southwest Islands of Sonsorol, Pulo Anna, and Tobi, a journey of 2–3 days. A critical component of these outreach visits is to identify and train a reliable family member to assist patients with medication compliance. Between visits to the distant islands, behavioral health staff follow up with patients by telehealth (phone/CB radio).

Federated States of Micronesia

The FSM Behavioral Health and Wellness Program (BH&WP), under the Department of Health and Social Affairs, coordinates mental health and substance abuse prevention and treatment services among FSM's four states, whose population is scattered across over 600 separate islands. Each state also has its own BH&WP with 10–20 staff, including counselors, nurses, prevention educators, and community outreach workers, working in collaboration with the FSM national psychiatrist, local physicians, and health assistants who staff community dispensaries. Innovative outreach strategies, including "house-to-house" patient care and CB radio communication, ensure access to services for all island communities.

Yap. The Yap BH&WP is part of Yap State Hospital in Yap Island. Services are provided through the hospital and five community health centers on Yap's four main islands. To reach the state's 17 inhabited outer islands, BH&WP staff travel aboard government ships on semiannual month-long trips, which briefly visit each island community along the 2000-km circuit between Yap and the state's easternmost atolls.

Chuuk. The Chuuk BH&WP is at Chuuk State Hospital on the main island of Weno in Chuuk Atoll. As Chuuk's population is dispersed across more than 40 islands, community outreach is crucial to the program's mission. Services are provided to 17 islands of Chuuk Atoll and 24 outer islands, with community outreach workers stationed on six islands. The Weno-based staff visit the nearby islands of Chuuk Atoll by motorboat weekly and participate in semiannual public health trips by ship to the outer islands.

Pohnpei. The Pohnpei BH&WP is located on the island of Pohnpei next to Pohnpei State Hospital. Services are provided in Pohnpei and two of the state's five outer islands to the south and east of Pohnpei—Pingelap and Sapwuahfik—where community outreach workers are stationed. Services to outer island communities include semiannual visits by the Pohnpei-based staff who make the 2-day journey by government ships or on the *Okeanos Pohnpei*, a double-hulled traditionally styled sailing canoe.

Kosrae. The Kosrae BH&WP is located on the island of Kosrae close to Kosrae State Hospital. As the only FSM state comprising a single high island, the program's services are easily accessed by the entire population.

Republic of the Marshall Islands

RMI's behavioral health programs are based in the capital, Majuro, where half of the nation's population reside. Of the 34 atolls and coral islands comprising this archipelagic nation, 24 are inhabited. Substance abuse services are provided through the Single State Agency under the Ministry of Finance, by approximately 10 paraprofessionals who conduct substance use prevention programs. Mental health services, on the other hand, are provided through the Ministry of Health and Human Services by approximately 10 staff including a psychiatrist, four nurses, and one counselor. Both programs collaborate with faith-based and nongovernmental organizations focused on community empowerment, such as WAM (*Waan Aelõñ in Majel*—Canoes of the Marshall Islands) and WUTMI (Women United Together Marshall Islands). Mental health services are based within Majuro Hospital and include an outpatient clinic for medication, psychotherapy, and counseling and a full range of community outreach and prevention services. Behavioral health care is also provided at Ebeye Hospital in Kwajalein Atoll by two mental health staff and the MOH psychiatrist who flies monthly to the densely populated island of Ebeye. For residents of RMI's many outer islands, access to behavioral health care is available through 56 government health centers, each staffed by a health assistant trained to provide basic medical services. When working with patients with mental disorders, the health assistants consult with mental health staff at Majuro Hospital by CB radio. Additionally, a behavioral health team from Majuro travels by plane or boat to each of the outer islands quarterly to evaluate new cases, provide follow-up care for current patients, and educate families and the community about mental health.

Conclusion

Throughout the Micronesian region, traditional cultural beliefs and practices continue to play a critical role in the community's response to mental illness. Of particular importance are the extended family networks and traditional community associations in which people take responsibility for each other. However, within some of Micronesia's traditional belief systems, mental illness is viewed as a curse placed on a family or an individual because of a past transgression. Thus, social stigma is prevalent, especially in the more remote island communities, and many of those who might benefit from behavioral health treatment are reluctant to reach out for help. It is primarily for this reason that behavioral health staff often go out to the homes of their patients to provide services. Traditional healers are often the first line of treatment, and many individuals with mental health problems respond well to the herbal medicine, massage, and spiritual healing provided. However, some aspects of traditional healing can contribute to stigmatization by perpetuating the belief that mental illness is caused by supernatural forces, such as a curse, black magic, or ancestral spirits. Local government education and prevention programs focus on providing alternative biopsychosocial explanations.

Perhaps the most widespread cultural practice in responding to mental illness is the support provided by families. As there are no residential care facilities for persons with mental illness (except in Guam), the primary caregivers are almost always family members, who play a vital role. In general, when there is strong family support for a person with mental illness, behavioral health interventions including medication and counseling tend to be successful. In cases where family support is not available, village chiefs sometimes step in to assign a relative or member of the community to serve as the primary caregiver. In many communities, churches also play an important role in providing faith-based support. In sum, although Western behavioral health services have brought relief to many individuals and families throughout the Micronesian region, it is important to recognize that these relatively new approaches to mental health care supplement Indigenous approaches to helping and healing that continue to take place within families and village communities in every island in the region.

Acknowledgments The authors gratefully acknowledge the following individuals who assisted with the preparation of this chapter: Theresa Arriola and Carissa Pangelinan (Guam Behavioral Health and Wellness Center); Dr. Esther Lizama Muña, Reyna Saures, and Wilbert Rospel (CNMI Commonwealth Healthcare Corporation); Joy Mascardo (Palau Ministry of Health); Benido Victor and Juveena Jose (FSM Behavioral Health and Wellness Program); Stanley Ruemgol and Tony Torwan (Yap Behavioral Health and Wellness Program); Veronica Andon, Serlino Wichep, and Kathrine Harry (Pohnpei Behavioral Health and Wellness Program); Nette Kinere and Carsila Tosie (Kosrae Behavioral Health and Wellness Program); Maybelline Ipil (Marshall Islands Epidemiology and Prevention Initiatives); and Rickson Katwon (RMI Ministry of Health and Human Services).

References

Cash, H. (2013). *Palau state epidemiological profile: An update on substance abuse and mental health in Palau*. Palau State Epidemiological Outcomes Workgroup.

CNMI Commonwealth Healthcare Corporation (CHCC). (2021). *Suicide death master listing, 2000–2020* [Unpublished raw data].

David, A. M. (On behalf of Guam SEOW). (2021). *Suicide in Guam, 2019*. Guam State Epidemiological Outcomes Workgroup.

FSM Department of Health & Social Affairs (DHSA). (2019). *Epidemiological profile: 2019 update*.

FSM Department of Health & Social Affairs (DHSA). (2021). *Suicide cases in FSM, 2015–2020* [Unpublished raw data].

FSM Statistics Division. (2020). *FSM statistics*. FSM Department of Resource & Development. https://www.fsmstatistics.fm/

Guam Department of Public Health & Social Services (DPHSS). (2021). *Guam suicide data 1998–2019* [Unpublished raw data].

Hezel, F. X. (1989). Suicide and the Micronesian family. *The Contemporary Pacific, 1*(1/2), 43–74. https://www.jstor.org/stable/23701892

Hezel, F. X. (2016a). *Severe mental illness in Federated States of Micronesia: 25 year follow up of mental illness survey*. FSM Department of Health & Social Affairs.

Hezel, F. X. (2016b). *A survey of suicide over the last half-century: Update on suicide in FSM*. FSM Department of Health & Social Affairs.

Hezel, F. X. (2017). Suicide in Federated States of Micronesia: A new direction. *Pacific Studies, 40*(3), 408–429.

Hezel, F. X., & Wylie, M. A. (1992). Schizophrenia and chronic mental illness in Micronesia: An epidemiological survey. *ISLA: A Journal of Micronesian Studies, 1*(2), 329–354.

Majuro Hospital. (2021). *RMI suicide cases annually 2000–2020 by gender* [Unpublished raw data].

Palau Ministry of Health. (2021). *Leading cause of death, 2013–2019* [Unpublished raw data].
Purcell, D. (1987). *Suicide and mental illness in Japan's Pacific mandate* [Unpublished manuscript]. Department of History, University of Hawai'i at Hilo.
RMI Epidemiological Workgroup. (2018). *Republic of the Marshall Islands behavioral health epidemiological profile 2018.*
Rubinstein, D. H. (1987). Cultural patterns and contagion: Epidemic suicide among Micronesian youth. In A. B. Robillard & A. J. Marsella (Eds.), *Contemporary issues in mental health research in the Pacific Islands* (pp. 127–148). University of Hawai'i Press.
Rubinstein, D. H. (2002). Youth suicide and social change in Micronesia. *Occasional Papers, 36*, 33–41. https://core.ac.uk/download/pdf/144568373.pdf
Sullivan, R. J., Allen, J. S., & Nero, K. L. (2007). Schizophrenia in Palau: A biocultural analysis. *Contemporary Anthropology, 48*(2), 189–213. https://doi.org/10.1086/510474
Workman, R. L., & Rubinstein, D. H. (2019). *Suicide in Micronesia: Guam's historical trends and patterns*. In Guampedia. https://www.guampedia.com/contemporary-guam-suicide-in-micronesia/
Worldometer. (2021). *Population by country*. https://www.worldometers.info/

Chapter 2
Psychology in Fiji: Complexity and New Horizons for the Isles of Smiles

Neeta A. Ramkumar, Ofa Swann, and Tima Tuvuki

The Fiji Islands are internationally coveted as a remote vacation destination with paradisiacal white sand beaches and a friendly local population. The island nation is known as "the Isles of Smiles" in tourism with its official name being the Republic of Fiji. The country is an archipelago of Melanesia in Oceania consisting of 332 islands, a third of which are permanently inhabited. About 75% of Fijians live on the coast of the largest island, Viti Levu. Fiji is the most urbanized Pacific Island Country (PIC) and serves as an educational, commercial, and cultural hub for the South Pacific region. Despite a worldwide survey, which pegged Fiji as the happiest place on earth (Gallup International Association, 2017), the country faces severe mental health vulnerabilities that require local psychology expertise. This chapter reviews cultural meanings of mental illness in Fiji, as well as the past, present, and future context for mental health services and psychology education.

Country and Human Security Overview

Fiji became independent in 1970 after being under British rule for 96 years. The current Fiji population is approximately 900,000 and consists of three major ethnic divisions (Fiji Bureau of Statistics (FBoS), 2018). The *iTaukei*, indigenous (meaning "owner" of the land), make up 45% of the population. An almost equal portion are Fijian people of Indian descent, or Indo-Fijians. Large numbers of *Girmitiyas*

N. A. Ramkumar (✉)
Psychology Across Borders, Austin, TX, USA

O. Swann · T. Tuvuki
University of the South Pacific, Suva, Fiji
e-mail: ofakilomaloma.swann@usp.ac.fj; tima.tuvuki@usp.ac.fj

G. J. Rich, N. A. Ramkumar (eds.), *Psychology in Oceania and the Caribbean*, International and Cultural Psychology, https://doi.org/10.1007/978-3-030-87763-7_2

were brought as indentured laborers from India for the colonial sugar industry. The complicated history of the sugar colonies is violent and devastating (Quishile & Pillay, 2021). The exploitation of indigenous, enslaved, and indentured communities continues to impact the Caribbean and Pacific regions today. In Fiji, colonial policy laid out ethnic divides between iTaukei and Girmitiyas and placed both communities in opposition which continues today.

The rest of the population is comprised of Chinese, European, Polynesian, Melanesian, and Micronesian communities who have made Fiji their home. Fiji is a multicultural and multireligious society with 64.4% Christian (primarily Methodist and Catholic), 27.9% Hindu, and 6.3% Muslim (FBoS, 2018). English remains an official language and is spoken by the majority of the population as a second language. Vernacular Fijian is a type of Austronesian language of the Malayo-Polynesian family. There are several dialects and variations among regions and island groups. Fijian Hindi is also an official language and combines elements of dialects from Awadhi and Bhojpuri, Fijian, Arabic, and English. The capital of Suva is particularly reflective of this diversity; however, ethnic tensions are entangled with Fijian politics.

Forty percent of Fijians were estimated to live in poverty in 2010, and the standard of Fiji living continues to decline overall (FBoS, 2011). Since independence, subsequent governments have been democratically elected, but there were recurrent coups d'état in 1987, 2000, and 2006. The military takeovers destabilized the nation and drastically impacted the people and their livelihoods. Several studies document severe personal losses (Ramasamy et al., 2008), social effects (Gepul, 2004), and economic setbacks (Jayaraman & Choong, 2008; Stauvermann & Kumar, 2009). While Indians were once the ethnic majority in Fiji (by 1946), many migrated after the coups and because of tensions due to land rights (Lal, 2013). Tens of thousands of Indian families have been displaced since the 1990s as land leases from the colonial administration expire (Narayan, 2008). Urban areas have become flooded with squatter settlements, and 87% of the land in Fiji is owned by iTaukei Mataqali or the state.

In many developing regions, neoliberal policies have affected global food systems and made high-quality fresh foods and healthy diets increasingly unaffordable (Phillips et al., 2019). The Pacific region has one of the highest rates of noncommunicable diseases (NCDs) worldwide. In Fiji, the shift from traditional whole foods to nutrient-poor and energy-dense processed foods has been associated with premature death due to cardiovascular disease, cancer, and diabetes. Only 16% of Fiji's population lives past 50 years of age (World Health Organization, 2011b). In addition, a survey of NCDs found a high rate of binge drinking and that 37% of the adult population smokes (Chung, 2002). In children, both underweight/malnourishment and obesity have increased in the population. While breastfeeding is associated with improved childhood dietary habits, in 2004, only 40% of babies were being breastfed at 6 months (World Health Organization (WHO), 2019)—likely due to widespread marketing implying that infant formula was as healthy as or better than breastmilk. The pressures for economic growth and multinational corporations in Fiji are often at odds with effective public health policy. Interventions have largely placed the burden on changing lifestyle and food choices on the individual without addressing larger environmental influences such as poverty and scarcity of healthier options.

Like other PICs, Fiji is faced with rising sea levels and heightened exposure to natural disasters such as tropical disturbances, tsunamis, earthquakes, and severe flooding. Cyclone Winston, one of the largest cyclones recorded in the Southern Hemisphere, hit Fiji in 2016 with devastating impact on lives and the environment—especially coral reefs. Some rural communities were relocated as a result. The cyclone revealed the urgent need for the country to prepare for climate change adaptation in terms of mental health and food/water security (Mangubhai, 2016). Extreme weather events have also been associated with increased outbreaks of dengue, malaria, cholera, filariasis, leptospirosis, and ciguatera fish poisoning.

In addition to political, economic, and environmental complexities, Fiji faces many social challenges. Urbanization, breakdown of traditional family systems, and substance abuse are an ongoing challenge (Chang, 2011). There is a high prevalence of child abuse, gender-based violence (64% of partnered women as estimated by the Fiji Women's Crisis Centre, 2013), and violence towards LGBTQ+ minority groups (George, 2008). Geographically, Fiji's islands are spread across vast distances that make it difficult to access healthcare and social services (Chang, 2011). Poverty, NCDs and ill-health, social exclusion, and unemployment are known to have a cyclical relationship with mental health. As climate change and global shifts are only exacerbating existing vulnerabilities, the need for mental health expertise is only expected to increase. The COVID-19 pandemic has been the latest setback drastically impacting Fiji's tourism, health, and education sectors and is still unfolding.

Prevalence and Mental Health Needs

Three-quarters of the world's global burden of mental illness is situated in lower- and middle-income countries (WHO, 2011a), and Fiji is no exception. There is no systemic baseline data collected regarding the prevalence of mental illness in the South Pacific. Most countries have used global estimates from the 2004 WHO Mental Health World Survey to predict that 13% of adults live with mental illness. Using 2017 census data, population estimates for Fiji are nearly 88,500 with mild-to-moderate mental illness and 26,500 with severe (FBoS, 2018).

In annual medical service camps to Fijian villages, Sivakumaran et al. (2015) noted mood and anxiety disorders as the most frequently endorsed clinical presentation for mental health from 2011 to 2014. Men generally reported psychosocial concerns related to substance abuse (kava and alcohol), employment and financial stability, and grief/loss. Women reported issues related to "domestic violence, poverty, abandonment from family (especially in old age), relationship stressors, family planning and fertility issues, grief and loss issues, general anxiety and some conversion and psycho-somatic presentations where emotional distress was culturally inappropriate to be displayed."

Some of the highest estimates of suicide in the world—for youth suicide in particular—are found among Pacific populations (Booth, 1999). In Fiji, the average age for attempting suicide is 16 years old with Fijians of Indian descent being the most vulnerable demographic (Delaibatiki, 2017). However, officially reported suicide cases (attempts and completions combined) indicate that 66% are male (FBoS, 2018). There is reason to believe that reported rates underestimate the gravity of the situation (Booth, 1999). Haynes (2018) contends that the historically low status of the Indian population and the "invisibility" of other groups such as rural women and the aged have contributed to insufficient public attention.

Sivakumaran et al. (2015) concluded that "the health service in Fiji does not have the capacity or infrastructure to support people with mental illness [...] With the study of psychiatry still not considered a priority, the local medical practitioners and medical students expressed a lack of understanding on how to diagnose, treat and provide guidance in caring for someone with mental illness." Fiji is among the most-resourced countries in the South Pacific in terms of physical and mental healthcare access, yet in 2011, only 6000 people were seen at St. Giles, the only national psychiatric facility (Singh et al., 2013). Without accounting for the skills of traditional healers or nonprofessional providers, this indicates over a 90% treatment gap in Fiji across all mental disorders (mild, moderate, and severe). The estimate is among the highest in global research on the mental health treatment gap (Kohn et al., 2004). Previous research found that 42% of a Fijian sample disliked taking medications for mental illness and 25.5% dislike being labeled with a mental health diagnosis (Aghanwa, 2004). The paucity of integrated behavioral and psychological interventions to complement psychiatric medication management is likely contributing to this pronounced treatment gap.

Cultural Meaning of Mental Illness and Treatment

Culture and social contexts play an influential role in ways in which the illness is understood and treatment decided (McDonald, 2015). In Fiji, as in other PICs, there is a commonly held belief that trained mental health professionals only work with severe mental illness, which stigmatizes help seeking. Indeed, one of the theorized reasons for low utilization of available mental health services by Pasifika peoples is cultural perceptions of mental illness (Te Pou o Te Whakaaro Nui, 2010). Mental health and mental illness seem to still be relatively new concepts in Fiji and can be understood in diverse ways.

There is a general perception that people with mental illness are a violent lost cause, so they should be kept on the periphery of society (Nabukavou, 2017). They are often ostracized by their families and communities. Words commonly "used to describe mental illness are *lialia* (Fijian: crazy/mad/stupid), *pagala* (Fijian-Indian: crazy/mad) or 'St. Giles,' referring to the psychiatric hospital in Suva" (McDonald,

2015, p. 28). The stigma associated with mental illness is linked to indigenous interpretations of madness and shame brought to the family (Backe, 2013). Traditional perspectives among both iTaukei and Indian ethnic groups often attribute mental illness to curses or possession by evil spirits. Sorcery or black magic in Fiji is typically linked to jealousy, revenge, and hatred (McDonald, 2015) and brings about misfortune. Curses also are thought to come about from breaking cultural protocols (transgressing taboos) or not fulfilling one's familial customary obligations.

Interestingly, both traditional Indian and iTaukei interpretations of health and wellness are holistic and generational in nature. The *Vanua* is an important concept to indigenous Fijians as it consists of "physical, social and cultural dimensions which are interrelated" (Ravuvu, 1995, p. 70). In a study done by Orcherton (2017), research participants believed that some illnesses are caused by the *Vanua (mate ni Vanua)* and some are attributed to the *sau ni Vanua* (wrongdoings to the *Vanua*). In Fiji, various spiritual perspectives of the consequences of one's actions on the future (e.g., the Hindu concept of *Karma*, the Muslim concept of *Kifarah*, and the Christian concept of *Sin*) are all culturally understood to play out across generations. It is believed that if black magic was practiced by one's ancestral line without requesting for pardon, descendants are bound to be punished by a curse. Such consequences may be mental or physical and this spiritual explanation of illness may inhibit medical treatment-seeking.

For the iTaukei, assistance may be sought from traditional healers or *na veisorosorovi* or *bulubulu* to facilitate the process of forgiveness so that amicable relationships can be reestablished. Witch doctors were once considered pivotal in psychotherapeutic situations (Gluckman, 1969; Aghanwa, 2004; Chang, 2011). In rural areas, traditional healers are still consulted for a variety of health problems, which can range from minor health ailments to more life-threatening diseases like cancer and poisoning (WHO, 2011b). Postnatal depression is a known condition that may be treated through herbal remedies or spiritual healing; *cavuka* is when women experience a severe psychotic illness, and *tadoka ni vasucu* describes somatic symptoms for a short duration (Becker & Lee, 2002). Pride in traditional medicine, faith in prayer, and beliefs about spiritual risk contribute to preference of the iTaukei ethnomedical paradigm—which sometimes complements and sometimes contradicts biomedical models and explanations (Phillips, 2020). *Tevoro* (adaptation of Christian devil) could possess doctors to give the wrong diagnosis and sudden death. Prescribed medication may be unaffordable, inconsistently available, or in opposition to sociocultural explanations of illness, and was often disregarded. Villagers with physical illness were more likely to feel a sense of safety in relying on herbal remedies and faith-based approaches to uncertainty. Medication management for mental illness likely faces the same interplay with alternative paradigms.

While counseling is thought of as a collaborative change process in Western contexts, Auxier et al. (2005) stated that counseling in Fiji is likely to be viewed as "directive advising" or a "corrective process administered by elder family members, village leaders, clergy, and teachers who counsel those who stray from cultural or religious norms." Nabukavou (2017) quoted a family member on indigenous Fijian mental health:

> The challenge inherent in always thinking, deciding and acting in the interest of the community is that a person is not encouraged to express his feelings about things that concern him as an individual. Therapy is about personal space and the self, which is foreign to the iTaukei context. A person does not have the luxury of having his own space in which to heal himself as he is always deemed to be part of a larger picture. It is difficult to restore oneself in such circumstances if there are community expectations, taboos and protocols hanging over you all the time. A person's preoccupation with cultural considerations and group identity hinders the opportunity to focus on one's wellbeing and find a pathway for therapy. Self-motivation, self-awareness and self-fulfillment are unfamiliar concepts in iTaukei culture.

For all ethnic groups, the seeking of professional counseling may be viewed as a norm violating itself as it involves taking personal concerns beyond the boundaries of traditional family and social groups. Consistent with this perspective of counseling, preparation to be a counselor may be more related to maturity, social status, or experience in a related field rather than the understanding of counseling as a professional credential. Although traditional healers, spiritual leaders, and informal counseling often fill in the gap and are a significant component of care, this can perpetuate misconceptions about mental illness if not integrated into the healthcare system (Leckie & Hughes, 2017).

Colonial Legacy

Christian missionaries introduced Western medicine to the South Pacific Islands from the nineteenth century. Healthcare and provision of training was typically institutionalized by the colonial state. In 1884, the first asylum in the region was established in Fiji. Attention to mental health made a relatively late entry into the region due to Pacific colonies being considered peripheral, but some colonial officials expressed a need for the management of "lunatics" and, later, for the psychological impact of dislocation and modernization that followed World War II (Leckie & Hughes, 2017, p. 255). While psychopharmacology and socialization were provided as hospital treatments, psychotherapy and assessment were not; thus, psychiatric approaches inevitably prevailed over the psychological.

The introduction of hospitalization brought a new alternative to local communities unable to cope with the severely mentally ill, but there was "little evidence of traditional concepts of aetiology having any influence over the application of psychiatry to Fiji" (Roberts et al., 2017, p. 238). Colonial and missionary authorities specifically targeted indigenous healing practices and beliefs (NiaNia et al., 2017). In the early years of the Fiji asylum, Europeans were separated from "natives" which lumped iTaukei with Girmitiyas. Wilson (1965) explored admission rates from 1941 to 1962 and found that Indians were admitted approximately twice as much as indigenous patients. Wilson concluded this was because Indians were more likely to be affected by "Europeanisation" while indigenous Fijians were accommodated at the tribal level. Still, all "native" patients sustained high mortality rates by comparison to their European counterparts.

Mental health infrastructure originated in the transfer of modern medical care to the colonies along with public health, policing, and prisons. Presumptions of mental normality were therefore linked to colonial legal and social control in the management of the insane: "Madness at one level was framed as a homogenous other but this could pertain to unsettled bodies and minds of both colonisers and colonised. Within this, demarcations of madness were defined, incarcerated, controlled and occasionally treated, according to colonial stereotypes of gender and ethnicity" (Leckie, 2007).

Despite this colonial legacy, mental health services and specialists remain centralized at St. Giles Hospital which continues to operate as Fiji's only psychiatric facility today (WHO, 2011b). Although there are no sub-specialist psychiatric services, there are now separate units for alcohol and drug abuse, children and adolescents, and a psychogeriatric clinic. St. Giles operates in the community through a network of public health facilities. Stress Management Wards were integrated into each of the divisional hospitals and outreach clinics. St. Giles also has regular forensic clinics at Suva Prison and Naboro. Increases in psychiatric admissions and outpatient services utilization are likely due to growing public awareness of mental health and improved referral systems (Roberts et al., 2017). Even with these improvements, being a patient of St. Giles continues to carry considerable stigma. It is known by most of the population to be for those with serious mental illness and when traditional interventions have failed.

The British colonial administration in Fiji adopted Western psychiatry without community discussion. Prevention and awareness will require healthcare professionals who can reconcile traditional etiologies with biomedical frameworks (Backe, 2013) and explain using basic scientific terminology for the general public to understand. With the profession of psychology in Fiji in its infancy, psychologists have the additional challenge of educating the public on who they are and what they do. On one hand, psychologists must distinguish behavioral interventions from psychiatric medication management. On the other hand, talk therapies and assessment must complement dominant traditional and spiritual explanations.

Counseling Services

Beyond psychiatric care, there is a developing network of NGOs that provide varying degrees of counseling and support services in Fiji. These include Pacific Counselling and Social Services, Fiji Council of Social Services, Empower Pacific, and some faith-based organizations. Initial crisis counseling with referral is provided by Fiji Lifeline Counselling Service (via phone) and the House of Sarah, carers to survivors of domestic violence (Australia's Department of Foreign Affairs and Trade (DFAT), 2017). Medical Services Pacific provides mobile counseling along with physical health visits especially as it relates to reproductive health, forensic reports for sexual assault, and legal services. The Fiji Women's Crisis Centre also takes a comprehensive approach from training programs to counseling and case management of practical support services such as shelter and medical care.

Counselors come from various training backgrounds and qualifications. A comprehensive review of counseling services across the Pacific revealed that the vast majority of organizations lacked counselors with a diploma or degree in counseling, social work, psychology, etc. and staff may only have a couple weeks of training and/or practical experience (Australia's DFAT, 2017). In developed country contexts, high-level health professions such as psychologists and psychiatrists historically trained and supported the development of counselors and community workers. In the Pacific Islands, formal mental health capacity building expanded in the reverse direction—from the ground up. This approach was necessary to respond to immediate community needs and resulted in a proliferation of people working in counseling roles. At early stages, short courses and training were less expensive and more practical than coordinating masters or doctoral level education (Auxier et al., 2005). Informal counselors may have benefitted from sporadic workshops or short courses conducted by clergy or other interested groups. The current challenge is supporting mental health workers in their scope of practice. They may be assigned complex cases with limited knowledge or resources to respond effectively. Psychologists were identified as effectually absent across specialization levels (Australia's DFAT, 2017).

A more in-depth review of national services (Fiji Health Sector Support Program, 2017) found many case managers, mental health nurses, and basic counseling counselors at lower levels of service provision, but only one to two clinical psychologists or psychiatrists in the entire country to "refer up" to. This indicated little change in the previous decade of 0.24 psychiatrists and 0.12 psychologists per 100,000 people in Fiji (Fiji Ministry of Health Women Social Welfare & Poverty Alleviation, 2008). The consequences of the shortage of high-level mental health professionals in the current care system have also been documented. Both the Pacific and Fiji reviews of counseling services identified similar barriers, including:

(a) Inconsistent or lack of supervision/evaluation of counselors
(b) Lack of skills in counselors or intervening beyond counseling capacity (especially in the case of trauma and complex problems and were even "intrusive and upsetting to patients")
(c) Noncompliance with key ethical principles of counseling (e.g., confidentiality violations or unmonitored standards)

These kinds of outcomes only perpetuate the stigma against mental health and work against attempts to establish trustworthy relationships between mental health professions and the public. Quality assurance, ethical compliance, and accountability must be an integrated part of service delivery. Although mental health capacity building in the Pacific context has been well underway in recent decades, the current system has become unbalanced with the potential to do more harm than good.

Urgency in action is required to lift the professionalism of services and earn public trust in providers.

Education and Career Paths

Regular clinical and process-oriented supervision are foundational aspects of mental health training in psychology, psychiatry, and counseling professions. Supervised practice allows trainees to build skills gradually and endorse their competency to practice independently. Like other lower- and middle-income countries, however, Fiji severely lacks the infrastructure for supervision. As a consequence, no internationally recognized pathway for independent practice for either psychology or counseling professions exists in the South Pacific region to date. Mental health providers who seek training overseas (typically in Australia or New Zealand) often migrate permanently due to the higher salaries, and thus, "brain-drain" issues contribute to the problem of capacity building. Additionally, training programs in other countries are unlikely to be contextualized to the needs, resources, or cultures of Fijian communities. There is a genuine need for such programs to be offered locally.

The University of the South Pacific (USP) is a regional university serving much of the anglophone Pacific. The university's main campus is located in Fiji, and there are satellite campuses in each member country: Cook Islands, Kiribati, Marshall Islands, Nauru, Niue, Solomon Islands, Tokelau, Tonga, Tuvalu, Vanuatu, and Samoa. The USP was the first to formalize counseling education in 1993 with the introduction of undergraduate counseling courses. A Certificate in Guidance Counseling evolved to a Certificate of Basic Counseling in 2006 (Auxier et al., 2005). It consisted of five courses and 40-hour practicum at a community site, but was phased out in 2011 in hopes of offering a professional psychology program at the postgraduate level. Despite several iterations of such program proposals, the USP has yet to launch a replacement to the certificate. Obstacles have included insufficient staffing and constraints that require new university programs to be both accreditable and profitable. Current graduates of a general psychology postgraduate program receive two theory-based counseling courses. They may continue on to a master's program in research and are often hired for clinical roles with no prior field training. Until such time as the USP is in a position to offer supervised training for professional psychological practice, a nascent partnership established with Massey University in New Zealand has potential as a bridge between USP's current postgraduate offering in psychology and local supervised practice training. Massey University has opened a small number of places in their post-master's internship offering to USP psychology graduates, with supervised practice training structured to support students to practice adaptively when they return to their respective PIC. The USP houses the only postgraduate psychology program in the region at this time of publication.

The Fiji School of Medicine introduced psychiatry training to medical students in 1968 and nursing students in 1996 as part of their curriculum (Chang, 2011).

After joining Fiji National University, it began to offer the region's first psychiatry training program (graduate diploma in mental health for doctors) in 2011 and implemented additional certifications in mental health for nurses (2006 and 2013) to assist with the treatment gap in primary care settings. Through these medical professions, psychiatry as a field continues to advance in Fiji deficit of referral options to counselors and psychologists specializing in behavioral interventions (i.e., alternatives to psychopharmacology). In 2017, the USP and the Australian Pacific Technical College began offering a pre-bachelor's/vocational certification in counseling. Despite high enrollment numbers, graduates require regular supervision to advance in the counseling profession, and no counseling organizations reviewed were resourced to provide supervision at international benchmarks (Australia's DFAT, 2017). Thus, mental health capacity building in the region is bottlenecked by the shortfall of adequate supervision infrastructure for both psychology and counseling professions.

Despite their ability to fill supervisory roles, practicing psychologists are the least represented mental health profession in Fiji with counseling, social work, and psychiatry programs already in place. Part of the dilemma rests in educating decision makers about the overlapping but distinctive services in mental healthcare. For instance, given a scarcity of designated school counselors with supervised training in Fiji, teachers were selected to serve as counselors in their schools with blended roles. This contributed to the perception that counseling interventions are part of teacher education rather than a separate profession. Industry stakeholders must demand distinct academic and training programs for universities to implement. Psychology must be reclassified as a health science in addition to being a social science. Increasing capacity involves developing each service level and type so that mental healthcare works as a system with support networks and referral processes.

A Sustainable Future for Psychology in Fiji

Since community agencies and nongovernmental organizations do not have the infrastructure, long-term training pathways for applied psychology training require university partnerships. The major barrier is that training programs typically run at a financial loss to universities. Universities are rarely able to offer these programs without subsidies from other sources (their undergraduate programs, government funding, grants, etc.). A further hurdle for Fiji is the current absence of psychology field supervisors external to the university who could assist with the clinical training workload.

Still, university training programs are often the most cost-effective way for low- and middle-income countries to increase capacity to provide quality care. A desirable feature of graduate professional practice programs is the inclusion of university-based training clinics (Walz & Bleur, 2012). Training clinics are able to offer low-cost services to communities while providing students a safe environment to practice under close supervision according to their level of proficiency (Hittner &

Fawcett, 2012). The facility could also be a joint endeavor by multiple programs such that psychology, social work, and counseling students could train alongside each other as allied mental health professionals. This experience would facilitate integrated care models in their future workplaces. Thus, the investment in first generation of supervised trainees then becomes a long-term sustainable solution as local graduates become field supervisors in health centers and community agencies.

Further, a regional university such as the USP would be able to offer services via telepsychology and videoconferencing across multiple PICs. This model of care is a quickly growing means of service delivery worldwide in light of the COVID-19 pandemic. Evidence-based training models have already taken off in the United States (McCord et al., 2015), Australia, and New Zealand. Telepsychology is particularly suited for remote communities found in the geographically dispersed island countries. The reality is not only insufficiency of specialist services in rural areas, but also the lack of economic resources to make follow-up visits in the city. Utilization of newly available technology is already available for distance and online learning across USP campuses. The telehealth model supports building community partnerships across the region. For instance, students from Tonga could be supervised in Fiji while providing mental health services and/or consultation to their home country. This model carries enormous potential for contextualizing delivery to the needs of the Pacific region.

The Fiji Psychological Society (FPsS) was founded at the end of 2019 as the nation's first professional network of psychology degree holders, students, and allied professionals. Professional societies are charged with standardizing and regulating qualifications for service delivery. In psychology, advocating for legal enforcement of ethical codes of conduct to ensure accountability is typically done through the society. There will be questions of how to maintain standards while "grandfathering in" practicing professionals who did not have access to new educational programs. Beyond these logistical considerations, new professional societies have to reckon with many theoretical and value-based issues. They must consider the extent to which psychology should align itself with the medical model (e.g., develop mechanisms for insurer reimbursement) and engage in an ongoing process of what constitutes evidence-based practice for their communities.

Implicit in the process are steps towards self-determination. These debates, discussions, and formulations are decolonization and indigenization processes with transformative potential. Fijian psychologists will be tasked with applying psychological knowledge in "new" sociocultural domains. They must identify cultural norms, adapt prevailing models, build on traditional social structures, and define the ethical practice of psychology for their people. This is a deeply creative process of reclaiming in which the representation of Fijian psychologies and peoples will shape the future of the region and the field of psychology itself.

Conclusion

Paradisiacal images of the Isles of Smiles mask the complex realities of the various threats to Fijian well-being and human security. Enrollments in certificate and academic programs missing supervised experience have resulted in a proliferation of people working in counseling roles with no pathways for independent practice. Although public awareness and interest in mental health treatment is growing in Pacific communities, there is little trust in quality care. Fiji has a lot to gain from investing in high-level psychology professional practice programs and even more to lose by delaying it. A collective effort is necessary to strengthen existing mental healthcare systems. The future for psychology in the Fiji Islands is exciting to consider. There is much to discover about mental health and cultural ways of healing. There are ample opportunities to apply psychological knowledge in Pacific Island contexts and for the benefit of Fijian communities.

References

Aghanwa, H. (2004). Attitude toward and knowledge about mental illness in Fiji islands. *International Journal of Social Psychiatry, 50*(4), 361–375. https://doi.org/10.1177/0020764004050336

Australia's Department of Foreign Affairs and Trade. (2017). *Review of counselling services in the Pacific final report*. Pacific Women Shaping Pacific Development.

Auxier, C. R., Forster, P. M., & Kuruleca, S. (2005). Counseling in Fiji. *Journal of Mental Health Counseling, 27*(2), 142–148. https://doi.org/10.17744/mehc.27.2.jg83yyqdtp7ewdel

Backe, E. L. (2013, December 22). *Mental health and mental illness in Fiji*. Retrieved from Emma Louise Backe Blogs: http://www.linkedin.com › emma-louise-backe-10285156.

Booth, H. (1999). Pacific Island suicide in comparative perspective. *Journal of Biosocial Science, 31*(4), 433–448. https://doi.org/10.1017/S0021932099004332

Becker, A. E., & Lee, D. T. (2002). Indigenous Models for Attenuation of Postpartum Depression. In World mental health casebook (pp. 221–236). Springer, Boston, MA.

Chang, O. (2011). Mental health care in Fiji. *Asia-Pacific Psychiatry, 3*, 73–75.

Chung, E. (2002). *Fiji non-communicable diseases (NCD) step survey 2002*. Fiji Ministry of Health.

Delaibatiki. (2017, May 4). Children's suicide statistics shocking. *Fiji Sun.* Retrieved from: https://fijisun.com.fj/2017/04/05/childrens-suicide-statistics-shocking/

Fiji Bureau of Statistics. (2011). *Report on the household income and expenditure survey for Fiji: 2008–09*. FBoS.

Fiji Bureau of Statistics. (2018). *Fiji 2017 population and housing census*. FBoS Fiji Bureau of Statistics. Retrieved from: https://www.statsfiji.gov.fj/index.php/statistics/population-censuses-and-surveys

Fiji Health Sector Support Program. (2017). *Review of counselling services in Fiji*. Fiji Ministry of Health.

Fiji Ministry of Health Women Social Welfare & Poverty Alleviation. (2008). *Annual report 2008*. Government Printers. Retrieved from: https://www.health.gov.fj/wp-content/uploads/2018/03/Annual-Report-2008.pdf

Fiji Women's Crisis Centre. (2013). *Somebody's life is everyone's business – National research on women's health and life experiences in Fiji (2010/2011): A summary exploring the prevalence, incidence and attitudes to intimate partner violence in Fiji.* Retrieved from: http://www.fijiwomen.com/wp-content/uploads/2017/11/National-Survey-Summary.pdf1

Gallup International Association. (2017). *Gallup International's annual global end of year survey: Happiness, hope, economic optimism.* Retrieved from: https://www.gallup-international.com/fileadmin/user_upload/surveys/2017/2017_Happiness_Hope_Economic-Optimism.pdf

Gluckman, L. K. (1969). Drau ni Kau: The Ethnopsychiatry of Fiji in Historical and Clinical Perspective. *Australian & New Zealand Journal of Psychiatry, 3*(3), 152–158.

George, N. (2008). Contending masculinities and the limits of tolerance: Sexual minorities in Fiji. *The Contemporary Pacific*, University of Hawai'i Press, *20*(1), 163–189.

Gepul, J. W. (2004). Economic development and nation building in the South Pacific: In search of a new paradigm. *Ritsumeikan Journal of Asia Pacific Studies, 14*, 113–130.

Haynes, R. H. (2018). *Suicide and social response in.* A Historical Survey. Published online by Cambridge University Press. https://doi.org/10.1192/bjp.151.1.21

Hittner, J., & Fawcett, M. (2012). Developing a counselor education training clinic: The first year. *Ideas and Research You Can Use: VISTAS 2012, 1*, 1–7.

Jayaraman, T. K., & Choong, C. K. (2008). Exchange market pressure in a small Pacific island country: A study of Fiji: 1975-2005. *International Journal of Social Economics, 35*, 985.

Kohn, R., Saxena, S., Levav, I., & Saraceno, B. (2004). Policy and practice: The treatment gap in mental health care. *Bulletin of the World Health Organization, 82*(11), 858–866. https://doi.org/10.1590/S0042-96862004001100011

Lal, B. V. (2013). *Fiji Islands: From immigration to emigration. Migration information.* Retrieved from: www.migrationinformation.org/

Leckie, J. (2007). Unsettled minds: Gender and settling madness in Fiji. In S. Mahone & M. Vaughan (Eds.), *Psychiatry and empire* (pp. 99–123). Palgrave Macmillan.

Leckie, J., & Hughes, F. (2017). Mental health in the smaller Pacific states. In H. Minas & M. Lewis (Eds.), *Mental health in Asia and the Pacific: Historical and cultural perspectives* (pp. 253–272). Springer.

Mangubhai, S. (2016). *Impact of tropical Cyclone Winston on coral reefs in the Vatu-i-Ra Seascape.* (Report No 01/16). Wildlife Conservation Society.

McCord, C., Saena, J., Armstrong, T., & Elliott, T. (2015). Training the next generation of counseling psychologists in the practice of telepsychology. *Counselling Psychology Quarterly, 28*(3), 324–344. https://doi.org/10.1080/09515070.2015.1053433

McDonald, N. N. (2015). *A 'St. Giles case': Negotiating mental illness, treatment and the adverse impact of stigma in Suva, Fiji.* Macquarie University.

Nabukavou, T. (2017). Our personal journey in the Fijian context. Invited talk. *Creating Futures Conference 2017*, Suva, Fiji.

Narayan, S. (2008). Racial discrimination in Fiji. *Journal of South Pacific Law, 12*(1), 68–75.

NiaNia, W., Bush, A., & Epston, D. (2017). *Collaborative and indigenous mental health therapy: Tātaihono – Stories of Māori healing and psychiatry*. Routledge.

Orcherton, M. (2017). The Social and Cultural Refocusing of iTaukei Landscapes of Identity through Traditional Healing Practices (Doctoral dissertation). Retrieved from USP electronic Thesis Collection: http://digilib.library.usp.ac.fj/

Phillips, T. (2020). The everyday politics of risk: Managing diabetes in Fiji. *Medical Anthropology, 39*(8), 735–750. https://doi.org/10.1080/01459740.2020.1717489

Phillips, T., Ravuvu, A., McMichael, C., Thow, A. M., Browne, J., Waqa, G., Tutuo, J., & Gleeson, D. (2019). Nutrition policy-making in Fiji: Working in and around neoliberalisation in the Global South. *Critical Public Health, 31*(3), 316–326. https://doi.org/10.1080/09581596.2019.1680805

Quishile, C., & Pillay, E. (2021). *Coolie cut cane: The sugar empire of the South Pacific.* Published on the occasion of the online exhibition Coolie Cut Cane, Bad Fiji Gyals Collective. Retrieved from https://badfijigyals.com/

Ramasamy, S., Krishnan, V., Bedford, R., & Bedford, C. (2008). The Recognised Seasonal Employer policy: Seeking the elusive triple wins for development through international migration. *Pacific Economic Bulletin, 23*, 171–186.

Ravuvu, A. (1995). Vaka i Taukei: The Fijian Way of Life. Suva: Fiji Times.

Roberts, G. J., Leckie, J., & Chang., O. (2017). The history of mental health in Fiji. In H. Minas & M. Lewis (Eds.), Mental health in Asia and the Pacific: Historical and cultural perspectives (pp. 237–251). New York, NY: Springer.

Singh, S., Chang, O., Funk, M., Shields, L., Andrews, A., Hughes, F., Sugiura, K., & Drew, N. (2013). *WHO Profile on mental health in development (WHO proMIND)*. World Health Organization. Retrieved from: https://apps.who.int/iris/bitstream/handle/10665/85325/9789241505659_eng.pdf?sequence=1&isAllowed=y

Sivakumaran, H., George, K., Naker, G., & Nadanachandran, K. (2015). Experience from mental health clinics held during medical service camps in Fiji. *Australasian Psychiatry, 23*(6), 667–669. https://doi.org/10.1177/1039856215592321

Stauvermann, P. J., & Kumar, S. (2009). Can the Fijian economy be saved by ethanol production? *Pacific Economic Bulletin, 24*, 92.

Te Pou o Te Whakaaro Nui. (2010). *Talking therapies for Pasifika peoples: Best and promising practice guide for mental health and addiction services*. Retrieved from: https://www.tepou.co.nz/resources/talking-therapies-for-pasifika-peoples/152

Walz, G. R., & Bleuer, J. C. (2012). Developing a counselor education training clinic: The first year. *Ideas and Research You Can Us: VISTAS 2012, 1*, Article 22.

Wilson, G. D. (1965). "Europeanisation" and admission to mental hospital in the Fiji Islands. *New Zealand Medical Journal, 64*(395), 364–367.

World Health Organization. (2011a). *Global burden of mental disorders and the need for a comprehensive, coordinated response from health and social sectors at the country level*. World Health Organization.

World Health Organization. (2011b). *The Fiji Islands health system review. Health Systems in Transition* (Vol. 1 (1)). WHO Regional Office for the Western Pacific.

World Health Organization. (2019). *Nutrition Landscape Information System (NLiS)*. World Health Organization. Retrieved from http://apps.who.int/nutrition/landscape/report.aspx?iso=FJI&rid=1621

Chapter 3
The State of Psychology and Mental Health Services in Vanuatu

Christopher R. Brown and Jimmy Obed

The role of psychology has historically had little relevance in Vanuatu. The reason for this has its roots in Vanuatu's isolation and geography, in its language and culture, in its colonial past and in its place as a newly developing nation. This has led to there being effectively no mental health services in the country until relatively recently. However, in the last decade, there has been a growing recognition of the benefits that good mental health care can provide the community. Over that time, Vanuatu has produced significant mental health policies and begun the process of providing mental health care across the country. This chapter will discuss the state of psychology and mental health care in Vanuatu, consider the changes that have occurred in recent times and will look at some of the ways that this new focus on mental health care is benefiting the community.

Demographic Overview

Geography

Vanuatu is an archipelago in the South Pacific. It is around 1770 km (1100 mi) east of Australia and 800 km (500 mi) west of Fiji. The archipelago stretches approximately 1300 km (810 mi) from north to south and comprises 83 separate islands. Of these, 65 are inhabited. There are only 14 islands that measure more than 100 km^2. The three largest are Espiritu Santo, Malekula and Efate – the most populated island and home to the capital Port Vila.

C. R. Brown (✉) · J. Obed
Vanuatu Ministry of Health, Port Vila, Republic of Vanuatu

G. J. Rich, N. A. Ramkumar (eds.), *Psychology in Oceania and the Caribbean*, International and Cultural Psychology, https://doi.org/10.1007/978-3-030-87763-7_3

Population

The population of Vanuatu is approximately 300,000 (Vanuatu Demographics, 2020). Around 98% are indigenous Ni-Vanuatu who are of Melanesian descent. The remaining population is predominantly comprised of people from European, Micronesian, Chinese and Vietnamese descent (Vanuatu National Statistics Office, 2009). The average life expectancy in Vanuatu is 71 years (72.8 female; 69.4 male). Infant mortality is somewhat below the global average, being 22.8 deaths per 1000 live births of children under the age of 5 years (global average = 39/1000 under 5; Worldometer, 2020). There has been a steady increase in population over the last decade (approximately 3.5% per annum).[1] This has led to a demographic shift which shows 54% of the population below the age of 25 (Vanuatu – The World Factbook, 2021).

Economy

Vanuatu is considered a low-income developing country. It was upgraded from least developed country status by the UN in 2020 (UN News, 2020). It is estimated that around 75% of the population lives outside of urban areas (Vanuatu National Statistics Office, 2009). Rural populations live a largely agrarian lifestyle, with family groups tending to their own land as the predominant means of subsistence (Vanuatu National Statistics Office, 2009).

Languages

There are three official languages in Vanuatu. Bislama is the common national language and the primary language of politics and government (Cox et al., 2007). It is a pidgin that is largely based on English. There are variations of this pidgin language spoken throughout the Pacific, including in Papua New Guinea, the Solomon Islands and the Torres Strait. The variations are grammatically distinct but are sufficiently similar to allow for cross-cultural communication. The other two official languages are French and English, which are indicative of Vanuatu's colonial history.

There are also over 100 local languages spoken throughout the archipelago, with several dialects spoken within most islands. Crowley (2000) suggests that Vanuatu is one of the largest linguistically diverse populations in the world. It is common for people living away from their home island to communicate using their local language with others from their communities. This attachment to ones 'mother tongue'

[1] This is based on the average change since the last official census in 2009.

has seen a significant maintenance of indigenous languages throughout the country. It is worth noting that a large proportion of the Vanuatu community are multi-lingual.

The Political System

The Republic of Vanuatu is 40 years old, having gained independence from colonial rule in 1980. The Vanuatu national parliament is a 'Westminster' style democracy that comprises representatives from each of the islands. Multiple political parties stand for election across the country, and government is typically formed on the basis of coalition arrangements between these parties. These coalitions are generally not based on ideological alignments but rather formed on the basis of political expedience (Cox et al., 2007).

The national government of Vanuatu provides a centralising role for the distribution of services. National ministries work with provincial authorities across the country's six provinces (Torba, Sanma, Penama, Malampa, Shefa, Tafea – presented from north to south). Each province is responsible for service provision to their regions in conjunction with and under the purview of the national ministries. Unlike most other parliamentary democracies, the Vanuatu constitution codifies a role for customary chiefs across the islands. This is embodied in the Malvatumauri, or National Council of Chiefs. The Malvatumauri was originally convened after independence in order to codify kastom law – an indigenous regulatory system of rights and responsibilities in island communities. It currently plays a significant role in ensuring that kastom law is represented in the decision-making process of parliament (for a detailed description of the role of kastom in Vanuatu, see Bolton, 2003; Cox et al., 2007; Goddard & Otto, 2013).

The Health System

The Ministry of Health is responsible for the provision of health care across the archipelago. Around 85% of health services are in rural areas. The need for health services across such a large geographic area places great demands on government expenditure. The health budget represents the second largest expense to the country (World Bank Group, 2018). In order to provide services, there is a multi-layered approach to service delivery.

Health services in Vanuatu are provided by two groups – the Southern Health Care Group that provides services to 2 southern provinces (11 islands) and the Northern Health Care Group that provides services to 4 northern provinces (17 islands). There is one primary hospital to service each group. The largest referral hospital – Vila Central Hospital (VCH) – is located in the capital, Port Vila, on the island of Efate. It has 131 beds and 52 doctors, including 15 specialists. The second referral hospital – the Northern Provincial Hospital (NPH) – is based on the island of Espiritu Santo and has 112 beds as well as 9 doctors including 3 specialists.

The majority of health services are provided at a local level. There are six provincial hospitals – one in each province – that are serviced by 11 medical officers, nurse practitioners (who can stand in for doctors in their absence) and trained nursing staff. There are 35 health care centres staffed by nurse practitioners and general nursing staff. They provide medical services to individual islands. There are 92 dispensaries distributed across the country that are staffed by nurses who can prescribe medications, and there are 202 health posts that are staffed by community workers.

Mental health facilities are predominantly located in the two major hospitals. There are four dedicated mental health beds at Vila Central Hospital, which also has one qualified psychiatrist and three mental health nurses. The Northern Provincial Hospital has one dedicated mental health bed and one mental health nurse. There is also a mental health nurse based at the Vanuatu College of Nursing Education.

Psychology and Mental Health Care in Vanuatu

Psychology in Vanuatu

Psychology has traditionally had very little relevance in Vanuatu. Forster (2005) wrote a small and most likely the only review into the role of psychology in Vanuatu. He noted that, at that time, there was no perceived need for psychological service in the country. Furthermore, he noted that there were no psychological associations, no mental health facilities and no clear understanding about the role that psychology could play in the development of the country. Unfortunately, since the writing of that review, the status of psychology has not changed significantly. There has been no systematic attempt to scientifically understand psychological traits in the Ni-Vanuatu population. There are currently no indigenous trained research or clinical psychologists. There are also no psychological counselling or social work services in the country. Furthermore, the opportunity to study psychology at a tertiary level is not available in Vanuatu. The University of the South Pacific does offer a course in psychology. However, it is only offered in Fiji, and students who have the means to study in another country are more likely to study relevant disciplines, like engineering and medicine, rather than psychology. Overall, the discipline of psychology has not been historically recognised in Vanuatu. However, with the growing recognition of the need for effective mental health care in the country, it is hoped that the place of psychology will gain greater relevance in the future.

Cultural Factors and Psychological States

The reasons why psychology is not prominent in Vanuatu may be due to both linguistic and cultural practices. There are few words that describe psychological states in either local languages or Bislama, and descriptions tend be clinically non-specific. For example, in Bislama, someone who is sad may describe the feeling as '*wota fol blo aes*'. Literally, 'water falls from your eyes'. Symptoms of depression may be described as '*hart blong mi i hevi*' – a heavy heart. These descriptive epithets are indicative of the limited psychological literacy within the country. Furthermore, aberrant behaviours evident in mental illnesses have typically been interpreted through a cultural, religious and superstitious lens. References to demon possession, black magic and other spiritual descriptions were, and are, still common throughout the country (George, 2010; Benson et al., 2011; Blignault & Kaur, 2020).

In spite of there being a lack of psychological literacy in the country, the people of Vanuatu show high levels of well-being and psychological resilience. In fact, Vanuatu ranks as one of the happiest places on earth (Happy Planet Index, 2021). This apparent contradiction may be explained by the strong social connections evident in the country. The role of family is central to the community, and kastom tradition obliges family members to care for each other. This includes supporting and caring for people at times of psychological distress. It has been suggested that the presence of tight-knit communities and regular social meetings provide significant material and emotional support and are most likely to be the key contributing factors that are responsible for the high levels of well-being in Vanuatu (Vanuatu National Statistics Office, 2012).

It is worth noting that the rapidly increasing population and the large youth demographic have produced a growing trend for movement towards major town centres. The effect of increased urbanisation of the youth population is producing a fracturing of traditional cultural ties. It can be argued that the effect of urban dislocation and modernisation has the potential to reduce the beneficial psychological effects that are provided by strong family ties. This will increase the mental health burden and most likely see the need for more mental health services over time (see Charlson et al., 2015).

The Mental Health Policy of Vanuatu

Historically, there has been a lack of emphasis on the need for mental health services in Vanuatu. In 2005, a situation analysis of mental health needs across the Pacific noted that mental health services in Vanuatu were effectively non-existent (Hughes et al., 2005; see also Hughes, 2009). In response to this review, the Ministry of Health analysed the state of mental health in Vanuatu. It found that basic mental health services were unavailable on most of the islands in Vanuatu. It also found that there were no trained mental health nurses or doctors, no inpatient facilities in outlying islands, no community care facilities for people with mental disorders and no NGOs in the community dedicated to mental health. Furthermore, there was a heavy reliance on traditional or religious approaches to mental health care at the village level (Ministry of Health, 2009). This led to the development of the first mental health policy in Vanuatu.

The Mental Health Policy (2009–2015) represented the first recognition of the need for mental health services in Vanuatu. It aimed to modernise the approach to mental health care service delivery across the country. In order to do so, a strategic plan was developed to deal with the limited infrastructure available for mental health care and treatment, the lack of mental health professionals, the limited financial resources available for mental health and the lack of services in primary health care (for details, see Ministry of Health, 2009).

In the decade that followed the development of the inaugural Mental Health Policy, there have been significant improvements in the provision of mental health services in Vanuatu (see Tarivonda et al., 2012). The most notable of these have been the development of updated mental health legislation, increases in human resources, the provision of mental health services at the primary care level and recognition for the role of mental health care in the wake of natural disasters. These improvements reflect the country's commitment to creating a mentally healthy and literate community through access to equitable mental health care.

Mental Health Legislation

Mental health legislation in Vanuatu has not been updated for a very long time. The current mental health act dates back to 1965 and simply provides for '… the reception and detention of persons of unsound mind in the mental hospital in Port Vila' (Mental Hospital Act, 1965). This legislation is reminiscent of the British system of 'moral management' for the treatment of the mentally ill that has been evident in many former colonies (e.g. in the Caribbean; Smith, 2010).

As a result of the focus on mental health and the growing need for appropriate mental health care in the country, work began on redrafting the mental health act for Vanuatu in 2016. The redrafted mental health act aims to bring mental health practices in line with modern standards. Some key priorities in the act are the guarantee that mental health care is provided on a voluntary basis where possible and that patients have access to the best possible mental health care based on internationally accepted standards. The new act should ensure equity, access to treatment and the guarantee of human rights to people with mental illnesses. At the time of writing this piece, Vanuatu still does not have a revised mental health act as it is presently under review and awaiting parliamentary approval.

The Mind Care Clinic

One of the greatest advances in mental health treatment in Vanuatu has been the development of the Mind Care Clinic. This clinic, based in the Vila Central Hospital, deals with mentally ill patients from around the country. It has one fully qualified psychiatrist, three fully qualified mental health nurses and four dedicated beds to treat the mentally ill. It also provides a visitation service to remote communities. Since its inception in 2014, it has seen increasing demand for its services, such that the clinic conducted 520 consultations in 2020.

Psychosis, mood disorders, depression and anxiety are the profile of psychiatric disorders that are most typically treated in the clinic. However, there is growing evidence for the critical need to provide interventions around substance abuse and suicide prevention, both of which represent a significant problem in the community.

It can be argued that the disorders that are most frequently treated by the clinic typically represent only the most acute and intransigent psychological disorders; those that produce the greatest behavioural challenges to communities. Less problematic although equally severe psychiatric disorders are not commonly seen. For example, childhood, personality, conduct and paediatric disorders, as well as pre- and post-natal disorders, are less likely to present for treatment at the Mind Care Clinic. The fact that these disorders are not being treated is most likely a result of systemic issues in the provision of health care, rather than their absence in the community.

Some of the systemic challenges that prevent the utilisation of mental health services include a lack of trained personnel in regional health care centres and a lack of psychological services (both of these can be seen to impede effective referral pathways to treatment); a lack of appropriately qualified mental health professionals, a lack of financial resources, a lack of infrastructure and a lack of access to appropriate medication and other resources (all of which put constraints on the number and types of services that can be provided); and a lack of psychological literacy and education in the community (as described above), the role of stigma associated with mental illness and patriarchal dominance (all of which can reduce help-seeking behaviours).

The Mind Care Clinic is the preeminent organisation for the provision of mental health services in the country. Staff at the Mind Care Clinic consider addressing the systemic challenges to the provision of mental health care a key priority. As such, the Mind Care Clinic provides feedback to government on the need for appropriate resources for mental health service provision. It is also developing human resources through training and internship programs (Obed et al., 2020) and is educating the community about mental health, which is helping to destigmatise mental illness and increase psychological literacy across the community.

A Vanuatu Specific Approach to Mental Health Care

An interesting approach to have come out of the Mind Care Clinic is the inclusion of culturally relevant practices in the treatment of mental illness. In Vanuatu, patients suffering psychological distress are typically unlikely to self-refer to psychiatric services. It is more likely that their behaviours will have become so problematic that family members are no longer able to cope and will organise for patients to receive treatment. The decision to seek help for a family member is a significant undertaking. As most people live in remote areas that have limited facilities to treat mental illnesses, the process of seeking treatment can be both expensive and time consuming. Beyond the ostensible cost of travelling from outlying islands, it will typically require family members to accompany the patient to hospital, and remain with them, sometimes for weeks at a time. This takes members of the family away from their responsibilities at home. As a result, it is often only the most intransigent of problems that present for treatment. It is unclear how many people are going without treatment as a result of not being able to afford the time and expense.

The fact that patients are accompanied by family members has provided an opportunity for practitioners at the Mind Care Clinic to adapt treatments in a more culturally relevant way. Traditional Western psychiatric practices have often required patients who are exhibiting severe psychotic symptoms to be placed in seclusion and isolation in order to protect them and others. However, it became clear over time that this practice resulted in increased agitation and a lengthening of the time it took for patients to settle and begin treatment. This observation led practitioners at the Mind Care Clinic to begin allowing the patients to be attended to by their family. As noted above, family connection plays a significant role in resilience and well-being in the country. Anecdotal evidence has suggested that including family members in the treatment of patients, even when they are extremely agitated and in isolation, has helped to settle patients more quickly and has made them more amenable to treatment.

The involvement of family members in a patient's treatment has had an added benefit. It has allowed them to be better educated about the person's condition and their treatment needs. This has been beneficial in the ongoing assessment, treatment and care of the patient once they have returned to their communities. It has also allowed family members to be cognisant of warning signs that may lead to relapse. This family-centred approach is showing promising results. Further study is needed to see how this approach can be better utilised in the Vanuatu context.

Mental Health Psychosocial Support and Natural Disasters

The need to provide post-disaster mental health services has increased with the growing severity and frequency of natural disasters across the Pacific (Dawes et al., 2019). Vanuatu is considered one of the most at-risk countries for natural disasters in the world (World Risk Report, 2019). It is regularly subjected to earthquakes, tsunamis, volcanic eruptions, tropical cyclones and droughts. It is also vulnerable to the effects of climate change and rising sea levels. In response to these disasters, there has been a growing recognition of the need to provide mental health services throughout the country.

In the last 6 years, Vanuatu has been subjected to a series of unprecedented events. In 2015, Vanuatu was impacted by what might be considered the worst series of natural disasters in living memory (Shultz et al., 2018). These included a 6.4 magnitude underwater earthquake, just north of Efate, a small-scale tsunami and the eruption of the volcano on the island of Ambrym. These three events caused widespread damage and dislocation to communities. However, the most significant event occurred a few weeks later. Tropical Cyclone Pam, a category 5 system, passed directly over Vanuatu on March 13, 2015. The destructive effect of TC Pam was felt across the entire archipelago, with wind speeds that reached up to 250 km/h producing extensive damage to many islands. It took many years for Vanuatu to recover from the devastating impact of this cyclone. Shultz et al. (2018) noted that in the wake of these disasters, high levels of psychological distress were reported. They also noted that there was a severe shortage of health care workers, particularly in the mental health sector.

There was a growing recognition for the need to improve access to psychological care following TC Pam (see WHO, 2015; Government of Vanuatu, 2015). In what was the first example of its kind in the country, the Ministry of Health supported a team of trained mental health personnel from the Mind Care Clinic, in partnership with IsraAID – an Israel-based not-for-profit organisation – to provide Mental Health Psychosocial Support (MHPSS) training across affected communities. This team trained community leaders, including chiefs, pastors, police and nurses, about the psychological impacts of natural disasters. The aim was to develop the capacity of communities to deal with natural disasters, through awareness training, and increasing their ability to identify persons of concern (POC). Participants reported that the training was highly relevant to them and that it provided information that they had not previously been aware of (IsraAID, 2015). As part of this program, the team initiated provincial MHPSS committees. These committees were responsible for monitoring the community for signs of psychological distress and liaising with mental health professionals. Overall, this program had the effect of putting control of mental health needs into the hands of local communities and increased awareness of the types of psychological services that were available.

In 2017, the eruption of the Manaro Voui volcano resulted in the evacuation of the entire population of the island of Ambae (approximately 11,000 people). As a result, a large proportion of the population were permanently relocated to neighbouring islands. The effect of relocation produced a significant sense of loss of property, of cultural ties and of belonging to community. Zahlawi et al. (2019) found that 53% of the community were showing signs of high distress following this disaster. In order to deal with the consequences of this disaster, 101 volunteers and community leaders were provided with MHPSS training. This included psychological first aid (PFA), psychosocial support (PSS) and distress awareness training, which enhanced the volunteer's ability to identify persons of concern. The trained volunteers were sent to affected communities and were able to provide psychological support to more than half of the members of the community. IsraAID (2018) noted that this training elevated the role of community leaders and volunteers, allowing them not only to provide psychosocial support in their communities but also to pass information on to others. The result of this was the creation of an enhanced support network within the community.

In 2020, Vanuatu was once again impacted by a severe category 5 tropical cyclone. TC Harold wrought destruction over three northern provinces of Vanuatu, affecting several islands and killing five people (Reliefweb, 2021). In response, a team of trained volunteers along with trained mental health personnel were once again sent to affected communities to provide MHPSS training. This program provided psychological support to community members and increased the awareness of the effects of psychological distress. As had been seen previously, this program enhanced the ability of affected communities to manage the harmful effects of the disaster.

Mental Health Psychosocial Support training has become a commonly used tool to assist affected communities to cope with the effects of natural disasters. It has improved the reach of psychological support across the country. It has also educated communities about the availability of services to assist people that have been affected by disastrous events. It is hoped that this program will continue to provide much needed mental health care to communities affected by natural disasters.

Conclusion

Vanuatu is a proud, resilient and culturally vibrant nation. As with many post-colonial developing countries, it has many challenges to overcome. These include isolation, limited economic resources, a widely distributed rural population, cultural and linguistic diversity, limited psychological literacy, a need to deal with its colonial history and frequent natural disasters. These concerns have all played some role in the way that psychology and mental health has historically been understood throughout the country. However, in the last decade, there have been significant advances in understanding the need for mental health care in Vanuatu. This has produced significant improvements in the provision of mental health services across the country. It is hoped that, by continuing to focus on the need for mental health care and the continued development of mental health care services, Vanuatu will become a psychologically literate and mentally healthy country, which will allow it to deal with the many future challenges it will face.

References

Benson, J., Pond, D., Funk, M., Wang, X., & Tarivonda, L. (2011). A new era in mental health care in Vanuatu. *International Journal of Family Medicine, 2011*, 1–7.

Blignault, I., & Kaur, A. (2020). Integration of traditional and Western treatment approaches in mental health care in Pacific Island Countries. *Australasian Psychiatry, 28*(1), 11–15.

Bolton, L. (2003). *Unfolding the moon: Enacting women's kastom in Vanuatu*. University of Hawaii Press.

Charlson, F. J., Diminic, S., & Whiteford, H. A. (2015). The rising tide of mental disorders in the Pacific region: Forecasts of disease burden and service requirements from 2010 to 2050. *Special issue: Health Policy Challenges in Asia and the Pacific, 2*(2), 280–292.

Crowley, T. (2000). The language situation in Vanuatu. *Current Issues in Language Planning, 1*(1), 47–132.

Cox, M., Alatoa, H., Kenni, L., Naupa, A., Rawlings, G., Soni, N., & Vatu, C. (2007). *The unfinished state drivers of change in Vanuatu*. Vanuatu.

Dawes, N., Franklin, R., McIver, L., & Obed, J. (2019). Post-disaster mental health servicing in Pacific Island communities: An integrative review. *International Journal of Disaster Risk Reduction, 38*, 1–9.

Forster, P. M. (2005). Psychology in Vanuatu. *The Psychologist, 18*(5), 288–289.

George, K. (2010). Vanuatu: Happiest nation on earth, mental health and the Church. *Australian Psychiatry, 18*(1), 63–65.

Goddard, M., & Otto, L. (2013). *Hybrid justice in Vanuatu: The island courts* (Justice and development working paper series). World Bank.

Government of Vanuatu. (2015). *Tropical cyclone pam humanitarian action plan*. Retrieved from https://www.humanitarianresponse.info/sites/www.humanitarianresponse.info/files/documents/files/vanuatu_tc_pam_hap.pdf

Happy Planet Index. (2021). Retrieved from http://happyplanetindex.org/countries/vanuatu

Hughes, F., Finlayson, M., Firkin, M. P., Funk, M., Drew, N., Barrett, T., Wang, X., & Fristch, F. (2005). *Situational analysis of mental health needs and resources in Pacific Island countries*. World Health Organisation: Centre for Mental Health Research, Policy and Service Development.

Hughes, F. (2009). Mental health in the Pacific: The role of the Pacific Island mental health network. *Pacific Health Dialog, 15*(1), 177–180.

IsraAID. (2015). *MHPSS capacity building, ToT. developing a mental health foundation and referral system*. Vanuatu.

IsraAID. (2018). *Ambae volcano disaster response program mental health & psychosocial support disaster interventions program report*. Vanuatu.

Mental Hospital Act. (1965). Retrieved from http://www.paclii.org/vu/legis/consol_act/mha172/

Ministry of Health. (2009). *The Vanuatu mental health policy and plan 2009–2015*. Retrieved from https://mjcs.gov.vu/images/disability_desk/MH_Policy.pdf

Obed, J., Bush, A., Stathis, S., & Hunter, E. (2020). The Vanuatu Psychiatry Mentorship Programme: Supporting the development of a fledgling mental health service in the Pacific. *Australasian Psychiatry, 28*(1), 24–26.

Reliefweb. (2021). *Vanuatu: Tropical Cyclone Harold – Final Report, DREF n° MDRVU008*. Retrieved from https://reliefweb.int/report/vanuatu/vanuatu-tropical-cyclone-harold-final-report-dref-n-mdrvu008

Shultz, J. M., Rechkemmer, A., Rai, A., & McManus, K. (2018). Public health and mental health implications of environmentally induced forced migration. In *Disaster medicine and public health preparedness* (pp. 1–7).

Smith, L. (2010). Caribbean Bedlam: The development of the lunatic asylum system in Britain's West Indian colonies, 1838–1914. *The Journal of Caribbean History, 44*(1), 1–47.

Tarivonda, L., Funk, M., Kaloris, P., Iaruel, J., Hughes, F., Shields, L., Sugiura, K., & Benson, J. (2012). *WHO profile on mental health in development (WHO proMIND): Vanuatu*. World Health Organization.

UN News. (2020). Retrieved from https://news.un.org/en/story/2020/12/1079252.

Vanuatu Demographics. (2020). Retrieved from https://www.worldometers.info/demographics/vanuatu-demographics/

Vanuatu National Statistics Office. (2009). *National population and housing census 2009*. Retrieved from https://vnso.gov.vu/images/Public_Documents/Census_Surveys/Census/2009/2009%20Census%20Analytical%20Report%20-%20Vol2.pdf

Vanuatu National Statistics Office. (2012). *Alternative indicators of well-being for Melanesia Vanuatu pilot study report*. Retrieved from https://vnso.gov.vu/images/Special_Report/Altinative_Indicator_of_Wellbeing/Alternative_Indicators_of_Well-being.pdf

Vanuatu – The World Factbook. (2021). Retrieved from https://www.cia.gov/the-world-factbook/countries/vanuatu/

WHO. (2015). *Tropical Cyclone Pam, Vanuatu*. Retrieved from https://www.who.int/hac/crises/vut/vanuatu_donor_alert_25march2015.pdf

World Bank Group. (2018). *Vanuatu health financing systems assessment: Spend better*. World Bank.

World Risk Report. (2019). Retrieved from https://reliefweb.int/sites/reliefweb.int/files/resources/WorldRiskReport-2019_Online_english.pdf

Zahlawi, T., Roome, A. B., Chan, C. W., Campbell, J. J., Tosiro, B., Malanga, M., Tagaro, M., Obed, J., Iaurel, J., Taleo, G., Tarivonda, L., Olszowy, K. M., & Dancause, K. N. (2019). Psychosocial support during displacement due to a natural disaster: relationships with distress in a lower-middle income country. *International Health 11*, 472 –479.

Chapter 4
"Teu Le Va: We over Me" A Brief Overview of Mental Health Amongst Samoans in American Samoa

Jueta B. McCutchan-Tofaeono

Geography and History

Situated in the heart of the South Pacific and approximately 2200 miles southwest of the state of Hawaii, American Samoa (AS) is the southernmost US territory. American Samoa is recognized as an unincorporated, unorganized territory of the United States. As a result, individuals born in American Samoa are considered US nationals and not citizens, and in exchange, American Samoans retain control over their lands and system of governance. Widely dispersed over 150 square miles of open ocean, the seven individual islands of American Samoa (Tutuila, Aunu'u, Ofu, Olosega, Ta'u, Swains, and Rose Islands) equal 79 square miles. Pago Pago, the capital of American Samoa, is located on the main island of Tutuila (52 square miles). American Samoa has one of the most naturally well-protected deep-water harbors in the South Pacific Ocean, which became a point of interest for the United States and later resulted in a temporary Naval station on Tutuila in 1900. The US military influence remains prominent, with notably one of the highest rates of military enlistment of the US states and territories.

The 2010 US Census recorded 55,519 residents with a median age of 21 years in American Samoa. It takes at minimum 10 hours and two flights to land at the Pago Pago International Airport from the US mainland. The remoteness of American Samoa can yield both health promotional and health risk factors, particularly as it relates to mental health. This was most prominently demonstrated during the onset of the COVID-19 pandemic. In response to the pandemic, American Samoa Government leadership made the decision to close the borders to all incoming and outgoing travel in March 2020. Government leaders expressed concern that one

J. B. McCutchan-Tofaeono (✉)
Empowering Pacific Islander Communities/Pacific Youth Community Development, Pago Pago, American Samoa

G. J. Rich, N. A. Ramkumar (eds.), *Psychology in Oceania and the Caribbean*, International and Cultural Psychology, https://doi.org/10.1007/978-3-030-87763-7_4

community transmission case could result in devastation for a population where a majority are overweight or obese and the rate of diabetes is nearly three times that of the national average (American Samoa Government, 2018). While American Samoa has been able to remain COVID-19-free, there have also been mental health challenges associated with American Samoa citizens who were stranded off-island, facing uncertainty as to when they could return home due to border closures and other unintended consequences associated with recent increases in deaths by suicide.

People and Culture

The Samoan culture is founded on the concepts of "tu ma le aganu'u," whereby mutual respect, obedience, and service are observed and woven into the fabric of daily life. It is the force that governs the ways in which individuals interact with each other and the environment around them. It is likely one of the reasons that American Samoa has one of the highest rates of military recruits. The structure is remarkably similar to that of military culture. The success of *fa'asamoa* is largely dependent upon everyone's fulfillment of their predetermined roles, both within the family and society. The saying "*O Samoa o le atunu'u ua uma ona tofi*" is an important aspect of Samoan life. Translated, this means "Samoa is a place with individuals who have prescribed roles" (Stewart-Withers & O'Brien, 2006). Another saying, "*tu i lou tofi*," indicates the importance of one staying in one's place. Everyone has prescribed roles, and they are to remain in those roles and act accordingly.

In American Samoa lies a unique juxtaposition between traditional values and Western ideals, which is most evident when discussing those younger Samoans who choose to return. It is not uncommon to hear someone describe another who has recently returned to American Samoa as "smelling like America," meaning that their mannerisms or ways of engaging are perceived to be more Westernized. While often said in a facetious manner, it demonstrates the delicate balance that American Samoans face between traditional Samoan values and American influence.

The Samoan culture is based upon the notion of reciprocity, in which different systems are interwoven, with the success of one system dependent upon that of the others (Thornton et al., 2010). The structure is based upon the notion of "*fa'asamoa*," whereby individuals are expected to live according to the Samoan way and all members are expected to work to take care of the family unit (Stewart-Withers & O'Brien, 2006). The most important concepts within "*fa'asamoa*" are those of respect, reverence, and love. These virtues are taught to be bestowed by God, thereby governing the ways in which Samoans think, act, and live (Stewart-Withers & O'Brien, 2006).

Land, resources, and political power remain largely at the village level, with much of the decision-making conducted by the family leaders, comprised of *Matai*, or familial chiefs. The family structure for Samoans is comprised of the extended family and is hierarchical in nature, with the *Matai*, making decisions related to the collection, allocation, and division of resources within each family (Thornton et al., 2010).

The Samoan culture is based upon the foundation of mutual respect and trust that everyone will follow their roles for the good of the community. This is especially important when considering the ways in which Samoans might approach mental health treatment. Individuals may be more reticent to engage in mental health treatment for fear of how they might be perceived by others. When someone might be perceived as being "weak" or "not having enough faith," particularly in a territory where the motto is "God first," there may present significant challenges.

Everything is relational in the Samoan culture, and it is evident in the traditional practices and the language that is employed. The "Samoan fale" model is one that has been employed in multiple interventions (Pulotu-Endemann, 2009) to help explain the intersection of values and governance of not only the individual but the extended families. During *fa'alavelave* (e.g., funerals, weddings, or any other significant event that could cause disruption to daily living), families will visit with their assistance in either the form of a *fesoasoani* (translated as "help") or a Samoan *si'i*. During this time, a delicate exchange occurs in which the visiting family, through their representative *Matai* (chief), will proceed to explain the familial connection. During the *si'i*, a series of exchanges are made in which the visiting family will provide monetary gifts and fine mats, and the receiving family will provide items back as an expression of thanksgiving. This system of reciprocity is evident across different domains within the Samoan culture. Interconnection is also evident as one's identity is not solely about one's personal accomplishments. Rather, who they are in the context of those around them, including their lineage, is often discussed first. Understanding one's identity may help Samoans feel a sense of connectedness that can help buffer against potential stressors (Tamasese et al., 2005).

One cultural facet is the notion of what time looks like and how it is spent in the Samoan culture. Everything and everyone are relative to one another. While every culture has their corollary for "Samoan time," it highlights the cultural values that may differ from Eurocentric values of time. As previously discussed, the importance of honoring the sacred bond between people takes precedence. While this has been changing, the notion of time spent creating and establishing relationships as opposed to task based may impact those who place little value in time. This could explain reasons why others may not perform well on time-based tasks as they do not see the value.

Language and Communication

The Samoan culture has oral traditions. Wisdom was traditionally passed down through stories, or *fagogo*, in addition to myths and legends that help to tell the origin story of the American Samoa people. How one speaks has often been viewed as a reflection of one's upbringing. Sadly, it is becoming less common to see the younger generation uphold the same traditions. However, myths and legends continue to be passed down, either through traditional storytelling or within the public school system, within the context of American Samoan history.

A system of reciprocity demonstrating the pillar of *fa'aaloalo* (i.e., respect) is also woven into daily practices. During a funeral, for example, extended families will take gifts that are valuable in the Samoan culture (e.g., fine mats, money). At these ceremonies, the designated head of the family will first describe their connection to the person who is deceased, connecting back multiple generations, before they share their *fesoasoani* (i.e., assistance) in support of the family. The system of reciprocity may also be seen in daily exchanges, particularly amongst people who are just getting acquainted. This is important to remember when considering mental health service delivery. Individuals who seek out mental health services may begin to ask questions about the clinician's background and history as this is a way to help orient them to who you are. While there may be some hesitation amongst some Western-trained clinicians in terms of boundaries, this is likely more of an attempt by Samoans to establish rapport and meaningful connection. As previously mentioned, context is key and one's identity is also connected to the larger context (e.g., family history, etc.).

Language in itself is hierarchical, with the high talking chief (HTC) designated as the individual to speak in formal family gatherings. It is largely a top-down system in which individuals are directed by the chiefs. There is typically little question amongst the extended family system once a decision has been made by the *Matai*. This is important to remember when thinking about the role that someone in a perceived position of authority (e.g., an examiner) might play in a Samoan's responses in therapy, whereby deference might lead to a more superficial relationship with their clinician. When things are governed according to what is best for the collective, individuals experiencing mental health challenges may continue to silently suffer or endure without the support that could help buffer against certain effects.

The ways in which one communicates may also depend upon whom one is referencing, offering further evidence of the importance of relationships in the Samoan culture. One prominent example is the way in which siblings are referenced according to the respective gender of the primary subject. Therefore, a woman would refer to her brother (i.e., "tuagane") differently than an identified man (i.e., "uso").

There is the everyday language that is employed by all and then the *gagana fa'aaloalo* (Esera, 2001). Therefore, the ways in which one speaks with those who are in positions of authority (e.g., elders, *Matai*, etc.) are different from others. A common saying in American Samoa is "*O le ala i le pule o le tautua*," which when directly translated means "the path to leadership is through service." This indicates that one cannot assume a leadership role without first adhering to the values taught, and respecting their elders, serving others before being served themselves (Tuia, 2013). Samoans grow up learning certain customs through doing and observing. It is expected that you attend family events in order to better understand the nuances in the communication. When you make a mistake, others may openly scold with the intention of helping you to recall for next time. Overall, individuals are taught that one is judged according to the ways in which they communicate with others and behave. Through these interactions, a young Samoan steeped in the traditional customs learns the delicate nuances and art of communication.

Religion and Spirituality

While Christianity is not germane to the Samoan culture, the integration of Christian principles is evident in everyday life. Esera (2001) maintains that many of the Samoan spiritual principles pre-Christianity were aligned with those concepts introduced by early missionaries. The church plays an integral role in the Samoan culture, with the parishioners assuming responsibility to support the pastor, his family, and his residence. Religious leaders are highly respected within the Samoan community, and families commonly defer to them for guidance on various issues. Indeed, the *Matai* who are bestowed prominent titles are held in high esteem and seen as anointed by God and blessed by the ancestors before them (Esera, 2001). The church has also been identified as a powerful educative agent in the Samoan community, with many children having attended pastor school (commonly known as "a'oga Samoa") and learning to read and pronounce both Samoan and English words through religious discussion and lessons with their families. The practice of attending pastor school is still prevalent, though appears to be less common as the years progress.

Despite the emphasis on community, individual families continue to feel the strain of balancing the expectations of the church with the realities of having to provide for their families. A study by Thornton and associates (2010) estimated that approximately 41% of the Samoan household income designated for "social use" is dedicated to the church. Although families might struggle to keep up with the demands of tithing, whereby families are responsible for allocating a percentage of their income to the church, some reported that when faced with a decision, they sacrifice other needs (e.g., schooling) to maintain their contributions to the church (Thornton et al., 2010). The high esteem to which the church is held in the Samoan community may make it difficult for families to prioritize other seemingly important aspects, such as one's well-being or that of his or her family.

Despite many of the stressors that can be faced, both socially and financially, there are also buffers, particularly as it relates to connection. Individuals may cite their position in church to be a primary reason motivating them to persevere despite challenges that they encounter. Within households, there may be multiple generations residing together; therefore, there is less opportunity for someone to isolate for extended periods of time without others attempting to connect. While this may be seen as a nuisance for those experiencing mental health challenges, overall, being surrounded by others who will continually check in can mean the difference between life and death for some.

Gender and Sexuality

Gender can be seen as more fluid amongst different Pacific Islander populations. In American Samoa, in addition to the binary gender identities of male and female, there are individuals who also identify as *fa'afafine*, which literally translated means "in the manner of a woman" (Schmidt, 2017). While traditional Western views may interpret *fa'afafine* as transgender, some *fa'afafine* would argue that the term does not encapsulate their experiences. *Fa'afafine* may hold prominent positions in government and nongovernment organizations, including church activities. The problematic label of gender dysphoria within the Western medical model further increases the stigmatization of one's gender identity, which tends to be more fluid (Schmidt, 2017). *Fa'afafine* continue to experience stigma amongst those with more conservative views; therefore, there is a delicate balance that they have to navigate, which can also be a source of distress.

Migration

Despite the rich cultural heritage found in the Samoan islands, many have chosen to relocate to the mainland United States to pursue opportunities that are assumed to assist family members remaining in the islands (Fiaui & Hishinuma, 2009). Approximately 300,000 Samoans reside outside of the Samoan islands, with a majority having migrated to the United States, New Zealand, and Australia. Opportunities such as ready access to education and ranks of distinction in the military are predominant reasons for the migration of many Samoans to the United States (Fiaui & Hishinuma, 2009). It has been hypothesized that since they are native to the United States, most American Samoans were not provided the tools necessary to aid in the transition from a communal, noncompetitive way of life to an urban and highly competitive society (Stafford, 2010).

One concern regarding this mass migration is the notion that Samoans are moving further from the traditional cultural customs that are commonly practiced in the Samoan islands. Another consequence of this migration has been the loss of language for many Pacific Islanders, including Samoans (Faleafa, 2010). While this is true for many Pacific Islanders, the language barrier remains for those Samoans whose first language is Samoan, particularly those of the older generation (Stewart-Withers & O'Brien, 2006). This presents unique challenges with regard to the knowledge necessary to access services that are vital to one's success in the United States. Since they are assumed to be native to the United States, little attention is currently afforded to the struggles they face, as evidenced by the minimal resources that are allocated to Samoans or the Pacific Islander community as a whole outside of their respective island homes.

Health Status

American Samoa residents suffer from a myriad of health-related issues, particularly noncommunicable diseases (NCDs). In a recent hybrid survey, about 94.7% of American Samoa residents were identified as obese, with diabetes rates almost three times the national average (33.6% vs. 12.2%). NCDs are the leading cause of morbidity and mortality across the US Pacific Islands, including American Samoa (ASG, 2018). According to the World Health Organization (2021), four identified health risk factors associated with NCDs are tobacco use, unhealthy diet, physical inactivity, and the harmful use of alcohol. Research indicates that those with a diagnosable mental health condition smoke at two to four times the rate of the general population (Smith et al., 2014). Therefore, Samoans who experience mental health challenges may also be at increased risk to develop health complications that could further exacerbate their mental health concerns.

Traditional Conceptualization of Mental Illness

Mental illness was typically viewed through the lens of religion and spirituality, although this viewpoint slowly appears to be evolving as more information comes to light. Traditional views associated mental illness with punishment from God or an indication of a spiritual rupture. Healing was sought through pastors or traditional healers (Huakau & Bray, 2000). It is often believed that consistent prayer and other healing conducted by priests or other religious figures, particularly when conceptualized to be a spiritual challenge, are the most appropriate course of action to remediate symptoms (Huakau & Bray, 2000). Traditional medicinal practices are still commonly utilized amongst Samoans today (Srinivasan & Guillermo, 2000). Some families may visit traditional healers for guidance in addressing somatic complaints rather than seeking assistance from medical professionals in the Western medical model. As previously enumerated, there may still exist views that God has set each person's role and position in life (Esera, 2001). Now, imagine someone who might hold beliefs about their role in life experiencing mental health challenges that affected their abilities to complete their assigned tasks. If mental health challenges were only viewed within the context of a rupture in the spiritual sense (e.g., upsetting ancestors which resulted in a curse), it is suspected that their willingness to seek out or even understand potential resources might be significantly impacted. Traditional views might also impact one's willingness to seek social support, thereby creating further distance from factors that might be protective in nature (e.g., family, roles within the larger community, etc.).

Mental Health in American Samoa Today

As is common across various regions, stigma continues to impact those with identified mental health concerns. According to the American Samoa Government Hybrid Survey (2018), 7.4% of adults reported signs of depression with no significant gender differences. The survey also indicated that approximately 7.7% of adults reported experiencing signs of anxiety. At the end of 2020 into the new year, there has been an increase in deaths by suicide, with an estimated 11 deaths by suicide in the latter part of last year and then a cluster of three within the first month of the new year (Talanei, 2021). While this may seem miniscule in comparison to the mainland United States, there is a ripple effect that seems to reverberate through smaller communities more prominently.

In response to the recent cluster of deaths by suicide, Empowering Pacific Islander Communities (2021) screened 1125 high school students across three high schools in the territory, for suicide risk to identify those at highest need for intervention. Of those screened, one in three adolescents has seriously thought about suicide and nearly 30% endorsed having attempted to die by suicide in the past year (EPIC, 2021). Screening yielded prominent risk factors to include (1) family problems such as domestic violence, abuse in the family, and loss; (2) school issues such as bullying and constant social media exposure; (3) community and church risk factors such as easy access to drugs and alcohol, exposure to violence; and (4) individual factors such as depression, lack of connection, and previous attempts to die by suicide (EPIC, 2021). Family risk factors identified in this most recent survey are consistent with historical risk factors documented for Pacific Islanders in general (e.g., Else et al., 2009).

While there are some organizations (both religious and nonprofit alike) reaching out, stigma is still highly prevalent. Examples of outreaches are those conducted by religious leaders to a few of the schools every month to offer words of encouragement and words of affirmation to the students. While outreach opportunities are implemented by different organizations and government agencies locally, there continues to exist a gap in needs for youth and young adults with regard to understanding their mental health needs. As a juxtaposition, rates of veteran deaths by suicide appear to be so low that as a composite with other US territories, none of the information could not be reliably interpreted (U.S. Department of Veteran Affairs, 2019).

Most primary prevention services are offered by the local Department of Health. In 2007, the WHO STEPS reported that amongst adults aged 25–64 in AS, 93.5% were obese, 47.3% were diabetic, and 29.9% smoked cigarettes daily. This has resulted in the refocusing of healthcare resources to the prevention and treatment of noncommunicable diseases such as diabetes, hypertension, and cancer. According to the American Samoa Hybrid Survey, approximately 45% of American Samoa citizens did not engage in an annual checkup, with approximately 12% not having gotten a checkup at all (ASG, 2018).

As is the case in the many rural locations, particularly remote Pacific Islands such as American Samoa, there are a limited number of qualified health professionals; therefore, the local system is focused mainly on acute care. There are severely limited resources with regard to mental health service provision on island. There are currently two US trained psychologists, one US trained psychiatrist, two US trained licensed clinical social workers, and two foreign-trained psychiatrists for a population of approximately 60,000. Aside from Medicaid and Medicare, there is no health insurance program for the territory; therefore, residents will need to pay out of pocket for services. This presents a challenge as most individuals are unable to afford out-of-pocket fees, particularly if they are not residents of American Samoa. Therefore, many residents will likely only seek out healthcare services only during acute needs (U.S. Department of Health and Human Services, 2021). One can imagine that preventative services, particularly for mental health, are not discussed or emphasized.

Confidentiality is a prominent area of concern for a small community such as American Samoa where most people are connected in different ways. This concern may escalate when meeting a clinician of Samoan descent. Whereas others might perceive this as helpful, for some, there may be more comfort in having an established distance with a non-Samoan clinician. When considering therapy resources, there is the real possibility that the closest available support is over 2500 miles away in Honolulu. Therefore, providing clear and concrete recommendations of things that can be feasibly done is important. While there may be some resources available to qualified veterans and their families, the same may not be the case for the general population. Given the limited resources available, community and family support are a vital aspect.

Promoting Resiliency in American Samoa

Whereas the traditional Western model of therapy might only involve the individual, given the communal nature of American Samoa life, it would be important to consider the ways in which family can be involved. Tamasese et al. (2005) reviewed the importance of providing classes or training to include the families of Samoans in need in New Zealand. Given the importance of the identified family unit, providing opportunities to help foster resilience amongst caregivers may also help foster stronger bonds. While risk factors such as domestic violence were identified by local youth (EPIC, 2021), active family involvement could also serve as a protective factor. It is surmised that the more others involved in an individual's care understand, the less stigmatizing it might be to discuss mental health concerns. There is concern that the more American Samoa adapts traditional Western principles, the more the *fa'asamoa* values become sacrificed; however, resilience does not have to be seen as a "*palagi*" ("non-Samoan," or, most often, "White") concept. There are factors that are already in place within the community that allow American Samoa to thrive. Therefore, it is particularly important for discussions around mental health to continually occur, so that there can be a continual weaving of traditional teachings with newer concepts around growth, communication, and connection.

References

American Samoa Government. (2018). *American Samoa adult hybrid survey.* Retrieved from https://cdn.who.int/media/docs/default-source/ncds/ncd-surveillance/american_samoa_steps_hybrid_2017-2018-final-report.pdf?sfvrsn=2d828855_1&download=tru

Else, I. R., Goebert, D. A., Bell, C. K., Carlton, B., & Fukuda, M. (2009). The relationship between violence and youth suicide indicators among Asian American and Pacific Islander youth. *Aggression and Violent Behavior, 14*, 470–477. https://doi.org/10.1016/j.avb.2009.07.009

Empowering Pacific Islander Communities. (2021). *Youth suicide in American Samoa* [infographic]. Retrieved from https://www.facebook.com/photo?fbid=4182050261806504&set=a.276033979074838

Esera, F. I. (2001). *If a client is operating from a Samoan world view how can s/he be holistically and appropriately treated under the western medical model?* [Unpublished Master's Thesis]. Victoria University of Wellington, Wellington, New Zealand.

Faleafa, M. (2010). *Talking therapies for Pasifika peoples: Best and promising practice guide for mental health and addiction services.* Te Pou o Whakaaro Nui.

Fiaui, P. A., & Hishinuma, E. S. (2009). Samoan adolescents in American Samoa and Hawaii: Comparison of youth violence and youth development indicators: A study by the Asian/Pacific Islander Youth Violence Prevention Center. *Aggression and Violent Behavior, 14*, 478–487. http://www.apiyvpc.org

Huakau, G., & Bray, A. (2000). Talking disabilities from a Pacific perspective. Dunedin Academic Press: Donald Beasley Institute.

Pulotu-Endemann, F. K. (2009, Sept). *Fonofale model. Workshop on Pacific health promotion models: A partnership between the Health Promotion Forum of New Zealand & Pasifika@ MasseyWellington Campus*, Massey University, New Zealand. Retrieved from http://www.hauora.co.nz/~hpforum/resources/Fonofalemodel.pdf

Schmidt, J. M. (2017). Translating transgender: Using Western discourses to understand Samoan fa'afafine. *Sociology Compass, 11*(5) https://doi.org/10.1111/soc4.12485

Smith, P. H., Mazure, C. M., & McKee, S. A. (2014). Smoking and mental illness in the U.S. population. *Tobacco Control, 23*, 147–153. https://doi.org/10.1136/tobaccocontrol-2013-05146

Srinivasan, S., & Guillermo, T. (2000). Toward improved health: Disaggregating Asian American and Native Hawaiian Pacific Islander data. *American Journal of Public Health, 90*, 1731–1734

Stafford, S. (2010). Caught between "the rock" and a hard place. *American Journal of Public Health, 100*, 784–789. https://doi.org/10.2105/AJPH.2009.191064

Stewart-Withers, R., & O'Brien, A. (2006). Suicide prevention and social capital: A Samoan perspective. *Health Sociology Review, 15*, 209–220. https://doi.org/10.5172/hesr.2006.15.2.209

Talanei. (2021, Jan 26). *We are at a crisis with youth suicides.* Retrieved from https://www.talanei.com/2021/01/26/we-are-at-a-crisis-with-youth-suicides/

Tamasese, K., Peteru, C., Waldegrave, C., & Bush, A. (2005). Ole Taeao Afua, the new morning: A qualitative investigation into Samoan perspectives on mental health and culturally appropriate services. *Australian & New Zealand Journal of Psychiatry, 39*(4), 300–309.

Thornton, A., Kerslake, M., & Binns, T. (2010). Alienation and obligation: Religion and social change in Samoa. *Asia Pacific Viewpoint, 51*, 1–16. https://doi.org/10.1111/j.1467-8373.2010.01410.x

Tuia, T. T. (2013). *Re-contextualizing and re-theorising cultural values in teacher education practices: A Samoan standpoint* [Unpublished Doctoral Thesis]. Queensland University of Technology, Queensland, New Zealand.

U.S. Department of Health and Human Services. (2021, May 01). *HRSA maternal child health program overview-American Samoa 2020.* https://mchb.tvisdata.hrsa.gov/Narratives/ExecutiveSummary/be7a1b90-b6cb-4716-ac6e-a27b897be87a

U.S. Department of Veteran Affairs. (2019). *U.S. territories veteran suicide data sheet, 2017* [Fact sheet]. https://www.mentalhealth.va.gov/docs/data-sheets/2017/US_Territories_Veteran_Suicide_Data_Sheet_2017.pdf

World Health Organization. (2007, March). *American Samoa NCD risk factors STEPS report.* https://www.who.int/ncds/surveillance/steps/Printed_STEPS_Report_American_Samoa.pdf

World Health Organization. (2021). *Addressing non-communicable diseases in the Pacific islands.* https://www.who.int/westernpacific/activities/addressing-ncds-in-the-pacific

Chapter 5
Psychology in Samoa and Throughout the Diaspora

Faafetai Faaleava and Siautu Alefaio

Samoa was made famous in psychological literature through the writings of the renowned anthropologist, anthropological psychologist, and developmental feminist Margaret Mead (Mead, 1928). As a research hub of exploration, Samoa was discovered and made a worldwide phenomenon through Mead's work with Samoan adolescents (Frame, 1983; Shankman, 2013; Shore, 1982). Despite the controversy that ensued from the challenge by Derek Freeman (Freeman, 1983), Mead had already achieved the impact of influencing societal change in America (Langness, 1975). Her discovery (or exploitation) of Samoan adolescents challenged psychology's notions of development and sparked a revolutionary movement for women in America during the 1920s (Frame, 1983). The perception of freedom lived by young Samoan women was researched from an outside-in perspective that ultimately changed the understanding of adolescent development for developmental psychology despite inaccuracies unearthed later. The historical Mead vs. Freeman debacle based on "nature vs. nurture" or "biology vs. environment" scientific understandings of human development (Shore, 198) lies at the heart of inaccuracies still current today (Shankman, 2013). In Freeman's refutation of Mead's superficial accounts of Samoan young women, she was "played" or misled. Essentially, Samoan adolescents made up accounts of everyday life as a joke which Mead as a Palagi (European) outsider could not comprehend. As a result, Samoa continues to be a bone of contention for the anthropological (and social science) world to diffuse and debate. While America's psychology was revolutionized by Mead's

F. Faaleava (✉)
California Department of Corrections and Rehabilitation, Mule Creek State Prison, Ione, CA, USA

S. Alefaio
School of Psychology, College of Humanities and Social Sciences, Massey University, Albany Auckland, New Zealand
e-mail: S.Alefaio@massey.ac.nz

G. J. Rich, N. A. Ramkumar (eds.), *Psychology in Oceania and the Caribbean*, International and Cultural Psychology,
https://doi.org/10.1007/978-3-030-87763-7_5

research, Samoa with its groundbreaking ways of "knowing, being, and doing" remains a cultural enigma for psychology. This chapter authored by Samoan psychologists living outside of Samoa shines a light on Samoan indigenous cultural knowledge as the bedrock of understanding Samoa's psychology.

Samoan History and Identity

At the turn of the twentieth century, the islands of Samoa were split into two sections, eastern and western islands, as a result of colonization. The eastern islands (Tutuila and Manu'a) were acquired by America. It remains a territory of the USA at the present time and is known as American Samoa. The western islands (Savai'i and Upolu) were taken by Germany in 1899 and later seized by New Zealand in 1914 at the outbreak of World War I (Field, 2002). Western Samoa gained its independence in 1962 from New Zealand and formally changed its name from Western Samoa to Samoa in 1997 (Coleman, 2015). Samoa is located south of the equator in the Polynesian region of the Pacific Ocean. It lies approximately 1800 miles northeast of New Zealand and 2600 miles southwest of Hawaii. The population of Samoa is just under 200,000 people, with the native language being Samoan.

As the first Pacific nation to become independent after a period of New Zealand administration, Samoa's founding document "*O le Faavae o le Malo Tutoatasi o Samoa*" (1960) prescribes the constitution in which the Independent State of Samoa would be governed. It begins with a statement acknowledging Samoa's sacred heritage as a Christian nation "based on Christian principles and Samoan custom and tradition." The motto on the public seal of Samoa is "*Fa'avae i le Atua Samoa*," which means "God be the foundation of Samoa." Therefore, Samoa was historically changed through its encounter and connection to Christianity through the missionaries. The early years of this encounter shaped Samoa's cultural milieu where the imposition of middle-class England was birthed in the Island Paradise. For example, cold-weather clothing was imposed upon the warm-climate people of Samoa, and cooking was transferred to women when it was historically the domain of young men (Meleisea et al., 1987, p. 68).

Despite the influence and subsequent cultural change in Samoa during this encounter with early missionaries, Meleisea contends that "although there is evidence that Christianity 'revolutionized' Samoan culture during the mid-nineteenth century, these changes were absorbed and Sāmoanized" (Meleisea et al., 1987, p. 69). The Samoan language, in which its cultural histories, genealogy, cosmological artifacts, values, and beliefs were retained, was maintained within the realm of "oratory." Salesa (2009) describes a deeper phenomenon housed within Samoan language: "although most cultures, no doubt, have proverbs, Samoans' understandings of language, and words – and *alaga'upu* as 'the path to knowledge' – are distinctive" (p. 226). As Samoan language moves and encounters new and foreign lands, it is transported across time (history) and place (cultural context). Therefore, in the realm of psychological "talking therapies," an exploration of language is imperative, especially as the theoretical knowledge which undergirds these talking therapies (traditional psychology) is derived from a vastly different cultural-philosophical knowledge base.

By drawing on Samoa's first scholar and cultural authority, the late Professor Aiono Fanaafi Le Tagaloa, Samoa's holistic culture is defined within the auspices of *aganu'u*:

> In the philosophical and religious consideration, what maintains unity between man and God; the unity between the material and spiritual; the unity between the physical and psychic; the unity between the social-political and the economic; the unity between the practical and aesthetic; the unity between male and female - is of absolute importance. The word for culture defines this unity. *Aganu'u* speaks of nature and nurture in the same breath; for *aga* is the essence of nature and things, while *nu'u* represents the sum of man's learned experience. (Cited in Meleisea, 2004, p. 171)

Through *aganu'u*, Meleisea (2004) advocates that "Samoans have developed a number of peaceful values based on positive concepts of social distance and mutual respect. These are reflected in public etiquette and social institutions that maintain peace and harmony and promote reconciliation in Samoan communities" (p. 171). Furthermore, Meleisea (2004) in this case study of Samoa presents core values of peace and harmony that exist within the fabric of *Fa'aSamoa* (Samoan indigenous ways of knowing, being, and doing). Historical accounts of violent encounters with Western colonial expeditions were allayed through Samoa's leadership advocacy for peaceful resistance illustrated in the Mau movement of the 1930s. It is imperative to understand that the Samoan individual is not singular. Every individual carries his or her family, village(s), and nation. When a Samoan individual does something good or bad, Samoans do not query about the individual; instead, they ask who are the parents, to which family do they belong, or what village(s) are they from (Faaleava, 2020). It is also important to understand the essence of the Samoan individual, their outlook on life, and their perspective of themselves. Samoa's former head of state, the Honorable Tui Atua Tamasese Efi (2003), eloquently described his Samoan identity as the following:

> I am not an individual; I am an integral part of the cosmos. I share divinity with my ancestors, the land, the seas and the skies. I am not an individual, because I share my *tofi* (inheritance) with my family, my village and my nation. I belong to my family and my family belongs to me. I belong to my village and my village belongs to me. I belong to my nation and my nation belongs to me. This is the essence of my belonging. (Efi, 2003)

The definition of being Samoan is not only a categorization of an ethnic identity; it expands beyond the typical cultural and traditional practices; it includes values of respect, humility, and hospitality for family and strangers. In addition, the definition of Samoan culture is often intertwined with Christianity and religion (Faaleava, 2020). Others have even asserted that religion and Samoan culture are one.

Religion

When John Williams, a Christian missionary from the London Missionary Society, first arrived on the shores of Samoa in 1830 (Robson, 2009), his message of Christianity was easily accepted in Samoa. The King of Upolu and Savai'i at the time, Malietoa Vainu'upo had long awaited the fulfillment of a prophecy that was spoken upon one of his predecessors. The prophecy is often told in the well-known Samoan legend of the warrior goddess Nafanua. She had defeated and conquered her enemies and controlled all of the *āo malo* (authority) in Samoa. When Malietoa went to Nafanua to request a *āo malo* for himself, Nafanua had already given them all away. Thus, Nafanua urged Malietoa to be patient and wait for his *āo malo* that will one day come from the heavens (Meleisea et al., n.d.). Hence, years later, when John Williams arrived in Samoa to spread the message of Christianity, Malietoa accepted it as the *āo malo* from heaven that was promised to his forefathers and perceived it as the fulfillment of Nafanua's prophecy.

As Christianity spread throughout Samoa, kings of Samoa surrendered their royalty status to God. Malietoa was addressed like other kingly titles, as *afioga* (majesty). However, after the arrival of Christianity, Malietoa gave the salutation of *afioga* to reference God while he assumed the lower address of *susuga* (mister). This change in the formal address of the Malietoa chief title is still recognized in Samoan culture and oratory practices today. All those who carry a Malietoa chief title are addressed as *le SUSUGA i le* Malietoa as opposed to what was formally *le AFIOGA i le* Malietoa out of reverence to God. The Tui-Manu'a, who was the king of the Manu'a islands in the eastern side of Samoa (American Samoa), renounced his kingship over Manu'a and urged his people to take the God of the Christians as their only king. Thus, the Tui-Manu'a title no longer exists.

Many Samoan scholars will acknowledge the deep intertwined nature of Samoan culture and religion. Pouono (2017) supported this notion by saying that "the Samoan church is to the Samoan people what water is to fish" (p. 45). He emphasized that religion and the church have become a central part of the Samoan life and elaborated that the core of Samoan culture, both socially and politically, evolves around the church and Christian values (Pouono, 2017). The significance of the intertwined nature between church and culture is often demonstrated in Samoan migration around the world. It is common practice for Samoans to build and establish new Samoan churches in whatever community or country they live in. Samoan cultural and traditional practices are often carried out by the Samoan churches in foreign countries (Pouono, 2017). Consequently, psychology for Samoa needs to co-exist with theology in the scaffolds of church-village contexts.

Psychology Through Mental Health Services in Samoa

Currently, psychology as a discipline, practice, and profession is nonexistent in Samoa. There is limited psychology curriculum in Samoa's national university – NUS (National University of Samoa) – and what is taught sits within other disciplines such as nursing and education under the umbrella of mental health. As such, an overview of mental health services in Samoa is critical to understand the confluence of psychology within Samoan society.

Data and literature pertaining to Samoa's mental health services are scarce. However, a review of Samoa's mental health policy released by the Ministry of

Health in 2006 offers a clinical picture of the overall landscape of mental health within the country at present. The Mental Health Unit (MHU) in Moto'otua provided mental health care to the entire country. In 2006, this MHU was staffed with five mental health nurses who completed their postgraduate course at the National University of Samoa in 2004, a part-time psychiatrist from Australia who worked 9 hours a week, and a full-time medical officer who was on leave, studying and working in New Zealand. During this time, the nurse-patient ratio was 29.8:1 with the majority of patients being between the ages of 14 and 40 years old (Government of Samoa, 2006). The salient diagnosis among those who received mental health services was schizophrenia and other psychotic-related disorders. Due to the lack of inpatient treatment facilities, patients exhibiting symptoms that were a risk to others were detained by the police in jail cells until psychiatric care was arranged. Alternatively, some patients received day treatment and were returned home to their families in the evenings (Government of Samoa, 2006).

The Samoan mental health infrastructure has two components, clinical and a family-focused community component (Enoka et al., 2013). The clinical component includes the holistic assessment, management, security, seclusion, and rehabilitation, while the community component summoned the assistance of the patient's family (nuclear family, extended family, village). The component of care that is received by a patient is determined from the mental status examination conducted at the initial point of care. When a patient is discharged from the mental health inpatient care, a daily follow-up is conducted for the first week. This follow-up is then titrated down to a fortnightly basis, then monthly. Patients who live far from the MHU are seen by the village community nurses on behalf of the MHU; any urgent issues are communicated via phone. Of note, the staff in the MHU provide mental health care to the entire country of Samoa and visit all islands on a quarterly basis (Enoka et al., 2013). It is evident that the mental health system in Samoa is in dire need of reinforcements. However, despite the shortage of mental health professionals, lack of adequate facilities, and funding limitations, the communal approach towards the care of mental health patients between nurses, families, and communities permeates the values of *Fa'aSamoa* (the Samoan way), which will be discussed further in the latter part of this chapter.

Contributing Factors to Mental Health Issues in Samoa

The issues that were identified by Samoa's Ministry of Health (Government of Samoa, 2006) as salient contributors to the mental health status in Samoa include increasing urbanization, financial hardship, substance use, migration, and utilization of services.

Increasing Urbanization Samoa's population has incurred shifts that have indicated an increase in the urban population and a decrease in the rural population. These changes have been associated with less people living in the traditional village structures and thus a decrease on family systems to support individuals with mental health issues. Religious and nongovernment organizations have also increasingly conveyed homelessness among mentally ill individuals in Samoa.

Hardship Samoa has a significant number of individuals who are economically disadvantaged compared to the rest of the population. As such, hardship serves as both a risk factor and a consequence of mental health issues. The stressors from day-to-day hardship may precipitate mental health issues. Similarly, the chronic nature of a mental health issue may disrupt an individual's ability to maintain their income/resources.

Substance Use Alcohol and marijuana use within the community were reported to be on the rise. The use of the aforementioned substances is linked with a higher prevalence of mental disorders especially among young Samoans.

Migration Migration to neighboring countries for education and employment opportunities is common in Samoa. This has resulted in the loss of many experienced health workers and therefore weakening the overall health system. In addition, this leaves fewer individuals in the home to care for elders, disabled, and/or mentally ill individuals. Fewer caretakers at home, combined with caring for a higher number of family members, may increase the stress upon the caretakers, thus making them susceptible to mental health issues.

Utilization of Services The MHU offers community support for individuals suffering from long-term mental health issues. The primary diagnoses treated in the MHU are those with psychotic disorders including schizophrenia, bipolar, and drug-induced psychosis. The most common referrals to the MHU comes from the hospital, families, and self-referred individuals. The limited capacity of the MHU in its infrastructure, employees, funding, and general resources makes mental health services in Samoa difficult to access.

Psychology Throughout the Samoan Diaspora

There are more Samoans living outside of Samoa with over 75,000 in Australia, 183,000 in Aotearoa New Zealand (NZ), and over 200,000 in America. Altogether close to half a million Samoans live outside Samoa compared with just under 200,000 in Samoa (Alefaio, 2020). The Samoan diaspora living in mainly Euro-American societies have encountered psychology through the countries in which they live such as America, Australia, and Aotearoa NZ. From within these countries, Samoa's diaspora have experienced psychology either as those studying and practicing as psychologists or those receiving psychological services and treatment. To date, there are roughly 11 Samoan psychologists in Aotearoa NZ, 3 in the USA (Hawaii, California, American Samoa), and none that are known in Australia. The Samoans working in psychology cover a range of areas in psychology: educational, clinical, health, forensic, counselling, community, and humanitarian-disaster resilience. Experiences of the Samoan diaspora are shared to highlight the importance of grounding any development for psychology in *Fa'aSamoa* (Samoan indigenous cultural knowledge). For youth of Samoan heritage born, bred, and raised in the new lands of migration (Aotearoa New Zealand, Australia, and America), identity formation and development are inextricably linked to *aiga* (family). As Pilato, Su'a, and Crichton-Hill (1998) explained:

> The preservation of family unity, integrity and credibility is of paramount importance.... The prevailing belief of Pacific Island people is that individual achievements are directly related to the nurturing and support of the family. In almost every case the individual edifies and attributes the source of their success to their family. (p. 5)

References by various Samoan researchers, practitioners, and writers feature *aiga* (family) as the nurturing force of *Fa'aSamoa* (Lui, 2003; Meleisea et al., 1987; Tamases et al., 1997; Tofaeono, 2000). Lui (2003) describes the affinity of Samoan culture with "kinship and family" as one that is connected to a "strong sense of identity and belonging" (p. 3). Regardless of migratory encounters in new lands reflected in the movements of Samoa's diaspora, *Fa'aSamoa* remains embedded in the hearts and minds of its migrant settlers and is regarded as a primary source of "understanding" which houses language, cultural artifacts, nuances, and ways of "knowing, being, and doing" (Alefaio, 2007; Anae, 1998; Fairbairn-Dunlop, 1998; Tofaeono, 2000). Family values, roles, and traditions are therefore fundamental to the worldview of *Fa'aSamoa*. Identity development can be viewed as occurring within the heart of *aiga* for Samoan youth, as the context of each young person's family defines who he or she is, in character, and deed. Therefore, Samoan youth must be embraced as a product of the "*we*," since the majority do not consider themselves as individuals but rather as part of the family. Roles within *aiga*, although at times very difficult, are powerfully influential in the development of their identities and worldviews (Alefaio, 1999).

Samoa's Church-Village Contexts of Psychology Reformation

In the broader sociocultural milieu, the church for Samoans is viewed as an extension of *aiga* (family) and plays a vital role in the developmental journey of identity. When migration to New Zealand occurred, churches became the epicenter of community life. Samoan youth highlight the importance of church-village support systems for providing holistic sustenance:

> Family's important but it's not the central thing that holds us together, it's mostly our Christian relationship with God and just the fellowship we have with our Christian brothers and sisters...the church within my life is really important, I really enjoy it, helping me out in my fa'aSamoa. (Cited in Alefaio, 1999, pp. 39–40)

Church-village communities in Aotearoa NZ have become for Samoan families the sociocultural contexts in which cultural knowledge traditions are practiced and maintained. As outlined by Tuala-Warren (2002):

> Samoan society is one of the strongest in the world, in terms of cultural solidarity and adherence. It has enabled the Samoans to absorb, rather than to be absorbed into Western institutions. In New Zealand, Samoans are holding fast to their language, to their belief in God, to their cultural practices and to their customs and beliefs. In New Zealand, the Samoan communities that are established have organised themselves around the churches. The Church congregation becomes akin to a Samoan village. They are searching for a community-like structure to feel comfortable in. (p. 25)

The values and beliefs of Samoans are very similar to the neighboring Pacific nations that are underpinned by the credence of Christian love (Meleisea et al., 1987; Tofaeono, 2000). When migration to New Zealand occurred, churches became the epicenter of community life, replicating the Samoan village, which is an extension of Samoan families. The church-village phenomenon in Aotearoa NZ plays a vital role in supporting families and especially those in crisis such as violent offenders that often encounter psychologist practitioners. The linking together of Christian principles with ancient cultural knowledge epistemologies throughout the Pacific has led to the formulation of *niu*[1] (new) indigenous "understandings" of the holistic nature of humanity, divinity, and creation (Alefaio-Tugia, 2015).

The role of the church as a *community of cultural artifacts* is imperative in the exploration of the *language of rehabilitation*. The journey of rehabilitation symbolizes the road to redemption for Pacific offenders. The "Message of the Cross" illustrated through the life of Jesus Christ thereby symbolizes hope, forgiveness, and reconciliation. The importance of highlighting this *narrative of change* lies in the conceptualization of this transformational phenomenon through *ifoga* (*Samoa ceremonial apology for restorative justice*). Cultural practices are therefore synonymous with Christian principles, but it is the interconnectedness between culture and Christianity that gives rise to a value system that is indispensable to any development process within Samoa and for Samoans. Some of these notable values include a strong sense of identity or belonging to an ethnic group, attitudes of cooperation, self-help, unity within and among communities, and the strength and support of the family and family discipline. It is in this context that the role of churches in the lives of Samoans needs to be recognized and emphasized, especially within the professional domain of psychology. Within the paradigm of cultural-spiritual encounters, Taufe'ulungaki (2004) highlights the need to identify "core values that are consistent with the rebuilding and reconstruction of relationships that promote health and well-being for all our people" (p. 8).

[1] Literally translated *niu* means baby coconut. It is used in text as a "symbolic representation" of new encounters in knowledge formation.

New Psychological Innovations Grounded in *Fa'aSamoa*

Highlighting and understanding the cultural origins, traditions, and societal understanding of *ifoga* is an example of how cultural artifacts or rituals are essential knowledge traditions that can help inform and make visible reconciliatory processes of healing needed in the language of psychology's therapeutic environment. This can inform and engage participants more effectively according to the principle of responsivity in offender rehabilitation literature (Bonta & Andrews, 2007). *Ifoga* is a Samoan cultural ritual of reconciliation enacted when a deep transgression of *tapu* (sacred) has occurred, and has been described as a "ceremony of apology and reconciliation" (Meleisea, 2004) which "involves aiga (family) and villages rather than individuals" (Tuala-Warren, 2002). *Ifoga* is a holistically complex and highly sacred ritual which numerous Samoa writers collectively describe as an act of humiliation and humility (Meleisea, 2004; Tamasese Efi, 2003; Tofaeono, 2000; Tuala-Warren, 2002) on the part of the offender, offender's *aiga* (family and extended family), and *nu'u* (village, community, society).

Presently, in many *ifoga*, a minister of the church goes with the *ifoga* party in an attempt to induce the receiving party to accept the *ifoga* peacefully and quickly. The church has had a major influence in the acceptance of *ifoga*. Currently, in Christian Samoa, it is extremely rare for an act of *ifoga* to be rejected. The extent and strength of the Christian values of an *aiga* are judged by their acceptance of an *ifoga*. A refusal to accept a traditional apology from the wrongdoers would be considered un-Christian like, unforgiving and in profound, spiritual terms, a repudiation of Jesus Christ's sacrificial act through which he died to forgive the sins of mankind (Tuala-Warren, 2002).

Through a description of *ifoga*, the process of psychological intervention is not an act of introspection or located within an individual's mind. It involves *aiga* (family), *nu'u* (village), spiritual engagement (church), and one's own humility. From this cultural practice, Samoa's psychology through *Fa'aSamoa* permeates every area of life, and as the diaspora moves, it is noted that *Fa'aSamoa* is not lost.

> Ifoga has not become lost as a custom for Samoan people in New Zealand, the dynamics of ifoga as performed in New Zealand are vastly different from that which is performed in Samoa, however the same spirit of genuine apology underlies it. (Tuala-Warren, 2002, p. 27)

Ifoga provides embedded cultural knowledge used in the context of a cultural-psychological innovation – *Saili Matagi*, a forensic rehabilitation program for Pacific violent offenders (Alefaio-Tugia, 2015). *Saili Matagi* as a Samoan metaphorical proverb was used to describe a forensic group psychotherapeutic rehabilitation initiative pioneered by the Department of Corrections in Aotearoa NZ. In the redevelopment of the program, Samoan cultural knowledge was contextualized within a psychological practitioner framework which was groundbreaking for offender rehabilitation in Aotearoa NZ. *Saili Matagi* in its redevelopment brought to the core of psychological science Samoa's indigenous cultural knowledge as tools for healing in therapeutic intervention, where the "dialogue" of therapy is shaped first and foremost by cultural knowledge/principles and second by the method of talking therapy used. It is a starting point in the indigenous retheorizing (Jackson, 2005) of psychology from *Fa'aSamoa* (Samoan indigenous cultural knowledge). Understanding the social constructs of *Fa'aSamoa* is crucial for combating the effects of offending and crime, especially with reference to the Samoan ritual of *ifoga*. Therefore, Samoan cultural values help future generations of the Samoan diaspora engage with a way of living that exudes "peace and harmony."

Conclusion

Much of psychology as currently known and practiced throughout Oceania (a region with the world's largest ocean), in which Samoa is located, has been imported from the global north (North America and Europe). This chapter reviewed the current state of mental health services in Samoa and offered an in-depth exploration of cultural factors that should be considered when providing clinical care to the Samoan population. Contrary to the Eurocentric notion of individualism, the Samoan population must be conceptualized through a collectivistic lens, specifically one that captures the essence of *Fa'aSamoa* (Samoan indigenous ways of knowing, being, and doing), which includes *aganu'u* (Samoan appropriate response in various situations), *aiga* (family), and religion.

References

Alefaio-Tugia, S. T. (2015). *Galuola: A NIU way for informing psychology from the cultural context of Fa'aSamoa (Version 1). figshare*. Retrieved from https://doi.org/10.4225/03/58abad465cdc1

Alefaio, S. (1999). *Impact of family structure and family environment on the ethnic identity of Samoan young people in New Zealand* [Unpublished master's thesis, University of Auckland].

Alefaio, S. (2007). Supporting the wellbeing of Pasifika youth. In P. Culbertson, M. N. Agee, & C. O. Makasiale (Eds.), *Penina uliuli: Contemporary challenges in mental health for Pacific peoples* (pp. 5–15).

Alefaio, S. (2020, Sept 4). Mobilizing the Pacific diaspora: A key component of disaster resilience. *East-West Wire*. Retrieved from https://www.eastwestcenter.org/publications/mobilizing-the-pacific-diaspora-key-component-disaster-resilience.

Anae, M. (1998). *Fofoa-i-vao-'ese: The identity journeys of NZ-born Samoans*. [Unpublished Doctoral dissertation, University of Auckland].

Bonta, J., & Andrews, D. (2007). Risk-need-responsivity model for offender assessment and rehabilitation. *Rehabilitation, 6*.

Coleman, D. Y. (2015). *Samoa:2015 Country Review*, 1–221. Retrieved from www.library.alliant.edu

Efi, T. A. T. T. T. (2003). In search of meaning, nuance and metaphor in social policy. *Social Policy Journal of New Zealand, 20*, 49–63.

Enoka, M. I. S., Tenari, A., Sili, T., Peteru, L., Tago, P., & Blignault, I. (2013). Developing a culturally appropriate mental health care service for Samoa. *Asia-Pacific Psychiatry:*

Official Journal of the Pacific Rim College of Psychiatrists, 5(2), 108–111. https://doi.org/10.1111/j.1758-5872.2012.00201.x

Faaleava, F. (2020). *Identifying colonial mentality among Samoans in America* [Doctoral Dissertation, Alliant International University]. Retrieved from www.proquest.com

Fairbairn-Dunlop, P. (1998). *Tamaitai Samoa: Their stories*. Suva, Fiji: Institute of Pacific Studies.

Field, M. (2002). Kiwis say sorry. *Herald Sun (Melbourne)*. Retrieved from www.library.alliant.edu.

Frame, R. (1983). Sex without love (discussion of Margaret Mead and Samoa and the end of sex). *Christianity Today, 27*, 24.

Freeman, D. (1983). *Margaret Mead and Samoa: The making and unmaking of an anthropological myth*. Harvard University Press.

Government of Samoa. (2006). *Ministry of Health-Samoa Mental Health Policy.* Retrieved from http://www.who.int

Jackson, P. R. (2005). Indigenous theorizing in a complex world. *Asian Journal of Social Psychology, 8*(1), 51–64.

Langness, L. L. (1975). Margaret Mead and the study of socialization. *Ethos: Journal of the Society for Psychological Anthropology, 3*(2), 97–112.

Lui, D. (2003). *Family-a Samoan perspective*. Paper presented at the Keynote presentation to the SF National Conference, Christchurch Convention Centre 13-14th September 2003.

Mead, M. (1928 [1943]). *Coming of age in Samoa: A study of adolescence and sex in primitive societies*. Penguin.

Meleisea, M., Meleisea, P. S., Leatio'o, K., Fitisemanu, T., Sib, G. P. S., Tavale, T., & Fido, P. (n.d.). *Chapter Four: Christianity.* Retrieved from samoanstudies.ws

Meleisea, M., Schoeffel-Meleisea, P., Pesteta-Sio, G., Va'ai, I., Suafole, L., & Tavale, T. (1987). *Lagaga: A short history of Samoa*. Institute of Pacific Studies and the Western Samoa Extension Centre of the University of the South Pacific, Fiji.

Meleisea, P. S. (2004). Teaching Asia-Pacific core values of peace and harmony. *Anthropologist,* Auckland: University of Auckland, 163.

Pilato, T., Su'a, T., & Crichton-Hill, Y. (1998). A Pacific Islands perspective. *Social Work Now, 11*, 25–29.

Pouono, T. (2017). Replanting the transplanted Christian churches: Missio dei and the twenty-first century diaspora Samoan church. *Stimulus: The New Zealand Journal of Christian Thought and Practice, 24*(1), 45–50.

Robson, A. E. (2009). Malietoa, Williams and Samoa's embrace of Christianity. *Journal of Pacific History, 44*(1), 21–39.

Salesa, T. D. (2009). Remembering Samoan history. In T. Suaalii-Sauni, I. U. Tuagalu, T. N. Kirifi-Alai, & N. Fuamatu (Eds.), *Su'esu'e Manogi: In search of fragrance Tui Atua Tupua Tamasese Ta'isi and the Samoan indigenous reference* (pp. 215–228). National University of Samoa, APIA: The Centre for Samoan Studies.

Shankman, P. (2013). The "fateful hoaxing" of Margaret Mead: A cautionary tale. *Current Anthropology, 54*(1), 51–70. https://doi.org/10.1086/669033

Shore, B. (1982). *Sala'ilua, a Samoan mystery*. Columbia University Press.

Taufe'ulungaki, A. (2004). Fonua: Reclaiming Pacific communities in Aotearoa. In *LotuMo'ui: Pacific health symposium counties-Manukau District Health Board [Symposium].* Waipuna Hotel.

Tofaeono, A. (2000). *Eco-theology: Aiga, the household of life. A perspective from living myths and traditions of Samoa*. Erlanger Verlag für Mission und Ökumene.

Tuala-Warren, L. (2002). *A study in ifoga: Samoa's answer to dispute healing*. Te Mātāhauariki Institute, University of Waikato.

Tamases, K., Peteru, C., & Waldegrave, C. (1997). Ole taeao aqua: the new morning: A qualitative investigation into Samoan perspectives on mental health and culturally appropriate services: A research project carried out by The Family Center. Lower Hutt, Wellington, New Zealand: The Family Center.

Chapter 6
Native Hawaiians and Psychology: The Cultural and Historical Context of Indigenous Ways of Knowing

Laurie D. McCubbin and Anthony Marsella

Historical events have shaped Native Hawaiian peoples' survival and identity over the course of the past two centuries. The colonial domination of Native Hawaiians that began with the arrival of the Westerners has affected the design, delivery, and treatment of health services for Native Hawaiians, as well as the psychological research conducted on this population. The most recent four decades have encompassed a resurgence of Native Hawaiians' reclamation of their traditional cultures and practices and restoration of their indigenous identity. During this same period, educational opportunities for Native Hawaiians with an emphasis on language emersion, culture-based teaching in K through 12 education, program evaluations, and academic assessments have resulted in an increase in Native Hawaiians conducting psychological research that has challenged the conclusions of prior studies by offering indigenous perspectives and interpretations. The resulting revisions and rewriting of Native Hawaiian history and culture and resurgence of the native language have had a salutogenic impact on this ethnic group. Native Hawaiian psychologists and scholars from other disciplines (e.g., education, cultural studies, anthropology, history, archeology, and social work) play a critical role in the correction of past misrepresentations in Hawaiian history, cultural preservation, and cultivation of indigenous knowledge and research. These developments have also

McCubbin, L. D., & Marsella, A. (2009). Native Hawaiians and psychology: The cultural and historical context of indigenous ways of knowing. *Cultural Diversity and Ethnic Minority Psychology, 15*(4), 374-387. https://doi.org/10.1037/a0016774

L. D. McCubbin (✉)
University of Louisville, Louisville, KY, USA
e-mail: mccubbin@wsu.edu

A. Marsella
Department of Psychology, University of Hawaii at Manoa, Honolulu, HI, USA

G. J. Rich, N. A. Ramkumar (eds.), *Psychology in Oceania and the Caribbean*, International and Cultural Psychology,
https://doi.org/10.1007/978-3-030-87763-7_6

exposed the profession to serious gaps in psychological research on Native Hawaiians that demand attention if this line of scientific inquiry is to enlighten the profession and apply knowledge to enhance the well-being of the Hawaiian people.

Given the limited awareness and knowledge about this ethnic group among the psychology profession, a brief profile of Native Hawaiians in the United States in terms of age, gender, and socioeconomic status would be appropriate (McCubbin et al., 2008; Pacific American Foundation, 2004). According to the U.S. Census in 2000, there are 401,168 Native Hawaiians who live in the United States which is an increase of over 90,000 people since 1990 (estimate: 310,747 Native Hawaiians; U.S. Census, 2000). Approximately 60% of Native Hawaiians live in the State of Hawaii, and approximately 40% in the continental United States. Among the Native Hawaiians, 49.9% are male and 50.1% are female which is similar to the national population distribution (49.1% male and 50.9% female; U.S. Census, 2000). Native Hawaiians on average are significantly younger in comparison to the national age distribution (25.6 years old compared to 35.3 years old, respectively) with slightly over 40% of Native Hawaiians being 19 years or younger (as compared with the national rate at 28.6%). Native Hawaiian families are more likely to be considered poor (12%) compared to the national rate (9.2%). In terms of unemployment, Hawaiians are more likely to be unemployed, with a rate of 5.7% for unemployed women (national rate: 3.3%) and a 7.0% rate for unemployed men (national rate: 4.0%). Hawaiians are more likely to live with families and have a higher number of people living in the household despite having smaller houses and are more likely to rent rather than own their home (Pacific American Foundation, 2004) when compared to the national average. Hawaiians are more likely to graduate from high school (85%) as compared with the national rate of all high school graduates (80.4%). While these results are promising, the data also show that Native Hawaiians are almost half as likely to receive a bachelor's degree (4.6%) as compared with the national rate (8.9%).

Challenges to Defining Native Hawaiians

As an ethnocultural group, Native Hawaiians have not received much attention in psychological studies of racial and ethnic minorities. The dominant reason for this phenomenon is the historical orientation of social scientists to subsume Native Hawaiians under the broader racial category of Asian Americans and Pacific Islanders. Until the 2000 Census, this categorization masked differences within the subgroups of these ethnicities. This same strategy, observed in multiple US government studies and demographic publications, persisted until the 2000 Census. This "collapsing" of racial groups has resulted in the conspicuous absence of meaningful and accurate data on Native Hawaiians including (a) population demographic patterns and trends; (b) specific health needs and resources; (c) critical social and historical forces that shape health and illness; and (d) the poverty, discrimination, and abuse of these populations and of other indigenous groups (Srinivasan & Guillermo, 2000). Also, by combining Native Hawaiians with Asian Americans, elementary, secondary, and postsecondary students have acquired only a limited understanding about the best practice strategies for improving the educational profile and development of Native Hawaiians.

The shifting classification systems used to place Native Hawaiians in a social context have added to the challenge of social and behavioral scientists' efforts to understand and explain the variability within ethnic groups. Native Hawaiians have also been categorized as Pacific Islanders, Polynesians, Oceanic People, and the classic Asian-Pacific Islanders. As the psychology of race and culture has evolved, Native Hawaiians have been marginalized or left out of the Federal and State funding strategies for promoting psychological research on at-risk populations, and particularly indigenous groups as the Native American Indians and Alaskan Natives. The ethnic classification challenge is exacerbated by contextualized definitions of Hawaiians. The classification "Hawaiian" has been used loosely to describe all citizens and residents of the Hawaiian Islands (e.g., Japanese, Puerto Rican, Chinese, and Filipinos) who were born on the islands or were long-term residents of the islands. There is confusion about a geographical identity referred to as "local" as opposed to Hawaiians as indigenous/Native people of the Hawaiian Islands. For the purposes of this chapter, Pacific Islanders will be referred to as a race and Native Hawaiians as an ethnic group within this racial category.

Two important population trends need to be clarified when describing the Native Hawaiian people as a separate entity for psychological inquiry. First, the Native Hawaiian population, due to its colonial history, faced a rapid decline in population similar to that of American Indians in the nineteenth and twentieth centuries. This dramatic decline in the population of Native Hawaiians is often referred to as cultural genocide or "holocaust" (Stannard, 1989). Population reports from the time period of the first Western contact in 1778 to 1876 indicate that over 90% of the Native Hawaiian population died within the first 100 years after Western contact. In contrast, the 2000 U.S. Census accounted for over 400,000 Native Hawaiians living in the United States, with projections of this number increasing to almost 1 million by 2050 (Malone, 2005). However, paradoxically, the number of pure-blooded Hawaiians (those of 100% Hawaiian blood quantum) in the twenty-first century has been estimated at less than 5,000 currently and projected that by 2050, there will be no more "pure" Native Hawaiians left (Noyes, 2003).

The second population trend among Native Hawaiians is the extensive interracial partnerships and marriages, which have resulted in the majority of Native Hawaiians being multiethnic or multiracial. Estimates range from 66% (from the U.S. Census, 2000) to 98% to 99% of Native Hawaiians (Noyes, 2003; Office of Hawaiian Affairs, 1998) as being multiethnic. In psychological research, it is common to see classifications of Native Hawaiians separated by those who are "full-blooded" Hawaiians and those who are multiethnic or multiracial as "part-Hawaiian." Researchers often report Native Hawaiian samples as either a combination of Hawaiians and part-Hawaiians or separated (e.g., Kanazawa et al., 2007; Nishimura et al., 2005). For the purposes of this review, the term Native Hawaiians will refer to both Hawaiians with 100% Hawaiian ancestry and those who are considered part-Hawaiian.

Definition of Native Hawaiians

The 1959 Statehood Admissions Act of Hawai'i defines a Native Hawaiian person as "any individual who is a descendant of the aboriginal people who, prior to 1778, occupied and exercised sovereignty in the area that now constitutes the State of Hawaii" (Statehood Admissions Act of Hawai'i, 1959). The term "Hawaiian" is not necessarily the preferred Native Hawaiian term within this ethnic group; rather, the proper term in the Hawaiian language is "*Kanaka Maoli*," which translates as "true" or "real" person (Blaisdell, 1989; for a more thorough review about Hawaiian identity and the varying definitions of Native Hawaiian, see McCubbin & Dang, in press).

A Brief Overview of Indigenous Psychology

Indigenous psychology is the scientific study of human behavior that is native, unique, not transported from other regions, and designed *by* the people *for* the people (in this case the indigenous or Native people). It involves the systematic examination of knowledge, skills, beliefs, and values a population may have about themselves. Theories, concepts, and methods are developed to correspond with psychological phenomena (Kim & Berry, 1993). This specific domain of psychology explicitly encompasses the content and context of research and is a vital part of scientific inquiry because existing psychological theories are not universal, but represent the psychology and cultural traditions of Europe and North America. Indigenous psychology as it relates to Native Hawaiians emphasizes the examination of psychological phenomena in ecological, historical, and cultural contexts and involves multiple perspectives and methods to create a comprehensive and integrated picture of the population. The scientific process acknowledges that the Native Hawaiians have complex and sophisticated understandings of themselves as individuals and part of a collective whole. It is a formidable challenge to translate their worldview into analytical knowledge, a process which characterizes the Western/European approach to psychology. Although descriptive analysis may be the starting point of indigenous research, its ultimate goal is to discover cultural patterns through indigenous epistemology that can be theoretically and empirically verified. Of importance, indigenous psychology embraces the cultural and anthropological sciences' tradition of incorporating meaning and context into the research (Kim et al., 2006).

A Worldview of Native Hawaiians: An Indigenous Perspective

Understanding the traditional *Kanaka Maoli* psyche requires an understanding of a worldview of human nature that is different from Western theories and assumptions about human nature and behavior. It is especially different from those Western theories about the structure and dynamics of personality that consider the individual psyche to be the source of human behavior (Marsella et al., 1995).

The Native Hawaiian concept of self is grounded in social relationships (Handy & Pukui, 1972) and tied to the view that the individual, society, and nature are inseparable and key to psychological health. Such relational and emotional bonds are expected to support and protect each member (Ito, 1985) which in turn can promote psychological well-being. However, if these same relational bonds are out of balance and are harmful to the individual, community, or nature, this can result in maladaptive behaviors or psychopathology. This relational harmony or balance is referred to as *lōkahi.*

Lōkahi (which means accord or unity according to Pukui & Elbert, 1986) is a concept that can be visualized as a triangle formed by *'aina* (nature), *kanaka* (humankind), and *ke akua* (gods). Native Hawaiian health requires *lōkahi*, or a sense of harmony, which can consist of the following elements: mind, body, spirit, and land. From a Native Hawaiian perspective, mental health is viewed holistically encompassing body, mind, and spirit and is embedded in family, land, and the spiritual world (Judd, 1998; Marsella et al., 1995).

The concept of land or *'aina* (translated can also refer to earth or nature; Kanahele, 1986; Pukui & Elbert, 1986; Rezentes, 1996) within a Native Hawaiian worldview is fundamentally different from a Western definition of land as a location or geographic place that can be owned, sold, or bargained with as a commodity. According to Kanahele (1986) and Rezentes (1996), *'aina* has three dimensions: physical, psychological, and spiritual. The environment embodies physical *'aina*, marking both ancestral homelands and the substance required to nourish the body. Psychological *'aina* is related to mental health, particularly in regard to positive and negative thinking. Spiritual *'aina* speaks to daily relationships between Native Hawaiians and the spiritual world. Traditionally, the spiritual world has been—and continues to be—a source of great guidance and strength for Native Hawaiian people. Casken (2001) points out the need for Native Hawaiians to protect the land and the ocean, as these aspects of *'aina* are essential to the health of the *Kanaka Maoli*.

Mana refers to the energy of life that is found in all things, animate and inanimate. Mana also refers to divine or spiritual power (Kanahele, 1986; Rezentes, 1996) and evokes respect for one's gods. *Mana* emanating from ecological elements or nature has the power to calm, energize, heal, and relax (Oneha, 2001). It is the *mana* that binds and connects person, family, land, and the spirit world.

Mana is reflected in the felt or experienced connection between the psyche and the many life forms around it (i.e., gods, nature, family), thus creating a sense of relationship—perhaps even obligation—to act or to behave in such a way that the *mana* is increased, enhanced, and sustained and brought into harmony or *lōkahi*. It is our speculation that *mana*, *lōkahi*, and the various expressions or manifestations of life for the Native Hawaiians, including their gods, nature, family, and way of life, form a psychic unity that creates an inherent and/or implicit epistemology (i.e., way of knowing), praxiology (i.e., ways of acting), and ontology (i.e., view of human nature) that offers a model of causality, morality, and cosmology for the Native Hawaiian. External controls for this including social controls, rules, axioms, and moral codes (e.g., taboos) add to the generational transmission and perpetuation of this cultural construction of reality.

This generational transmission and perpetuation of cultural construction is found in the *'ohana*, meaning family or kin group (Kanahele, 1986; Pukui & Elbert, 1986; Rezentes, 1996). *'Ohana* can consist of extended family members, as well as informal relationships, such as friends and family members of friends. Central to this concept of family is the emphasis on harmony and balance among all the key components of family life: nature, the spiritual life, community, culture, and interpersonal relationships (McCubbin & McCubbin, 2005). Thus, *'ohana* can be considered an extended and complex arrangement of roles and relationships that include all of the following:

- *Ke Akua* (God)
- *Aumākua* (family guardian gods)
- *Kūpuna* (family elders)
- *Makua* (parents)
- *Ōpio* (children)
- *Mo'opuna* (grandchildren)
- *Hānai* children (those offspring of other families incorporated into another family to be raised and cared for)

- With an understanding of these Hawaiian concepts, an example of the Native Hawaiian psyche is presented (see Figure 6.1). As Figure 6.1 indicates, the person is located within a series of interdependent and interactive forces that extend from the family (*'ohana*) to nature (*'aina*) and to the gods and spirits (*'akua*). The force holding these elements together in a unified manner is *mana*. This is the optimum relationship for health and well-being. What is special about this conception of the human psyche is that it is based on an embeddedness or contextual model of personhood that is more consistent with contemporary views in psychology advocating contextual, ecological, and interactional models of human behavior.

Within this framework, health and illness are considered to be a function of those forces that serve either to promote or to destroy harmony. Given the importance of the complex social fabric for Native Hawaiians, many of these forces reside in events and behaviors that support or undermine social and spiritual relations. For example, things that destroy the social fabric include the following behaviors:

- Hate (*ina'ina*)
- Jealousy (*lili*)
- Rudeness (*ho'okano*)

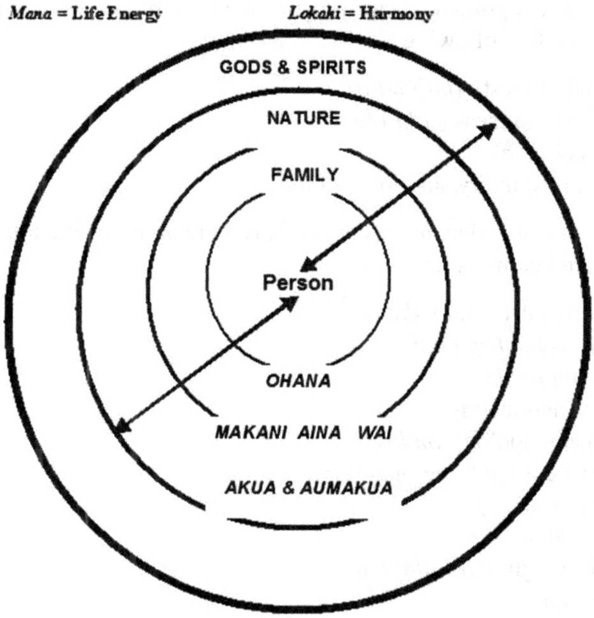

Fig. 6.1 Traditional Native Hawaiian conception of psyche: person, family, nature, and spiritual world. *Mana*, life energy; *Lōkahi*, harmony

- Being nosy (*niele*)
- Bearing a grudge (*ho'omauhala*)
- Bragging (*ha'anui*)
- Showing off (*ho'oi'o*)
- Breaking promises (*hua'ōlelo*)
- Speaking bitter thoughts (*waha 'awa*)
- Stealing, fighting, and hostile (*huhu*) behavior

Destruction of the spiritual fabric occurs when forces come into play when an individual or a family violates certain taboos or restrictions, thus opening the door for supernatural forces seeking propitiation or mollification to enter their lives. These forces are:

- Offended ghosts (*lapu*)
- Natural spirits (*kupua*)
- Spirit guardians (*aumākua*)
- Ancestor/elders (*kūpuna*)
- Black magic or sorcery (*ana'ana*)
- Curse (*anai*)

The resolution of both social and supernatural conflicts can occur by using prosocial behaviors and certain rituals that can restore and promote *lōkahi*. Prosocial behaviors include adopting the behaviors of a *Kanaka Makua* (a good person); these behaviors include the following:

- Humility and modesty (*ha'aha'a*)
- Politeness and kindness (*'olu'olu*)
- Helpfulness (*kokua*)
- Acceptance, hospitality, and love (*aloha*)

Ritualistic behaviors that can restore and promote harmony include the following Native Hawaiian healing arts:

- Herbal treatments (*la'au kahea*)
- Purification baths (*kapu kai*)
- Massage (*lomi lomi*)
- Special diets and fasting
- Confession and apology (*mihi*)
- Dream interpretation (*moe 'uhane*)
- Clairvoyance (*hihi'o*)
- Prayer (*pule ho'onoa*)
- Transfer of thought (*Ho 'olulu ia*)
- Possession (*noho*)
- Water blessings (*pi kai*)
- Spirit mediumship (*haka*)

Thus, the Native Hawaiian worldview encompasses a complex system that is rooted in the interaction of body, mind, and spirit and is directly tied to prosocial human relations and prospiritual relations. The restoration of health and well-being requires the adoption of prosocial behaviors and engagement in the healing arts and protocols that can reestablish interpersonal and psychological harmony.

Native Hawaiians in a Historical Context

In order to understand the psychology of Native Hawaiians, it is important to have the cultural context as described earlier and the historical context. The history of Native Hawaiians can be viewed in two segments: (a) precolonization (prior to Western contact; see Table 6.1) and (b) postcolonization (after Western contact; see Table 6.2). Based on archeological evidence, the exploration and settlement of Polynesian populations on the islands of Hawaii occurred sometime between 200 and 600 AD (Graves & Addison, 1995). By the eighteenth century, the Hawaiian cultural traditions were well established with a population estimated from 400,000 (Schmitt, 1968) to 875,000 (Stannard, 1989).Hawaii was governed by a system under the control the *ali'i* (chiefs) class and thus was viewed as in a state of flux (Handy & Pukui, 1972). The major source for understanding the Native Hawaiian culture prior to Western contact is the work by Handy and Pukui (1972) on the Polynesian family system. Two fundamental units of social organization existed, the

Table 6.1 Chronological history of Native Hawaiians (Kanaka Maoli) 1 CE to 1899

1 AD	The first Native Hawaiian people arrived in the Hawaiian Islands from the Marquesas, Tahiti, or the Society Islands sailing double-hulled canoes.
1–1400	Migration between Polynesia and the Hawaiian Islands continued and the Islands grew in population. Settlement occurred across all major islands (i.e., Hawaii (Owhyhee), Maui (Mowee), Molokai (Morotoi), Lanai (Renai), Oahu (Woahoo), and Kauai (Atooi)). Different kingdoms led by various chiefs or royal families (ali'i) were established across the islands. Land was cultivated and hierarchical societies were established. Around 1400, travel between Polynesia and Hawaii ceased.
1778	Captain James Cook arrived in the Hawaiian Islands with two ships: HMS Resolute and HMS Discovery. This was the first contact between the Native Hawaiians and Europeans. Captain Cook named the Hawaiian Islands the "Sandwich Islands." Population estimates at the time of Captain Cook's arrival varied from 300,000 to 800,000.
1778–1878	Many Native Hawaiians became ill and died from diseases spread by Captain Cook's men (e.g., tuberculosis, measles, smallpox, syphilis). Within 100 years from Cook's arrival, it is estimated that less than 10% of the Native Hawaiians remained.
1779	Captain Cook was killed by the Native Hawaiians in a battle at Kealakekua Bay on the Island of Hawaii.
1810	All the Hawaiian Islands were united for the first time under the leadership of Kamehameha I. Prior to this time, different islands were separate kingdoms. A Hawaiian monarchy was established.
1819	First whaling ships arrived in Kealakekua, Hawaii, signaling the beginning of a thriving whaling industry and the further demise of the Native Hawaiian people.
1820	First American missionaries arrived in Hawaii to spread Christianity and to further destroy Native Hawaiian cultural traditions. Missionary families soon joined with Caucasian businessmen in taking ownership of land, politics, and the economy. Hawaiian language use and cultural practices were discouraged as pagan and primitive.
1850	Because there were so few Native Hawaiian men (i.e., estimates of less than 3000) during this period, the Legislature approved the hiring of foreign laborers from China, Japan, and Portugal to work in the growing sugar and pineapple industries. Floods of workers from these countries came to Hawaii. They were followed by workers from Puerto Rico and the Philippines. In combination with the Caucasians (from America and Europe), these populations soon outnumbered the Native Hawaiian people, who were rapidly dying from disease and who were intermarrying.
1876	One of the lowest points in the population decline of the Native Hawaiian people was reached in 1876 when only 53,900 Native Hawaiian people were reported to be living in the Kingdom of Hawaii. King David Kalakaua states of his people: "One day their words will be heard no more forever."
1893	On January 16, 1893, the U.S. Minister to Hawaii, John Stevens, with a group of American businessmen and the help of the US Navy, invaded the sovereign Hawaiian nation without permission or approval of the US government. On January 17, 1893, Queen Lili'uokalani, the last queen, and the Hawaiian monarchy were overthrown by a group of American businessmen. This tragic event was called the *Onipaa* by Native Hawaiians.
1894–1895	President Cleveland investigated the overthrow of the monarchy, declared it an "act of war," and called for restoration of the Hawaiian monarchy. The provisional government declared itself as the Republic of Hawaii.

(continued)

Table 6.1 (continued)

1895	The annexationists put down a Native Hawaiian rebellion to restore Queen Lili'uokalani and tried and convicted her for treason on January 7, 1895. She was sentenced to 5 years in jail (she actually served 21 months).
1898	On July 7, Hawaii became a territory of the United States without a single Native Hawaiian vote. The United States annexed the former Kingdom of Hawaii.

'ohana (family) and the *'aina* (land). The *'aina*, or land, was divided into the *ahupua'a*, or "pie-shaped" segments of the island consisting of running from the mountains to the ocean. The two main food sources for Native Hawaiians, the ocean with fishing and the land with agriculture, were therefore available in each *ahupua'a*.

The *ahupua'a* was the domain of the *ali'i* (the high chiefs). No one chief ruled all of the Hawaiian Islands. However, the Native Hawaiians had a hierarchy of social classes with the chiefs on the top of the order, followed by commoners and slaves, with each status having its own duties and roles in society. The chiefs were responsible for the welfare of their people living on the *ahupua'a*. An elaborate system of *kapu* or taboo was created to maintain harmony and balance with nature while also providing subsistence for its people. This was considered the cornerstone that supported the ancient Hawaiian culture (Lind, 1934).

The religion consisted of four major gods, *Ku* (god of war and chiefs), *Kane* (creator of man), *Lono* (god of agriculture), and *Kanaloa* (god of the ocean), and also additional lesser but powerful gods and spirits including *aumakua* or spiritual ancestors (Pukui et al., 1972a). Within this worldview, humankind, the *Kanaka Maoli*, had the duty to protect all other species. Thus, the core of the Hawaiian culture was built on two belief structures: (a) the *Ihi Kapu* or the consecrated law that enabled the Hawaiian people to live in harmony with one another, with nature and the spiritual realm; and (b) the *Huikala* which is the psycho-spiritual process of untangling oneself (involving the *mihikala* protocol of repentance of error) and healing which allows a person to "elevate their earthly presence to a place where their divining self can express itself in this material world, allowing its influence to bring about conditions of health and prosperity for all" (Cook et al., 2003, p. 3). Even in the isolation of 2,000 miles of ocean surrounding the Hawaiian Islands, the Hawaiians were able to achieve cultural stability and self-sufficiency prior to Western contact in 1778.

During Captain James Cook's journeys of the Pacific Islands, which took him from Tahiti to other islands, he arrived on January 18, 1778, at Hawaii, signifying Native Hawaiians' first contact with Western culture. Captain Cook and his crew cultivated many stereotypes about the Native Hawaiian people; for example, they were characterized as friendly and hospitable with a propensity toward thievery (Lind, 1934) and also were "dreadful, mercenary, artful villains" (Meares, 1788–1789).

Additional contacts with the Western world included the first missionaries who arrived on March 20, 1820, from New England in order to spread Christianity among Native Hawaiians. Manly (1929 as cited in Lind, 1934) described the natives as "wretched creatures," "savages," with the appearance of "half-men and half

Table 6.2 History of Native Hawaiians: 1900 to present

1900–1930	Arrival of Asian immigrants, especially Filipino, Chinese, and Japanese plantation workers, continued.
1909, 1911	Queen Lili'uokalani established an organization dedicated to the welfare of orphaned and destitute children in the State of Hawaii, with preference given to Native Hawaiian children; this became the Queen Lili'uokalani Children's Center.
1922	Hawaiian Homes Commission Act was passed by the US Congress in an effort to rehabilitate Native Hawaiians and restore the population.
1940s	US military began to use Kaho'olawe, an island off the coast of Maui, as a bombing range.
1941	Japanese bomb Pearl Harbor. Hawaii became a major location for American military operations for the Pacific War. The landscape and cultural life of Hawaii was permanently altered.
1953	President D. Eisenhower transferred Kaho'olawe to the jurisdiction of the US Navy.
1959	Hawaii became the 50th US State.
1964–1974	During the Vietnam War era, American military once again used Hawaii as a major base for military campaign.
1970–present	A resurgence of activism has arisen among Native Hawaiian people, including numerous civil protests, and cries for Native Hawaiian sovereignty and nationhood. Many schools have been opened to teach Hawaiian languages. Native Hawaiian activists are calling for the preservation of Native Hawaiian culture and are pushing for various kinds of national and international recognition of Hawaiian people. The restoration of Kaho'olawe becomes an important issue for Native Hawaiians and serves as a catalyst for Native Hawaiian Renaissance.
1972	Mary Pukui, a revered Native Hawaiian *Kupuna* (respected elder), published *Nana I Ke Kumu* (*Look to the Source*) in collaboration with E. Haertig and C. Lee. This work (Volumes 1 and 2) discusses traditional Native Hawaiian wisdom, values, and beliefs using Mary Pukui's rich store of personal memories.
	The US Congress included Native Hawaiians in American Indian/Alaskan Native legislation; the first grantee from the Administration for Native Americans was Alu Like, Inc.
1973	Attempts were made by Dean Windsor Cutting to allow nontraditional students to enroll in medical school as "guests" to increase the number of underrepresented minorities, including Native Hawaiians.
	Herb Kane, Ben Finney, and Tommy Holmes founded the Pacific Voyaging Society.
1974	The *Hokule'a*, a Polynesian voyaging canoe, was launched and became a symbol of Native Hawaiian pride and navigational skills.
	The vessel sailed to Marquesas and Tahiti Islands using traditional navigation methods, repeating historic voyages.
	Alan Howard, a University of Hawaii professor in anthropology, with long experience among Pacific Island cultures, published *Ain't No Big Thing: Coping Strategies in a Hawaiian-American Community*. Honolulu, HI: East-West Center Press.
1975	Alu Like, Inc., a nonprofit organization, was established to assist Native Hawaiians toward social and economic self-sufficiency.
1976	Nine people, known as the Kaho'olawe Nine, occupy Kaho'olawe to protest the bombing of the island.

(continued)

Table 6.2 (continued)

1980s	The Bishop Estate, an educational, cultural, and financial trust created at the turn of the century as the legacy of Princess Bernice Pauahi Bishop, emerged as a major social force in Hawaii through its ownership of leased land. Its mission is to promote educational development of students of native Hawaiian ancestry.
1980	Benjamin Young, MD, a psychiatrist of Hawaiian-Chinese ancestry, published a chapter entitled "The Hawaiians" in J. McDermott et al. (Eds.) *People and Culture of Hawaii*. Honolulu, HI: University Press of Hawaii.
	A consent decree was signed with the members of the Protect Kaho'olawe 'Ohana (PKO) with a memorandum of understanding requiring the US Navy to begin soil conservation, revegetation, and goat eradication of the island.
1981	Gene Kassebaum, a sociology professor at UH, published *Crime and Justice Related to Native Hawaiians in the State of Hawaii* (Alu Like, Honolulu, Hawaii), which documented disproportionate numbers of Native Hawaiians in penal system and sentencing offenses.
1982	Andrew White, a psychiatrist, and Marilyn Landis, a sociologist, published *The Mental Health of Native Hawaiians*. Honolulu, HI: Alu Like, Inc. White is a psychiatrist who works in the Native Hawaiian communities on Leeward Oahu.
1983	US Congress produces the Native Hawaiians Study Commission Report—21-month study of the culture, needs, and concerns of Native Hawaiians.
1985	*E Ola Mau* Native Hawaiian Health Needs Study Report (E Ola Mau) was published by Alu Like, Inc. which identified the physical, mental, spiritual, and dental health needs of Native Hawaiians.
	Victoria Shook published *Ho'oponopono*. Honolulu, HI: University Press of Hawaii.
1986	The Hawaiian Studies Program at University of Hawaii was languishing. The only faculty member was a 0.50 nontenured track elderly Hawaiian, Abraham Pi'ianai'a. At the same time, Haunani Kay Trask, a female Hawaiian activist, was petitioning for tenure and promotion in the American Studies Program where she was an assistant professor. However, internal conflicts in the American Studies Program emerged regarding her petition.
	The Office of the Vice President for Academic Affairs (OVPAA) mediated the conflicts that emerged in an effort to resolve differences. A decision was reached to assign Professor Haunani Kay Trask and her 1.00 FTE to the Hawaiian Studies Program. Professor Trask thus became the first full-time tenured member of the Hawaiian Studies Faculty.
	The University of Hawaii initiated a report on the status of Native Hawaiians and higher education needs. This report, entitled *KA'U*, was prepared by Native Hawaiians, including some of the most prominent members of the UH system faculty (e.g., Isabel Abbot, Kekuni Blaisdell, Larry Kimura, Haunani Kay Trask, Abe Pi'ianaia) and talented graduate students who assume future leadership roles (e.g., Lilikala Kame'eleihiwa, Davianna McGregor). The *KA'U* Report calls for the development of Native Hawaiian Studies Center with four tenured faculty positions and funds to support teaching, research, and outreach activities. It was the birth of the now famous Native Hawaiian Studies Center that became part of the new School for Hawaiian Asian and Pacific Studies (SHAPS).
1986	The *E Ola Mau* Report on Native Hawaiian health status was submitted to the US Congress by Alu Like, a Native Hawaiian research and training organization. The report documented the serious medical, psychological, and dental problems of the Native Hawaiian people. Federally funded programs were designed and implemented to address the problems.

(continued)

Table 6.2 (continued)

	For the first time, a person of Native Hawaiian ancestry, John A. Waihee, was elected governor of the State of Hawaii. He served for two 4-year terms. The Native Hawaiian Studies Program was initiated at the University of Hawaii with tenured faculty positions.
	There was an increase of Native Hawaiian students attending the University of Hawaii.
1986	George Kanahele, a Hawaiian business leader, published *Ku- Kanaka (Stand Tall): A Search for Hawaiian Values*. Honolulu, HI: University Press of Hawaii.
1987	Britt Robillard and Anthony J. Marsella published *Contemporary Issues in Mental Health Research in the Pacific Islands* (Social Science Research Institute, University of Hawaii, Honolulu, Hawaii). This volume contains several chapters on Native Hawaiian mental health including a chapter on the cultural accommodation of mental health services for Native Hawaiians by Nicholas Higginbotham.
1988	The US Congress passed the Native Hawaiian Health Care Improvement Act (PL 100–597), Sect. 2(3)—42 USC 11701; the purpose was to raise the health status of the Native Hawaiians.
	Papa Ola Lōkahi was formed with representatives from 25 public agencies and private organizations; this was the first effort to establish an infrastructure to address Native Hawaiian health issues.
1989	*Papa Ola Lōkahi's* Native Hawaiian Health Master Plan was created to develop appropriate and culturally acceptable health care programs and delivery for Native Hawaiians.
1990	The population of State of Hawaii exceeded 1,100,000 people distributed across the islands—ethnocultural minorities make of more than 75% of the State's population: Caucasian (262,604), Japanese (222,014), part-Hawaiian (196,367), other mixed race (190,789), Filipino (123,642), Chinese (51,293), African American (16,180), Korean (11,597), pure Hawaiian (8711), Samoans (3235), and Puerto Ricans (3140).
	These population figures are inaccurate for 1996. Rapid influxes of legal immigrants into Hawaii (e.g., Filipino, Korean, and Vietnamese populations) and illegal immigrants by other groups (e.g., Chinese, Mexican) within the last decade resulted in sizeable increases in the population of these groups and proportionate reductions in the population distribution of other groups.
	The Native Hawaiian Mental Health Research Development Project (NHMHRDP) at the University of Hawaii at Manoa was established with the goal to conduct interdisciplinary, cross-cultural, mental health-related research for Asian and Pacific Islanders.
1990s	The US government returned the Island of Kaho'olawe to the State of Hawaii, along with a congressional appropriation exceeding $400 million for its restoration, following decades of military use/abuse including constant practice bombing operations.
	Sizeable Federal Government grants and entitlement funds for health, education, economic, and social demonstration projects became available to the Hawaiian people and the State of Hawaii.
	Sovereignty movement grew in strength and determination. The Office of Hawaii Affairs managed an election procedure to determine Native Hawaiian interest in various forms of self-government.
1991	The Office of Hawaiian Health declared a serious health crisis for the indigenous people of Hawaii.

(continued)

Table 6.2 (continued)

	The Native Hawaiian Health Scholarship Program was established in order to train Native Hawaiians to become health professionals in Hawaii, including clinical psychologists.
	The Native Hawaiian Center of Excellence (NHCOE) at the John A. Burns School of Medicine (JABSOM) was established.
1992	The first graduate course in Native Hawaiian Culture and Behavior was taught in University of Hawaii Psychology Department by A.J. Marsella, Kamanao Crabbe, and Patrick Uchigakiuchi.
	Lilikala Kame'eleihiwa published *Native Land and Foreign Desires: How Shall We Live in Harmony*. Honolulu, Hawaii: Bishop Museum Press. The volume documents abuses of Native Hawaiian culture and exploitation of Native Hawaiian people and served as a rallying point for emerging Hawaiian activism.
	Legislation amended and reauthorized the Native Hawaiian Health Care Improvement Act (Public Law 102–396).
1993	Haunani Kay Trask, the first tenured professor of the Hawaiian Studies Center, published *From a Native Daughter: Colonialism and Sovereignty in Hawaii*. Monroe, MA: Common Courage Press. The volume documents historical violations and abuses of Native Hawaiians and their culture and calls for a sovereign Hawaii under Native Hawaiian rule.
	Congress passed a resolution and President Clinton signed Public Law 103–150 which acknowledged the 100th year commemoration of the overthrow of the Kingdom of Hawaii and a formal apology to Native Hawaiians for the improper role of the US military in support of the overthrow (Hawaii Advisory Committee to the U.S. Commission on Civil Rights, 2001).
1996	William Rezentes published *Ka Lama Kukui: Hawaiian Psychology: An Introduction*. Honolulu, Hawaii.
1998	The first Native Hawaiian Health and Wellness Summit was held in September, as well as publication of the special issue The Health of Native Hawaiians in the *Pacific Health Dialog: Journal of Community Health and Clinical Medicine for the Pacific*.
1999	*Decolonizing Methodologies: Research and Indigenous Peoples*, written by Linda Tuhiwai Smith, was published by Zed Books. 2000 Senator Daniel Akaka introduced a bill, the US Senate Bill 344, called the Native Hawaiian Recognition Act which would allow for federal recognition of Native Hawaiian people as a distinct indigenous entity similar to the Native American tribal status.
	The creation of the Rural Hawaii Behavioral Health Program (RHBHP) was established, incorporating Native Hawaiian cultural values, beliefs, and practice in conjunction with primary care psychology.
	Hamilton McCubbin, a native Hawaiian, was named the first CEO and Chancellor of the Kamehameha Schools (formerly Bishop Estate); a multibillion dollar trust was dedicated to the education of Native Hawaiians.
2001	*Pacific Health Dialog: Journal of Community Health and Clinical Medicine for the Pacific* published a special issue in September, entitled "E Ola Na Kini: The Health of the Native Hawaiians."
2003	*Ho'oulu: Our Time of Becoming Hawaiian Epistemology and Early Writings* written by Manulani Aluli Meyer was published by 'Ai Pohaku Press.
2005	Native Hawaiian Educational Assessment by S. Kana'iaupuni, N. Malone, and K. Ishibashi was published by Pauahi Publications including a model of Native Hawaiian well-being.

(continued)

Table 6.2 (continued)

2006	The Native Hawaiian Recognition Act, US Senate Bill 344 (also referred to as the Akaka Bill), was defeated.
2007	Hawai'inuiakea School of Hawaiian Knowledge became the newest school at the University of Hawaii at Manoa. In approving its establishment on ay 16, 2007, the Board of Regents created one of the largest schools of indigenous knowledge in the United States.
	I Ola Lahui, a rural behavioral health program, was created to address the mental and behavioral health care needs of rural populations in Hawaii, including the integration of cultural and community-based perspectives and approaches in program development, implementation, research, and evaluation processes.
2008	Myron B. Thompson School of Social Work became the new name of the professional school to honor a distinguished leader of Hawaiian ancestry; the naming is reflective of the school's commitment to the advancement of indigenous knowledge for profession in the behavioral sciences.

beast." An officer stated, "Well, if I never before saw brutes in shape of men, I have seen them this morning" (Manly, 1929, as cited in Lind, 1934). When these Westerners came to the islands, they brought with them various diseases including syphilis, gonorrhea, tuberculosis, influenza, typhoid, and smallpox which reduced Hawaii's population to 84,000 from an estimated 500,000–800,000 in 1853 (Diamond, 1999). In the 1860s, Reverend Rufus Anderson witnessed the genocide of the native population; however, he declined to see this as a tragedy. He thought this potential extinction of a race as "only natural" and equated it to "the amputation of diseased members of the body" (Anderson, 1865, p. 274).

Concomitantly, Native Hawaiians had established their own monarchy with the unification of the Hawaiian Islands by King Kamehameha I the Great in 1810 (see Figure 6.2). Subsequent kings continued to establish Hawaii's government, constitution, and international policies and treaties that established Hawaii as a nation. The Hawaiians have never relinquished their status as a sovereign nation (Sai, 2008). However, while Native Hawaiians began to find a balance between Western notions of leadership and government and maintaining their own indigenous culture, values, and knowledge, Westerners continued to hold a firm perception of these Natives as inferior savages in need of Western salvation.

Adams (1934) wrote how transient sailors and white exploiters broke down the native order and subsequently made claims of native incompetence, thus establishing the need for foreign governments to set up control of these people and their lands. The Native Hawaiian monarchy at times was forced to submit to unjust demands "backed up by foreign warships ..." (p. 157) and that the character of these demands were never to come to the attention of the civilized world" (Adams, 1934). In addition, the stereotype of Native Hawaiians as lazy was derived from the planters who regarded these indigenous people as being indolent and in need of constant supervision. Brown (1847 as cited in Lind, 1934) described Native Hawaiian laborers as deceptive and thus required constant supervision.

These observations, writings, and beliefs about Native Hawaiians influenced how these indigenous people of Hawaii viewed themselves. These perspectives

Fig. 6.2 King Kamehameha the Great

influenced the psyche of the Native Hawaiian people, particularly as their society and culture began to succumb to Western ideology. In Rufus Anderson's *The Hawaiian Islands* (1865), a Native Hawaiian stated, "We, the ancient men of Kamehameha's time were once idolaters, murderers … were once buried in darkness, sunk to the lowest depths of ignorance, roaming the fields and woods, like wild beasts … plunging into the darkness of hell. Now we are clothed like civilized beings" (p. 166). The stereotype of the savage was therefore imprinted on the psyche and soul of the Native Hawaiian people and contributed to Hawaiian leaders to express little hope for the future.

King Kalakaua, the last king of the Hawaiian people (see Figure 6.3), wrote in 1888:

> … the natives are steadily decreasing in numbers and gradually losing hold upon the fair land of their fathers. Within a century they have dwindled … to landless, hopeless victims to the greed and vices of civilization. They are slowly sinking under the restraints and burdens of their surroundings, and will in time succumb to social and political conditions foreign to their natures … [until] finally their voices will be heard no more forever. (Kalakaua, 1888, pp. 64–65, as cited in Nordyke, 1989, p. 27)

By 1876, only 53,900 Native Hawaiian people were reported living in the Kingdom of Hawaii.

On January 16, 1893, the U.S. Minister to Hawaii, John Stevens, with a group of American businessmen and the help of the US Navy invaded the sovereign Hawaiian nation without the permission or approval of the US government. On January 17,

Fig. 6.3 King Kalakaua

1893, Queen Lili'uokalani (see Figure 6.4), the last queen, and the Hawaiian monarchy were overthrown by a group of American businessmen. President Cleveland investigated the overthrow of the monarchy, declared it an "act of war," and called for restoration of the Hawaiian monarchy (Osborne, 1998). However, Cleveland's words went unheeded and the provisional government declared itself as the Republic of Hawaii in 1894 (Hawaii Advisory Committee to the U.S. Commission on Civil Rights, 2001). On July 7, 1898, Hawaii became a territory of the United States without a single vote from the Native Hawaiians. As a testimony of her struggle to save the Native Hawaiian Kingdom and her strength and resilience drawn from her heritage and spirituality, Queen Lili'uokalani wrote to her adopted daughter:

> I could not turn back the time for political change but there is still time to save our heritage. You must remember never to cease to act because you fear you may fail. The way to lose any earthly kingdom is to be inflexible, intolerant and prejudicial. Another way is to be too flexible, tolerant of too many wrongs and without judgment at all. It is a razor's edge, it is the width of a blade of *pili* grass. (Lili'uokalani, 1917)

Lili'uokalani (1917) described the struggle of Native Hawaiians as finding the delicate balance between navigating the Western world and its notions while also reaffirming the roots of the Hawaiian culture. It is this struggle not only for the Hawaiian psyche, but also for the Hawaiian people and its community as a whole, that has been dealt with over multiple generations. As the colonization in the nineteenth century resulted in negative views of Native Hawaiians, significant events in the twentieth century (see Table 6.2) helped shape the movement for Native

Fig. 6.4 Queen Lili'uokalani

Hawaiians to again navigate and chart their own path toward the reemergence and reclaiming of their indigenous ways of knowing, being, and living.

In an attempt to make amends for the illegal overthrow, Congress passed the Hawaiian Homes Commission Act in 1921 which set aside 200,000 acres of the land to be used to establish homelands for Native Hawaiians with 50% or more Hawaiian blood (Council for Native Hawaiian Advancement, 2005; Hawaii Advisory Committee to the U.S. Commission on Civil Rights, 2001; Spoehr et al., 1998). The beginning of the twentieth century is also the beginning of the remolding and stabilizing character of the Hawaiian (Lind, 1934). With the development of secret societies and lodges, a growing sense of pride and respect for oneself as a Hawaiian emerged. Local and international entities recognized and appreciated Native Hawaiians' contributions in their traditional music, folklore, dance, and chants which provided a more positive view of the Hawaiian people. A part-Hawaiian dean of a church articulated this newfound pride and development of a strong Hawaiian psyche:

> … the Hawaiian, no matter how dark or poor he may be, must have a conscientious pride and faith and belief in his ability … he must possess a well-calculated faith … No race that despises itself … can stand secure on the onward march of the world's forces. And no individual that belittles or hates his race can ever be a respectable and vital ingredient in the life of that race. (pp. 243–244, Lind, 1934)

In 1959, Hawaii became the 50th state with the federal government returning the ceded lands (i.e., the lands that were once property of the Hawaiian monarchy, which is approximately 1.8 million acres) to the state. One purpose for the use of the ceded lands was to enhance the quality of life among Native Hawaiian people. The Office of Hawaiian Affairs was created in 1978 to manage this share of the ceded land revenues (Bolante, 2003) with the mission to protect Native Hawaiian rights and the environmental resources in order to perpetuate the culture and promote the health of this indigenous group (Office of Hawaiian Affairs, 2003). Significant events occurred in the 1970s which created opportunities for the resurgence of the Hawaiian culture. This revival of the Hawaiian culture is commonly referred to as the Hawaiian Renaissance. This rebirth resulted in a renewed interest in traditional language, music (*mele*), dance (*hula*), arts, and crafts (McCubbin & McCubbin, 1997). On May 1, 1976, the *Hokule'a*, a Polynesian voyaging canoe, made its maiden voyage to Tahiti, which proved the exploration and voyaging skills of the Polynesian people. This journey and its subsequent voyages provided a sense of deep cultural pride for Native Hawaiians, and "the *Hokule'a* emerged as a cultural icon credited with helping spark a general cultural renaissance among the Hawaiians" (Finney, 2004, p. 299). Another significant event was the occupation of Kaho'olawe (an island off the coast of Maui) in 1976 by a group of nine people, including Native Hawaiians and an American Indian to protest the US Navy's bombing of the island (Blacksford, 2004). This historical event was followed by many other occupations and protests against the US military and the need for restoration of this island. This movement for the restoration of Kaho'olawe became an important issue for Native Hawaiians and also served as a catalyst for the Renaissance (Blacksford, 2004). In 1993, the history of oppression of the Hawaiian people and the Kingdom of Hawaii was formally recognized by the United States and the State of Hawaii. President Clinton signed Public Law 103–150 which acknowledged the 100th year commemoration of the overthrow of the Kingdom of Hawaii and a formal apology to Native Hawaiians for the improper role of the US military in support of the overthrow (Hawaii Advisory Committee to the U.S. Commission on Civil Rights, 2001). This historical event was a formal acknowledgment by the US government of the "illegal overthrow" of 1893 and represented a step forward toward reconciliation between the US and the Native Hawaiian people (Hawaii Advisory Committee to the U.S. Commission on Civil Rights, 2001). This event infused a sense of optimism and renewed energy in the sovereignty movement. In 2000, Senator Daniel Akaka introduced a bill which would have allowed for federal recognition of Native Hawaiian people as a distinct indigenous entity similar to Native American tribal status. However, this bill, US Senate Bill 344, called the Native Hawaiian Recognition Act was defeated in 2006.

Native Hawaiians continue to struggle and face challenges in protecting their indigenous rights and ceded lands. Individuals and groups with legal representation have been leading a campaign against Native Hawaiian entitlements including challenging the funding of the Office of Hawaiian Affairs, Native Hawaiian Homelands, and educational programs for Native Hawaiian children on the premise that these programs are violating the US Constitution due to its race-based criteria for the distribution of services and resources (see McCubbin & Dang, in press).

The revival of Hawaiian culture, language, and practices and the increasing number of people in the United States identifying themselves as Native Hawaiians are indicators that this ethnic group is strong and thriving. The historical trends found in this overview of Hawaiian history, from the oppression and colonization of the nineteenth century to the rebirth and renewal of the Hawaiian culture in the twentieth and twenty-first centuries, can be seen in the history of psychology and the research and methodologies used to study this indigenous population.

Trends in Psychology and Research on Native Hawaiians

Psychology applied to the study of Native Hawaiians was shaped and influenced by the colonial history of the Hawaiian people and the Islands. The postcolonial period after 1778 within the field of psychology can be characterized by three specific approaches: (a) the deficit approach (1800s to 1950s), (b) the cultural interaction approach (1960s to 1970s), and (c) the indigenous approach (1970s to present day).

The Deficit Approach

According to Ridley (1995), the deficit model views ethnic minorities as having predetermined deficiencies which are used to relegate minorities to an inferior status (Thomas & Sillen, 1972). This perspective, also referred to as scientific racism, encompasses research conducted under the guise of studying racial differences when in fact the studies were linked with White supremacist notions (Guthrie, 2004; Sue & Sue, 2003). This deficit approach has a long history in psychological research and has been used in researching Native Hawaiians. In reviewing the literature on Native Hawaiians in the late 1800s and the first half of the twentieth century, multiple studies were conducted, solely ranking racial groups by their superiority and thus determining the inferiority of the Hawaiian race.

Samuel George Morton, a leader among American polygenists, conducted one of the first research studies based on a deficit model. Morton's work ranked the mental capacity of different races using the volume of the cranial cavity as his measure (Gould, 1996). This research was used to provide empirical evidence of the mental worth of human races, with the Caucasian group as having the highest mental worth, followed by Asians, then Polynesians (where Native Hawaiians were categorized), American Indians, and lastly African Americans (Morton, 1849, as cited in Gould, 1996). Morton failed to take into account gender, body type, nutrition, and various other confounding variables that would impact the volume of the cranial cavity. This was the beginning of 100 years of research comparing Native Hawaiians to other racial groups in the United States to demonstrate this indigenous group's "inferiority."

G. Stanley Hall, the founder of organized psychology as a science and profession and a national leader in education, wrote about Native Hawaiians in 1904 as part of his multivolume work on adolescence. He referred to the Hawaiians as similar to other tropical races and that Hawaiians did not suffer from ignorance but rather from "weakness of character, idleness and the vices it breeds" (Hall, 1904, p. 658). He described Hawaiians as behaviorally lacking control, morally inert and sluggish, and developmentally like "infants," similar to Adam and Eve in Eden, people who had not encountered hardship. He articulated a process of strengthening the race and changing the natives' mental abilities through interracial marriage. His characterization of Hawaiians was the predominant view of indigenous people in psychology, and subsequently these stereotypes heavily influenced research methodology and interpretations of empirical findings.

Various studies conducted in the first half of the nineteenth century made racial comparisons on the following variables: IQ (intelligence) or TQ (test quotient; Livesay, 1942; Porteus, 1930), recall ability (Louttit, 1931a, 1931b), and neurotic tendencies (Smith, 1938). Each of these studies included a subsample of Native Hawaiians. Porteus (1930) compared racial groups on "mentality" examining Chinese, Japanese, part-Hawaiian, Hawaiian, Portuguese, and Caucasian children from ages 9 through 14 years. When compared to Caucasians, Hawaiians scored lower on mental alertness. It was interesting that those children who were identified as part-Hawaiian with a mixture of White or Chinese scored higher on mental awareness than pure Hawaiians, yet still lower than Caucasians. Overall, Portuguese, Hawaiians, and part-Hawaiians scored significantly below Asians and Caucasians on intelligence testing. Only the Japanese children scored higher on various intelligence activities when compared with Caucasian children. All other racial groups tended to score lower than the Caucasian group. Each of these studies provided limited information on the methodology of the testing and little commentary on additional environmental factors that may have affected their findings. Livesay (1942) examined racial differences in scores on the American Council Psychological Exams among high school seniors in Hawaii. According to the researcher:

> … it is immaterial in this connection whether these tests really measure innate mental ability or reflect environmental differentials … the manifest differences are real and must be allowed for in educational, vocational, and civil and social activities of a community. (p. 90)

Caucasian students scored higher than all the other groups including Chinese, Hawaiian, part-Hawaiian, Japanese, Filipino, Korean, and Portuguese students. Caucasian-Hawaiian students were second and Asiatic-Hawaiian students were above Portuguese and Filipino students. All Hawaiians were considered a "hybrid" of two races, and therefore no sole Hawaiian category was included. These hybrid rankings also yielded an own interesting racial hybrid hierarchy with Caucasian-Hawaiians before Asiatic-Hawaiians or Portuguese-Hawaiians. Research during this time was used to support the racial hierarchy of the society along with support for Hall's conclusions that racial mixing would lead to increased mental ability. Louttit (1931a) examined racial comparisons of memory ability, specifically studying immediate recall of logical and nonsense material among 12-year-olds and university students in four racial groups: White, Japanese, Chinese, and Hawaiian. Whites only tested favorably (i.e., superior) to the other racial groups on 10 out of 24 comparisons. However, the author concluded there were no real differences between the racial groups studied. In addition, Louttit (1931b) provided empirical evidence to support Hall's assertion that racial mixing would increase the mental capacity of Native Hawaiians with mixed-race Hawaiians scoring higher than pure-blooded Hawaiians on various intelligence tests. However, racial bias, socialization, prejudice, and discrimination were not measured as possible reasons for these differences during this time period.

Smith (1938) examined racial group differences using scores on the Thurstone Neurotic Inventory. The study found that part-Hawaiians and Koreans scored significantly higher, and therefore were considered to be the most neurotic groups, as compared with Japanese, Chinese, Caucasian, and Portuguese groups. One explanation for the higher neurotic tendency of part-Hawaiians was due to the "difficulty of adjusting themselves to the problems of mixed ancestry" (p. 400). The investigator also pointed out that Caucasians may have less neurotic tendencies due to their "greater prestige in the Islands" (p. 411). Upon further examination of the scores for Native Hawaiians, this group was found to show more self-confidence and ease in social situations; however, they were the "most discontented group," because they thought they were unlucky and deserved a better lot in life. Environmental factors, such as the overthrow of the monarchy or the cultural genocide of their people, were not mentioned. Considering the historical context, these findings could be interpreted as outcomes of the impact of colonization and oppression among Native Hawaiians. However, this theme of neurosis among part-Hawaiians due to problems of mixed ancestry was seen in other psychological research. The problem of mixed ancestry was used to explain discontent or racial discrepancies when compared with their Caucasian counterparts. Stonequist (1937) in his book *The Marginal Man* included part-Hawaiians in his investigation of the marginalization of mixed-race men.

Adams (1934) wrote a chapter entitled *The Unorthodox Race Doctrine of Hawaii* where he presented the unique race relations found in the Hawaiian Islands where races at some level were treated as "equal" and how this was unorthodox from the standpoint of English-speaking White people. He pointed out the trend of White men, who had preconceived notions about race and privilege, had to change their behaviors to adjust to Hawaii's ritual of race relations. White men had observed the racial equality traditions on the Islands such as calling every male of any race by the title of "Mister" in order to transition from being a *malahini*, a new person who was not sympathetic to the local race relations, to a *kama'aina*, a person who was a part of the society and followed the racial doctrines set in Hawaii. However, Adams (1934) documented that although a "White man" may have observed these traditions, these behaviors were not linked to changes in racial ideology or beliefs about racial equality. For example, a young White man from a southern state sang the following words, "You may call 'em Hawaiians, but they look like niggers to me" (p. 154), despite living in Hawaii, marrying a Native Hawaiian woman, and having part-Hawaiian children.

The negative stereotypes of Hawaiians also impacted educational psychology and research on Native Hawaiian children's performance in schools. Pratt (1929), upon examination of school achievement among Japanese, Chinese, part-Hawaiian, and Hawaiian students (ages 12 through 15), found Hawaiians scoring the lowest on every section in the Stanford Achievement Advanced Examination. In her conclusions, Pratt explained that all teachers were familiar with the "typical Hawaiian 'misfit'" and that Hawaiian students were "older, big, nice, pleasant and agreeable" yet "indolent" and "inefficient in schools" (Pratt, 1929, p. 667). She also stated that the educational system at the time was trying to force the Native Hawaiian into a model by which "he is, by native ability and by interests, completely unfitted" (p. 668). Pratt summarized that there were a large percentage of Native Hawaiians who were in fact "retarded." Pratt alluded to contextual factors such as curriculum and teaching styles for these racial discrepancies, but referred to these as necessary to take care of the misfits in any racial group.

The Cultural Interaction Approach

The comparison of Hawaiians with other races in the early 1900s continued during the 1950s through the 1970s. During these two decades, there seemed to be a subtle shift from looking for evidence to support a racially inferior hypothesis toward investigations on Hawaiians while examining them within the context of their culture. During this time period, the conceptualization of culture ranged from a very broad construct to a rather narrow one, depending upon the researcher(s)' definition. The second trend of psychological research on Native Hawaiians lies in the words "on" and "them." The researchers were still "outsiders" observing Native Hawaiians as a separate and unique cultural phenomenon. A belief in the objectiveness of the scientific methodology used by Western researchers still persisted with limited awareness of these social scientists being potential prisoners of their own cultural conditioning (Ridley, 1995) as well as perpetuating forms of oppression. Despite studies using Native voices and Native stories, authorship and "discoveries" were still made by the Western researcher rather than including Native Hawaiian scholars. Very few Native Hawaiian scholars and researchers were acknowledged for their contributions within the psychology field during this time. In their book *Culture, Behavior and Education: A Study of Hawaiian Americans*, Gallimore et al. (1974) viewed the behavior of Hawaiians as a product of a "coherent cultural system" rather than as a deficit or an innate pathology of these indigenous people. The researchers viewed the differences in educational outcomes, not as an indicator of deviance, but rather due to (a) the conflict between two cultures (majority culture and Hawaiian) and (b) the failure of researchers and teachers to interpret the students' behavior in a culturally relevant context. The data were collected over a 5-year period in a rural Hawaiian community, with the researchers having a long-term involvement with the families and the communities, while also collecting data through standardized interviews and questionnaires. The researchers investigated the community, the family system, infants, school-age children, socialization processes, peer effects, and school experience, help-seeking behavior, and achievement-oriented behavior.

The authors drew several conclusions worthy of note: (a) achievement was defined by the culture in terms of contribution to the family and the needs of others; (b) school conflicts may have occurred due to cultural conflicts, such as Hawaiians' emphasis on sharing as a group rather than the school's focus on individual evaluation; (c) conflict or contrast of a youth's important role as a contributor to the family to their "status as underachieving students in school" (p. 263); (d) differences in how the native youth dealt with conflict; and (e) the misinterpretation of Hawaiian children's peer interactions in the classroom as negative rather than the children supporting one another as a group. The authors indicated the absurdity in referring to Hawaiians as unmotivated or lazy because the values, goals, and definitions of achievement (i.e., group affiliation and interaction rather than individual achievement) differed depending on culture and therefore their behaviors needed to be viewed as motivated and successful based on their cultural context.

This work is a clear example of the second trend in research, the cultural interaction approach. Specifically research on Hawaiians shifted from a deficit approach toward a more constructive perspective interpreting Native Hawaiians' behavior within their cultural context. The "outsiders" rather than the indigenous people themselves were still conducting the majority of psychological research on Native Hawaiians.

The Indigenous Approach

With the establishment of the Office of Hawaiian Affairs and the voyaging of the Hokule'a in the 1970s, a new paradigm of research was on the horizon for the Native people of the Hawaiian Islands. The reclaiming of the Native culture, traditions, values, and practices during the Hawaiian Renaissance influenced multiple professions including mental health providers and social scientists. Learning from the limitations and biases of past research on Native Hawaiians by others outside of the culture, Native Hawaiian professionals and scholars implemented programs, organizations, and research projects for Native Hawaiian people incorporating indigenous knowledge. The two-volume *Nana I Ke Kumu, Look to the Source* (Pukui et al., 1972a, 1972b), an indigenous resource and reference on Native Hawaiians' ways of living, knowing, and being, was published and set the stage for the third trend in psychological research on Native Hawaiians. The publication of this key work was an example of the merging of (a) the reclaiming of the Hawaiian culture and (b) the emergence of indigenous ways of knowing as a separate and valuable entity for scholarship.A commitment toward indigenous scholarship was demonstrated through the establishment of the Hawaiian Studies Program at the University of Hawaii at Manoa. This program provided an academic space where scholars from all over the Pacific could engage in the study and research of Native

Hawaiian culture and the perpetuation of the Hawaiian language. Subsequently, in the 1970s through the 1990s, with the help from various private and governmental funding agencies, mental health agencies and research institutions were also established specifically focusing on Native Hawaiian people and their well-being.

The Native Hawaiian Mental Health Research Development Project (NHMHRDP) at the University of Hawaii at Manoa was established in 1990 with the goal to conduct interdisciplinary, cross-cultural, and mental health-related research for Asian and Pacific Islanders. Another program at the University established a year later was the Native Hawaiian Center of Excellence at the John A. Burns School of Medicine. This program focused on multiple levels in its commitment to indigenous people and native knowledge including the education of Native Hawaiians into the field of medicine while also conducting research to address and reduce the health disparities found in this population. These programs clearly demonstrate the shift in Native Hawaiians reclaiming their identity and knowledge and utilizing these assets in the perpetuation of their people and culture.

Organizations established by the foresight and leadership of the Hawaiian monarchy which still exist today also focus on the physical and psychological well-being of Native Hawaiians based on indigenous practices. One key organization is the Queen Lili'uokalani Children's Center (QLCC), which is committed to the development of healthy children, strong families, stable home environments, and caring communities for the welfare of children. The QLCC has been instrumental in providing cultural indigenous practices to strengthen *'ohana*. For example, QLCC has used family strengthening techniques including the Hawaiian process of *ho'oponopono*, an indigenous family healing process.

In addition, various academic and nonprofit institutions have made significant contributions in developing and conducting culturally relevant and responsible psychological research for Native Hawaiians. These organizations have made a clear commitment to having research on Native Hawaiians conducted by "insiders," that is, fellow Native Hawaiians. This represents a significant shift from the past where an "outsider" who had limited knowledge of the culture usually conducted research on Native Hawaiians. This shift has empowered Native Hawaiians to conduct their own evaluations and research in psychology for their respective communities using their cultural perspective and standards.

In a collaborative effort, various community-based agencies with the leadership of Lois-Ellen Datta came together and formed the Evaluation *Hui* (meaning club or organization in Hawaiian) with the purpose to discuss indigenous research and evaluation standards when working with Native Hawaiians. This group worked toward the development of Native Hawaiian guidelines for culturally responsible evaluation and research. The *Hui* highlights the challenges and issues researchers face in working with Native peoples and the need to respect the language, culture, and relationships within the community when conducting research. The Evaluation Hui also expanded beyond the principles of professional organizations (such as the American Educational Research Association and the American Psychological Association) to include indigenous standards of research. The team emphasized the need to rely on cultural elders, *kupuna*, for knowledge and to include Native

Hawaiians as researchers in the investigative process. Similar to the holistic model, the team outlined the necessity of using a comprehensive framework in research including emotional, spiritual, and relational factors.

Given the historical trauma the Native Hawaiian people have faced, one important factor in the research of Native Hawaiians is the need to consider participants' and researchers' cultural awareness and perpetuation of the culture as ideal outcomes and their effects on the psychological well-being of this indigenous population. It is this fundamental aspect, the indigenous ways of knowing and being, which may be critical and vital to Native Hawaiian mental health.

Starting in the twenty-first century, several institutions and organizations have been created to promote the well-being of Native Hawaiians based on indigenous practices and methodologies. Two examples of these types of activities occurred at the University of Hawaii at Manoa. First, the Hawai'inuiakea School of Hawaiian Knowledge under the leadership of Native Hawaiian educator Dr. Maenette Benham was established in 2007, thus creating one of the largest schools of indigenous knowledge in the United States. In addition, the School of Social Work was renamed the Myron B. Thompson School of Social Work after a prominent Native Hawaiian who dedicated his life to public service for the benefit of the Hawaiian people. Community organizations have also been established such as the I Ola Lahui, a rural behavioral health program which focuses on the health care needs of rural populations in Hawaii including the integration of Native Hawaiian cultural practices in clinical practice, research, and evaluation. This program and other community health organizations are focused on serving Native Hawaiians and were created by emerging Native Hawaiian scholars including Drs. Aukahi Austin, Jill Oliveira Gray, Kamana'opono Crabbe, and Keawe'aimoku Kaholokula. Other emerging Native Hawaiian scholars are Drs. Hannah Preston-Pita, Hoku Hoe, Kaliko Change, Halona Tanner, and Kaniala Kekaulike.

These are just a few examples of multiple projects, organizations, and research that have emerged over the past 30 years, which are dedicated to the well-being and healing of Native Hawaiians by their own people through their own practices. This emergence of culturally congruent and relevant practices and research demonstrates a new trajectory for the mental, spiritual, and physical health of Native Hawaiians.

The Future of Psychology and Native Hawaiians

With these trends firmly in mind and presented as a chronology, one could infer that utilizing indigenous epistemology is the wave of the future for psychological research among Native Hawaiians. Indigenous ways of knowing can be applied to theory, clinical practice, and research in the counseling and psychology field. There is little doubt that other disciplines, such as sociology, anthropology, psychiatry, education, and social work, have already found this indigenous focus promulgated by the writing and investigations of the Maori nation, as well as Native Hawaiians (Smith, 1999; Ah Nee-Benham, 1998). The widely referenced work of Smith (1999) entitled *Indigenous Methodologies* focused on the mandate for theories, research methods, policies, and practices based on indigenous knowledge. Indigenous populations are unique in their worldview, their holistic perspective to life and well-being, and, thus, their psychology. Furthermore, indigenous knowledge has already given rise to indigenous practices for physical healing, psychological health, conflict resolution, interpersonal problem-solving, family relationships, community building, spiritual healing, and general well-being. With the revival of the Hawaiian language and the translation of Hawaiian publications written in Hawaiian, new insights and knowledge continue to flow into the psychological literature, thus giving birth to theories and practices embedded in Hawaiian history and knowledge, thought to be lost to the dominance of colonialism. An enriching future lies ahead with the proliferation of indigenous psychology.

History and historical markers buttressed by Census data highlighted in this chapter offer new challenges and potential promises to the advancement of psychology in the study of the Hawaiian people. There are compelling data pointing to the multiethnic nature of the Hawaiian people. In spite of the passion underlying the renaissance movement to find meaning in the historical roots of this indigenous population, the parallel and ever emerging emphasis on multiethnic and multiracial Hawaiians to understand their development, identity, health, and well-being is equally apparent. Empirical evidence is emerging, starting with the 2000 Census and more recent studies of all ethnic groups in Hawaii, which point to the significant positive differences in the health, education, occupation, academic achievement, and income of multiethnic Hawaiians from those who identify themselves as solely Hawaiian (Hart & McCubbin, 2005).

These two directions of research are not mutually exclusive nor in competition with each other, for they do both have much to offer the psychology profession and advancing understanding of the Hawaiian population. Indigenous knowledge brings new insights and potential confirmatory evidence of the importance of past practices and beliefs to Native Hawaiians. Colonization was accompanied by a loss of culture, language, traditions, beliefs, values, esteem, vision, and well-being all in the name of Westernization, which places a premium on assimilation and subordination of indigenous people. Yet, history affirms time and time again the gradual but definitive resurgence of cultures, identities, and beliefs buttressed by the realization that indigenous knowledge is vital to the future of peoples whose roots have long and rich histories. It is the demand for survival that resurgence and revitalization of the Hawaiian culture and its people have found their place in the twenty-first century. How well these indigenous populations negotiate their way through the dominance of the Western culture is determined, in large part, by an understanding and revitalization of indigenous knowledge and its application and integration into research and clinical practice. In this chapter, we offered a perspective of the evolution of psychology of the Hawaiian people underscored by a belief that history paired with indigenous knowledge could if not should play a salient role in guiding the profession's contributions to the psychological health, well-being, and self-determination of all indigenous peoples.

References

Adams, R. (1934). *The unorthodox race doctrine of Hawaii*. McGraw-Hill.

Ah Nee-Benham, M. (1998). *Culture and educational policy in Hawaii: The silencing of native voices*. Erlbaum Associates.

Anderson, R. (1865). *The Hawaiian Islands: Their progress and condition under missionary labors* (3rd ed.). Gould & Lincoln.

Blacksford, M. (2004). Environmental justice, Native rights, tourism, and opposition to military control: The case of Kaho'olawe. *The Journal of American History, 91*. Retrieved from www.historycooperative.org/journals/jah/91.2/blackford.html

Blaisdell, K. (1989). Historical and cultural aspects of Hawaiian health. *Social Process in Hawai'i, 32*, 1–21.

Bolante, R. (2003). What happened to sovereignty? *Honolulu, 116*, 94–97.

Casken, J. (2001). Improved health status for Native Hawaiians: Not just what the doctor ordered. *Wicazo SA Review*, 75–89.

Cook, B. P., Withy, K., & Tarallo-Jensen, L. (2003). Cultural trauma, Hawaiian spirituality and contemporary health status. *California Journal of Health Promotion, 1*, 10–24.

Council for Native Hawaiian Advancement. (2005). *The Hawaiian Homes Commission Act: National policies for Native needs*. Author.

Diamond, J. (1999). *Guns, germs and steel: The fates of human societies*. Norton.

Finney, B. (2004). Playing with canoes. In B. V. Lal (Ed.), *Pacific places, pacific histories*. University of Hawai'i Press.

Gallimore, R., Boggs, J. W., & Jordan, C. (1974). *Culture, behavior, and education: A study of Hawaiian-Americans* (Vol. 11). Sage.

Gould, S. J. (1996). *The mismeasure of man*. Norton.

Graves, M. W., & Addison, D. L. (1995). The Polynesian settlement of the Hawaiian archipelago: Integrating models and methods in archaeological interpretation. *World Archaeology, 26*, 257–282.

Guthrie, R. V. (2004). *Even the rat was white: A historical view of psychology* (2nd ed.). Pearson/Allyn & Bacon.

Hall, G. S. (1904). *Adolescence: Its psychology and its relations to physiology, anthropology, sociology, sex, crime, religion, and education* (Vol. 2). D. Appleton and Company.

Handy, E. S., & Pukui, M. K. (1972). *The Polynesian family system in Ka'u*. Tuttle.

Hart, H., & McCubbin, H. (2005). *Multi-ethnic Hawaiians are making strides in educational achievement, income and occupation, Honolulu, Pacific American Foundation*. Pacific American Foundation.

Hawaii Advisory Committee to the U.S. Commission on Civil Rights. (2001). *Reconciliation at a crossroads: The implications of the apology resolution and Rice v. Cayetano for federal and state programs benefiting Native Hawaiians*. (Summary Report of the August 1998 September 2000 Community Forums in Honolulu, Hawai'i). Honolulu, HI: Author.

Ito, K. L. (1985). Affective bonds: Hawaiian interrelationships of self. In G. M. White & J. Kirkpatrick (Eds.), *Person, self, and experience: Exploring Pacific ethnopsychologies* (pp. 301–327). University of California Press.

Judd, N. (1998). Laau Lapaau: Herbal healing among contemporary Hawaiian healers. *Pacific Health Dialogue, 5*, 239–245.

Kanahele, G. H. S. (1986). *Ku kanaka: Stand tall*. University of Hawaii Press.

Kanazawa, A., White, P., & Hampson, S. (2007). Ethnic variation in depressive symptoms in a community sample in Hawaii. *Cultural Diversity & Ethnic Minority Psychology, 13*, 35–44.

Kim, U., Yang, K. S., & Hwang, K. K. (2006). *Indigenous and cultural psychology: Understanding people in context*. Springer.

Kim, U., & Berry, J. W. (1993). *Indigenous psychologies: Experience and research in cultural context*. Sage.

Lind, A. W. (1934). *Modifications of Hawaiian character*. McGraw-Hill.

Livesay, T. M. (1942). Racial comparisons in test-intelligence. *American Journal of Psychology, 55*, 90–95.

Louttit, C. M. (1931a). Racial comparisons of ability in immediate recall of logical and nonsense material. *Journal of Social Psychology, 2*, 205–215.

Louttit, C. M. (1931b). Test performance of a selected group of part-Hawaiians. *Journal of Applied Psychology, 15*, 43–52.

Malone, N. (2005). *Laupa'i Kānaka: Native Hawaiian population forecasts for 2000 to 2050: Statistical overview of Native Hawaiian population trends and implications for young Native Hawaiian learners.* Retrieved from http://www.ksbe.edu/pase/pdf/Reports/Demography_Well-being/04_05_34.pdf

Marsella, A. J., Oliveira, J. M., Plummer, C. M., & Crabbe, K. M. (1995). Native Hawaiian (Kanaka Maoli) culture, mind, and well-being. In H. I. McCubbin, E. A. Thompson, A. I. Thompson, & J. E. Fromer (Eds.), *Resiliency in ethnic minority families: Native and immigrant American families* (pp. 93–113). University of Wisconsin.

McCubbin, H. I., & McCubbin, L. D. (1997). Hawaiian American Families. In M. K. DeGenova (Ed.), *Families in cultural context: Strengths and challenges in diversity* (pp. 239–266). Mayfield Publishing Company.

McCubbin, L. D., Ishikawa, M., & McCubbin, H. I. (2008). Kanaka Maoli: Native Hawaiians and Their Testimony of Trauma and Resilience. In A. Marsella, J. Johnson, P. Watson, & J. Gryczynski (Eds.), *Ethnocultural perspectives on disaster and trauma: Foundations, issues and applications* (pp. 271–298). Springer.

McCubbin, L. D., & McCubbin, H. (2005). Culture and ethnic identity in family resilience: Dynamic processes in trauma and transformation of indigenous people. In M. Unger (Ed.), *Handbook for working with children and youth: Pathways to resilience across cultures and contexts* (pp. 27–44). Sage.

McCubbin, L. D., & Dang, T. (in press). Native Hawaiian identity and measurement: An ecological perspective on indigenous identity development. In J. G. Ponterotto, J. M. Casas, L. A. Suzuki, & C. M. Alexander (Eds.), *Handbook of multicultural counseling* (3rd ed.). Sage.

Meares, J. (1788–1789). Voyages made in the years 1788 and 1789 from China to the Northwest coast of America. *Hawaiian Historical Society Reprints, 1*, 47.

Nishimura, S., Goebert, D., Ramisetty-Mikler, S., & Caetano, R. (2005). Adolescent alcohol use and suicide indicators among adolescents in Hawaii. *Cultural Diversity & Ethnic Minority Psychology, 11*, 309–320.

Nordyke, E. C. (1989). *Comment*. University of Hawaii Press.

Noyes, M. H. (2003). *Then there were none*. Bess.

Office of Hawaiian Affairs. (1998). *Native Hawaiian data book*. Author.

Office of Hawaiian Affairs. (2003). *OHA mission statement.* Retrieved from http://www.oha.org/cat_content.asp?contentid 20&catid 22

Oneha, M. F. M. (2001). Ka mauli o ka oina a he mauli kanaka: An ethnographic study from a Hawaiian sense of place. *Pacific Health Dialog, 8*, 299–311.

Osborne, T. J. (1998). *Annexation Hawaii, fighting American imperialism.* Island Style Press.

Pacific American Foundation. (2004). *A Snapshot of Native Hawaiians in the United States* (Native Hawaiian Research Center Rep. No. 04 – 01). Honolulu, HI: Author.

Porteus, S. D. (1930). Race and social differences in performance tests. *Genetic Psychology Monographs: Child Behavior, Animal Behavior, and Comparative Psychology, 8*, 93–208.

Pratt, H. G. (1929). Some conclusions from a comparison of school achievement of certain racial groups. *The Journal of Educational Psychology, 20*, 661–668.

Pukui, M. K., & Elbert, S. H. (1986). *Hawaiian Dictionary*. University of Hawaii Press.

Pukui, M. K., Haertig, E. W., & Lee, C. A. (1972a). *Nana I Ke Kumu (Look to the source)* (Vol. 1). Hui Hanai.

Pukui, M. K., Haertig, E. W., & Lee, C. A. (1972b). *Nana I Ke Kumu (Look to the source)* (Vol. 2). Hui Hanai.

Queen Lili'oukalani. (1917). *Letter to hanai daughter (Lydia).* Retrieved on September 8, 2009, at https://onipaa.org/pages/kainoa-ailatinted#:~:text=Our%20Queen%20is%20one%20of,be%20inflexible%2C%20intolerant%20and%20prejudicial

Rezentes, W. C. (1996). *Ka Lama Kukui Hawaiian Psychology: An introduction.* A'Ali'i Books.

Ridley, C. R. (1995). *Overcoming unintentional racism in counseling and therapy: A practitioner's guide to intentional intervention.* Sage.

Sai, D. K. (2008). A slippery path towards Hawaiian indigeneity: An analysis and comparison between Hawaiian state sovereignty and Hawaii and indigeneity and its use and practice in Hawai'i today. *Journal of Law and Social Changes, 10*, 68–133.

Schmitt, R. C. (1968). *Demographic statistics of Hawaii: 1776–1965*. University of Hawaii.

Smith, L. T. (1999). *Decolonizing methodologies: Research and indigenous peoples*. Zed Books.

Smith, M. E. (1938). A comparison of the neurotic tendencies of students of different racial ancestry in Hawaii. *The Journal of Social Psychology, 9*, 395–417.

Spoehr, H., Akau, M., Akutagawa, W., Birnie, K., Chang, M., Kinney, E., Nissanka, S., et al. (1998). Ke Ala Ola Pono: The Native Hawaiian community's effort to heal itself. *Pacific Health Dialog, 5*, 232–238.

Srinivasan, S., & Guillermo, T. (2000). Toward improved health: Disaggregating Asian American and Native Hawaiian Pacific Islander data. *American Journal of Public Health, 90*, 1731–1734.

Stannard, D. E. (1989). *Before the horror: The population of Hawaii on the eve of western contact.* University of Hawaii Press.

Statehood Admissions Act of Hawai'i of 1959, 25 U.S. C. 32 S 3001–10. Retrieved from http://www4.law.cornell.edu/uscode/html/uscode25/usc_sec_25_00003001—-000-.html

Stonequist, E. V. (1937). *The marginal man: A study in personality and culture conflict.* Charles Scribner's Sons.

Sue, D. W., & Sue, D. (2003). *Counseling the culturally diverse: Theory and practice* (4th ed.). Wiley.

Thomas, A., & Sillen, S. (1972). *Racism and Psychiatry*. Brunner/Mazel.

U.S. Census. (2000). Retrieved from http://factfinder.census.gov/servlet/DTTable?_bmy&-geo_id01000US&regDEC_2000_SF2_U_PCT003:001|062;DEC_2000_SF2_U_PCT005:001&-ds_nameDEC_2000_SF2_U&_lang en&mt_name DEC_2000_SF2_U_PCT003&-mt_nameDEC_2000_SF2_U_PCT005&-format&-CONTEXTdt

Chapter 7
Hawaiian National Re-emergence from US Colonization: Community Strength, Mental Health, and Traditions

Poka Laenui and Izaak Williams

Hawai'i is an archipelago, which consists of eight major islands, several atolls, numerous smaller islets, and seamounts in the North Pacific Ocean that extend some 1500 miles (with an additional 200 miles running along the outer lines of the archipelago in accordance with the Law of the Seas Convention) from the island of Hawai'i in the south to northernmost Kure Atoll (Van Dyke et al., 1988). It is here where the Hawaiians established themselves followin4g years of exploration across the world from Asia throughout the Pacific that the history of Native Hawaiians originates. According to the traditional Hawaiian Kumulipo chant, the genealogy of the islands' people began before time, in what is known as Pō or darkness, and out of that darkness came light, the separation of the waters from the land, and the many living forms, including eventually the kanaka or people (Kamakau, 1992). The gods created the lands of Hawai'i as well as the people who traveled to these islands and formed societies, becoming the Hawaiian people. These inhabitants' (Nā Kanaka Maoli) ancient chants and other sources indicate that people were called Kanaka, which means person, people, or individual(s) which is also ancient based on the legendary mystical northern land called "Hawaiki" (Dudley, 1990; Fornander, 1996). They touched upon many lands including the most isolated land mass in the world: Hawai'i. Hawaiians conducted commerce with other Polynesians in the Pacific many years after arriving in Hawai'i and had infrequent contacts with Japan, the Great Turtle Island (today "North America"), South America, and other Pacific rim peoples. The people of these islands spoke a common language with some

P. Laenui (✉)
Private Practice of Law, Waianae, HI, USA
e-mail: plaenui@hawaiianperspectives.org

I. Williams
University of Hawaii, Honolulu, HI, USA
e-mail: izaakw@hawaii.edu

G. J. Rich, N. A. Ramkumar (eds.), *Psychology in Oceania and the Caribbean*, International and Cultural Psychology, https://doi.org/10.1007/978-3-030-87763-7_7

dialectic variations and followed generally common rules of conduct or *kapu* (prohibitions) that formed the social norms of conduct for this nation. The society was divided into a class structure of ali'i (with authority due to a combination of mana, spiritual descent from gods or lesser gods), kahuna (priests), maka'ainana (general people), and kauwa (lower-level servants) (Kamakau, 1992). Hawai'i remained relatively unknown to Europe until January 25, 1778, when British Navy Captain James Cook arrived to find a highly developed society, kindling widespread knowledge of the islands and its people to the American and European world. Once this door was opened, immigrants from all parts of the world came to Hawai'i. Sailors from Europe and North America married into Hawaiian families and became part of the Hawaiian society, while Chinese and Japanese laborers came to work on sugar plantations or accompanied such workers (McDermott & Andrade, 2011). Christian missionaries also came to Hawai'i, with some remaining even after their formal missions were terminated, taking important roles in Hawaiian society (Merry, 2000). Many others, including those of African descent and other Polynesians, also established homes in Hawai'i (Jackson, 2005). As they did this, many renounced their former citizenship and took up Hawaiian citizenship (see also Husted, 1890).

In 1810, Hawai'i became united as a nation-state under the unification of Kamehameha I (1779–1819). The ensuing global influx to Hawai'i coincided with trade exchanges between Hawai'i and China, Great Britain, and the United States as well as other nations (Gonschor, 2019). In 1840, Hawai'i's first written constitution was passed, containing a declaration of rights often referred to as the Hawaiian Magna Carta, that effectively transitioned the Hawaiian state from an "absolute monarchy" to a constitutional monarchy (Sai, 2013). For the next 70 years, the kingdom transformed from an elitist society based on the rule and rank authority of ali'i and kahuna to an egalitarian one in which high-ranking chiefs and commoners were viewed as equal before the law (Osorio, 2002). The government also developed a system of schools, boosting Hawai'i's literacy rate to one of the highest in the world (Sai, 2013). It was a modern society with a public health system and even had electricity and telephones at its 'Iolani Palace before the US White House. Its international stature as an independent nation (99 counselor and diplomatic posts) was without question holding treaties and executive agreements with almost every nation-state that existed at the time (Hawaiian Islands, 1887): from the German Empire to the lesser known country of Bremen, and from the imperial superpowers Great Britain and the United States to the "has been" imperial powers of Portugal and Spain. From 1810 until 1893, Hawai'i underwent many changes in its political formation, economy, demographics, educational quality, and international presence (McGregor & MacKenzie, 2014). Hawai'i was undergoing its course of development, unfolding into its future based on its own internal culture, hopes, and dreams for its future so that by 1892 it was a vibrant multiracial, multicultural nation engaged in intellectual and economic commerce throughout the world (Gonschor, 2019; Husted, 1890); but due to outside forces, this development did not continue.

Avaricious desire for wealth and power among remnants of the Christian missionaries, who aligned with US military interests, resulted in a conspiracy to land US forces in Hawai'i, wresting the power from the constitutional monarch, Queen

Lili'uokalani, and placing it in the hands of the "Missionary Boys," who then became known as the provisional government (Dudley & Agard, 1990). The provisional government (PG) attempted to cede Hawai'i to the United States in a treaty of annexation, but President Cleveland intervened and rejected the treaty. Previously formed by proclamation, the PG ratified a self-serving constitution, blocked the vast number of Hawaiians from participating, changed its name to the Republic of Hawai'i, and resubmitted another annexation treaty when a new president, McKinley, took charge 4 years later. The treaty was again resisted by widespread Hawaiian protest (Minton & Silva, 1998) as well as by those in the United States who recalled Cleveland's Congressional address (Cleveland, 1893). Realizing the "treaty" could not get the 2/3 Senate approval required of the US Constitution, the conspirators circumvented that requirement and settled for only a joint resolution of Congress, known as the Newlands Resolution, which, over the outcry of the vast majority of people, was passed in Hawai'i on July 7, 1898 (30 Stat. 750; 2 Supp. R.S. 895). The McKinley administration circumvented the constitution (Art. 2, Sec. 2, Clause 2, US Constitution) and declared Hawai'i annexed by a joint resolution of both houses of Congress (Richardson, 1908). It took up a third of the Hawaiian lands for its military and imposed its colonial control over all public education, travel outside of Hawai'i, and international trade. In addition, the US president appointed a territorial governor, all judges to courts, and instituted taxes on the Hawaiian people. The United States would obtain the choicest lands and harbors for their Pacific armada. Queen Lili'uokalani's protests that the occupation was a breach of treaties international law were simply ignored (Lili'uokalani, 1898).

When the United Nations was formed in 1945, territories such as Hawai'i were to be given three options: independence, free association, or integration (UN Charter, Article 73; UN G.A. Resolution 66(1) 1946). The United States took no action toward the option of independence or free association, leaving only integration as the "choice," i.e., remaining a territory of the United States or become the "State of Hawai'i" (Admission Act of March 18, 1959, Pub L 86–3, 73 Stat. 4; see also Laenui et al., 2020).

In 1993, the United States adopted an apology resolution (Pub L 103–150, 107 Stat. 1510)—echoing the sentiment of President Grover Cleveland (Gillis, 1897)—admitting its wrongdoing nearly 100 years after the Queen's government was overthrown. The "Apology Bill," as it became known as, was symbolic in meaning but without legal traction in the court of US law, so although granting a major concession that validates the grievances of Native Hawaiians was welcome, legal, and just, it does little to assuage the material realities faced by Hawaiians as a consequence of the illegal overthrow of the Kingdom (SB 2899 & HB 4909, 106th Congress, second Session).

It is against this historic backdrop that mental health or behavioral health services are situated in the Hawaiian Islands—once administrated by the kingdom's government, they are now controlled by the US government and the State of Hawai'i. The social, political, environmental, economic, health, and educational systems impinging upon behavioral health services are no longer under the functional control of the kingdom's government.

DIE Culture in Contemporary "Systems of Care" and OLA Cultural Care Models

There are cultural codes in the collective subconscious of all societies that define what is right and wrong, what is moral and natural, and which forms of behavior are appropriate in any given circumstances (Laenui, 1997a). These codes derive from myths and legends, deep national memories, environmental conditions, and internal conflicts, along with a multitude of other processes that have occurred over long periods in a society (Laenui, 2013). These codes are not to be found in a constitutive document or in some explicit statement but are generally unwritten and usually unspoken; yet they are so ingrained in a society; they become its very driving force. You can often observe these norms and beliefs in the routines and habits of people, in their fears and pleasures, in their dreams and expectations, and in their systems of reasoning. In Hawai'i, at least two distinct deep cultures touch on every area of life. One is prominent in the formal and the other in the informal systems of community life. The first of these cultural codes, identified by the acronym DIE (Domination, Individualism, and Exclusion) (Laenui, 1997b), is emblematic of the Americanized social order and wedded to the Hawai'i Islands as a multiethnic colony (Baumhofer & Yamane, 2019; Fojas et al., 2018; Fujikane & Okamura, 2008; Irwin & Umemoto, 2016; Kaholokula et al., 2020):

Domination—especially reflected in the formal economic, education, political, military, and judicial systems. Central to this colonialist characteristic is the idea of expansion in terms of an ever-widening territory, market, or other field of conquest as part of the natural order of things. Colonialism has for years led Indigenous people to believe they are outside of, and unwelcome in, mainstream culture while diluting the influence of a traditional Indigenous influence at the same time (Blume, 2020; Duran, 2019; Muller, 2020). This social control and cultural containment structure is a reflection of the multiethnic dominance of the State bureaucracy extending its governance to colonial-induced poverty and inequities as well as the over-incarceration synergistically contributing to the systemic and systematic "clientization" of (darker-skinned and poorer) Native Hawaiians (Office of Hawaiian Affairs (OHA), 2019). As a result, Native Hawaiians are grossly overrepresented as subjects of "treatment" within the State's human services in addition to its criminal justice and social welfare systems (OHA et al., 2010; OHA, 2019). Hawaiians, who are thereby redefined as "clients," "consumers," and "patients," are human bodies signifying value—reconstituted as Medicaid (Med-Quest) sponsored commodities—integral to the fiscal viability of many public (and private) substance abuse treatment and behavioral health programs. Subsidized by the State, treatment programs and human services agencies form part of the social control infrastructure within State apparatuses and can be viewed as a modern form of colonial domination. Top-down administrations of contemporary "systems of care" generally replicate forms of control, containment, regulation, punishment, penalty, and coercion of Indigenous people as a feature of colonial bureaucracies (Blume, 2020; Muller, 2020). Moreover, any program bearing the term of *culturally integrated* usually means that Native Hawaiian practice is, at best, offered separately on a parallel treatment track and consequentially fragmented within the treating agency (Williams et al., 2019). As a certain eventuality of colonization and coloniality, Hawaiian cultural practices are subordinated to the cultural dominance of Western/American approaches and not given full recognition; that is, the language, history, protocol, values, and healing traditions are largely ignored, excluded, or tokenistic in "systems of care" (see also Williams, Rezentes et al., in press). Conversely, cultural practices may be visibly displayed and touted in treatment programs while processed through top-down bureaucratic control mechanisms and conducted in such a fashion as to institutionally undermine the legitimate value of Native Hawaiian cultural practices as a form of treatment (Williams, 2019; Williams et al., 2019).

Individualism—protected in the legal system, elevated in the expression of history, and dominant in Western philosophies. Central to this formal characteristic is the idea of singularity—a continual separate parceling and fragmenting of things, concepts, and people. Although the treatment modalities in most treatment settings may include groups, for instance, the treatment is clearly targeted at *individual clients* (Blume, 2020; Duran, 2019; Linklater, 2014; Muller, 2020). Hence, treatment models focus on individuals avoiding risk (exposure to people, places, environs, re-experiencing tragic moment which brings up sense of guilt, substance use, etc.) rather than on decision-making at the familial and community level (Blume, 2020). All aspects of care, from treatment plans and goals to specific care regimes, are focused on the individual. Although this perspective is necessary to a large extent given the Americanized "systems of care" and its expression of cultural values, expectations, and norms, it is in itself incomplete and certainly does not fit in the worldviews of Native Hawaiians. The more traditional view of Native Hawaiians is to perceive health and well-being collectively in relation to the societal contexts of family and community in an interplay between relational pressures and health-related norms impacting both treatment and Hawaiians receiving services. Additionally, from a more complete historical perspective of continuing American occupation of Hawai'i—coloniality—and the associated intergenerational trauma is essential. As a subject of treatment recovery as well as a material reality to be confronted and engaged in as a means of therapy (e.g., see Williams, Makini Jr., & Rezentes III, 2021), the fact of coloniality in the Hawai'i Islands and its health-related ramifications are largely absent from conventional behavioral health and drug treatment procedures, processes, and outcome measures. The contemporary form of mental, behavioral, and addiction treatments is often directed to experiences and training that emanate from colonial societies and their "best practices" as "proven" and normalized to a colonial culture and society. Ultimately, this becomes another attempt to impose a set of values and beliefs—a morality—on the Hawaiian person that can be self-sabotaging and antithetical to Hawaiian cultural identity and nationalism. Successful adaptation to the conditions of State-sanctioned incarceration is contingent on self-preservation or a highly selfish survival-oriented morality, for example, State-subsidized drug abuse treatment programs and the State's criminal justice system coercively compel Hawaiian people into abstinence-oriented lifestyles and regard any substance use—whether for spiritual reasons, communal bonding, cultural revitalization of indigenous psychoactive drug use, or motivated by other social activity with therapeutic purpose (e.g., Williams, Davis, et al., 2021; Williams, Makini Jr., & Rezentes III, 2021; Williams et al., in press)—as problematic and emblematic of failure worthy of treatment termination and warranting suspension of free will.

Exclusion—often accomplished by the depersonalization of the "other," the stranger. One patent colonial technique is to refer to others as nonhuman entities—"heathens," "pagans," or "savages"—as missionaries did in the early nineteenth century when they clashed with native ways of being and the persisting traditional religion of Hawai'i, known commonly as the kapu or mana belief system (Merry, 2000). The colonial system elevates academic achievements in specialized fields and the accumulated entitlements from academic circles while contemporary traditional healers of the Hawaiian community, the kupuna, kahuna, and kanaka makua (identified as people with the maturity of parents) are erased, degraded, and generally eliminated from the treatment community. Their "credentials" of experience and training in fishing, farming, warfare, hunting and gathering, and their resolution of inter-family or inter-gang conflicts in communities are given no credibility in the State's colonial "systems of care." The tools of traditional healers such as prayer, ho'oponopono practices, la'au lapa'au (herbal and other traditional medicine including water treatments), la'au kahea (treatment by the use of a "call," such as a chant or prayer, used to work on the spiritual level), or other counseling activities conducted by such traditional healers are discredited and therefore not reimbursed. The healers have no regular place to practice their treatment, which is generally performed in informal community settings such as farms (Hoa'aina o Makaha) or fishing training facilities ('Opelu Project) or on ocean vessels (Hokule'a, Hikianali'a, etc.).

Moreover, agencies buttress their services on individual assumptions, emphasizing the client's individual psychology at the expense of the client's relational concerns within their environment and the political positioning and/or economic situation. For instance, mainstream treatment practices may coexist with "Native Hawaiian culture" under the auspices of cultural competence and cultural humility, but the individualized treatment model lies outside the legacies of forced acculturation and intergenerational trauma of the American colonization of Hawai'i negatively reverberating on Hawaiian genealogies of the past, present, and future. This, however, is at the foreground of Hawaiians' cultural understandings of mental health and well-being regarding the root causes of the psychological, cultural, social, environmental, political, and economic losses pervading Hawaiian communities (Rezentes III, 1996). Lacking a communalistic focus, treatment modalities create a fundamental cultural mismatch that excludes the material realities of Hawaiians and results in a mode of treatment that casts behavior as a discrete function of individual autonomy and individual beliefs through the paradigms of motivational enhancement and behavioral modification (Blume, 2020). Further, these treatment modalities are employed in an office-based setting that undermines the communal embeddedness of the individual as a whole being and do not materialize improvement in community conditions or the attendant social problems elevating risk for mental illness and drug misuse (Duran, 2019). As such, service delivery for Native Hawaiians compartmentalizes the individual and largely ignores or excludes the person's familial and communal interdependence—a reductionist paradigm of the Hawaiian psyche/psychology (Rezentes III, 1996). While State funding of human services and other treating agencies mostly benefit non-Hawaiian employees representing "systems of care," the State nonetheless highlights in its own reports the total funds exceedingly "expended for Native Hawaiians" as (a hypocritically self-congratulatory) testament to its commitment to cultural sensitivity toward a "special group" (e.g., see *Alcohol and Drug Treatment Services Report* issued by the Department of Health's Alcohol and Drug Abuse Division (ADAD), 2021; see also Williams, 2019).

The second deep culture stream contains elements of the following characteristics:

ʻOluʻolu—a person who is amiable and agreeable and who creates harmonious relationships; who displays a high degree of respect and trust when interrelating with others, even their competitor; the ability to find contentment with what one has; of staying within the bounds of one's kuleana (territory, property, or responsibility). One way to ensure ʻOluʻolu in the behavioral health center is to include the voices of service recipients in ways that allow their worldview to positively shape and impact the development of services. This can be partially achieved by gathering data either from feedback-informed treatment or measurement-based practice, asking the Native Hawaiians who have experienced treatment to rate the benefits of various components of it (Williams et al., 2019). Such measures do not refer to any subjective "satisfaction," but aim to discover which components have been beneficial in achieving recovery. Respondents could also be asked to suggest changes they believe should be made and to mention any instances of feeling demeaned or disrespected by providers. Specific areas where the answers cluster can prove illuminating and serve in identifying which program components are helpful and which are not. Once the salient topics are identified, many of the constructs could be quantified on a Likert scale. If the construct is "real," it should be measurable and can be grouped and scored. ʻOluʻolu also entails gathering information grounded in the needs and preferences to tailor treatment matching, where deemed culturally appropriate by Native Hawaiians in terms of ascribing: *procedures* (e.g., use of Hawaiian cultural protocols monitored and supervised by cultural experts), *processes* (e.g., behavioral health interventions meet Hawaiian people where they are at; in their respective communities and families), and *outcome measures* (e.g., a rise in Hawaiian national consciousness linked to improved mental health or remission of drug misuse).

Lokahi—a collective effort, with many working toward a common goal that leads to a clearer view of the wider implications of all things, both large and small. Similarly, positive outcome measures for wellness could include how "systems of care" have impacted the individual's holistic well-being as well as that of their families and communities. Efforts toward recovery are too commonly institutionally controlled and directed in a situation isolated from the relationships to (extended) families and the broader environment/land that surround and support Hawaiians, rather than community grounded (Rezentes III, 1996). Moreover, an individual's positive treatment outcome would mean an improvement in their overall quality of life (Blume, 2020), to include acknowledging and addressing the consequences of coloniality and the mental health impact of the continual US occupation of the Hawaiian Islands affecting Native Hawaiian cultural well-being.

Aloha—a propensity toward the inclusion of other people and different philosophies; a search for the humanity within others and an effort to draw that humanity to the surface of relationships. The all-inclusive Aloha draws into the family all of the surrounding environmental elements, which carry a spirituality that unites the family to the whole environment. From a Hawaiian perspective, recovery means restoring the correct relationships with the Hawaiian Islands as Indigenous people, alongside the healing in the proper relationships that are central to the holistic frameworks of the sovereignty, political self-determination, independence, and autonomy essential to wellness and recovery. Treatment therefore includes the haumana or client and others associated with the client (including the spouse, partner, boss, and children). Together with an addiction expert, cultural informant, nurse, etc., they can impart a program of recovery that ideally would include certain cultural features relevant to the specific condition of the haumana.

Taken together, this "OLA" is generally attributed to the underlying Hawaiian culture and the multiplicity of added cultures to Hawai'i. Entrenched in the informal economy of sharing and caring, the spirit of OLA infuses the nonformal education as well as the traditional healing and the indigenous methods for resolving disputes; it also influences the organization of the community. In the Hawaiian language, as in other Polynesian languages, OLA means both health and life. The word itself is sometimes used in healing prayers when the healer breathes it into the hands and then spreads them over the places that need healing. The acronym DIE is an easy reminder of the elements of that deep culture stream, which is prevalent in the formal systems, even within the religious and healthcare practices. It would, of course, be rare to find a purely DIE or OLA perspective in the general community, as these ingrained cultures constantly mix, conflict, and sometimes work together within and between individuals and families, as well as within certain systems and situations. The presence of these beneficial practices and beliefs justifies a cultural assessment of the entire treatment setting to provide a framework of culturally appropriate ideas on which to build mutual relationships, pursue a healthy interaction with the environment, and reshape attitudes to time, family justice, sharing and caring, and medicine (Rezentes III, 1996). The acronym DIE is also a reminder that colonial practice is essentially one based on DIE at its core (see also Laenui, 2000b).

Hale Na‘au Pono: Cultivating OLA Against the Forces of DIE

Since the 1960s, a vibrant development of indigenous and Hawaiian national consciousness has occurred that questions the sanctity of American entitlements across the world and the superiority of moral stature in US territories (Laenui, 1993). This Hawaiian cultural awakening has underscored questions and implications related to Native Hawaiian self-determination, independence, and sovereignty (Laenui, 1996). This momentum raised questions concerning primary and behavioral healthcare as it came to the attention of Wai‘anae, which is a community of the largest number of Native Hawaiians in Hawai‘i.

Hawai‘i was undergoing changes in mental health treatment as part of the Community Mental Health Act of 1963 (also known as the Mental Retardation and Community Mental Health Centers Construction Act of 1963), which drastically altered the delivery of mental health services and inspired a new era of optimism in mental healthcare. It established comprehensive community mental health centers throughout the State and helped people with mental illnesses who were "warehoused" in hospitals and institutions to reintegrate into their communities.

In the 1970s, the State opened a clinic to service the population of approximately 40,000 residents of Wai‘anae. A community elder, Marie Olson, who wanted to gauge the utilization of services, spent a week sitting in the waiting room of the clinic, counting the number of clients who attended for service; but she counted only three in the course of the week. Olson and other community elders petitioned the Hawai‘i State Department of Health to devolve service responsibility to the community. The State took up this opportunity, agreeing to spin off the Wai‘anae "catchment area" to a not-for-profit community entity, using this experience to see whether a model could be established for community empowerment in mental health services. With this "go ahead" from the State, the community organized a not-for-profit organization, the Wai‘anae Coast Community Mental Health Center, and obtained a 4-year grant to develop a center to reflect the possibility for a model for communities to run their own centers for behavioral healthcare. The new organization adopted a name, Hale Na'au Pono (House for Inner Balance), and over a period of several years transitioned with personnel, leadership, and a clear statement of its community and cultural connection to services. It began a private funding campaign for a modern building in the heart of the community and, through its location, established a central presence there. Hale Na'au Pono's community-based board of directors selected a member of the community who had previously served as a volunteer board member to steer the organization through the coming years. Several unique approaches and services to the community were rolled out while still operating within the confines of an Americanized model of behavioral health practice and a colonized system of healthcare delivery. As Hale Na'au Pono proceeded to develop its Wai‘anae style of practice, it had to begin with the basic format of the practice already established by the State system and its regulators/standard-setters (Laenui, 2001a). Upon that established practice, Hale Na'au Pono adopted a number of unique principles and processes—traditions, as part of its effort to imbue an OLA approach to health (Laenui, 2001b), which are listed in the following section.

The ABC Triangle of Peace and Violence

The practice of behavioral health services can be thought of as a twofold challenge: understanding and/or altering behavior, then bringing such behavior within an acceptable range for the target community or wider society (Laenui, 2002). Hale Na'au Pono (HNP) borrowed from Johan Galtung, distinguished professor of peace studies and HNP's executive director, to understand and appreciate peace and violence as simply as ABC.

The apices of an equilateral triangle—A, B, and C—help us set the framework for an understanding of peace, violence, and other behaviors, as well as the possibilities for change: Point A for attitudes at the left lower side, B at the top for behavior, and C on the right lower end for conditions. At Point A, position basic attitudes, assumptions, and aspirations on the individual, community, or societal levels. Point A describes frames of mind that cause people to project anger, assume an argumentative stance, project a peaceful nature, submit, or any combination thereof. At Point A, we find cultural belief systems so deeply rooted within people that they are usually accepted as normal and natural, part of the make-up of life. This rootedness is a result of upbringing; living conditions; model behavior of elders, peers, and national figures; and social propaganda. Male superiority, the attitude of "payback," property as a measure of individual worth, physical strength as a determinant of one's value, and the idea of triumphant psychology are all examples of such beliefs and goals that are presumed to be the natural order!

Point B stands for Behavior: direct and indirect. Direct behavior is the direct conduct and physical violence including aggressive national acts (e.g., fighting, shooting, stabbing, bombing raids). In response, we create institutions to imprison, develop programs to modify direct behavior, and continually develop different techniques to suppress direct physical violence. Indirect conduct is violence to the human spirit. This behavior takes the form of disparate treatment based on race, religion, size, gender, sexual orientation, etc. Examples of indirect violence are continual nagging, teasing, harassing, and other forms of verbal and psychological abuse. On a national scale, it may be "economic sanctions" or demonizing a national leader at international conferences. Often, this indirect violence begets responsive direct violence, which society immediately reacts to and chastises as being the primary fault.

Point C is where we place conditions, conflicts, and contradictions. This point may include the hypocrisy between a nation's creed and deeds—proclaiming equality for all men while prohibiting Black Americans from registering to vote, attending white schools, or sitting at the front of buses. It can also be a society whose government admits to the theft of one's national life contrary to accepted international norms but thumbs its nose at any call for effective remedy, forcing the victims to conform to the imposed colonial structure. Additionally, it can describe the economic situation of an ohana (family) in which the father lost his job 6 months ago, including family esteem, and begins to use physical violence on his wife and children to regain his stature.

Recall that Point B (Behavior) is at the top. Thus, behavior is a direct result of either or both A and C. Thus, if we hope to change behaviors, we need to address Points A and C for individuals, communities, and their institutions, keeping in mind the way in which culture—and the conditions surrounding and affecting the other—impacts the wider influences upon individuals and societies. Actions that respond to violence by merely criminalizing or suppressing behavior, by separating offenders from the rest of the community, or through other responses limited to dealing solely with behavior without tackling the deeper problems of attitudes and conditions are of no long-term value and will not lead to appropriate provision of services.

Ho'oponopono

Ho'oponopono, a traditional Native Hawaiian healing practice of reconciliation and forgiveness, brings things or relations back into pono (proper balance, repair) (Laenui, 2000a). This could mean restoring relationships or cleaning away the hihia, or entanglement, that has caused problems. All the many styles of Ho'oponopono all seem to involve invoking spiritual forces. One style which comes from Ka'u on Hawai'i Island involves a very orderly "group therapy": calling together all family members involved, as well as invoking ancestor spirits, family guardian spirits (aumakua), and God or gods. Another form of Ho'oponopono is a specialized process or order of prayers, led by one with a special power (Shook, 2002).

Ho'oponopono can be useful in the gap where "traditional" healing ends. A war veteran came into HNP. He said the Veteran Administration services told him they could not help him any further and that he should seek help from HNP. Asked what was his pilikia (trouble), he said, "I lost my soul in the war in Vietnam and don't know how to call it back!" One of the forms of Ho'oponopono spiritual work is called 'uhane hele (spirit travel). A Hawaiian Ho'oponopono practitioner, kahuna pule (prayer specialist, generally also Christian), may either ask the client to explain his pilikia or may simply observe the individual(s) to see the spiritual forces that have entered the room or detect other problems or tensions brought by the client(s) (Pukui et al., 1979).

Before beginning the prayer, one approach is a cleansing. A mixture of water, sea salt, 'olena (turmeric root), and the young shoot of the ki or tea plant is prepared and blessed by the kahuna pule. Then, it is dabbed on the client's shoulders and the back of their neck. Then, the client sips the mixture. The kahuna (or a helper) will begin the prayer, and the kahuna will receive the "showing" or revelation of the problem. In the case of a person who has suffered from 'uhane hele, the spirit can be called back after understanding why the spirit traveled and the conditions for its return. In one circumstance, a Japanese mother died at a train station in the United States, but her spirit would not return home to Hawai'i. When the spirit was asked why she would not return, the spirit replied it was because there was too much hilahila (shame) as her son had left his wife and gone with another woman. So, her spirit chose to remain away from her home. A similar spirit consultation would be done for the Vietnam War veteran. Then the appropriate procedure or rites would be done.

Practitioners of Ho'oponopono use a variety of tools. In addition to water or a liquid mixture as mentioned above, just the force of words—hua 'olelo (fruit of speech)—can be sufficient to form and carry the spiritual significance of the practice. This can be done via the Christian Bible, having God speak to them through the open Bible (wehe i ka paipala). Others use prayers, revelations, or visions that come to them. All these practices incorporate words from the person leading the process and/or the participating parties to the process. These elements carry strong representations of features of God. Indeed, the awareness of a higher spiritual power than the participants is always present, often in the form of ancestral spirits and in a God element (Pukui et al., 1972).

Environment and Spirituality

Another area of cultural consideration for Hale Na'au Pono's care model lies in the overlap between the environment and spirituality unfolded into addiction and serious mental illness recovery pathways, especially the aspect of balance or harmony (Laenui, 2006). Returning a client to the ocean is often a washing away of tensions and negative spiritual moods, a spiritual cleansing via an immersion into the original amniotic fluid (i.e., the Pacific Ocean) (Rezentes III, 1996). Some would explain this cleansing as the balancing of the Yin and Yang energies, where the Yang/land energy needed the opposite, softer, calming energy that the Yin/ocean energy provided. In addition to the ocean, the mountains and valleys provide healing for many clients, as do plants. The belief is that natural elements (e.g., plants) carry mana (spiritual energy), assisting in healing by correcting energy imbalances (Rezentes III, 1996).

Conclusion

The manner in which Hawai'i's sovereignty was lost to illegal colonization is constitutive in the national history and memory that is carried by Hawaiians to this day (Blaisdell, 2002; Crabbe, 2007; Laenui 2019). This reality is still profoundly felt and expressed through strong oral traditions, tight-knit communities, and expansive familial networks that span the Hawaiian archipelago (Paglinawan et al., 2020; Trask, 1999).

This chapter has underscored the Hawaiian national consciousness in the practice of behavioral health, highlighting a collection of experiences, practices, readings, discussions, and consultations distilled into the Hale Na'au Pono training materials developed for its Adult Mental Health Division. Hale Na'au Pono adopted an OLA cultural care model for application in the indigenous context—centralizing the cultural views of the community and family, emphasizing spirituality and the environment, and adopting general models such as the ABC triangle and Ho'oponopono. Specifically, this model follows a basic structure called the Kumu Ola Pono (Wai'anae Wellness Model) that calls for balance among three realms: the spiritual, the personal/familial, and the environmental (Laenui, 2006). Each is harmonious within itself and between the others. Hale Na'au Pono's system of OLA evolved within the broader constraints of a DIE culture propagated through State and federal laws and regulations that stress risk management, liability, and solving individual problems by taking a deficits-based approach. The system uses a so-called strengths-based perspective with a psychocentric focus on individuation and with office-based funded interventions defining the discrete and siloed nature of service provisions. At odds with the assumptions underlying the treatment modalities cultivated by the philosophy of OLA, those ontological strands of a DIE culture represent challenges, especially in terms of funding—the *colonial bureaucratic hammer*, if you will—through which the State has controlled the development of programs as well as orchestrating pressure and punishment (i.e., financial duress) to channel the efforts of Hale Na'au Pono into conformity. Other Indigenous scholars with direct practice experience in Canada, America, and Australia have alluded to some of the contaminants of DIE or noxious cultural pollutants generated and present within colonized "systems of care" (Blume, 2020; Duran, 2019; Linklater, 2014; Muller, 2020).

In gleaning the potential differences in mental health and addiction treatment services informed by OLA, compared to that underpinned by DIE, we hope this chapter will overall be of interest to any practitioner operating within a context of colonization and coloniality, implementing locally developed behavioral health models that offset the cultural infringements of DIE. While the focus of this chapter has been on the Hawaiian psyche/psychology in relationship to health services, the dimensions of DIE/OLA—a conceptual framework—is also a unifying reference point for Indigenous people and other social groups in circumstances envisaging a treatment milieu conducive to OLA as they struggle to express their own self-determination for community strength, mental health, and traditions.

References

Alcohol and Drug Abuse Division [ADAD]. (2021). *Alcohol and Drug Treatment Services Report.* https://health.hawaii.gov/substance-abuse/prevention-treatment/treatment/

Baumhofer, K. N., & Yamane, C. (2019). Multilevel racism and native Hawaiian health. In C. L. Ford, D. M. Griffith, M. A. Bruce, & K. L. Gilbert (Eds.), *Racism: Science and tools for*

the public health professional (pp. 1–17). American Public Health Association Press. https://doi.org/10.2105/9780875533049ch19
Blaisdell, K. (2002). Historical and cultural aspects of Native Hawaiian health. In P. Spickard, J. L. Rondilla, & D. H. Wright (Eds.), *Pacific diaspora: Island peoples in the United States and across the Pacific* (pp. 279–285). University of Hawai'i Press.
Blume, A. W. (2020). *A new psychology based on community, equality, and care of the earth: An indigenous American perspective*. Praeger.
Cleveland, G. (1893, December 18). Message about Hawai'i [Speech]. *Senate and House of Representatives*. https://www.congress.gov/congressional-record
Crabbe, K. O. M. (2007). Kupa'a I ke kahua o Hawai'i: Stand firmly behind the foundations of Hawai'i. *Journal of Pacific Rim Psychology, 1*(2), 25–30.
Dudley, M. K. (1990). *A Hawaiian Nation I: Man, gods, and nature*. Nā Kāne O Ka Malo Press.
Dudley, M. K., & Agard, K. K. (1990). *A Hawaiian Nation II: A call for Hawaiian sovereignty*. Nā Kāne O Ka Malo Press.
Duran, E. (2019). *Healing the soul wound: Trauma-informed counseling for Indigenous communities* (2nd ed.). Teachers College Press.
Fojas, C., Guevarra, R. P., & Sharma, N. T. (2018). New politics of race in Hawai'i. In C. Fojas, R. P. Guevarra Jr., & N. T. Sharma (Eds.), *Beyond ethnicity: New politics of race in Hawai'i* (pp. 1–18). University of Hawai'i Press.
Fornander, A. (1996). *Ancient history of the Hawaiian people to the times of Kamehameha I*. Mutual Publishing.
Fujikane, C., & Okamura, J. Y. (Eds.). (2008). *Asian settler colonialism: From local governance to the habits of everyday life in Hawai'i*. University of Hawai'i Press.
Gillis, J. A. (1897). *The Hawaiian incident: An examination of Mr. Cleveland's attitude toward the revolution of 1893*. Lee and Shepard.
Gonschor, L. (2019). *A power in the world: The Hawaiian kingdom in Oceania*. University of Hawai'i Press.
Hawaiian Islands. (1887). *Treaties and conventions concluded between the Hawaiian kingdom and other powers since, 1825*. Elele book, card and job print.
Husted. (1890). *1892: Directory and handbook of the kingdom of Hawai'i*. F.M. Husted.
Irwin, K., & Umemoto, K. (2016). *Jacked up and unjust: Pacific islander teens confront violent legacies*. University of California Press.
Jackson, M. M. (Ed.). (2005). *They followed the trade winds: African American in Hawai'i* (Rev. ed.). University of Hawai'i Press.
Kaholokula, J. K., Miyamoto, R. E. S., Hermosura, A. H., & Inada, M. (2020). Prejudice, stigma, and oppression on the behavioral health of Native Hawaiians and Pacific islanders. In L. Benuto, M. Duckworth, A. Masuda, & W. O'Donohue (Eds.), *Prejudice, stigma, and oppression* (pp. 107–134). Springer.
Kamakau, S. M. (1992). *Ruling chiefs of Hawai'i* (Rev. ed.). The Kamehameha Schools Press.
Laenui, P. (1993). The rediscovery of Hawaiian sovereignty. *American Indian Culture and Research Journal, 17*, 79–102. https://doi.org/10.17953/aicr.17.1.v520565l30116036
Laenui, P. (1996, August 16). *Statehood and sovereignty* [Speech transcript]. Hawai'i Public Television.
Laenui, P. (1997a, January 27). DIE & OLA: Two deep cultures in Hawai'i. *Institute for the Advancement of Hawaiian Affairs*.
Laenui, P. (1997b, October 22). On deep cultures and colonization: A Hawai'i case study. *Institute for the Advancement of Hawaiian Affairs*. http://www.Hawai'ianperspectives.org/
Laenui, P. (2000a). Correcting wrongs: Ho'oponopono [Paper presentation]. Church of the Cross Roads, Honolulu, Hawai'i. *Institute for the Advancement of Hawaiian Affairs*. http://www.Hawai'ianperspectives.org/
Laenui, P. (2000b). Processes of decolonization. In M. Battiste (Ed.), *Reclaiming indigenous voice and vision* (pp. 150–160). UBC Press.

Laenui, P. (2001a, March 8). *Asian Pacific Americans and our political involvement, access and future* [Paper presentation]. UCLA School of Law.
Laenui, P. (2001b, March 9). Walking the crooked path straight. *Hale Na'au Pono, Wai'anae Coast Community Mental Health Center.* http://www.Hawai'ianperspectives.org/walking-crooked-path-in-ms-word-updated-2020/
Laenui, P. (2002, September 25). The ABC triangle of peace and violence. *Institute for the Advancement of Hawaiian Affairs.* http://www.Hawai'ianperspectives.org/
Laenui, P. (2006). Voyage to recovery. Hale Na'au Pono, Wai'anae coast community mental health center. Institute for the Advancement of Hawaiian Affairs. http://www.Hawai'ianperspectives.org/
Laenui, P. (2013). Cultural sensitivity in delivery of social services. *Journal of Indigenous Social Development, 2*(1), 1–9.
Laenui, P. (2019). The 2016 Na'i Aupuni congregation: A brief study in a practice of indigenous self-determination. *Hūlili: Multidisciplinary Research on Hawaiian Well-Being, 11*(1), 83–154.
Laenui, P., Dudley, K., Siu, L. K., & de Zayas, A. (2020, April 20). A call for review of the historical facts surrounding UNGA resolution of 1959 that recognized attainment of self-government for Hawai'i. Transcend Media Service: Solutions-Oriented Peace Journalism. https://www.transcend.org/tms/?s=Poka+Laenui
Lili'uokalani. (1898). *Hawai'i's story by Hawai'i's Queen.* Lee & Shepard. https://digital.library.upenn.edu/women/liliuokalani/Hawai'i/Hawai'i.html
Linklater, R. (2014). *Decolonizing trauma work: Indigenous stories and strategies.* Fernwood Publishing.
McDermott, J. F., & Andrade, N. N. (Eds.). (2011). *People and cultures of Hawai'i: The evolution of cultures and ethnicity.* University of Hawai'i Press.
McGregor, D. P., & MacKenzie, M. K. (2014). *Mo'olelo Ea O Nā Hawai'i: History of native Hawaiian governance in Hawai'i.* Office of Hawaiian Affairs.
Merry, S. E. (2000). *Colonizing Hawai'i: The cultural power of law.* Princeton University Press.
Minton, N., & Silva, N. K. (1998). *Kū'ē: The Hui Aloha 'Āina Anti-Annexation Petitions, 1897–1898.* http://libweb.Hawai'i.edu/digicoll/annexation/petition/pet-intro.php
Muller, L. (2020). *A theory for indigenous Australian health and human service work: Connecting indigenous knowledge and practice.* Routledge.
Office of Hawaiian Affairs. (2014). *Income inequality and Native Hawaiian communities in the wake of the great recession: 2005 to 2013.* http://www.oha.org
Office of Hawaiian Affairs. (2017). *Native Hawaiian health fact sheet 2017: Native Hawaiian health status (Vol. 4.1).* http://www.oha.org
Office of Hawaiian Affairs. (2019). *Native Hawaiian data book.* http://www.ohadatabook.com/DB2019.html
Office of Hawaiian Affairs, Justice Policy Institute, University of Hawai'i, and Georgetown University. (2010). *The disparate treatment of Native Hawaiians in the criminal justice system.* http://www.oha.org
Osorio, J. K. K. (2002). *Dismembering lāhui: A history of the Hawaiian nation to 1887.* University of Hawai'i Press.
Paglinawan, L. K., Paglinawan, R. L., Kauahi, D., & Kanuha, V. K. (2020). *Nānā I Ke Kumu—Look to the source* (Vol. 3). Lili'uokalani Trust.
Pukui, M. K., Haertig, E. W., & Lee, C. A. (1972). *Nānā I Ke Kumu—Look to the source* (Vol. I). Hui Hānai.
Pukui, M. K., Haertig, E. W., & Lee, C. A. (1979). *Nānā I Ke Kumu—Look to the source* (Vol. II). Queen Liliuokalani Children's Center.
Rezentes, W. C., III. (1996). *Ka Lama Kukui–Hawaiian psychology: An introduction.* 'A'ali'i Books.
Richardson, J. D. (1908). A *compilation of the messages and papers of the presidents: 1789–1908 (Vol. 11) and index (1908).* Bureau of National Literature and Art.
Sai, D. K. (2013). *Ua mau ke ea–Sovereignty endures: An overview of the political and legal history of the Hawaiian Islands* (2nd ed.). Pū'ā Foundation.

Shook, V. E. (2002). *Ho'oponopono: Contemporary uses of a Hawaiian problem-solving process*. University of Hawai'i Press.

Trask, H. -K. (1999). *From a Native daughter: Colonialism and sovereignty in Hawai'i* (Rev. ed.). University of Hawai'i Press.

Van Dyke, J. M., Morgan, J. R., & Gurish, J. (1988). The exclusive economic zone of the Northwestern Hawaiian Islands: When do uninhabited islands generate an EEZ? *San Diego Law Review, 25*, 425–494.

Williams, I. L. (2019). Does Native Hawaiian culture-based treatment deserve more funding than treatment-as-usual? *Journal of Ethnic & Cultural Diversity in Social Work, 28*, 246–261. https://doi.org/10.1080/15313204.2018.1555500

Williams, I. L., Laenui, P., Makini, G. K., Jr., & Rezentes, W. C., III. (2019). Native Hawaiian culturally based treatment: Considerations and clarifications. *Journal of Ethnicity in Substance Abuse*. Advance online publication. https://doi.org/10.1080/15332640.2019.1679315.

Williams, I. L., Makini, G. K., Jr., & Rezentes, W. C., III. (2021). Indigenous Hawaiian psychoactive drug use before European contact, and after 1778. *Journal of Psychoactive Drugs, 53*(2), 111–126. https://doi.org/10.1080/02791072.2020.1833114

Williams, I. L., Rezentes, W. C., III, Nunes, A., & Makini, G. K., Jr. (in press). Native Hawaiian healing to treat substance misuse: History through the looking glass. *Journal of Social Work Practice in the Addictions*. https://doi.org/10.1080/1533256X.2021.1933844

Williams, M. T., Davis, A. K., Xin, Y., Sepeda, N. D., Grigas, P. C., Sinnott, S., & Haeny, A. M. (2021). People of color in North America report improvements in racial trauma and mental health symptoms following psychedelic experiences. *Drugs: Education, Prevention and Policy, 28*(3), 215–226. https://doi.org/10.1080/09687637.2020.1854688

Chapter 8
Psychology in Aotearoa New Zealand

Barbara J. Kennedy, Natasha A. Tassell-Matamua, and Benita Stiles-Smith

Introduction

In this volume, which seeks to map the emergence, development and current status of psychology in Oceania and the Caribbean, Aotearoa New Zealand (NZ) is a study in contrasts. In comparison to OECD averages (2020), disposable household income in NZ lags behind and financial inequality is higher, with 14.7% of the population living in poverty (Child Poverty Action Group, 2021). Despite this, in general, New Zealanders are more satisfied with their life than the global average (OECD Better Life Index, 2020). The government and the profession emphasise a bicultural Māori/non-Māori approach, which recognises the identity of the Indigenous peoples of the country while also acknowledging all those with non-Indigenous heritage. Approximately 36% of the psychology workforce is multicultural, having migrated or been recruited from overseas. The profession became a legal entity only 40 years ago and yet, since 2006, registration has been competency based, ahead of many nations in taking up this approach. Although developed, the nation is small and predominantly un-urbanised, which presents challenges and opportunities for psychology training and service delivery. However, it has perhaps been able to maintain a nimble approach more easily than places with a larger and more established workforce.

The following chapter outlines the current state of psychology within the timeline and components of its development in NZ. To make sense of that current state, socio-cultural histories of both nation and profession are essential, offering insights

B. J. Kennedy (✉) · N. A. Tassell-Matamua · B. Stiles-Smith
Massey University, Palmerston North and Auckland, Aotearoa, New Zealand
e-mail: b.j.kennedy@massey.ac.nz; n.a.tassell-matamua@massey.ac.nz; b.stiles-smith@massey.ac.nz; benita.stiles-smith@mail.waldenu.edu

G. J. Rich, N. A. Ramkumar (eds.), *Psychology in Oceania and the Caribbean*, International and Cultural Psychology, https://doi.org/10.1007/978-3-030-87763-7_8

of potential value to nations where there is opportunity for psychology to emerge and develop more rapidly and deliberatively.

Current Overview

With a land mass of just over 100,000 square miles, NZ lies at the southernmost reach of Polynesia and some 1200 miles east of its nearest neighbour, Australia. The nation has a population under 5 million, of whom 16.5% identify as Māori (Stats NZ, 2018). The census further indicates other ethnic groups of European/Pākehā (70.2%), Pasifika (8.1%), Asian (15.1%) and other (1.2%).

In 2021, the New Zealand Psychologists Board recorded 3583 psychologists holding a current practising certificate, comprising 4 scopes and 239 psychologist interns/trainees (Gina Giannios, NZPB, personal communication, May 7, 2021). This is just short of a threefold increase from 2009 when the total was 1225 (NZ Ministry of Health, 2010). Of the current total of 3583, 232 (6.5%) identify as Māori and 72 (2%) as Pasifika; this is less than half of what might be expected when considering the proportion of Māori and Pasifika in the general population. According to workforce data collected by the Ministry of Health (Emmanuel Jo, Ministry of Health, personal communication, May 7, 2021), some 7% of practising psychologists identify as Asian which therefore constitutes another group under-represented in the profession in relation to population. Government employs a majority of psychologists between secondary mental health, education and corrections services. Psychologists also work in both the non-government sector and private practice, across diverse fields including addiction, aged care, behaviour issues, children in care, coaching psychology, community, disability, family, family violence, forensic, health, industrial/organisational, health conditions, hospice, Kaupapa Māori, pain management, primary mental health, refugees, rehabilitation, sexually concerning behaviour, sport psychology, trauma, youth and youth justice.

Socio-historical Context

Navigating the oceans of the South Pacific, the peoples that came to be known as Māori arrived in NZ over 1000 years ago. Roughly translating as "normal" or "natural", the term *Māori* was adopted after the arrival of the early European settlers, as a way of distinguishing *tāngata whenua* ("people of the land" or Māori) and settlers. *Aotearoa* was the name given by Kuramarotini, wife of the chief navigator of one of the voyages that first brought Māori to the country. Aotearoa was subsequently given the European name of Zeeland in 1642 by Dutch navigator Abel Tasman. By the time of Captain Cook's visits in 1769, Māori had established communal living according to immediate kinship ties within groups. These were categorised as *whānau*, or families, *hapū*, or extended relational ties which comprised several *whānau* groups, and in specific geographical localities comprising several *hapū*, were *iwi* (Mead, 2016; Roberts, 2013). From 1814, British missionaries settled in NZ seeking to influence Māori and complaining to the Crown of the unruly traders, sailors and adventurers who were also attracted to the island nation. Ostensibly to control the British, James Busby was appointed British Resident, though without means to exert control. He did however assist with the 1835 Declaration of Independence, which was signed by 34 northern *Rangatira*, chiefs and leaders and recognised by Britain. By late 1839, there were perhaps 100,000 Māori across the two islands of New Zealand, and 2000 Europeans, mostly in the north of the North Island. Europeans were purchasing land from Māori, whose relationship to the *whenua*, land, was at once pragmatic and also imbued in spirituality and subsequent notions of guardianship, protection and sustainability for future generations. This was in contrast to the permanence of individual ownership and intergenerational entitlement assumed by the Europeans in such purchases.

Initially reluctant to intervene, Britain eventually became formally involved with the intent to protect Māori interest, gain legal control over its own subjects and improve relationships among Māori and settlers. Thus, at a meeting on February 5, 1840, a proposed treaty was presented in *te reo*, the Māori language, and English to some 500 Māori and 200 Europeans at Waitangi in the Bay of Islands. Despite lengthy discussion, agreement was not reached that day, and as English language history records, it appears more was said about possible benefits for Māori than restrictions or losses, especially through the absolute nature of the transfer of authority to the British Crown. The *hui*, or meeting, was to resume on the 7th, but as some Māori wished to leave early, signing began on the 6th at Waitangi, and with copies of the documents, the collection of signatures continued on around the country until September when British sovereignty was declared. Notably, not all *iwi* signed the documents and therefore were not subject to the conditions of the Treaty, a point which has remained contentious since that time (Wilson, 2020).

By the 1858 census, numbers of European and Māori were approximately equal (Berliner, 2014); from this point, Māori numbers declined to approximately 50,000 by the 1890s from a total population of some 800,000 (Te Ahukerau, 2013). As with many other Indigenous peoples around the globe, Māori experiences of settler occupation were coloured by opportunity, but also exploitation, marginalisation and oppression (Walker et al., 2006). This included the dispossession of ancestral lands, subjugation of cultural practices, newly introduced diseases and socio-economic disadvantage, which some Māori suggest effectively resulted in epistemicide. This continues to have ongoing impacts on contemporary Māori through the perpetuation of systematic and systemic bias.

From 1886, the majority of non-Māori people living in NZ were of British origin, but had been born in NZ. Before World War II, there were only very small numbers of migrants, French, German, Scandinavian, Chinese and Dalmatians, and after the war, Dutch and a larger number of English and Scots. From the mid-1960s, attracted by work opportunities, there was significant migration from the Pacific Islands. Changes to immigration policies in the mid-1970s and 1980s that placed emphasis on qualifications and skills rather than race increased numbers of immigrants from Asia and South Africa. By 2004, it was said that after Australia, NZ had the world's second highest proportion of immigrants in its workforce (Callister & Didham, 2010). Spoonley (2014) termed contemporary NZ as a "settler society", due to its composition of "….national minorities comprised of indigenous peoples who have been colonized, and ethnic minorities whose presence and compositional characteristics are the product of both historical and contemporary immigration policies and a nation building project that revolves around immigration" (pp. 651–652).

Tertiary Education in NZ

The following series of subsections outline the current description of education for psychologists and the historical underpinnings and progression to date.

Overview

Domestic students pay fees, subsidised by the government, typically by taking out an interest-free student loan to be repaid from earnings after graduation. Students may also access a government-provided student allowance, but this typically applies only to a first degree, such as a bachelor's. There are few scholarships, mostly providing assistance rather than full provision of fees and living expenses. Therefore, many university students also hold employment alongside their study. The fact that student allowance is not available for students to finish their professional training in psychology constitutes a barrier to increasing the socio-economic diversity of those preparing for professional practice; this affects all students, but most significantly those from minority groups, who are already experiencing the effects of systemic biases.

History

Tertiary education in NZ began in the last quarter of the 1800s, with early academic staff generally from overseas. By 1900, 500 men and 305 women were enrolled in tertiary institutions. Examination papers were marked in the United Kingdom from 1879 to 1939 (Pollock, 2012).

However, prior to the introduction of colonial education systems, knowledge acquisition was an essential component of Māori life, beginning in the womb and extending across the life course, and perhaps best captured by the term *mōhiotanga*, or understanding and perception. Although oral transmission was the most common mode of knowledge acquisition, e.g. in the form of narrative, song and chanting, it also occurred through the arts, notably via carving and weaving. Māori understandings of *wairuatanga*, or spirituality, the natural environment as well as the interrelativity between the human condition and the wider ecosystem were astute, with remnants of such understandings trickling through in contemporary times, despite the colonial history of cultural near-erasure. *Whare wānanga*, which were physical and/or intellectual sites of advanced and systematic learning in specialist areas akin to metaphysics, were reserved for those of chiefly descent or identified with specific potential or capability.

Although Māori had these established systems of learning and knowledge acquisition, their initial engagement with western *literacy* was via missionaries who translated scripture to *te reo*. Schools for assimilation were incorporated in 1847, with Indigenous language loss and cultural suppression resulting and the English language being enforced as the mode of communication. Compulsory education introduced in 1877 further forced assimilation, though Māori retained Native Schools in some communities. Land loss and systemic marginalisation led to migration to cities in search of work, which increased acculturation-focused education with manual and technical instruction being prioritised. This stereotyping of Māori as best suited to labour vocations continued through the early twentieth century, effectively sidelining an extensive and purposive history of knowledge transmission and acquisition. Toward the latter part of the century, Māori influence and initiatives in higher education became more evident, which had the concomitant relative effect of increasing Māori engagement with education for the professions (Walker, 1991).

Development of the Discipline of Psychology in NZ

With the small population of Māori, settler societal norms and the rapidly increasing European population in the mid-1800s disregarded Māori ways of being as valuable. Indigenous psychologies or ways of knowing, particularly those related to *wairuatanga* and holistic notions of interconnectedness between all phenomena, were likely perceived as largely irrelevant. This became an embedded perspective in the majority of the non-Indigenous population with the emergence of the industrial revolution and scholarly traditions rooted in ancient Greece.

Despite William James and other historical figures in the discipline of psychology concerning themselves with matters of the spirit, this same focus did not extend to the shores of NZ when psychology landed. Berliner (2014) identified 1869 as the beginning of the history of westernised psychology in NZ as a subtopic of its parent discipline of philosophy at the fledgling institution of the University of Otago. In keeping with the convention of the time, psychology was taught by staff from Britain or by those who had travelled to study in Europe or the United States. Staff were instructed to bring their own teaching libraries. As the English university at that time existed primarily to teach a body of knowledge rather than to conduct research, there was little to motivate students in NZ to generate research that would likely be seen as being of little relevance to their English examiners (Berliner, 2014).

Applied psychology began generating substantive interest in education in the early 1900s, with compulsory education having been instituted and teachers' increasing awareness of psychology's mental testing and study of delinquency. The development of psychology was further fuelled by the devastating impacts of World War I and the subsequent pandemic. This stimulated government inquiry and the priority for more scientific and research-based expertise for health and social services, thus creating a timely opportunity for the fledgling discipline of psychology. An application of psychology focused upon addressing the needs of children, with a small number of Child Guidance Clinics being the first psychological clinics in NZ, and by the mid-1920s, psychology had crossed into mainstream consciousness (Berliner, 2014). In 1943, the Education Department began offering psychological services (Winterbourne, 1953).

It was not, however, until between 1948 and 1964 that psychology separated from philosophy at the four original university colleges, with clinical training first offered in 1976 at the University of Otago (Jackson, 1998). At the University of Canterbury, clinical teaching began in 1960 (University of Canterbury, 2020) as an additional paper in the master's degree, followed by a part-taught, part-practical certificate year; this became the foundation of a model used by other universities (Jackson, 1998). Initially available only to clinical practitioners but subsequently to selected students, by the 1980s, students had produced 37 clinical theses. Presumably, either none of these first practitioners training as clinical psychologists were Māori or cultural background was not considered noteworthy; in the sources available, only field of study and gender were analysed. However, at least one Māori student did become a clinical psychologist at Canterbury in this period, with Averil Herbert completing her training between 1966 and 1972 (Herbert, 2012). Victoria University and Massey University did not begin clinical training programmes until the 1970s. At Massey University, psychology grew substantially and by the time master's courses were introduced, they included a particular emphasis in I/O psychology. Lacking a large industrial base however, the development of I/O psychology was slower than was clinical (Jackson, 1998).

Interestingly, Jackson's (1998) analysis of taught courses and theses identified very little engagement with cross-cultural psychology across all NZ Universities in the decades he examined through the second half of the twentieth century. The notable exception was Victoria University's production of theses relating to cross-cultural psychology in the 1960s during the tenure of James Ritchie with the support of his mentor Ernest Beaglehole and his interest in Māoridom. The topic however then all but disappeared, with Beaglehole's death and Ritchie's move to Waikato University.

In 1965, formal application was made to the University Grants Committee to establish a Māori studies unit at the University of Waikato. The proposal had been made by Ritchie, by then the Foundation Professor of Psychology at the University of Waikato, but faced political opposition, resulting in an unfunded launch in 1972. Ironically, James Ritchie was the New Zealand-born son of Australian immigrants;

he had taught in Māori Schools and then gone to university to create an intellectual framework for his teaching experience with Māori.

Governance Shaping the Profession in NZ

Professional and legislative governance of psychology has been a developmental process of many years in length, and that process is detailed in the following subsections.

Overview

Although some early psychology scholars had limited engagement with the application of psychological knowledge as described above, professional training per se first became available in NZ in the 1970s and initially to very small numbers of students. That the very first clinical programme was approved by the Department of Health is noteworthy, and the first 50 years of professional training in psychology have been driven substantively to meet the demands of the core government services of secondary mental health, corrections and education. Diversification of the profession and its workforce in comparison to more populous developed nations has been delayed and slow.

Regulation

Prior to 1981, the profession was unregulated, with those interested in the applied practice of psychology joining the New Zealand Psychological Society (NZPsS), which had been established in 1968 (NZPsS, Timeline, 2018). Professional psychology was first recognised by law in 1981 with the Psychologists Act that established the New Zealand Psychologists Board (NZPB, 2021a), which was required to keep a register. The NZPB could also issue both provisional and temporary certificates of registration, investigate complaints and take disciplinary action. At that point, reflecting the limited training options available, there were four options for registration outlined with respect to degrees obtained from New Zealand Universities:

- Option A, a postgraduate diploma in any field of psychology or educational psychology or an applied master's degree in clinical and community psychology.
- Option B, a doctorate or master's degree in any field of psychology other than educational psychology plus a year's full-time practice in any field of psychology under supervision approved by the Board.

- Option C, a bachelor's degree with Honours plus 2 year's full-time practice in any field of psychology under Board-approved supervision.
- Option D essentially accommodated a specific variation for educational psychology.

These options were subsequently contracted into Option A and Option B. Option A was operationalised by graduation from a professional programme named for a specific type of psychological practice. These were either a clinical master's degree comprising advanced coursework, practice, thesis and the supervised practice of internship or a specific master's with internship or specific postgraduate diploma comprising master's thesis and internship (e.g. ABA, community, education). Option B remained a doctorate or master's degree plus 1 year's full-time practice under Board-approved supervision. Option B served to afford some diversity in professional practice beyond the necessarily small number of vocationally boundaried programmes and as a bridge into NZ psychology for immigrant psychology graduates and psychologists.

As numbers of psychology graduates increased, Board administration of the supervision component required for Option B became increasingly unwieldy. In an attempt to preserve the value of the pathway and address some of the quality control issues inherent in any system without clearly articulated parameters, the NZPsS developed the Supervision 2000 programme that identified supervisors, provided resources and training and articulated learning to be achieved by supervisees. By 2007, this proved economically unsustainable and was discontinued, thus effectively eliminating the Option B pathway.

The Psychologists Act (1981) was superseded by the Health Practitioners Competence Act 2003 (HPCA) covering all regulated health professions including psychology and itself amended in 2019. The core purpose of the HPCA is to protect the health and safety of the public by ensuring practitioners are competent and fit to practise (HPCA, 2019). Because the Act applies to multiple professions, functions such as specification of scopes of practice, competencies, prescription of required qualifications and accreditation of relevant courses are undertaken by each profession's Board in accordance with the HPCA.

Competence is addressed through specification of qualification for registration and demonstration of ongoing competence; the issue of fitness to practice falls under the disciplinary function of the Board. As such, the NZPB holds the responsibility of accountability to the public for both competence and fitness to practice of individual practitioners. The NZPB considers submissions of complaint against psychologists and, if warranted, undertakes further investigation. The Board has the power to place a condition on a practitioner's registration, requiring, for example, specific supervision or retraining, or to impose various disciplinary outcomes, up to and including deregistration.

Qualifications

The current base-level qualification for the practice of psychology in NZ is a NZ Master of Psychology or equivalent, plus 1500 hours of supervised practice; there are however some scope-specific requirements. Entry to the Master of Psychology is on the basis of strong academic performance in a bachelor's degree with specialisation in psychology. However, NZ retains a very liberal approach in which students may essentially construct their own selection of psychology courses with minimal prerequisites/prescription beyond broad survey courses at first year and methodology at bachelor's and master's levels.

The NZPB currently specifies seven scopes of practice: training scopes of intern and trainee; psychologist scope; and four vocational scopes including clinical, counselling, educational and neuropsychologist. Psychologists must all demonstrate the *Core Competencies for the Practice of Psychology in NZ* ([CC]; NZPB, 2018a), which includes practice in accordance with the *Code of Ethics for Psychologists Practicing in Aotearoa New Zealand* ([CoE]; NZPB, 2012). Those holding vocational scopes must also demonstrate additionally listed competencies that are specific to their field.

Psychologists who hold a vocational scope and who trained in NZ after a particular scope was specified will have completed a training programme with a name matching that of their scope of registration; these training programmes typically require completion of specified courses at least at the master's level, prior to internship. Clinical psychologist preparation is available as either master or doctor of clinical psychology. Completion of a PhD after a master's in psychology, either before or after internship, may occur in any of the scopes, including psychologist. Immigrant psychologists must demonstrate equivalence in their training or retrain in NZ, either wholly or in part.

Core Competencies

There are nine CC specified by the NZPB comprising discipline, knowledge, scholarship and research; diversity, culture and Treaty of Waitangi/Te Tiriti o Waitangi; professional, legal and ethical practice; framing, measuring and planning; intervention and service implementation; communication; professional and community relations, consultation and collaboration; reflective practice; and supervision (NZPB, 2018a). These are underpinned by a statement of Standards of Cultural Competencies (NZPB, 2018a). Specifically, "the Board acknowledges that the training and practice of psychologists in Aotearoa New Zealand reflects paradigms and worldviews of both partners to te Tiriti o Waitangi/the Treaty of Waitangi, and international cultural competence standards . . ." (NZPB, 2018a). In the practice of psychology in NZ, cultural competence is not only a distinct set of knowledge and skills but also, at least aspirationally, the lens through which psychological knowledge is apprehended and applied.

It has become evident, however, that aspiration has not yet resulted in meeting the standard needed to work in ways that minimally meet awareness of cultural nuance and honour *Te Tiriti*. The term *competence* itself is restrictive and implies that certain skill and knowledge levels have a minimum standard, beyond which competence is assumed and can be maintained through ongoing demonstration. Yet, a considered application of psychological knowledge to a heterogeneous Māori population born out of an often painful, socio-political history of colonisation requires continual in-depth reflection on one's own positioning as a psychologist and cultural bearer. How to demonstrate such reflection in a way that also authentically acknowledges one's own limitations and biases involves a further extension of one's self and perhaps suggests that the term *cultural compassion* for self and for others may be more apt than *cultural competence*.

A working group has been convened to further address cultural competence standards for psychologists in NZ. Bicultural guidelines and practices have become topics of discussion as leadership by Māori in the NZPsS has become more present over the past 25 years. The NZPsS joined the working party for developing the International Declaration of Competencies for Psychology in 2013 where Māori views were received with appreciation. This effort was followed by publication of *Te manu kai i te mātauranga*: *Indigenous Psychology in Aotearoa New Zealand* (Waitoki & Levy, 2016), and in 2018b the report, *Indigenous Psychology in Aotearoa: Reaching Our Highest Peaks for Māori Psychologists*, was released (NZPsS, Highlights from Our Bicultural Journey, 2018).

Accreditation

Both internship and traineeship programmes are subject to a regular schedule of accreditation by the NZPB. Accreditation is against a set of standards currently numbering 56, requiring the programme to provide significant documentation and evidence which is reviewed by an appointed Accreditation Team external to that university/organisation (NZPB, 2016). The NZPB currently monitors 21 courses of study in 7 universities and 2 trainee programmes. Areas of focus in addition to clinical psychology currently include counselling, rehabilitation, educational, applied behavioural analysis, health psychology, child and family and industrial/organisational (NZPB, 2021b).

All interns complete a degree comprising 1500 hours of supervised practice plus academic work, either as a stand-alone post-master's year or as the final year of a 3-year post-bachelor's programme. There are currently two trainee programmes, one each in the Departments of Defence and Corrections. Academic eligibility for these traineeship programmes is the Master of Psychology, but although successful completion of traineeship leads to registration as a psychologist, it does not result in a degree. Traineeship may begin at any time available in the host organisation and typically takes up to 2 years of supervised practice to complete the 1500 hours of practice and required learning outputs.

Continuing Competence Programme

All registered psychologists must hold an Annual Practising Certificate, have regular supervision and keep records of their ongoing learning and competence. These continuing competence records are subject to occasional and random audit by the NZPB. This programme was instituted in 2003 alongside the HPCA Act 2003, with the objectives of providing a framework for psychologists to address their ongoing competence and to give the NZPB a mechanism for ensuring this was being accomplished.

Interface Between Psychology and Government

In comparison to, for example, the United States, advocacy for the profession is very low key without use of professional lobbyists or other formal avenues. The NZ body representing the widest variety of psychologists, including some clinical scope psychologists, is the New Zealand Psychological Society. Clinical psychologists are also represented by the College of Clinical Psychologists. Both of these bodies interface with government and the media at intervals on behalf of the profession. They also collaborate with the Board in various endeavours, e.g. the *Code of Ethics for Psychologists Working in New Zealand* (NZPB, 2012). Academic and university-associated psychologists also assist the NZ government with working groups and other initiatives on occasion.

Psychology Workforce in NZ

Of the 3583 psychologists active on the register, clinical scope comprises the largest single group with 1897 psychologists. The psychologist scope follows with just over half that at 1017 psychologists. Together, scopes other than clinical totalled 1615 psychologists. The ageing profile of the psychology workforce is such that the increase of less than 6% represented by the 2021 trainee/intern psychologist numbers remains insufficient. Of the psychologist workforce, 10% is 65 or over and those aged 55–64 represent a further 16%. No differentiation of full time/part time is currently available (Gina Giannios, NZPB, personal communication, May 7, 2021).

Research on NZ's psychology workforce is sadly lacking; therefore, what follows is an informal and necessarily idiosyncratic perspective. The largest employer is the Ministry of Health which employs primarily psychologists in clinical scope for secondary mental health services and a small number of health and other psychologists. However, the Department of Health also contracts out a significant array of primary and other mental health services, mostly to non-government organisations which employ psychologists from a wider range of scopes. Other major employers are Department of Corrections and Ministry of Education.

Turnover in secondary mental health services is high, with many clinical scope psychologists migrating to private practice focusing on services beyond secondary mental health. A substantial portion of this work is contracted or subcontracted with government funding. For example, private contractors provide services via the Accident Compensation Corporation, a Crown entity which delivers psychological and other services for citizens sustaining physical and/or psychological injury through accident. Although a large proportion of the psychologist workforce in NGOs is registered under the psychologist scope, some of these practitioners are also choosing to work in private practice.

Given the bicultural underpinnings of NZ government and society, attention to Māori representation in the psychologist workforce is of import. In 2002, of the then approximately 900 psychologists, 18 identified as Māori. By 2014, this number had increased to 134, or 6% of the total Psychologists Board registrants (NZPB, 2018a). Even the current 232 Māori psychologists still represent only 6% of registrants. This constitutes a significant shortfall of representation given that the 2013 census indicated 14.9% of the population identified as Māori. At that time, Pacific peoples represented some 7% of the population, with fewer than 25 psychologists identifying as Pasifika (Faleafa et al., 2019). The historical legacy of the country and the contemporary systemic structures' bias against Māori and Pasifika likely perpetuate these figures, and both groups report over-representation for mental health burdens and within the forensic population as compared with the majority NZ/European/*Pākehā* ethnic groups.

The privileging of a psychological system that does not value spiritual realities with the same esteem as scientific realities means in some cases individuals' experiences constituting exceptional yet still normative experiences within Māori ontology may be perceived as pathological. This makes the low numbers of Māori and Pacific psychologists especially concerning given anecdotal and literary evidence that suggests the likelihood of transformative outcomes may be a function of cultural congruency between psychologist and client.

Culture and Psychology in Bicultural NZ

Although NZ psychology scholars are a dynamic group of productive researchers, literature from which academics and psychologists draw for training and practice remains predominantly from Britain and North America. This is unsurprising, given the privileging of knowledge generated from these contexts across the discipline in general, as well as the English roots of many people in NZ, and the small population for generating local research. Vital to the current practice of psychology in NZ is critical consumption of research. When utilising research generated around the world, the ability to think about the context and underlying assumptions is important as NZ psychologists consider the distinctions of the NZ socio-cultural setting and the practice of psychology in this country. Thus, generation of NZ-based research remains crucial.

Though always of import in the profession, critical thinking and debate in NZ regarding the inherent bias in the available theoretical and evidence base of the discipline is imperative for all students, academics and professionals. This is especially so if non-Māori are to work effectively alongside Māori. Until relatively recently, Māori students were receiving training from almost exclusively non-Māori academics whose understanding of cultures other than their own varied enormously, and who may not have given credence to spiritual realities in the same way that Māori do, or even at all. This has often left Māori students needing to not only work just as hard as others to achieve academic learning from an epistemic perspective that may differ from their own but also having the added challenge of reconciling (a) how another culture understands such intimate processes as thinking and behaving in the absence of spirituality, (b) how their own culture understands these processes through a lens of *wairuatanga* and (c) the relationship between the two and the applicability of western psychology in their own culture.

It would be fair to say that some decades ago most academics' expectation was without awareness of the inherent privileging of certain knowledge systems and perspectives over others in academia, perpetuating marginalisation of specific cultural/ethnic groups and their epistemologies. The predominating frame was simply that they were teaching their discipline and the student's job was to learn it, with no reference to self. Attempting to do just that cost the student heavily in terms of cognitive dissonance. Anecdotally, many Māori students/graduates report having resolved that by temporarily setting aside their own culture in order to learn psychology and then needing to return to home and *whānau*, or family, both nuclear and extended, in order to re-find themselves after their training in psychology. Such denying one's own identity in order to learn psychology has been an antithetical irony.

Attempts to redress such difficulties experienced by Māori students, as well as the longer-term outcomes of widespread socio-economic and systematic educational disadvantage, typically include the provision of additional learning support services and assistive scholarships specifically for Māori students. Māori academics have borne a huge workload burden in being called on to provide pastoral and academic support to Māori students, attending to a wide variety of duties specific to their culture. They have additionally also been expected to raise the cultural capital of their departments by providing guidance to non-Māori staff seeking to support their Māori students, as well as providing support to non-Māori students to be more culturally aware and competent. For example, providing cultural consultation to students regarding the ethical considerations inherent in their research as related to Māori has been considered necessary to attend to nuances that might not be general practice for many research projects. Within some universities in NZ, psychology has become a leader in at least attempting not only to support Māori students and staff but also to create a space in which it is hoped that the "partnership" value of *Te Tiriti* can emerge.

At Massey University, for example, an important and exciting development has been the recent establishment of the Centre for Indigenous Psychologies. This Centre developed from an identified need to ensure Indigenous knowledge systems and perspectives are privileged, and by doing so allow Indigenous students and staff to "see" themselves in psychology, and thus go some way to mitigating struggles felt by Māori staff and students in the past. The Centre for Indigenous Psychologies is an inclusive physical and intellectual space where Indigenous psychologies are explicitly acknowledged, practised and developed in all research and teaching undertaken. Although Māori perspectives are privileged as part of the Centre's commitment to giving full effect to *Te Tiriti o Waitangi*, the perspectives of other Indigenous peoples are respected and embraced as part of the inclusive ethos of the Centre. While the Centre for Indigenous Psychologies has appealed to Māori students studying psychology at Massey University, it has also been received favourably by non-Indigenous students wishing to engage with and learn more about Indigenous perspectives and how they, as future psychology practitioners, might work to better respect them in their working lives.

However, the growing emergence of Māori in the discipline and the profession is not the only important descriptor in the culture of psychology in NZ. The student body of senior psychology courses is generally upper middle class and western. Of course, multiple factors contribute, including advantaged schooling, tertiary-educated parents and the financial means to attend university and complete a long training course. The result has been a profession that is relatively homogeneous and influenced especially in years past by most NZ programmes producing clinical scope psychologists for providing government services. Broadly, in terms of match between the demographic of the profession and of the population most in need of the services of psychologists, the profession would benefit from a greater level of diversity of providers. Review of the profession in light of the expanded range of diverse services represented in the field would also be of benefit rather than the still-current assumption that clinical scope psychologists characterise the culture of psychology.

Taking steps to robustly examine the culture of the profession not only from an Indigenous psychology perspective but also from the multiple perspectives of diverse fields of psychological practice will benefit the profession as a whole and the society it serves. Such steps are currently being engaged, with increasing influence and input from Māori at national levels, as well as representation of an expanded range of psychological practice types at national advisor levels.

Looking Back, Looking Forward

Māori cosmology, ontology, epistemology and the social structures they informed had been long established prior to disruption by European settlement in NZ. *Te Tiriti o Waitangi*, the Treaty of Waitangi, sought to establish, however imperfectly stated, principles by which the bounty of the land and opportunities of trade could be shared among peoples. However, history shows that what ensued fell far short of those ideals, with Māori collectively paying an especially heavy toll. Less than 200 years later, it is perhaps unsurprising that the legacy remains, as the effects of systemic and systematic disadvantage, bias and epigenetic trauma are never simply erased. Rather, like a scar inflicted on a young tree, these must eventually be integrated in order to continue healthy development. Of course, in social histories, including that of Aotearoa New Zealand, this is inevitably complicated by the fact that both early settlers and subsequent waves of migration each brought their own histories of damage. Those who hold economic and political privilege and power inevitably inflict the legacy of their own damage on whomever does not, even if simultaneously seeking to act with at least some good intent. Perhaps more than most, those of us in psychology have a responsibility to be realistic about the fact that as much as we may idealistically wish, we cannot escape the human condition. People make errors and cause harm; people can also learn from error and recover from harm, but they remain flawed. Psychology does, however, have some knowledge and tools that can be used in service of healing the scars and supporting healthy development.

In NZ, mainstream western psychology emerged slowly from its parent discipline of philosophy, took out some of the parts that did not quite fit and began. It continued, however, dependent upon its parent universities in Britain and then on study visits to Britain, Europe and the United States. International research collaboration was difficult and slow, given the times. The profession's first roots took hold tentatively in the field of education some 50 years before training for clinical psychology became available in the last quarter of the twentieth century. This has been followed by limited diversification into other fields of psychological practice.

If NZ could begin the last two centuries again, perhaps Māori would bid those settlers immediate farewell. However, this seems unlikely given the inherent notion of *manaaki*, to care, uplift, be hospitable, that underpins Māori ways of being. With the grand benefit that is hindsight, though, how much different could the discipline and profession, indeed, the wider society be now, if equal honour were accorded the knowledge and cultures of both Māori and non-Māori? If from the start, each was to be valued for what it could best contribute, then each could become stronger by what it gained from the other. In psychology, it would still be wise to learn from scholars where the discipline was longer established. However, rather than proceeding on the basis of an unexamined assumption that the psychological findings from Europe or the United States were somehow universal truths, a more locally authentic vantage point might have been used. Established scholarship could have been examined alongside local research from both cultures, so that the braiding together of perspectives could begin at the start and provide an evidenced foundation from which to critically evaluate *the conditions under which* (Greenwald et al., 1986) research emanating from more populous nations with necessarily more extensive research programmes applies. Similarly, given the profession established elsewhere ahead of NZ, in a utopian opportunity, Aotearoa New Zealand could have studied what was socially beneficial elsewhere, and alongside fostering the development of its Indigenous psychology with both Māori and non-Māori voices, deliberately sought to build a heterogeneous profession whose membership reflected as well as possible the society it served through whatever range of roles met the needs of its people and structures.

However, there was no utopian opportunity, nor will there be for other nations currently at earlier points in developing psychology. There can, however, be an advantage in beginning a similar journey after another has gone before. There is always an opportunity to avoid some of the missteps, to contribute to the gaining of wisdom and to benefit from the experience of the other in order to make better choices.

In NZ, the discipline of psychology is embarking on the challenge of making space for the voices of Indigenous psychologies and learning how to listen to them, but also *hear* what they are saying. The same challenge is present in the profession, with a need to diversify both its workforce and the range of roles shaped and filled by psychologists in order to meet the increasing gap between need for mental health and other psychological services and the supply of practitioners.

References

Berliner, A. (2014). *A history of psychology in New Zealand : Early beginnings 1869–1929.* Master's Thesis. University of Canterbury. University of Canterbury Online. http://hdl.handle.net/10092/10579

Callister, P., & Didham, R. (2010). Workforce composition - Migration and work. In *Te Ara - the encyclopedia of New Zealand.* Retrieved on May 18, 2021, from http://www.TeAra.govt.nz/en/workforce-composition/page-6

Child Poverty Action Group. (2021). Retrieved on 5/15/2021 from https://www.cpag.org.nz/the-latest/current-statistics/latest-child-poverty-figures/

Faleafa, M., Kingi-'I;i'ave, D., & Stewart, M. W. (2019). *Growing the Pasifika Psychology Workforce; Current and Future Strategies.* Le Va. https://www.leva.co.nz/wp-content/uploads/2019/12/LV-190405-Growing-the-Pasifika-Psychology-Workforce-KeyFindings-final.pdf

Greenwald, A. G., Pratkanis, A. R., Leippe, M. R., & Baumgardner, M. H. (1986). Under what conditions does theory obstruct research progress? *Psychological Review, 93*, 216–229.

Herbert, A. (2012). Māori centred research and clinical programmes in Aotearoa/New Zealand. In R. Nairn, P. Pehi, R. Black, & W. Waitoki (Eds.), *Ka Tū, Ka Oho: Visions of a bicultural partnership in psychology*. NZPsS.

Jackson, P. A. (1998). *The mind of a nation: A philosophical and historical critique of psychology in New Zealand.* Doctoral Thesis. Massey University. Massey Research Online. http://hdl.handle.net/10179/1308

Mead, H. M. (2016). *Tikanga Māori (Revised Ed.): Living by Māori values.* Huia Publishers.

New Zealand Legislation (2003). Health Practitioners Competence Assurance Act 2003.

New Zealand Legislation (2019). Health Practitioners Competence Assurance Amendment Act 2019 No 11.

New Zealand Ministry of Health. (2010). *Psychologists, Health Workforce Annual Survey, 2010*. https://www.health.govt.nz/nz-health-statistics/health-statistics-and-data-sets/workforce-data-and-stats/health-professional-workforce-pamphlets/health-workforce-annual-surveys-2010

New Zealand Psychologists Act. (1981). http://www8.austlii.edu.au/nz/legis/hist_act/pa19811981n5222/

New Zealand Psychologists Board. (2012). *Code of ethics for psychologists practicing in Aotearoa New Zealand*. http://www.psychologistsboard.org.nz/cms_show_download.php?id=235

New Zealand Psychologists Board. (2016). *Standards and procedures for the accreditation of programmes and schemes leading to registration as a psychologist in Aotearoa New Zealand*. http://www.psychologistsboard.org.nz/cms_show_download.php?id=461

New Zealand Psychologists Board. (2018a). *Core competencies for the practice of psychology in Aotearoa/New Zealand*. Retrieved 5/1/2021 from http://www.psychologistsboard.org.nz/cms_show_download.php?id=533

New Zealand Psychologists Board. (2018b). *Reaching our highest peaks*. https://www.psychology.org.nz/journal-archive/Reaching-Our-Highest-Peaks-2018.pdf

New Zealand Psychologists Board. (2021a). *About the Board*. Retrieved on 5/1/2021 https://www.bing.com/search?q=About+The+Board+(psychologistsboard.org.nz)&cvid=22ba6aa72c6f44e1b40e43777d5613c3&aqs=edge..69i57.2007j0j9&FORM=ANAB01&PC=U531.

New Zealand Psychologists Board. (2021b). *Accredited training programmes*. http://www.psychologistsboard.org.nz/accredited-training-programmes2

New Zealand Psychologists Society. (2018). *From independence to registration: A timeline of activities*. https://www.psychology.org.nz/application/files/1815/7972/3126/A2-Independence ProfessionalRegistration-FINAL.pdf

New Zealand Psychologist Society. (2018). *Highlights from our bicultural journey* https://www.psychology.org.nz/application/files/2215/7972/3194/A2-Bicultural__NSCBI-FINAL.pdf

OECD Better Life Index. (2020). Retrieved May 17, 2021, from http://www.oecdbetterlifeindex.org/countries/new-zealand/

Pollock, K. (2012). Tertiary education. In *Te Ara - the encyclopedia of New Zealand*. Retrieved on May 17, 2021, from http://www.TeAra.govt.nz/en/tertiary-education

Roberts, M. (2013). Ways of seeing: Whakapapa. *SITES: A Journal of Social Anthropology and Cultural Studies. New Series, 10*(1), 93–120. https://doi.org/10.11157/sites-vol10iss1id236

Spoonley, P. (2014). New diversity, old anxieties in New Zealand: The complex identity politics and engagement of a settler society. *Ethnic and Racial Studies, 38*(4), 650–666. https://doi.org/10.1080/01419870.2015.980292

Stats NZ. (2018). 2018 Census. Retrieved from https://www.bing.com/search?q=2018+Census+%7C+Stats+NZNZ+Ministry+of+Health+(2010)+re%3A+psychologist+numbers&cvid=4a733883a3d64f22bb84f060c100d2da&aqs=edge..69i57.2418j0j1&pglt=547&FORM=ANNAB1&PC=U531.

Te Ahukerau, C. R. (2013). Māori decline and revival. In *Te Ara – The encyclopaedia of New Zealand*. http://www.Teara.govt.nz/en/Māori/page-4

University of Canterbury. (2020). *Postgraduate Diploma Clinical Handbook*. Retrieved on May 10, 2020, from ClinPsycHB-2020.pdf (canterbury.ac.nz).

Waitoki, W. Levy, E. (2016). Te manu kai i te mātauranga: Indigenous psychology in Aotearoa/New Zealand. New Zealand Psychological Society, Roopu Mātai Hinengaro.

Walker, R. (1991). *Liberating Māori from Educational Subjection* (Monograph No. 6). University of Auckland: Research Unit for Māori Education, Te Tari Rangahau o te Matauranga Māori.

Walker, S., Eketone, A., & Gibbs, A. (2006). An exploration of Kaupapa Māori research, its principles, processes and applications. *International Journal of Social Research Methodology, 9*(4), 331–344. https://doi.org/10.1080/13645570600916049

Wilson, J. (2020). *History*. In *Te Ara - the encyclopedia of New Zealand*. Retrieved on May 17, 2021, from http://www.TeAra.govt.nz/en/history

Winterbourne, R. (1953). A review of psychology in New Zealand. *Australian Journal of Psychology, 3*, 17–27.

Chapter 9
Psychology on The Rock: Mental Health System and Kanaké Indigenous Tradition in New Caledonia

Grégory Simon, John Dui Goropwojèwé, Yves-Béalo Gony, Gérard Sarda, Marlène Leloutre, and Emmanuelle Forsans

Historical and Sociological Overview of New Caledonia

New Caledonia is an archipelago in the South Pacific located 1500 km east of Australia and 2000 km north of Aotearoa-New Zealand. It comprises a main island, Grande Terre, extended by the Bélep Islands to the north and the Isle of Pines to the south, and bordered by the Loyalty Islands (Ouvéa, Lifou, Tiga and Maré). Located in Melanesia, the archipelago has been under French sovereignty since 1853. Since 2003, it has had the status of "an overseas country" within the French Republic. It

New Caledonia is often nicknamed "The Rock".
The word "Kanaké" is adopted in this text for its completeness, even if the word "Kanak" is usually used.

G. Simon (✉) · E. Forsans
Clinician psychologist and independent researcher, Nouméa, Drubea-Kapumë country, South Province, New Caledonia

J. D. Goropwojèwé
Kanaké initiate and traditional practitioner, Poindimié, Paicî-Camuki country, North Province, New Caledonia

Y.-B. Gony
Anthropologist and Kanaké traditional practitioner, Hienghène, Hoot ma Whaap country, North Province, New Caledonia

G. Sarda
Former healthcare administrator, Centre Hospitalier du Nord, Koumac, Hoot ma Whaap country, North Province, New Caledonia

M. Leloutre
Clinician psychologist and hypnotizer, Médipôle de Koutio - Centre Hospitalier Territorial Gaston Bourret, Dumbéa, New Caledonia, Drubea-kapumë country, South Province

G. J. Rich, N. A. Ramkumar (eds.), *Psychology in Oceania and the Caribbean*, International and Cultural Psychology,
https://doi.org/10.1007/978-3-030-87763-7_9

is administratively divided into three provinces (the South Province, the North Province and the Islands Province) but also according to eight indigenous linguistic and customary areas. With a maritime territory of 1,386,588 km^2, its population is approximately 271,407 inhabitants,[1] 67% of whom live in the capital Nouméa. New Caledonia is in the process of autonomy and unprecedented decolonisation involving a Caledonian society that is said to be "hyper-complex" due to its cultural diversity and the plurality of groups and identities to which it belongs (Carteron, 2008). Mainly, we find the following populations: indigenous Kanaké Melanesians, Europeans, Polynesians and Asians. The country's history and its multiple traumas bear witness to numerous cultural upheavals and failures of transmission and violence between generations (Sirota, 2017).

The first signs of human presence correspond to the Lapita period, the remains of ancient pottery found on the coastline more than 1000 years before Christ. Traces of food crops in descending terraces also testify to an ancient human occupation: their development is estimated to be around 1000 years after Christ (Terrier, 2010). However, some oral sources in Paicî-Camuki country identify "Lapita" as pottery given by navigators to the natives in exchange for fresh water (Simon, unpublished manuscript).[2] Thus, the origins of the Kanaké natives could be older. Let us also mention the mythical origins of the Paicî-Camuki Kanaké (Simon, unpublished). The first man, *Téâ kanaké*, is said to have appeared in the *Momaawé* region, coming out of a stone called *Yawé*, "the man-stone", and to have multiplied by visualising himself in several men and women. He is also called *katia kanaké*, the "metamorphosed man". From this first man and his transformations emerged three founding myths, sometimes symbolised by three concentric circles that can be found as petroglyphs in the country. The three founding myths form the basis of the Kanaké society and are known as *Téâ Kanaké* (the chiefs or kings), *Bwé Béalo* (the court) and *Dui Daoulo* (the warriors).

The voyage of Cook allowed him to "discover" the Caledonian archipelago in 1774, 50 years before the first whalers. The shock was prolonged by the arrival of Catholic missionaries in Balade, in the north-east of Grande Terre in 1840. The country was annexed by France in 1853. Twelve years later, the natives saw the arrival of the first transported people, immortalised on the "engraved bamboos". In 1868, the policy of "reserves" was put in place, reducing the cultivation land of the indigenous population and literally uprooting them. In 1878, the great Kanaké revolt of Ataï was put down in bloodshed. At the end of the nineteenth century, a "code de l'indigénat" was introduced, making the Kanaké "sub-citizens" by denying them the basic civil rights enjoyed by the colonists. Then, the "*grand cantonment*" completed, and considerably worsened, the policy of reserves. Despair set in for the Kanaké, who were deemed useful in 1917 to go and defend a homeland that they could not recognise as their own on the European front in World War I. The *Tipindje*

[1] Population census New Caledonia 2019, INSEE-ISEE

[2] SIMON Grégory, A la lumière de Momaawé. Ethnopsychologie du deuil, soins et rituels en pays kanaké Paicî-Camuki de Nouvelle-Calédonie

revolt was terrible and its repression ruthless: the gap of incomprehension and the despair of its victims was such that in the 1920s, a brutal demographic decline occurred, to the point that the missionary and ethnographer Leenhardt heard this message: "the Kanak will disappear". Paradoxically, it was World War II that revived hope among the indigenous population. New Caledonia became a military base during the Coral War against the Japanese. In the US federal army, which would see more than a million soldiers serve for 4 years, the Kanaké noticed that there were coloured and white people and that there was an apparent equality of treatment: an awareness that submission to "the whites" would not be eternal emerged.

In 1948, the "indigénat" was abolished and the Kanaké finally became French citizens, but they had to wait until 1957 to exercise universal suffrage. The Union Calédonienne and its motto "two colours, one people" were established. In 1978, the "red scarves", created by Kanaké and European students after May 1968, would give impetus to the demand for independence. Jean-Marie Tjibaou[3] was one of the first to understand that the emancipation of the Kanaké from colonial rule would first require the public affirmation of Kanaké culture, which the missionaries, administrators and numerous colonists had tried in various ways to reduce and forbid.

From 1984 to 1988, violence continued with deadly confrontations. The Matignon Accords, preceded by the "mission for dialogue", put an end to the violence, and the UN included the country in the list of territories to be decolonised and the Nouméa Accord brought considerable improvements for the Kanaké. But a process of truth and reconciliation between all citizens was still missing, which would finally give meaning to the "handshake" between Jean-Marie Tjibaou and Jacques Lafleur.[4] The Kanaké population had been severely reduced after the French had taken possession of New Caledonia, and only returned to its 1887 level in 1957. A majority of the Kanaké population is attached to customary law, and the gesture of the same name is crucial in social relations and events.

The New Caledonian Mental Health System

While New Caledonia is responsible for the health system and medico-social competences in the three provinces, the judicial and penal system is the responsibility of the State. However, people with special status are subject to customary jurisdiction. The financing of free medical aid is the responsibility of the French State, and the Health and Social Agency is a local feature for prevention and health promotion.

Most mental health care is provided by the Centre Hospitalier Spécialisé (CHS) Albert Bousquet, which also operates on the islands of Wallis and Futuna. The first hospital of its kind in New Caledonia, the CHS is now a member of the South

[3] Kanaké politician, assassinated in 1989

[4] European origin politician

Pacific Regional Hospital Federation (2006). It is composed of three main medical services: general psychiatry including inpatient and outpatient units in Nouméa and two medical-psychological units in the North Province (Koumac and Poindimié); child psychiatry in Nouméa and a medical-psychological unit in Lifou (Loyalty Islands); the clinical gerontology centre in Nouméa and a unit in Koné (North Province) (Visiting report, 2011). It should be noted that there is no inpatient unit for adolescents dispersed in the other units. Since the international crisis of COVID-19 began, the country has suffered from a lack of nurses and psychiatrists.

There are psychologists, educators and social workers who work for the Provincial Directorate of the Health and Social Agency in the three provinces, particularly in community centres in Nouméa and its suburbs. These departments include a child protection service, a prevention and health promotion service and a domestic violence treatment service. There is also a non-paying online listening platform, "SOS Ecoute", in the country, and a rich and developed psychology association. In particular, this group organised the Assizes of Psychology in order to move towards the possibility of protecting the title of psychologist in the country,[5] an unfinished project. In this respect, we do not have precise figures of the number of psychologists in the country, but according to associations and institutions, we would estimate that there are approximately 40 psychologists in institutions and a similar number in private practice and at service providers. According to the Health Directorate, in 2021, there were 16 institutional and 8 private psychiatrists in the country. The vast majority of these professionals are in Nouméa and its suburbs.

It should be noted that a mental health plan was voted on and approved by the Congress of New Caledonia in 2013. Its objectives are to optimise the coordination of care, to support a shared, common culture and to allow everyone access to adequate responses. Since 2019, Suzanne Devlin,[6] the coordinator of the mental health network, has been responsible for supporting the development of the patient process and the network approach, the destigmatisation of mental health, the setting up of psychological support cells in the context of crisis in schools at risk of trauma, the training of professionals in intervention with persons at risk of suicide and the consideration of the impacts on mental health of the communication strategy in the context of the COVID-19 health crisis.

Public Health Figures

In 2010, a survey[7] conducted with the assistance of the WHO estimated that 29% of New Caledonians had at least one mental disorder. In New Caledonia, almost 20% of 10–18-year-olds say they have experienced physical violence in the last 30 days:

---

[5] The title is recognised in the public administration but not globally.

[6] Personal communication

[7] Deliberation of the Congress. Official Journal of New Caledonia, 6 September 2013

53.9% of the cases were in the school environment, 44.1% in the home and 18.7% in the neighbourhood. Additionally, one woman in four experiences domestic violence (verbal, physical and sexual abuse, psychological harassment, etc.), and one woman in eight has been subjected to one or more sexual assaults before the age of 15.[8] More than one in two people use tobacco, three in ten young people aged 12–17, and more than one in ten deaths are attributable to tobacco over the 1991–2010 period. First-time tobacco use shows a strong tendency to start at a young age and more so among young women. Girls use tobacco as much as boys, which is a particularity of New Caledonia in the Pacific. Among 15–25-year-olds, one to two out of ten young people use cannabis daily, and there are approximately 40,000 regular users in the country. The average first use of cannabis is at 13 years of age, and alcohol and kava[9] at 11 years of age. One in four adults consume alcohol in a harmful way, and more than 60% of fatal accidents involve alcohol. In addition, 27% of the population is obese, and 45% of chronic diseases are heart diseases (ASSNC, 2015). Regarding the issue of suicide in New Caledonia, the START survey was locally conducted by a psychiatrist and a psychologist (Goodfellow & Selefen)[10] in collaboration with the WHO, the New Caledonian Government and the University of Australia (De Leo et al., 2013). The study shows that suicide is the second leading cause of death among 15–24-year-olds, that it affects mostly 25–44-year-olds (compared to 40–50-year-olds in Western countries) and that the Kanaké community (39% of the total population) remains the most vulnerable (57% of cases).

The Government's Do Kamo Public Health Plan

"*Do kamo*" has several meanings in the 28 Kanaké languages spoken in the country; "to be fulfilled" or "a beaming human being" are quite common ones. Following the findings related to public health expenditure and figures, the Caledonian Do Kamo health plan was commissioned in 2012 by the Government of New Caledonia to the Directorate of the Health and Social Agency. A strategy was implemented seeking a sustainable and equitable health model for New Caledonians. Implemented in 2017 and based on the Ottawa Charter (1986) as well as the Adelaide Declaration (2010), the objective was to promote a change in the health system through a concerted action plan with the actors of the health system themselves. This strategic plan focuses on promoting holistic health by supporting self-realisation in relation to others. The work to implement the Do Kamo plan should reflect the shared values of the population, develop the prevention of risk behaviour and promote community

[8] Inserm survey (2004, 2006) "Health, living conditions and security of Caledonian women"

[9] Plant whose pressed roots are widely consumed in Oceania

[10] Colloquium on 11 December 2019 at the South Province auditorium, Noumea

health, as well as the diversification of the care offer and the management of change in favour of better governance.

Three of the authors of this chapter were co-leaders (Gony, Simon) and participant (Goropwojèwé) in the "Representations and Social Practices" workshop of the Do Kamo health plan. This workshop helped to give meaning to health promotion and education actions by defining the determinants of well-being and living well together. They focused on Kanaké indigenous conceptions throughout life (birth, adulthood, marriage, death). The Kanaké conception of existence includes the presence of a concept of "life" (see below) which is essential for the balance of the human being ("*Momaawẽ*", Paicî-Camuki, or "*Marip*", Hoot Ma Whaap). Therefore, the "spiritual" sphere ("*avëaru*" – the inner being of Man) cannot be marginalised if we talk about psychological health in New Caledonia. Our workshop found that the existential reality of the *avëaru* should be affirmed and considered as complementary to the physical body and as an element of understanding of the Kanaké concept of life. After identifying a problem related to the fragility of self-esteem among New Caledonians, the powerful urge which supported the initiative of the Do Kamo plan is currently on hold due to the COVID-19 global pandemic and the uncertain political situation in the country.[11]

Psychology and Indigenous Health

Efforts have been made by the public health system to encourage the inclusion of Kanaké and Oceanian conceptions and representations in practices. However, culture tends to remain on the fringe of the system, and we can observe that some psychologists in the country are working towards a greater integration of indigenous fields of meaning. In particular, since the 2000s, New Caledonian psychologists have been conducting field research and developing clinical and therapeutic practices with Kanaké and Oceanian communities by focusing on the cultural dimensions of the populations.

Intercultural and transcultural work based on group psychoanalytical referentials with a socio-therapeutic aim has emerged. This work involves telling a story in a group in Kanaké, Wallisian and French as a holding for multi-disabled children (Thibouville & Wamowe, 2016), and freeing the speech of delinquent adolescents, in the symbolic place of the Kanaké hut, with a multi-generational group involving the group of ancestors in the discussions (Thibouville et al., 2018). These approaches integrate the languages, the relationships between the generations of the community and the symbolism of the traditional habitat involving the relationship to the ancestors. However, these approaches also retain a theoretical background and a grid for analysing relationships and the group as indicated by a modern Western

[11] The 17th Government of New Caledonia overthrew the previous one and took office on July 16 2021, five months after being elected

psychological cultural tradition. One of the authors of this text (Simon, 2015), favouring a socio-constructivist and pragmatic approach, demonstrated that giving voice to the dead (prosopopoeia) as a psychic care device for a complex persistent mourning can be decisive for the psycho-physiological healing of a New Caledonian woman of Polynesian origin (Tahiti-Tuamotu). The deceased loved one is involved in the care, and the clinician facilitates the relationship between the bereaved and her father. This psychotherapeutic practice is very suitable for the Kanaké because it integrates the relationship with the deceased, a notion that is very present in Oceania.

Let us also mention the work of Marlène Leloutre, another author of this text who has been practising Ericksonian hypnosis for 10 years at the Médipôle of Koutio (local general hospital) in Dumbéa, especially in the palliative care department. She offers breathing techniques, relaxation and active and positive visualisation to hospital patients suffering from serious illnesses such as cancer, by introducing modified states of consciousness thanks to hypnosis. This work emphasises connecting to a resource place and making it a sacred inner place, favouring the possibility of rituals of reconnection to one's values. The Kanaké and Oceanian people have a very strong connection with nature with which they evolve in close relationship, such as with waterfalls and certain trees, containing a recognised symbolic, spiritual and energetic value. More in-depth work can be carried out at a trans-generational level or around the problems of mourning. In this case, it is a question of proposing to people to let protective ancestors come to these symbolic places, to carry out rituals of forgiveness and thus to free the patient from his or her conflicts and fears. The fields of meaning of the people are thus summoned in these interior spaces (sacred places, protective ancestors) so that the patient reconnects with his or her internal resources. To provide a point of reference, about 10 years ago, palliative care patients did not feel legitimate or comfortable in using their own traditional healing resources in those Western healing spaces. They were suspicious and hid herbal potions or prayers on paper from the caregivers' eyes, which had been delivered to them by traditional practitioners. Today, a bond of trust more frequently allows for the integration of traditional resources into the hospital setting and for open discussions towards a holistic approach that takes into account the traditional care and spirituality of patients.

Some of the work is directly aiming at a better understanding and visibility of Kanaké indigenous psychology. Some ethnopsychiatric and ethnopsychological fieldwork focused on the rituals and relationships between the dead and the living during periods of mourning in Paicî-Camuki Kanaké country (Simon, 2020). Exchanges with several research participants made it possible to identify an indigenous psychology of mourning. This work highlights local existential conceptions, a theory of psychic mourning, evaluative and diagnostic knowledge, a cultural disorder of mourning and therapeutic practices and a relational care using a technique of cognitive-sensory visualisation that allows communication with the ancestors. In addition, Christine Qaeze,[12] the first Kanaké psychologist of the CHS Albert Bousquet based on the island of Lifou (Ne Drehu country), has spontaneously developed a clinical approach of the community psychiatric type. She conducts her interviews directly with the tribe in the indigenous Drehu language. She is currently working on a lexicon of the island's psychopathologies according to the indigenous tradition, in partnership with local traditional practitioners and Dr. Waminya, an ethnomathematician from the *Hnexujia* Centre.[13]

By the way, Grégory Simon co-developed an initiative of the Union of Liberal Psychologists of New Caledonia (UNI-Psy). He co-founded the "Circle of Voice Hearers of Nouméa" (2017), accompanied by Magali Molinié, psychologist and vice-president of the "Network of Voice-Hearers" in France. This innovative care practice stems from social psychiatry (Romme & Esher, 1993). These groups constitute extremely free, tolerant and integrative spaces with regard to the explanations and theories summoned on the origin of voices and about the discussions around spirituality. They have the advantage of sharing strategies for dealing with voices and restoring power and hope to people troubled by their voice(s). The participants in Nouméa are now interested in connecting with Kanaké traditional practitioners in order to nourish discussions and outings to feel connected to nature. The development of a network of voice-hearers in New Caledonia is underway with the support of the "Fondation de France", which is financing a position composed of two pairs (one health professional and one expert by experience).

Elements of Traditional Practitioner and Kanaké Initiates' Practices

In New Caledonia, traditional knowledge is still marginalised. Traditional practitioners have maintained a parallel network with the public health system and are consulted by both indigenous and non-indigenous populations. In the absence of recognition of their knowledge, practices and values, Kanaké traditional practitioners and initiates have tended to withdraw and become opaque in their practices, often not being taken seriously or considered. The contributions noted below reflect a long-term relationship of trust and friendship with one of the authors of this text (Simon).

[12] Personal communication

[13] The centre develops learning tools for children in the Drehu language.

Traditional Caregivers in Kanaké Hoot Ma Whaap Country

Yves-Béalo Gony, another author of this text, describes the concept of health in Hoot Ma Whaap country. The health is embedded in the general context of the knowledge of the Kanaké man and his environment, the "*gna men thau*". This translates into the terrestrial environment and people, the maritime environment and the sky and stars. Health is translated by the word "*marip*" in the Fwaî language of Hyeehen,[14] which also means "life", the source of well-being and self-esteem. Health is a concept organised according to the relationships between the different elements of the *gna men thau* and first and foremost "life", which is at the centre of the system of thought and the organisation of social structures. "Marip" is omnipresent in the facts and acts of daily life, customary ceremonies, political organisation and the spirit world. Life organises and manages human society, its environment and the spirit world.

The function of the traditional healers is essential because it allows each person to know his or her evolution within the group. The lack of knowledge of functions and roles results in illness, which is often the result of deviations and disobedience to the organised rules of life of the group. In Hyeehen country, the traditional practitioner, called "*ka po turek*", is the one who signals and dictates a diagnosis of a person's health. He has the knowledge of *gna men thau* and the power to heal people whose life or health is compromised by acts of incivility committed against their family or group. They are generally the "judges of the life of society and the health of social rules". They are organised by hierarchy according to the role of the group and their function within the chieftainship. Three categories of *ka po turek* can be observed. In order to carry out their diagnoses, the various practitioners must be in contact with the patient and above all know his or her cultural identity as well as the social practices of the group. Several media are used by traditional practitioners to diagnose the patient's health condition. The three practitioners presented here use, depending on the origin of their spirits (Totems), stone, wood (twigs, bark and leaves, buds, seeds), bird feathers and animal or human bones.

The "*ka thai hyarik*" are those who, in daily life, dictate the behaviour of the person by their spiritual knowledge. They listen attentively to the request made, observe actions and gestures and eventually place a hand on the patient. Intervening in a way carefully and precisely chosen by the practitioner in order to put the patient at ease, laughter is also used in cases of relational opacity. In this way, the practitioner establishes a relationship of trust between his spirits and those of the patient. The diagnosis will depend on this connection between his spirits and the energy (marip) of the patient, and the treatment can take two forms. The so-called "forgiveness" treatment includes a customary gesture[15] presented to the person(s) with whom there was an affront to the rules of life. On the other hand, another technique

[14] Hienghène, a village in Hoot Ma Whaap country (Northern Province)

[15] Based on a gift of presents accompanied by a speech

involves the taking of treatment by decoctions of plants whose virtues are recommended to cure the diagnosed physical or psychological illness.

The "*ka thai ceek*", literally "those who clear the path of the patient" to enable him or her to know his or her mistakes, are another practitioner type. The diagnosis that will be proposed is a solution that allows patients to see or perceive for themselves their mistakes made within their group.

The third type of practitioner, "*ka po noga*", refers to people who are consulted in the context of projects to be carried out or in situations of inherent difficulties. Unlike the other types of *ka po turek*, who carry out their consultations during the day, "*noga*" is practised at night. After receiving the patient's gesture, at nightfall, before lying down on a board representing his spirit (totem), the *ka po noga* consumes a herbal potion and dives into a deep sleep. During his sleep, he will be led to perceive visions that are close to a form of lucid dreaming. Several spirits, his own and those of the patient, give him a form of prescription to be applied to the patient. It is a kind of information regarding the guidelines, the set-up and the solution actions to be taken in order to better realise the project and make it succeed.

Thus, the interventions of traditional practitioners are of a preventive, diagnostic and curative nature. In the case of *noga*, the approach is on the side of risk prevention, but also of accompaniment, guidance and therefore of coaching and personal development through a relationship with the spirits of the invisible facilitated by the consumption of a plant which thus makes it possible to link the visible and invisible worlds.

The Seven Sources of Life of the Initiates in Kanaké Paicî-Camuki Country

The *avëaru* (the inner being of Man), the dead, the gods and the geniuses of the invisible world are initiators for the living (Simon, unpublished), a central element of Kanaké identity that touches on the notion of civilisation. Another author of this text, John Dui Goropwojèwé, explains us that an *abori*, literally "known and acquired", is an initiate in Paicî-Camuki country. He knows his inner being *avëaru*, which is effective for self-development and for treating oneself or others (Simon, unpublished). The initiates identify and name, in the human body, "seven sources of life", *Porê jèwé* in the Paicî language. Each source is assigned a specific existential and functional notion. These seven sources in relation can be understood as "the being expressed to present itself":

- *Peïri tëmèga coina*, principle of knowledge, which is located exactly at the top of the skull
- *Peïri pwéla*, principle of perception, located at the root of the nose
- *Peïri paicò mè patéré*, the principle of communication, located at the throat
- *Peïri papitiri*, the principle of gathering (love), found at the solar plexus
- *Peïri pwato*, the principle of fertilisation and creation, located just below the navel

- *Peïri wèdéari*, the principle of enjoyment, at the root of the sex
- *Peïri pwéjùwa*, the principle of matter, "Where we draw strength", at the level of the perineum

> The elders work on them, they concentrate on the sources to find peace and tranquillity, life forever ("Momaawé"), you have to make the connection between the sources and then you touch the initiatory world, which escapes people who are not initiated (Goropwojèwé)

From these seven related sources flows a healing "water of life", a light called *jio po*, literally "*the water that gushes forth*", which then allows the Rainbow Man to appear. The Maori Waitaha tradition (Brailsford, 2004) reports knowledge and exercises of consciousness that use images very similar to those of the Kanaké Paicî of the *Momaawé* region (Simon, unpublished), particularly when they evoke "*the river of the Rainbow Spirit*". We also note the myth of the rainbow snake among the Australian aborigines. While the seven Kanaké sources of life can also be related to the kundalini yoga chakras of the Bharati tradition in India (Baghel & Pradhan, 2015), we are here approaching this ontological reality through Kanaké eyes and conceptions. The ontological principle of the indigenous Kanaké of New Caledonia places us at the basis of a balance between the material and spiritual worlds, which is no longer the case in modern Western psychology, which remains strongly emptied of the spiritual sphere of the human being (Sotillos, 2021). The elements of Kanaké traditional practitioners' practices presented here demonstrate that not only relationships with the community, the environment and the ancestors are essential but also the relationship to the "inner being of Man".

Discussion and Conclusion

A consistent body of authors worldwide (Sotillos, 2021) consider modern Western psychology and psychiatry to be secular and culturally embedded disciplines, incomplete both in their understanding of human nature and in their ability to promote health and well-being. As such, they need to be transformed, as they currently remain inadequate in addressing mental health problems. Psychology implies a spiritual dimension to be more authentic, and under the dominance of modern Western culture, it remains too polarised on a materialism that values objectivity, rationality and empiricism, which implies a reductionist view of reality. Modern Western psychology has imposed itself through "universalising" conceptions of the person and of human behaviour, whether individualistic or group based. It would be favourable, even urgent, for health professionals to mobilise to modify their cultural professional posture, to integrate the knowledge system more fully and to develop an indigenous Kanaké psychology. To do this, it remains essential to recognise the expertise of indigenous communities, particularly knowledge holders who possess a level of competence that is not valued or understood by mainstream spaces of modern Western health (Wirihana & Smith, 2014).

This chapter aims to provide a better understanding of the approaches of Kanaké initiates and *traditional practitioners*. It also provides an overview of the mental health system and psychological work integrating Kanaké and Oceanian universes of meaning. If we were to characterise the Kanaké civilisation, we would say that it is a civilisation of relationship (Simon, unpublished). Among the Kanaké, health is linked to a notion of multidimensional relationship – the relationship to one's inner self (*avëaru*, spirituality), to the community (language, ceremony), to the environment (habitat, elements, land in connection with the clan name) and to the ancestors (genealogies, myths). This concept in New Caledonia regarding the relational nature of health and well-being is also a cornerstone of indigenous psychology among Aboriginal and Torres Strait Islander people in Australia and the Maori of Aotearoa-New Zealand (Waitoki et al., 2018).

Indigenous knowledge systems could be further lost if they are not protected and promoted. It would thus be appropriate to support and develop local healing by accompanying the restoration of therapeutic practices that have been marginalised over time. Kanaké understandings of being human, and of life and health, are valuable and necessary to provide more integrated and holistic psychic treatment options. These are also a process to develop self-awareness, as well as the awareness of others and the universe. We believe that all communities in the country would benefit from an indigenous Kanaké psychology and a more integrative psychology that would benefit from being enriched by the universes of meaning of all communities in the country.

Our country needs to receive the knowledge and healing practices that Kanaké traditional practitioners and initiates would like to share and develop. We believe that generalising the application of these practices would contain powerful possibilities for restoring the self-esteem of Kanaké and all Caledonians because they constitute a real lever for public health. We hope that the Do Kamo health plan can achieve the promotion of this development in the interest of all Caledonians who need to be part of a society in order to preserve peace and tranquillity in the country. Furthermore, as is the case in Aotearoa-New Zealand, research in indigenous psychology could enhance "our understanding of historical trauma" and highlight "the central role of indigenous therapeutic interventions" (Pihama et al., 2014) as a lever for transformation of the country itself. The terminology of "mental health" does not reflect the notion of health in Kanaké country or probably in Oceania more broadly. Today, we need to set up structures, not only for research and clinical practice, but also for health management, that are in favour of this "health of the Being". A holistic and integrative indigenous psychology could perfectly promote this concept.

Here, on the mythical Rock of New Caledonia, we have the resources to build a Directorate of Health of Being, that is, a health emancipated from individualism and the biological whole. We hope that the forces of the country can come together and allow us to live a more complete existential truth. To follow the current motto of the country, "Land of speech, land of sharing",[16] and the political affirmation of "common destiny" in New Caledonia, we certainly need "common care". To conclude, "We are all indigenous from somewhere", a Kanaké politician once said. "Today, however, I am also indigenous to the whole Earth. This feeling allows a special relationship to all life on Earth, whether visible or invisible. This generates respect, mutual understanding and harmony in time and space. In an age of trans-humanism, in which people and communities aspire to restore themselves from colonialist thinking and behaviour, being indigenous to the Earth makes sense. From the dialogue between local and global indigenousness comes an emancipatory covenantal relationship. This is actually part of a path to freedom that can be followed by all the nations of the world that are sensitive to it. In the end, we are left with "simply" knowing what it means to be "indigenous to the Earth". In short, this is probably one of the most important undertakings of our time, and then, through this understanding, perhaps we will know a little more about who we are as human beings" (Simon, unpublished).

Acknowledgements We express heartfelt thanks to Grand Chieftain Napwé and the Paicî-Camuki Customary Council, as they accepted and supported the works and research allowing the present chapter. And special thanks are addressed to Grant J. Rich and Neeta A. Ramkumar who invited us to publish our contribution in this book they are in charge of, as acting co-editors.

References

Agence Sanitaire et Sociale de Nouvelle-Calédonie (ASSNC). (2015). Assises de la santé 2015. Vers une amélioration du système de santé. Un plan stratégique de santé Calédonien. Être épanouï ! Do Kamo !

Baghel, S., & Pradhan, M. (2015). *Psychological significance of the chakras*. Conference at Banaras Hindu University Varanasi.

Brailsford, B. (2004). *Song of the old tides*. StonePrint Press.

Carteron, B. (2008). *Identités culturelles et sentiment d'appartenance en Nouvelle-Calédonie: Sur le seuil de la maison commune*. L'Harmattan.

Charte d'Ottawa pour la promotion de la santé. (1986, November 17–21). Conférence internationale pour la promotion de la santé "Vers une nouvelle santé publique". Ottawa, Ontario, Canada.

Contrôleur Général des lieux de privation de liberté. (2011). *Rapport de Visite*. Centre Hospitalier Albert Bousquet.

De Leo, D., Milner, A., Fleischmann, A., Bertolote, J., Collings, S,, & Amadeo, S., et al. (2013). The WHO START Study: Suicidal Behaviors Across Different Areas of the World. *Crisis The Journal of Crisis Intervention and Suicide Prevention, 34*(3),156–163.

Pihama, L., Smith, C., Reynolds, P., Smith, L. T., & Te Nana, R. (2014). Positioning historical trauma theory within Aotearoa New Zealand. *AlterNative: An International Journal of Indigenous Peoples, 10*(3), 248–262.

Rapport de la réunion internationale. (2010). *Déclaration d'Adelaïde sur l'intégration de la santé dans toutes les politiques. Vers une gouvernance partagée en faveur de la santé et du bien-être.*

Romme, M., & Escher, S. (1993). *Accepting voices*. Mind.

[16] Motto chosen by the Identity Signs Steering Committee

Simon, G. (2015). Deuil et prosopopée en Nouvelle-Calédonie: Prêter la parole aux morts en dispositif de soin psychique, La croissance mortifère, *Etudes sur la mort N°148, L'Esprit du temps*, 79–99.

Simon, G. (2020). Should we hide the eyes of the dead? Continuing bonds in Kanaké Paicî-Camuki country. *Death Studies, 45*(1), 29–39.

Sirota, A. (Ed.). (2017). *Violences entre générations. Transformation ou répétition?* Éditions Le Manuscrit.

Sotillos, B. S. (2021). The decolonization of psychology or the science of the soul. *Spirituality studies, 7*(1), 18–37.

Terrier, C. (2010). *L'Histoire de la Nouvelle-Calédonie*. Maison de la Nouvelle-Calédonie.

Thibouville, G., & Wamowe, J. (2016). Un "holding" interculturel pour des enfants polyhandicapés en pays "kalédonien": Dire un conte en groupe et en langues. *Enfances & Psy, 2*(2), 142–153.

Thibouville, G., Sirota, A., Sailuegejë, D., & Eurisouké, J. (2018). Écouter une figure du vide en groupe dans le contexte inédit de la décolonisation sur l'archipel calédonien. *Revue de psychothérapie psychanalytique de groupe, 2*(2), 113–126.

Waitoki, W., Dudgeon, P., & Nikora, L. W. (2018). Indigenous psychology in Aotearoa/New Zealand and Australia. In S. Fernando & R. Moodley (Eds.), *Global psychologies* (pp. 163–184). Palgrave Macmillan.

Wirihana, R., & Smith, C. (2014). Historical trauma, healing and well-being in Māori communities. *MAI Journal, 3*(3), 197–210.

Chapter 10
Melanesian Mental Health and Psychiatric Services: Perspectives from Papua New Guinea

Sanu Pal and Sutanaya Pal

Papua New Guinea (PNG) is geographically located north of Australia and its western part is connected with the eastern part of the Indonesian mainland. Ethnically, Papua New Guineans consider themselves as Melanesian, rather than as Polynesian or South Pacific. Papua New Guinea gained independence from Australia in 1975, but the colonial influence remained, both culturally and economically. PNG receives aid from Australia for education, medical training, and other forms of infrastructure (Noble, 1997).

Geographically, it has a central mountainous region, coastal areas, and many small islands, including the large Bougainville Island which is currently an autonomous island after the referendum. Bougainville is the biggest island of Solomon Island archipelago. Papua New Guinea has four regions which are further sectioned into 20 provinces for the purpose of governance, with the capital city at Port Moresby. The road infrastructure is limited, and people have to use air travel to make their way between the capital city and the provinces (Muga, 2006). Most of the rural areas are covered with dense tropical rainforest.

S. Pal (✉)
Te Whetu Tawera, Auckland City Hospital, Auckland, New Zealand

Department of Health, Papua New Guinea (1995 to 2000), Port Moresby, Papua New Guinea
e-mail: sanup@adhb.govt.nz

S. Pal
Department of Psychiatry and Behavioral Sciences, SUNY Upstate Medical University, Syracuse, NY, USA
e-mail: pals@upstate.edu

G. J. Rich, N. A. Ramkumar (eds.), *Psychology in Oceania and the Caribbean*, International and Cultural Psychology,
https://doi.org/10.1007/978-3-030-87763-7_10

Demographic Characteristics

The current population of Papua New Guinea is about 7.28 million as per 2011 statistics, with 3.77 million males and 3.50 million females. Most of the people (6.36 million) live in rural areas and only 0.9 million live in urban areas. The largest urban population is in the capital city Port Moresby (Demographic and Health Survey, 2021; Health: National Statistical Office: Papua New Guinea, 2021). The rural nature of PNG is one challenge to providing access to behavioral health treatment.

It is estimated that there are about 800 languages and dialects spoken in Papua New Guinea (Noble, 1997), but the official language is English. Most people speak Tok Pisin which is a local language. Hiri Motu is another spoken language, and it is mostly spoken in certain districts, such a Lae and in the central province. The current official languages are English and Tok Pisin. It is interesting to note that there is no script, and Papua New Guineans write using the Roman alphabet.

Another notable obstacle to treatment is that there are no official interpreters in Papua New Guinea, while I (this chapter's first author) worked as a psychiatrist there from 1995 to 2000. The interpretation is usually done by friends or family, or a social worker or nurses who happened to be involved in the care. Sometimes I had to use two interpreters (such as a local language to pidgin and then to English, or from a local language to Motu and then to English) for assessment. While this is not the ideal, it was the only option available in remote rural areas for getting information from family and even for some complex forensic cases.

Cultural Characteristics

Papua New Guinean society is an indigenous tribal society, and in villages family members live closely in wooden houses which are built above ground level. The houses close by usually have no boundaries, and in some communities, they share meals.

The head of the household is a male, and elders are very much respected. Women usually manage the household chores, look after the children, and at times do agriculture and other outdoor work, such as collection of firewood from the forest. As head of the family, men have the most control (both socially and financially) and have more leisure time than women. Some men marry more than one woman if they can pay the bride price. Currently, this situation is in a process of change, though men still may have relationships outside their marriage leading to family disharmony. It is estimated one in five married women (18%) report their husband has another relationship with a woman (Health: National Statistical Office: Papua New Guinea, 2021).

Religion and Spirituality

Christianity is the principal religion in Papua New Guinea's Constitution; thus, PNG is declared as a Christian country. In the nineteenth and twentieth centuries, Christian missionaries converted the tribal people to Christianity. Now a vast majority (96%) of the people are Christians (Health: National Statistical Office: Papua New Guinea, 2021). About two-thirds of Papua New Guineans are Protestants (Evangelical Lutheran 18.4%, United Church 10.3%, Seventh-Day Adventist 12.9%, Pentecostal 10.4%, Evangelical Alliance 5.9%, Anglican 3.2%, Baptist 2.8%, other Protestant 9.7%). Roman Catholics constitute only 26% (Grundy et al., 2019).

In Papua New Guinea, traditional beliefs, spirituality, and social values are greatly influenced by Christianity, and so all coexist in daily life. Ancestor worship is common, and animal totems, such as the crocodile, are important in the Sepik Region, where there is a large Sepik River (Belief systems and spiritual aspects in Papua New Guinea, 2021; Grundy et al., 2019). It is believed that most Papua New Guineans are animists, so they believe that both animals and plants have spirits like human souls. Their belief is that "spirits" need to be appeased or respected. So, to communicate with spirits, rituals are often performed to pacify or to dispel them (Belief systems and spiritual aspects in Papua New Guinea, 2021). It appears that traditional spiritual practices have declined since colonization. The tribal practice of cannibalism, which was reported by Western colonizers in earlier literature, is not practiced any more, possibly due to the spread of Christianity.

I (the first author of this chapter) did not receive much direct exposure to religious practices. However, I did note that marriages usually happen in Churches and that ministers participate in the process. After death, burials take place per the Christian rituals. I observed that Church activities such as Sunday Church attendance, community healing practices, and fellowship programs happen on a regular basis.

Healthcare System

Primary healthcare service is barely present even in urban areas and is mostly centered in regional hospitals. Among the regional hospitals, Port Moresby General Hospital is in the capital city, and it has all the basic specialties, including psychiatric service. The other regional hospitals are Goroka Hospital in Goroka and Base Hospital in the Eastern Highlands region. These hospitals have basic service, but do not cover most specialties.

There is no private medical service, such as GP service, or any private specialty service. The healthcare system has three tiers (Noble, 1997). Aid posts in the villages are staffed by community health workers with 2 years' basic medical training. Health centers are usually staffed by either a nurse or a health extension officer who has 3 years' training in a condensed medical course. These can be designated as primary service where there is no mental health service. The second tier is the provincial hospitals, which are run by doctors and are usually administered by the government or by missions (Christian missionaries). The third tier is the specialist hospital, located at Port Moresby General Hospital. Regarding psychiatric services, the only long-term psychiatric care is provided by Laloki Psychiatric Hospital, which is described in detail below.

Mental Health Services

Psychiatric services are regulated by the Social Change and Mental Health section of the Division of Curative Services. This is a part of the National Department of Health (Muga, 2006). A National Mental Health Programme was first established in 1962. Laloki Psychiatric Hospital was the first psychiatric hospital, and it was established in 1967. This is still the only psychiatric hospital in the country, and it has 80 beds. There are also psychiatric beds in Port Moresby General Hospital and in other provincial hospitals. Psychiatric patients are also seen in the clinics there (Grundy et al., 2019). At least two provincial hospitals have inpatient psychiatry units, run by psychiatric nurses. There are no doctors, as all the psychiatrists are based in the capital city of Port Moresby.

An independent review in 2011 revealed that mental health services have deteriorated due to multiple factors, including leadership and governance, and insufficient financial allocation in comparison with services and human resources at the district and grassroots level. Psychiatrists are scarce as medical trainees prefer to go into other specialties (Grundy et al., 2019).

Laloki Psychiatric Hospital and Correctional Services

The Laloki Psychiatric Hospital is located about 15 kilometers away from the capital city Port Moresby. It was opened in 1964 and replaced a small psychiatry unit attached to the country's jail at Bomana which is located a few kilometers away from the Laloki Hospital.

The first author was able to obtain the following information from a personal interview with Dr. Uma Ambihaipahar, who is the acting director of the Social Change and Mental Health section of the Division of Curative Services within the National Department of Health (U. Ambihaipahar, personal communication, May 26, 2021). Currently, the hospital has a CEO who is a psychiatrist, and who looks after the management of the hospital, including some clinical work. Apart from the CEO, there are two more psychiatrists posted at Laloki Psychiatric Hospital. There is one social worker for the whole hospital. The hospital has locked wards: for men, for women, an acute ward, and a forensic ward. There is an open ward, "Buna

Ward," where patients wait for discharge. The hospital has a rehabilitation annex and an occupational therapy unit. The wards have basic facilities, such as beds, but may not have mattresses as those may be destroyed by acutely unwell patients and not replaced due to lack of funding. There are common toilets and showers, with basic amenities. The hospital accepts patients from all over the country. The total number of current beds in the hospital is 60, and usually they may not be at full capacity. Currently, due to the COVID pandemic, there are only about 20 patients that are admitted there.

The clinical or medical supervision is varied but quite limited. The psychiatry registrars are based at Port Moresby, and they come over to Laloki Hospital for the reviews. Due to the posting of two psychiatrists, there appears to be a regular review of patients. Patients are mostly admitted informally, as the Mental Health Act is not used usually. Some may be admitted by court orders after they were taken to custody due to a criminal offence. There is no doctor onsite for any after-hours emergency, and usually the patients are transported to the Port Moresby hospital by a van which has no facility to manage any acute physical emergencies. In acute presentations, patients are usually admitted to the Port Moresby General Hospital, and from there, patients get transferred to Laloki Psychiatric Hospital for further treatment.

Bomana Correctional Institute Service, Psychiatric Services

Bomana Correctional Institute Service is the country's largest prison. It is located a few kilometers from Laloki Psychiatric Hospital and has about 630 prisoners. The prison has a clinic for inmates who are suffering from mental health issues. Inmates that have been charged with capital crimes and are suffering from a major psychiatric diagnosis are sent to Laloki Psychiatric Hospital for assessment and treatment. Two mental health nurses and two community health workers are employed by the Bomana Correctional Institute Service. From time to time, psychiatric consultation is provided by the psychiatrist at the Laloki Psychiatric Hospital (Hughes et al., 2005).

Mental Health Clinicians

Psychiatrists and other mental health professionals are scarce, along with a general scarcity of trained health professionals. Per Dr. Ambihaipahar, there are currently eight psychiatrists in the country (U. Ambihaipahar, personal communication, May 26, 2021). The Faculty of Nursing at the University of Papua New Guinea is the only center where nurses are trained, and about ten mental health nurses graduate every year, but most of them opt to work in general medical hospitals in the provinces (Grundy et al., 2019).

Among the eight psychiatrists, two are in the provinces, one at Southern Highlands Province and another in private practice at Manus Island, though there is no designated private psychiatrist in the capital city Port Moresby. Three psychiatrists are posted at Laloki Psychiatric Hospital. There is a psychiatrist at the university for teaching. The acting director of mental health is also currently a psychiatrist. The provincial psychiatry unit is usually run by psychiatric nurses who have 1 year of training in psychiatry after basic nursing training. The nurses at times get some brief specialty training in Australia. Social workers are rarely available in psychiatric hospitals and provincial psychiatry units. At Laloki Hospital, there is only one social worker and an occupational therapist.

In Papua New Guinea, as in other developing countries, there has been a dearth of social workers and occupational therapists in healthcare systems. The family takes the main initiative for follow-up and for providing the help, including monitoring medication adherence, managing self-care, activities of daily living, and meeting the social needs at home. There is no financial support from the state when people are disabled due to mental illness or by any other physical disability.

Psychotropic Medications

There is a limited supply of psychotropic medicines which are available in city hospitals or in provincial hospitals. There are basic antipsychotic medications, such as first-generation antipsychotics. Second-generation antipsychotics are rarely used, due to both cost and supply issues. Among the antidepressants, the only ones available are amitriptyline and fluoxetine. Most medications can be purchased from pharmacies outside when not available in the hospital pharmacies. Mood stabilizers are rarely prescribed and available. I had found no one who were prescribed mood stabilizers, even if they received a diagnosis of bipolar disorder.

Presentation of Mental Illness

Depression and anxiety in PNG present differently than in Western cultures. Feelings of depression may be identified as normal, and anxiety is often ignored. Thus, very few patients come to the clinic for the treatment for these conditions. They may end up receiving help from Church ministers in the form of counselling or prayers or from the community.

When presenting with symptoms of psychosis (hallucination, delusion, or disorganized behavior), the community may identify it as a supernatural phenomenon, such as a curse or sorcery. Thus, psychoses such as schizophrenia remain untreated for many years, due to these attitudes regarding mental illness. Another barrier to treatment is the lack of mental health services.

Case Vignette

Bereina is a rural or semi-urban area in the eastern coast, 90 kilometers away from Port Moresby. Sam, a 24-year-old man, was brought by a Church pastor to a Church clinic with complaints of odd behavior since his early teens. Sam isolated himself, stopped talking, appeared internally preoccupied, talked to himself frequently, and seemed to have poor understanding of what was happening around him. He was not sleeping well, was disorganized, easily agitated, and angry without any apparent reasons. Sam would not stay at home, would go into the bush, and return home only when hungry. He was unable to take care of himself and was malodorous and unkempt.

Sam refused to work in the field and his behavior was unpredictable. Some in the community felt that he had been possessed by spirits, while others believed he had become mentally retarded. His developmental milestones were normal, and he was attending school before his illness started. Collateral history from his family and his mental state examination revealed that Sam had schizophrenia which was untreated for many years. Due to compliance issues, he was started on a test dose of fluphenazine decanoate which was the only depot antipsychotic available in Papua New Guinea in 1997.

Two weeks later, during my second visit, his family reported some improvement in Sam. They noted that he was less agitated and angry, less internally preoccupied, and that his self-care had improved marginally. As he tolerated the test dose, he was administered a regular dose of depot IM every 2 weeks, and subsequently, in about 3 months, his mental state improved considerably. During his subsequent presentations, Sam was better groomed, somewhat pleasant in manner, not responding to any hallucination, not distressed, and said he wanted to work, get married, and have a family. His family was very thankful saying "it is a miracle that Sam is intelligent again."

Culture-Bound Syndromes

Culture-bound syndromes like "Amok syndrome" and "Spirit Possession Syndrome" are often associated with violent behavior (Pal, 1997).

Case Vignette: Culture-Bound Syndromes

Amok Syndrome

Mr. M was a middle-aged man (in his 40s), and a respected member of the clan, who had a history of social stress (as his sister had a child out of wedlock). He suddenly started brooding for a few days. Then he consulted the village magician and some doctors, as he thought he would become “long long” (mentally ill). After that brooding period, he returned home at midnight and killed his parents and two nephews with an axe. The following morning, he was found asleep, and he could not remember what he had done the night before. On admission, there were no psychotic symptoms, and he showed no abnormal mental symptoms during his stay in hospital for more than 14 years. He was acquitted of homicide charges due to the insanity defense (Pal, 1997).

Regarding the forensic aspect of Amok syndrome, it was suggested by Burton-Bradley (1985) that the apparent lack of motive and amnesia are primary. Epilepsy should also be excluded. Head injury also needs attention, as the “Amok syndrome” patient often becomes injured during the course of the attack (Pal, 1997). During the following years after his trial and acquittal, he was released from the hospital, but unfortunately his family refused to accept him back. He was given a place to live with a few others near the Bomana Prison, where he worked in the kitchen.

Spirit Possession Syndrome

Another important culture-bound syndrome to mention is “Spirit Possession Syndrome.” One example of this syndrome is the case of a middle-aged woman who killed her daughter’s father-in-law during the possessed state, after she had had a quarrel with him the night before. She was acquitted on the grounds of insanity. She had had mental illness in the past, and her sister had also suffered from mental illness (Pal, 1997).

Psychiatric Conditions

The most common psychiatric conditions seen at the clinics are depression and anxiety. However, psychosis, bipolar, and cannabis-related disorders make up a majority of the inpatient psychiatric diagnoses. Most of the patients admitted are young males, less than 30 years of age. Papua New Guinea does not yet have a problem with narcotic drugs such as heroin or cocaine (Muga, 2006).

It is interesting to note that personality disorders such as antisocial and borderline personality disorders are not reported or referred to mental health. This contrasts with what is found in Western cultures. Another important finding is that eating disorders which are noted in Western societies quite commonly are also not found or referred to mental health for treatment. I did not encounter any eating disorders such as anorexia and bulimia during my time in Melanesia.

Substance Use Disorder

Alcohol abuse has been the main substance use problem since colonization. Alcohol is one of the most common causes of motor vehicle accidents, particularly on weekends in Papua New Guinea.

The betel nut (which is a seed of areca palm plant) is a unique addiction which is pervasive in Papua New Guinean society with more than half of the population using it. Children as young as six start chewing betel nut. Most adults, men, and women of all ages chew betel nuts. Betel nuts are chewed day and night, and often persons can be seen chewing immediately after they wake up, at work, and in leisure time. Usually, the green betel nut is chewed, as opposed to ripe betel nut chewed in Southeast Asia. It is chewed with mustard sticks dipped in slaked lime powder, thus coloring the whole mouth red. Betel nut is known locally as "buai." In marketplaces, on the side of the streets, buai are sold with mustard sticks and lime (Prior, 2017).

Betel nut contains arecoline, which is a nicotine acid-based mild stimulant alkaloid. Many describe it like this: "Chewing buai makes me happy and gives me extra energy to complete my errands. Without the buai we would be tired and sleepy. It's part of our culture. Everyone in the family chews buai" (Prior, 2017). Mild withdrawal symptoms such as lethargy, irritability, feeling stressed, and being unable to relax have been reported when not taking buai for several hours. This has happened during recent COVID lockdowns in Port Moresby.

Apart from alcohol and betel nut, the most prevalent drug of abuse is cannabis, which is grown in most of the country, and there are no statistics about its abuse. Individual psychiatrists report that they rarely see problems with cocaine, heroin, and other drugs.

Migration and Substance Use

As in other developing countries, migration from rural areas into urban centers affected significant lifestyle changes. This led to the breakdown of cultural norms, unemployment, alcohol abuse, and other substance abuse such as cannabis use (Koka et al., 2004). Alcohol use has increased in the teenage population and among women. Alcohol abuse was estimated to be a major cause of morbidity in the 2001–2010 PNG National Health Plan. Most of this comes from trauma related to alcohol use, with about 90% of the admissions in hospitals due to trauma having some form of alcohol use.

There is no formalized national substance abuse treatment plan (Parker & Burton-Bradley, 1966). However, the PNG Narcotics Bureau has started a public awareness campaign. There are no treatment and rehabilitation centers for people with substance abuse problems or their dependents in PNG, although there is a proposal for one to be established (Mental Health Atlas, 2005). At the time of writing this chapter, there is no drug treatment facility in the country.

Suicide and Self-Harm

In 1966, Parker and Burton-Bradley reported that the indigenous population (as in Papua New Guinea) had the lowest suicide rate in the world (0.7/100,000). Shame was found to be an important and common motive for suicide. Other motives, such as depression and bereavement, are also discussed (Parker & Burton-Bradley, 1966). The current rate of suicide is 7.1 per 100,000 population, which is lower than the world average in 2016 based on 180 countries, which is 9.30 suicides per 100,000 people. The methods for self-harm in PNG have not been reported.

Community Mental Health Clinics or Centers

As noted, in developing countries, there are very few services at the community level. By writer's initiative, a community mental health clinic at Bereina in the eastern coastal area was started in 1999 to follow up with discharged long-term patients from Laloki Psychiatric Hospital.

In 2019, by the initiative of the acting director of mental health, a primary mental health clinic was started where patients can walk in for consultation. This clinic is located near the outskirts of Port Moresby City at Hohola at St. Teresa's Clinic, which is facilitated by a Church organization. I (this chapter's first author) am told services such as alcohol and drug clinics, child guidance clinics, and rehabilitation clinics are in operation. There is as such no other community mental health service in the community.

Psychiatric Facilities in the Provinces

Some provincial hospitals have small psychiatry units attached to the general hospital, managed by psychiatric nurses who also provide some outpatient services as well. In 2015, there were nine psychiatrists serving a population of about seven million. Of these, seven were based at Port Moresby. It was the first author's experience during 1995–2000 that there were only four psychiatrists in the country, and all were based at Port Moresby.

Mental Health Administration

The mental health administration is based at Port Moresby where the health ministry is located, along with a WHO office. The head of mental health or the "director of mental health" was then a psychiatric nurse, under whom was "the chief of psychiatry" who was responsible for the psychiatric and mental health services of the entire country. The chief of psychiatry is involved in teaching medical students, nursing students, and psychiatry registrars at the University of Papua New Guinea, mental health planning, and doing clinical work.

Political and Social Context in Papua New Guinea

Understanding the landscape of behavioral health in PNG requires understanding the nation's political, economic, and sociocultural context. Papua New Guinea has more natural resources such as minerals, agriculture, and wildlife when compared with the neighboring countries. It also has many languages and cultures. It shares a land border with Indonesia's West Papua – Irian Jaya – to its west. Papua and New Guinea used to be two different provinces that were colonized for more than 200 years by various powers including the Sultanate of Tidore, Holland Germany, Britain, and Japan, and finally by Australia.

In 1949, these provinces united, and Papua New Guinea finally attained independence in 1975 (Papua New Guinea: A brief history, 2021). Papua New Guinea is a tribal and traditional society, which is family and clan oriented. People mostly live in rural areas, and urban and city areas are a modern development. The people have close family ties, and the family live together in close-knit areas. Daily life closely involves the extended family, and people spend their day producing food for sustenance and rearing children. People use portions of land that they do not formally own for growing food as well as planting some cash crops (taro, sweet potato). They use the local forests to fish, hunt, and gather timber. Myth plays a major role in daily life, and many of these simple activities are accompanied by rituals. Sadly, some other rituals, such as the menarche ceremonies for girls and initiations for boys, are losing importance. Marriages are performed in Churches, and bride price paid by the groom to the bride's family is still a custom (Papua New Guinea: Daily life and social customs, 2021).

Due to many tribes and languages, there may be tensions among the tribes, leading to wars in between the clans. During clan wars, bows, arrows, and spears are used. Marriage within the clans is usual, but inter-clan marriages also happen. As noted earlier, polygamy is common in PNG, even though it is not usually accepted by the spouse. About 18% of married women say that their husbands are involved in other relationships. Two-thirds of women and about half of the men between the ages of 15 and 49 are married (Demographic and Health Survey, 2021). More than half of women aged 15–49 in Papua New Guinea have experienced physical violence since age 15, and about one-third have experienced sexual violence. Eighteen percent of women who have ever been pregnant have experienced violence during pregnancy (Demographic and Health Survey, 2021).

Spousal violence is quite common. About two-thirds of ever-married women reported spousal physical, sexual, or emotional violence, with the most common being physical abuse (54%), followed by emotional abuse (51%). Twenty-nine percent of these women report spousal sexual violence. Injuries, such as cuts and bruises, are frequently reported (Demographic and Health Survey, 2021). Most of the women who have experienced sexual or physical violence usually do not seek any help. Only 35% sought some help.

For recreation, due to the colonial influence, Papua New Guineans play rugby, which is their most popular game. The language for instruction in schools and other educational institutes is English only, though there are other languages spoken, such as Tok Pisin and Motu. Educational institutions are mostly related to, and some are affiliated with, Australian educational systems.

Consensus in Melanesia

In Papua New Guinea, and in Melanesia more broadly, consensus has been a way to solve difficult problems in the smaller, as well as in the larger, community involving issues such as tribal warfare or other disputes. Consensus was used to attain peace and reconciliation after major conflicts, such as the Bougainville crisis, which was estimated to be one of the biggest wars after WWII affecting the region. Consensus in Melanesia is defined as agreement of two or more groups regarding issues which have been contested for some time. Usually, the leaders, the big man, or chiefs are the persons at the center, and the people abide by and follow through the consensus.

During the conflict resolution, natural objects such as food and plants, as well as songs that have some symbolic meaning, aid the process. When a consensus is achieved, it is observed by a traditional or cultural way such as "breaking the spears used in fighting or eating sugar canes," killing of pigs, feasting, singing, shaking hands, and dancing to celebrate the occasion. These have a symbolic meaning of peace and response with the idea of long-lasting peace between the conflict groups (Marai, 2007). It is interesting to note that consensus is an essential part of Melanesian culture. It provides an avenue for emotions to be expressed and validated collectively which engenders empathy as both sides try to understand each other's positions. This is the very basis of universal conflict resolution that Melanesian society has ritualized into regular practice.

Role of the Church

The Church plays a major role in delivering medical and psychiatric care in Papua New Guinea. They have been involved in this work since the time of colonialism. The services provided by the Church help in bolstering government services. They provide resources and sometimes even governance in these remote areas (Kasse, 2008; Waiko, 1993). The Church is currently responsible for providing about half of the health services in these rural areas and with some subsidies by the state (Grundy et al., 2019).

My Personal Experiences in Transcultural Psychiatry in Melanesia

I (the first author of this chapter) did my medical and psychiatric training in India in the 1980s when the APA's DSM III was the leading authority. Even though the culture of the land where I lived and worked was predominantly non-Western, our formulations and recommendations were adapted from Western literature. This was also a time when cultural differences were not formally recognized by Western literature, and there was no mention of culture-bound syndromes in the DSM. I worked in some of the most remote tribal areas in Eastern India and later with a charitable organization for the destitute run by Mother Teresa where our resources were severely limited. Most of my practice consisted of improvising and adapting my training to suit the needs of the local population. It was a challenge finding culturally appropriate explanations for my patients' experiences and finding the right balance of Western science and Eastern philosophy during my therapy sessions.

I then received a unique opportunity to work as the superintendent of the only psychiatric hospital in Papua New Guinea in 1995. Although the culture was very different from India, the overarching issues with mental health seemed very similar. I was able to rely on my training and prior experience in India to bring culturally sensitive psychiatric practices to PNG. As superintendent of Laloki Psychiatric Hospital, I was able to deinstitutionalize almost half of the patients who were admitted there after being found not guilty of various crimes due to mental illness. A lot of these patients, as mentioned in the vignettes above, were suffering from culture-bound syndromes that resolved after the acute trauma that precipitated the condition had passed. I advocated to have them rehabilitated to their communities and set up a community psychiatry clinic for further follow-up. I also represented Papua New Guinea in the Pacific regional mental health plan with the WHO in Manila (1999).

I went on to work with refugees and was instrumental in developing a transcultural psychiatry service in Auckland, New Zealand, in 2000. I left the mental health landscape of PNG quite different from how I found it 5 years earlier. Regarding future directions, Papua New Guinea would benefit from adopting some of the methods that are being used in resource-poor regions in other parts of the developing world. Low-level psychological interventions, administered by laypeople or community health workers, have been effective in treating depression and anxiety in low- and middle-income countries (Rahman et al., 2013; Vanobberghen et al., 2020).

Summary

In sum, Papua New Guinean or Melanesian society is a traditional tribal society, exposed to modernity not long ago. PNG achieved independence about 46 years ago. Most people live in rural areas, and lead a community life, doing subsistence farming. The traditional values and rituals have been changed to some extent due to the influence of Christianity, though traditional/tribal culture is followed side by side. The provinces have not been well connected by roads or rails, only by air, but despite that transportation challenge, there is population movement to urban areas, which has led to increases in substance abuse and law and order problems.

Mental diseases often remain undetected due to lack of understanding and lack of service. Thus, depression, anxiety, and common psychotic disorders often remain untreated. There are hardly any community mental health services. There are no services for substance abuse disorders. There is no reliable data about suicide, which is often not reported. Suicidal overdose by chloroquine is unique in Papua New Guinea. Family violence is an issue, unreported mostly and addressed in the community in which they live.

Though patients received diagnoses such as schizophrenia and bipolar affective disorder, there was no report during my (the first author's) time in PNG of patients receiving personality disorder diagnoses, such as borderline or antisocial personality disorders. Eating disorders, such as anorexia nervosa and bulimia nervosa, have not been reported in contrast to Western cultures. Psychiatric medications are not easily available in most of the country. Regarding psychiatrists and nurses, there has been a shortage, and most services are available in urban areas. There is one psychologist based at the university. Most mental health support is provided by the Church clinics in urban and rural areas. In light of these challenges, recently, the government has been taking initiative to provide more resources to improve and deal with the lack of service.

References

Belief systems and spiritual aspects in Papua New Guinea: Culture of the countryside. (2021). Retrieved from http://www.cultureofthecountryside.ac.uk/resources/belief-systems-and-spiritual-aspects-papua-new-guinea

Burton-Bradley, B. G. (1985). The amok syndrome in Papua and New Guinea. In R. C. Simons & C. C. Hughes (Eds.), *The culture-bound syndromes* (pp. 237–249). Springer Netherlands. https://doi.org/10.1007/978-94-009-5251-5_22

Demographic and Health Survey. (2021). Papua New Guinea: National Statistical Office. Retrieved from https://www.nso.gov.pg/census-surveys/demographic-and-health-survey/

Grundy, J., Dakulala, P., Wai, K., Maalsen, A., & Whittaker, M. (2019). Independent state of Papua New Guinea: Health system review. *World Health Organization Regional Office for South-East Asia, 9*(1) Retrieved from http://www.searo.who.int/asia_pacific_observatory/publications/hits/hit_PNG/en/

Health: National Statistical Office: Papua New Guinea. (2021). Papua New Guinea: National Statistical Office. Retrieved from https://www.nso.gov.pg/statistics/health/

Hughes, F., Finlayson, M., Firkin, P., et al. (2005). *Situational analysis of mental health needs and resources in Pacific Island countries*. World Health Organization Regional Office for the Western Pacific.

Kasse, J. (2008). How the influence of missionaries and administrators strongly influenced the different developments in Papua New Guinea. Tribal Warrior. Retrieved from http://naturetropics.blogspot.com/2008/09/how-influenceof-missionaries-and.html

Koka, B. E., Deane, F. P., & Lambert, G. (2004). Health worker confidence in diagnosing and treating mental health problems in Papua New Guinea. *South Pacific Journal of Psychology, 15*, 29–42. https://doi.org/10.1017/s0257543400000146

Marai, L. (2007). The psychology of consensus in Melanesia. *Journal of Pacific Rim Psychology, 1*(2), 54–57. https://doi.org/10.1375/prp.1.2.54

Mental Health Atlas. (2005). Geneva, Switzerland: World Health Organization.

Muga, F. (2006). Psychiatry in Papua New Guinea. *International Psychiatry, 3*(3), 14–16. Retrieved from http://www.ncbi.nlm.nih.gov/pubmed/31507853

Noble, F. S. (1997). Long-term psychiatric care in Papua New Guinea. *Psychiatric Bulletin, 21*(2), 113–116. https://doi.org/10.1192/pb.21.2.113

Pal, S. (1997). Mental disorders in abnormal offenders in Papua New Guinea. *Medicine and Law, 16*(1), 87–95.

Papua New Guinea: A brief history from 8 – Papua New Guinea: RNZ. (2021). Retrieved from https://www.rnz.co.nz/collections/u/new-flags-flying/nff-png/about-png

Papua New Guinea: Daily life and social customs. (2021). Britannica. Retrieved from https://www.britannica.com/place/Papua-New-Guinea/Daily-life-and-social-customs

Parker, N., & Burton-Bradley, B. G. (1966). Suicide in Papua and New Guinea. *Medical Journal of Australia, 2*(24), 1125–1129. https://doi.org/10.5694/j.1326-5377.1966.tb91883.x

Prior, K. (2017, October 12). Is the traditional chewing of Betel nut killing Papua New Guinea? *BBC News*. Retrieved from https://www.bbc.com/news/world-asia-40884065

Rahman, A., Fisher, J., Bower, P., et al. (2013). Interventions for common perinatal mental disorders in women in low- and middle-income countries: A systematic review and meta-analysis. *Bulletin of the World Health Organization, 91*(8), 593–601. https://doi.org/10.2471/blt.12.109819

Vanobberghen, F., Weiss, H. A., Fuhr, D. C., et al. (2020). Effectiveness of the Thinking Healthy Programme for perinatal depression delivered through peers: Pooled analysis of two randomized controlled trials in India and Pakistan. *Journal of Affective Disorders, 265*, 660–668. https://doi.org/10.1016/j.jad.2019.11.110

Waiko, J. D. (1993). *A short history of Papua New Guinea* (2nd Revised Ed.). Sidney, Australia: Oxford University Press.

Chapter 11
The Polynesian Soul and the Modern World: Psychology Today in French Polynesia

Patrick Favro and Stéphane Amadéo

Introduction

"I hope that they will never be forgotten by us. [...] If therefore these good and friendly people are to be destroyed from our intercourse with them, unless they have timely assistance, I think it is the business of any of his Majesty's Ships that may come here to punish any such attempt". Thus wrote Captain Bligh upon leaving Tahiti in 1789 aboard HMS *Bounty* (Alexander, 2003).

The chapter will explore to what extent the statement is true from a psychological perspective. Indeed, FP went through dramatic changes over a period of 250 years, following what was later called the Contact. That started in 1767, with the landfall in Tahiti of the British ship HMS *Dolphin*, commanded by Samuel Wallis. From then on, FP evolved from a traditional society living in harmony with nature into a modernised territory. The colonisation strongly impacted the local population, mostly negatively, particularly seen from a traditional Polynesian perspective.

The so-called wider Pacific Island Blue Continent, especially Tahiti and Bora Bora, represents in the collective unconscious of Westerners idyllic places, with magnificent landscapes and a welcoming population. These descriptions, true to a very large extent, were born from the early writings by Europeans. The mutiny of HMS *Bounty* contributed to this international fame. Three movies (1935, 1962 and 1984) were shot after this dramatic episode. They are mostly romanticised versions and hardly reflect the pervasive violence, especially after the mutiny. It was not a

P. Favro (✉)
University of French Polynesia, EASTCO Laboratory, Tahiti, French Polynesia
e-mail: patrick.favro@upf.pf

S. Amadéo
Centre Hospitalier Universitaire de Fort de France, Inserm U1018, Paris, France

G. J. Rich, N. A. Ramkumar (eds.), *Psychology in Oceania and the Caribbean*, International and Cultural Psychology,
https://doi.org/10.1007/978-3-030-87763-7_11

happy story, as brutality, theft, rape and murder were rampant. Other writers (Pierre Loti, Victor Segalen and Herman Melville, to name but a few) and artists, most notably Gauguin, contributed to construct this paradisiac image.

This chapter will first present the geographical, historical, economic and societal context of this French part of the world. Then, it will give an overview of some issues related to the psychological scene, including a short description of ancient, and also new, approaches to psychology. To finish, it will attempt to assess the resources available now to deal with modern issues.

Context

Location and Geographical Description

FP occupies an exclusive maritime zone of 2.5 million km^2, virtually in the middle of the South Pacific Ocean. Tahiti is the main island (1042 sq. km). It is the economic and administrative centre of French Polynesia. FP has 118 islands (76 are inhabited) with an overall land area of around 4032 km^2. It is a group of five archipelagos: the Society Islands (including Tahiti), the Marquesas, the Tuamotus, the Gambiers and the Austral Islands. All islands are highly volcanic islands, except the Tuamotus and a few islands in the Gambiers, which are atolls, that is, low-lying coral islands. FP enjoys a hot and humid tropical climate, cooler in the Austral Islands, drier and hotter in the Marquesas. Hot and rainy from November to April, it is cooler and drier from May to October.

Demography

Its population is estimated at 279,300 in 2020, mostly urban, which is a problem per se. According to the last censuses, its population is ageing, and the demographic transition to a Western-style model is underway. Despite this ageing, the population of French Polynesia is younger than the French average. In FP, 3.2% of the population is 75 years old or over compared to 9.6% in mainland France (ISPF, 2020). FP is a multicultural society. The majority of the population is made up of so-called "native" Polynesians, whose ancestors came from successive waves of immigration by sea, from Southeast Asia. Then came Europeans, from the end of the eighteenth century, and finally the first Chinese in the 1860s, to work in plantations. The population is approximately divided as follows: two-thirds are Polynesians, one-fifth are *Demis* (mixed race between the three ethnic groups represented in Polynesia), 10% *Popa'a* (native from France) and 5% Chinese (*Les Nouvelles de Tahiti*, 2008). These percentages can only be estimates, because the distinction by ethnic group does not exist in the official censuses of the French Republic. Moreover, the mixing of races is so intricate that it is virtually impossible to classify the inhabitants according to race.

Languages

French is the dominant language, and it is used in business, teaching, law and domains open to other countries. It is spoken by over 90% of the population, with various degrees of fluency and command. Local languages are Tahitian, Marquesan, Pa'uomotu, Rapa and Mangareeviean. These languages were initially forbidden by the French colonisers, but they now enjoy a revival. Tahitian is taught in schools and at the University of FP. Quite a few television and radio programmes are in Tahitian.

History and Politics

According to certain hypotheses, the Polynesian people left the coasts of Southeast Asia to reach, over centuries, in turn, the islands of Samoa, Fiji and Tonga, before gradually settling in the Marquesas Islands, Easter Island, today's FP, Hawaii and eventually New Zealand. Europeans first arrived in Polynesia in the sixteenth century. Magellan was the first to land in the Tuamotus in 1521, followed by the Spaniards in 1595 in the Marquesas. The Society Islands were discovered at the end of the eighteenth century when Wallis landed in Tahiti in 1767. Bougainville, in 1768, compared Tahiti to Eden. Joseph Banks, the famous botanist on HMS *Endeavour* commanded by Captain Cook, described Tahiti as "An Arcadia of which we are going to be kings" (quoted in Price, 1958). It became a French protectorate in 1842, then a colony in 1880. It took the name of French Polynesia after WWII. In the 1960s, the construction of the Tahiti-Faa'a airport, and especially the installation of the Pacific Experimentation Centre (CEP), led to an upheaval of the economy and society. Politically, a local territorial assembly has authority over a number of areas (e.g. secondary education, health, local police, the economy). However, the French state retains its prerogatives in the fields of defence, foreign relations, higher education, law and order and finance.

Economy

French Polynesia went through an abrupt transition in the 1960s from a subsistence economy (fishing and agriculture) to a modern society with the domination of the tertiary sector. Today the economy is heavily based on tourism and on money transfers from France. Exports are minimal: black pearl (50% in 2019) and to a far lesser extent fish, copra and vanilla. Consequently, the local economy has been drip-fed from the late 1990s, since it heavily depends on financial transfers (about 34% of the GDP) from metropolitan France, as a compensation for the end of nuclear testing in 1996. The GDP per capita in 2019 was about half of that of France. However, FP is one of the richest territories in the South Pacific. The unemployment rate for the Society Islands is 14.7%. Taking a broader definition, 22% of the population are jobless. Unemployment particularly affects young people and the low-skilled: 40% of 15–24-year-olds are considered unemployed (ISPF, 2018). Homelessness (a few hundred people), sometimes related to psychiatric issues, is a side effect of unemployment and is reinforced by the erosion of family structures due to modernisation. According to the CTC (2020), FP employs too many civil servants, and many of them are underqualified. It recommends reducing the staff, which numbers over 8000 workers in various sectors (health, agriculture, housing, social services etc.).

Health

The health situation in FP, compared to France, is worrying, particularly for diseases linked to the risky behaviours (e.g. eating habits, sedentary lifestyle, obesity, smoking, alcoholism) of part of the population. The prevalence of these diseases is particularly alarming. Significant rate differences with metropolitan France and FP were observed in cardiovascular diseases (2.3 times higher rate in FP). Chronic pathologies (diabetes, obesity, arterial hypertension, cancers, ischaemic heart disease etc.) were responsible for 40% of premature mortality in 2005–2010 (Yen Kai Sun et al., 2016).

French Polynesia, like the islands and island states of the South Pacific, has a high prevalence of obesity. According to two surveys (1995 and 2010), 70% of the adult population is overweight, and 40% is in the obesity stage. This public health problem affects the infant population from an early age (Surpoids & obésité: https://www.service-public.pf/dsp/surpoids-obesite/).

Religion

One lesser well-known characteristic of French Polynesia is the significance of religion: "There is one point that does not fail to attract attention, it is the deeply religious character of the Polynesian people. Religious life is extremely lively and active in Tahiti and on all the archipelagos" (Garcia, 2006). This situation results from efficient Christianisation from the end of the eighteenth century (Protestants and Catholics), which continued into the nineteenth and twentieth centuries: Mormons, Sanito, Adventists and Jehovah's Witnesses, to name only the best-known churches. The most recent figures are from 1998 (Prenveille), with approximate percentages of the population for each group: Protestants, 45%; Catholics, 34%; Seventh-Day Adventists, 2.5%; Mormons, 5%; Sanitos, 2.5%; Jehovah's

Witnesses, 1.5%; others, 9.5%. Statistics on denominational membership are almost impossible to collect, as one would have to rely on the impressions of members of congregations. No recent official figures exist, due to legal restrictions related to questions on religious affiliation; they are absent from censuses.

The Polynesian Psyche

Many navigators, missionaries, travellers and anthropologists have provided observations on the Polynesian psyche. Ships were greeted with exuberance, for example, HMS *Bounty* (Kennedy, 1989). The missionaries of the LMS (London Missionary Society), when they sang religious hymns, were struck by the sensitivity to the melodies of the Tahitians, who were described as rather calm. Their theatricality was also noted, such as their way of expressing joy, anger and sorrow; paradoxically, they appear to be very stoic (Oliver, 1974). Dysthymia is perceived in the Tahitians' mood, which can present in sudden, superficial, rapid and unmotivated variations. Polynesians can go from laughter to tears with disconcerting ease. This playful appearance contributed to the image of the myth of Tahiti and its "childlike" people (Garcia, 2006). These observations come from the West and are potentially biased by Eurocentrism.

The issue of stereotypes in FP was partially addressed by Saura (2004): the *popa'a* are perceived by the Polynesians as "individualists" and "intellectuals". Research tends to confirm these clichés: the lexical field of speech and thought is often used to describe the *popa'a*. Some judgements are critical and mainly come from the *Demis* and Polynesians: "too authoritarian", "like to complain". Polynesians are described as, "not so hardworking", but also "welcoming", "kind", friendly", but also "aggressive", "shy", "spendthrift", "love their culture" and "carpe diem, impulse buying" (Favro, 2008). Anyone who has lived for some time in FP will confirm all or part of these comments.

Therefore, Polynesians are known to be smiling, welcoming, generous, joyful, friendly, happily living in the now and optimistic. Geographical determinism might provide an engaging explanatory hypothesis. Polynesians, before European arrival and settlement, lived in a bountiful environment (fruit, vegetable, fish) under a warm climate ideal for abundant tropical crops. The history of that population suggests other arguments. That population navigated over the Pacific Ocean in successive waves over centuries, and survived, potentially making survivors optimistic. Moreover, before the Contact, this population never went through invasions and occupation by foreigners; so, distrust is virtually absent. Even the first contacts and subsequent colonisation were not as violent as in other regions of the globe. Despite occasional fights and skirmishes, no significant war broke out there. To finish with, they do not bear the stigma of slavery, unlike in Jamaica, as explained in another chapter in this book. History often shapes national character, as in the United States. A similar process, together with a bounteous natural environment, may have shaped the collective identity of Polynesians.

The Polynesian mentality has been necessarily altered since the Contact due to the intermingling of races and acculturation. Walker, a *Demi* trying to revive ancestral Polynesian religion, talks about a cultural trauma caused by the arrival of missionaries and Western society. Polynesian culture was systematically denigrated and suppressed. Western culture and religion were seen as better, hence imposed on the natives, sometimes resulting in an inferiority complex among the latter. To this people described as "religious" by many observers, material ambitions only are offered, deplores Walker (2009) who notes, "We are in a world where materialism predominates, where the spiritual is side-lined, stifled, which means that the young, today, see the future only through concrete, material things, so they realize that the future is completely dark. That's unfortunate". He goes on to add, "attachment to a spirituality is a good solution [to manage discomfort], provided this is well organised and structured, so as to be as sure as possible, that it becomes an answer [to today's problems]". Because of secularisation in French Polynesia (Favro, 2009) that reflects a loss of the social significance of religion, Christianity often has become only a fragile protection against addictions. Consequently, gradually the weakened religious framework paved the way for new habits to develop in FP, including alcohol and cannabis consumption.

Culture and Psychology in FP

Saura (2008) underlines the difficulty of apprehending "Polynesian 'culture'" because it has been considerably ill-treated since the Contact. Only fragments have remained, which were reconstituted, or even reinterpreted, by Western-minded researchers. Their point of view is therefore potentially biased. However, this approach pervades a culturalist clinical current informed by ethno-psychology and is very influential within the AFAREP (Association for Training, Action and Research in Polynesia). This current postulates that psychic disorders are partly caused by a conflict between the values of the original Polynesian, but also Chinese (Sin Chan, 2002) cultures, and Western culture. The improvement of the psychic state of culturally uprooted individuals could occur if they can reconnect with their ancestral identities, in particular by an elaboration in psychoanalytical style or through some work with Tahitian names. This approach by "the members of AFAREP contributes to the development of some kind of neo-paganism in French Polynesia at the beginning of the 21st century" (Saura, 2008). "If clinical ethnopsychology, which connects the individual (private) dimension of conflicts and a (collective) cultural understanding has been very popular in Tahiti since the 1990s, it should not be forgotten that it is very controversial in France and elsewhere. More than a cultural approach of the psychic disorders of individuals and groups, it is sometimes (whatever its proponents may say) a form of culture-bound therapy. As such, it deserves the same critical perspective with which Western ethnocentrism should be taken" (Saura, 2008). From a more scientific perspective, intercultural psychology explores the role played by culture in structuring the psyche of ethnic groups (Guerraoui & Troadec, 2000).

Ancient Polynesian Psychology

Before the arrival of Europeans, there was no differentiation between physical illnesses and mental illnesses. Human beings were considered as having three dimensions: the physical body (*tino*), the mind (*mana'o*) and the soul (*varua*). *Varua* contains a divine essence because it is linked to the most distant ancestors. It goes back to the invisible world after death (Grand, 2007). Diseases can be caused by evil people (e.g. witch attacks and spells), the attack by a wandering spirit which can "possess" the living or the transgression of a taboo by the sick person or a relative. Transgression leads to the discontent of one of the many gods of the Tahitian pantheon against the one who transgressed rules or who neglected his religious duties.

The *tahu'a* is the healer, who works through both physical means (herbs, massage) and religious means (prayer, incantations, ceremonies) (Grand, 2007). Etymologically, the word *tahu'a* probably means "the one who lights the fire", but also "the one who casts words". These healers claimed to have received their knowledge directly from the gods or through contact with their ancestors. The role of the *tahu'a* corresponds to similar types of healers, such as shamans, medicine men or druids in other traditional cultures. As an intercessor, he mediates between the visible world (human beings and nature) and the invisible world (supernatural, transcendent dimensions). He represents religious and spiritual authority. He is responsible for maintaining order in the community (Blanchet, 2007).

Change took place under the influence of European thought, including Cartesian dualism. The *tahu'a* gradually lost prestige and authority because of Christianisation and colonisation. European priests took over, partly because traditional Polynesians healers were unable to cure foreign diseases. This traditional Polynesian psycho-spiritual paradigm, both animistic and polytheistic, gives a prominent place to the supernatural, which has been excluded from modern approaches to psychology.

Redefining Psychology

Etymologically, the word "psychology", coined in 1575 by Swiss humanist J. Freigius, means the study of the soul. Modern psychology was massively influenced by psychiatry, hence medicine, experimental psychology (Wundt and Pavlov) and Freudian psychoanalysis. Consequently, its potentially spiritual dimensions were dismissed to the benefit of behavioural, instinctual and intellectual characteristics. Later developments in psychology altered this reductionist trend. R. Assagioli created psychosynthesis. A. Maslow and Carl Rogers were the driving figures of humanistic psychology. Viktor Frankl was the founder of existential psychology, and later co-founded transpersonal psychology, with A. Maslow and S. Grof. In sum, today's psychology is predominantly materialistic and reductionistic, compared to the traditional Polynesian perception of human beings as presented above.

Key Issues Related to Psychology

Substance Misuse

FP has the highest rate of addictions among French overseas territories (e.g. alcohol, tobacco and cannabis, locally called *paka*), with one specific local consumption, *kava*, a traditional psychotropic plant. Alcohol consumption in FP is especially prevalent. Its use is even more widespread than in metropolitan France. Polynesian specificities for smoking stem from the rapid increase in consumption during adolescence, early initiations and a comparative over-representation of women. The spread of cannabis appears to be very strong in FP, where half of the consumers started at a young age (before 14). Among young Polynesians, girls are almost as impacted as boys by the consumption of *paka*. Ice is a new drug, and is highly addictive, hence leading to even more risky uses and behaviours, causing heavy damage. However, data on consumption, trafficking and production is scarce and insufficiently reliable (Obradovic, 2020).

A previous report highlighted similar issues (Beck & Brugiroux, 2010). It noted a trivialisation of these uses despite a good knowledge of the risks involved. Thus, the messages of prevention conveyed for several years have been heard, yet not heeded. These messages come up against the great availability of products and the fact that alcohol and cannabis often appear as the only means to face the hardships of life. Moreover, in FP, the well-established practices of consumption are associated with partying, at any age. The same report suggested some solutions based on improving emotional intelligence. Teenagers ask for information on improving self-confidence and self-esteem. The results confirm the need to set up prevention programmes based on the development of personal and social skills, including management of emotions, and communication. *Kava* was traditionally used as a psychotropic drug by Polynesians in a ritualised form, within a religious framework. According to S. Grand (personal e-mail), in the period of successive epidemics brought by Europeans, *kava* was consumed during mourning by the distraught populations. The missionaries considered everything Polynesian as diabolical, so they banned the use of *kava* and replaced it with tobacco and alcohol. These licit drugs have wreaked terrible havoc since then.

Suicide

Alcohol is a risk factor with regard to issues relevant to suicide, and thus religion becomes a protective factor, as churches discourage or forbid alcohol consumption (Amadéo, 1998; Kendler et al., 1997). Therefore, religion might be a potential protective factor against suicide. Religious values, practices and messages provide various types of support for individuals going through suicidal crises (Favro, 2009). Years ago, Jung (1958) pointed out that "modern man - Protestant or not - has lost the protection of ecclesiastical ramparts". Suicide did exist in French Polynesia in premodern times, as recounted in legends gathered by Henry (1928), but its prevalence has increased with modernisation (Amadéo, 2014). However, standardised suicide rates per year over the 25 years of the 1992–2016 period were relatively stable, and the rate for 2016 (8.3 suicides per 100,000 inhabitants) was close to that of 1992 (7.1 per 100,000 inhabitants) (Amadéo et al., 2021a). The comparison of suicide rates shows lower rates in Polynesia than in mainland France (Amadéo, 2014).

Mental Health Disorders

The recent Mental Health in the General Population: Images and Realities (MHGP) survey aimed at identifying issues related to mental health in FP. The survey found that lifetime prevalence of any mental disorder was 42.8%, with mood and anxiety disorders being the most frequent (20.5% and 26%, respectively). In the sample, all the mental disorders were correlated with a significantly higher suicidal risk. The high prevalence of suicidal risk in FP could therefore be explained by the high prevalence of mental disorders, since they were found at higher rates than in all the other sites of the MHGP survey. Greater impulsiveness of acting out, and hence less preparation for suicide attempts, is in keeping with the observation that deaths by suicide are less frequent in FP than in France, while suicide attempts are more frequent in FP. However, these figures should be taken with care, since they are based on self-report statements by the interviewees in the survey (Amadéo et al., 2021c).

Psychological Resources in French Polynesia

The French state is the main agent for organising and financing the psychological resources in FP, through various structures. The French state provides inpatient, outpatient, day treatment and community outreach, thanks to psychiatrists, psychologists and social workers. The first hospital that accommodated mental patients, Vaiami, was created in Papeete in 1913. Most mental health care has been provided by the CHPF of Taaone (main hospital) since 2003, after a transition in the Centre Hospitalier Territorial (CHT) of Mamao built in the 1970s. Vaiami was then converted into a mental hospital only, but was ill-adapted to modern psychiatry, in so far as the buildings were on the verge of being squalid ruins, badly understaffed and managed in military style. Non-psychotic patients (suicidal and depressed) were often taken care of in the CHT. The psychiatric department was fully transferred to the CHPF in 2003, with reinforcements in staff and improvement in treatments. Consultations were gradually extended to all Tahiti, then to all islands.

The department of psychiatry of the CHPF has 11 psychiatrists and 4 psychologists. A dozen psychologists work in other departments (oncology, general practice, maternity, haemodialysis etc.). However, mental health care is not as well provided in French Polynesia (1 psychiatric sector for roughly 150,000 inhabitants) as in metropolitan France (1 psychiatric sector for 56,000 inhabitants on average) (Projet de Service du Département de Psychiatrie, 2020). Pedopsychiatry was integrated in the CHPF in 2013; it is a unit of the department called Centre Thérapeutique à Temps Partiel (CATTP). Four psychiatrists, four psychologists and five social workers work there. The Department of Health has two psychiatrists. A project initiative for mental health in FP has been launched for the period 2019–2023 by the Ministry of Health (Plan de santé mentale, 2018). It aims at improving psychological well-being by working to ensure the whole population is able to access care and also strives to detect mental disorders earlier.

Several other public systems/organisations provide care for psychological issues to the population. The *Fare tama Hau* offers care for mothers and children and teenagers. The team of professionals working there includes two doctors, including a part-time nutritionist, three clinical psychologists, two nurses, three specialist educators and four social workers. The *CCSAT* is specialised in treating addictions, which are more prevalent in FP than in France, as described above. Currently, it has one doctor and two psychiatrists, five clinical psychologists, three nurses and one physiotherapist. The *DSFE* (Department of Solidarity, Families and Equality) employs 12 clinical psychologists, working for 10 administrative areas all over FP. Its main mission is to support, protect and counsel families and children in social and judicial issues. Psychologists may work according to different psychological influences and specialties, for instance, psychoanalysis, systemic psychology, child development, psychopathology and gerontology. They provide free counselling for individuals of any age, with any type of mental or social issue, when they go through psychological crises. These individuals are referred to psychologists by social workers and partners or can ask for help out of their own initiative. Group sessions are possible, and include collaboration with social workers. Supervision is carried out collectively, so as to analyse and improve interventions. They also take part in meetings in order to organise new projects, forever adapting to issues that may crop up. Research is also part of their professional activity (ad hoc communication from the DFSE). Moreover, psychologists can be found in a whole array of other organisations and settings: for instance, in training centres, with the police and in education. 35 educational psychologists (specialised in education, development and counselling in educational and vocational orientation) and 18 *EDA* psychologists (specialised in learning) work on the 5 archipelagos and contribute to facilitating schooling in FP.

Apart from these mental health professionals working in public settings, FP also has about 20 psychologists maintaining private practices with various levels of professional activity. Nine psychiatrists having private practices are identified by the CPS (local social security), but only six actually practice.

Role of Traditional Healing

The reported use of traditional Polynesian medicines is often mentioned in the MHGP study. The choice to directly ask about the use of traditional medicines, body care or healers with the corresponding Polynesian terms, may have helped to better reflect the importance of traditional medicine among Polynesians. Moreover, this use is mostly reported by people who identify themselves as Polynesian or of mixed race. This result is consistent with clinical practice. A large proportion of patients still use either traditional healers (*tahu'a*), monoi oil massage (*taurumi*) or herbal medicines (*raau tahiti*). These practices have been incorporated into the mental health plan for FP, which aims at improving mental health care and promoting mental health (Amadéo et al., 2021b). The still very significant use of traditional therapies was reported in an ethno-psychiatric study carried out in the "Polynesian triangle" (Grand, 2007). More recently, meetings between traditional practitioners and health-care personnel in the CHPF have begun, with a view to providing health care that takes traditional culture more into account (Poanui, 2019). Another example of this attempt at integrating complementary, traditional and modern care is a clinical trial of a suicide prevention programme. This scheme combines traditional practices (*monoi* massage) with psychiatric and psychological care. It has provided promising results in reducing the frequency of suicidal acts (Amadéo et al., 2020). These approaches are recommended by the WHO in order to develop integrative medicine (WHO, 2013). At the CHPF, in the palliative care unit, some physicians are assisted by traditional healers, and a young woman specialised in bridging the gap between the two worlds of care and cultures has been recruited. The psychiatric department also uses the collaboration of declared *tahu'a* (Grand, personal e-mail, 2021).

Conclusion

Modernisation is not evil per se. However, modernisation without a soul becomes evil. What has happened in FP over the last 250 years is a case study in that respect. A very similar destructive pattern can be observed in many other parts of the world, such as in Australia and in the Americas. Psychology as it is now in FP is woefully inadequate to deal with the damage done there by soulless modernisation. As shown in this chapter, the many changes that FP went through since the Contact were dramatic and not only from a psychological perspective. The scope of this article does not allow for the exploration of other issues, including the fallout from nuclear testing in Moruroa for the atoll and the local population. Damage to the natural environment, growing urbanisation and subsequent noise, unemployment and poverty, and homelessness are some of the many other dark facets of modernisation. Dropping out of school is also a problem; after leaving school, the idle youth may turn to petty crime and destructiveness. Local newspapers occasionally report these deviant behaviours.

To conclude, Captain Bligh's statement was visionary and insightful; he was also compassionate, an aspect of his personality sometimes ignored. The "intercourse" with "these good and friendly people" did not benefit them in all respects, even though quite a few Polynesians now enjoy domestic and international flights, massive FWDs, cable TV, the latest smartphones and fast Internet connections. Paradoxically Western civilisation also brought some means to try to solve the problems it created, i.e. psychology. On balance, however, the drawbacks have been greater than the benefits. In other words, modern psychology is a partial and limited solution to these deeply rooted issues, whose causes are imbedded in time and newly adopted destructive attitudes.

Mindfulness could help. Jon Kabat-Zinn has helped popularise its practice. Originally a Buddhist practice aiming at reaching nirvana, it has also been scientifically demonstrated to improve physical, emotional and mental health. It is taught in a few schools in FP, and used by one psychologist at the CHPF, and occasionally summarily presented in some classes at the University of FP. The modern world could also learn from ancient Polynesian wisdom and practices. S. Walker is the president of the *Te Hivarereata* association, which works at reviving the pre-Christian polytheistic animist religion. It is a very small minority movement, which promotes a potentially resilient and hopeful perspective. The purpose of this association, created in 1999, is to "bring us closer to the ancient *ma'ohi* [i.e. Tahitian] deities and to venerate them through ancient rites that we try to adapt to our mentalities today. In practice, it behoves us to immerse ourselves in ancestral spirituality by keeping the concepts and symbols relating to the values of wisdom, well-being among men and, as much as possible, symbiosis with our environment" (http://www.tehivarereata.com/pages/colloque_sur_la_mort_lintervention_de_moanaura_w-815135.html).

A return to ancestral ways of life is impossible. History cannot be undone, yet our destructive, disenchanting and disenchanted modern life could find inspiring approaches in almost extinct traditions. Indeed, unless novel approaches and solutions are considered, and unless a longer time perspective is adopted, the issues observed in FP and in other parts of the world could well spell disaster for mankind. A new attitude to, and interest in, nature and the environment is fashionable, and hopefully not superficial. Mentalities are slowly evolving. This chapter does not aim at painting too bleak a picture of what used to be pristine unspoilt islands. It aims to be soberly realistic, ideally. Soulful modernisation is the hope. Despite quite a few ugly aspects, including environmental, societal and psychological dimensions, FP is still a wonderful world, with beautiful people.

Acknowledgements Myriam Pain, President of the *CPFP* (Association of Psychologists in French Polynesia (FP)), for facilitating the writing of this chapter through communication within the association, the psychologists of *DSFE* (Department of Solidarity, Families and Equality) represented by Tumata Vaitoare and the association *Taputea Ora*, working for the promotion of mental health, which provided relevant information.

References

Alexander, C. (2003). *The Bounty: The true story of the mutiny of the Bounty*. Harper.

Amadéo, S. (1998). *Addictions: Étude des facteurs génétiques et culturels en Polynésie – maniaco-dépressions et suicides: Facteurs génétiques*. Doctoral thesis, Université Française du Pacifique.

Amadéo, S. (Ed.). (2014). *Suicide à Tahiti: Le paradoxe du suicide au paradis, éléments de compréhension et propositions de prévention*. Ed. L'Harmattan.

Amadéo, S., et al. (2020). Supporting effect of body mediation care with ylang aromatherapy and mobile intervention team in suicide prevention: A pilot study. *Journal of International Medical Research, 48*(9), 1–16.

Amadéo, S., et al. (2021a). Suicide in French Polynesia: A retrospective analysis based on medicolegal documents and interview with family. *Journal of International Medical Research, 0*(0), 1–15.

Amadéo, S., et al. (2021b, in submission). *Social representations, recourse to traditional care and other anthropo-cultural aspects of mental health in French Polynesia in the survey "Mental health in the general population: Images and Realities"*.

Amadéo, S., et al. (2021c). French Polynesia suicidal risk: Results of the survey mental health in general population: Images and realities.

Beck, F., & Brugiroux, M.-F. (2010). *Les conduites addictives des adolescents polynésiens*. Cerf.

Blanchet, A. (2007). Analyse critique des psychothérapies. In S. Ionescu & A. Blanchet (Eds.), *Psychologie clinique, pathologique et psychothérapie*. PUF.

CTC. (Chambre Territoriale des Comptes) – FP. (2020).

Favro, P. (2008). Perception d'une "discrimination positive" et des relations inter-ethniques à Tahiti, *Tahiti Pacifique Magazine*.

Favro, P. (2009). *Suicide attempts and religion*. Unpublished MD dissertation in Clinical Psychology.

Garcia, G. (2006). *Suicide et tentative de suicide en Polynésie française*. Université de la Méditerranée, Faculté de Médecine.

Grand, S. (2007). *Tahu'a, tohunga, kahuna. Le monde polynésien des soins traditionnels*. Au Vent des îles.

Guerraoui, Z., & Troadec, B. (2000). *Psychologie interculturelle*. Armand Colin.

Henry, T. (1928, 1997). *Ancient Tahiti. Tahiti aux temps anciens*. Société des océanistes.

ISPF. (2018). Etude Enquête Emploi.

ISPF. (2020). *Points Etudes et Bilans de la Polynésie française n° 2156*. 2020 – Bilan démographique 2020. Institut de la statistique de Polynésie française. Retrieved from https://www.ispf.pf/docs/default-source/publi-pf-bilans-et-etudes/1256-bilan-demographique-2020.pdf?sfvrsn=4

Jung, C. G. (1958). *Psychology and religion*. Routledge & Kegan Paul.

Kendler, K., Gardner, C., & Prescott, C. (1997). Religion, psychopathology, and substance use and abuse: A multimeasure, genetic-epidemiologic study. *American Journal of Psychiatry, 154*, 322–329.

Kennedy, G. (1989). *Captain Bligh: The man and his mutinies*. Abacus.

Les Nouvelles de Tahiti. 19 novembre 2008.

Obradovic, I. (2020). *Drogues et addictions dans les Outremers*. OFDT.

Oliver, D. (1974). *Ancient Tahitian society* (Social relations) (Vol. 2). The University Press of Hawaii.

Poanui, G. (2019). *Un projet polynésien de médecine intégrative. Analyse ethno-médicale de la rencontre entre Tradipraticiens et Professionnels de Santé à Tahiti*. Thèse de Médecine. Université Claude Bernard – Lyon 1.

Prenveille, E. (1998, May). *Horizon Magazine*, n°328, mai, pp. 33–34.

Price, G. (1958). *The explorations of Captain Cook*. Georgian House.

Projet de Service du Département de Psychiatrie Adulte. (2020). CHPF. Department of Psychiatry. Internal document.

Saura, B. (2004). *Des Tahitiens, des Français: Leurs représentations réciproques aujourd'hui*. Au vent des îles.
Saura, B. (2008). *Tahiti ma'ohi*. Au vent des îles.
Sin Chan, E. (2002). *Psychopathologie et identité des Hakka de Polynésie française*. Doctoral thesis.
Surpoids & obésité. (2021). Retrieved from https://www.service-public.pf/dsp/surpoids-obesite/
Walker, S. (2009). Interview in Pira'e, Tahiti.
WHO. (2013). *WHO strategy for traditional medicine for 2014–2023*. Retrieved from https://apps.who.int/iris/bitstream/handle/10665/95009/9789242506099_fre.pdf?sequence=1
Yen Kai Sun, L., Ghosn, W., & Rey, G. (2016). Les causes de décès en Polynésie française: Analyse de la période 2005–2010 et tendances évolutives de 1984 à 2010. *Buletin Epidémiol Hebd, 10*, 183–195. Retrieved from http://www.invs.sante.fr/beh/2016/10/2016_10_2.html

Part II
Psychology in the Caribbean

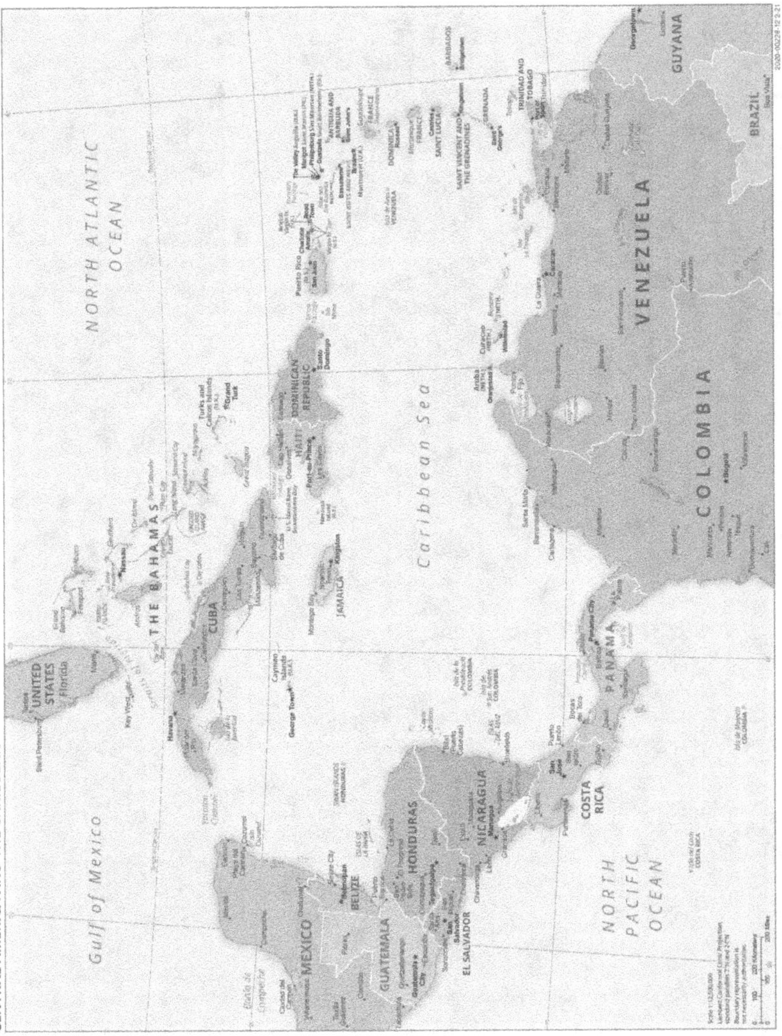

Fig. a *Political Central America Map. The World Factbook 2021*. Washington, DC: Central Intelligence Agency, 2021

Chapter 12
An Examination of the Landscape of Psychology in Jamaica

Gillian E. Mason and Kai A. D. Morgan

The history of psychology in the Caribbean, including Jamaica, is relatively new when compared to other geographical regions. The earliest evidence of a psychological examination of Jamaica or Jamaicans is the personality analysis done by an English social psychologist who in the late 1940s worked on the West Indian Social Survey (Rey, 1953). As it relates to psychological practice, starting from the 1960s the Government's health ministry employed clinical psychologists to work within their psychiatric services.

From these beginnings the field of psychology in Jamaica has experienced significant growth especially in the last two decades. Currently, we have over 100 psychologists from a range of subfields and approximately 15 degree programmes. It therefore appears that psychological resources in Jamaica are growing and there is great promise for the future. But the assessment of the state of psychology should be measured by whether the level of resources matches the needs of the country. To complete that assessment, one would therefore need to identify what psychological needs exist. So, what is Jamaica all about?

"*We likkle but we tallawah!*". This popular Jamaican saying can be translated as "we are physically small, but we are big in stature" and is the way some people describe the country. For many, this small island (just 146 miles long) is punching way above its weight class in terms of its worldwide popularity. With a population of less than 2.8 million (Statistical Institute of Jamaica, 2019), Jamaica has produced personalities who have had significant worldwide impact such as Marcus

G. E. Mason (✉)
Department of Sociology, Psychology, and Social Work, The University of the West Indies (Mona), Kingston, Jamaica
e-mail: gillian.mason@uwimona.edu.jm

K. A. D. Morgan
Jamaican Psychological Society, Kingston, Jamaica

G. J. Rich, N. A. Ramkumar (eds.), *Psychology in Oceania and the Caribbean*, International and Cultural Psychology, https://doi.org/10.1007/978-3-030-87763-7_12

Garvey, Bob Marley, and Usain Bolt. The seeming contrast between Jamaica's small physical size and its worldwide reach is one of many paradoxes that can be used to describe the country. Unfortunately, not all of Jamaica's paradoxes are as positive as this one.

For instance, Jamaica is simultaneously paradise for many due to its physical beauty, riveting music such as reggae, delectable food, and welcoming citizens and hell for many due to its high rates of violence, lack of basic resources, and poverty. Some may view it as a racial melting pot as its citizens are descendants from all races and many continents, and there are few reports of racial or nationalistic conflicts. However, many others perceive its racial structure as one of colourism or shadism with unofficial privileges existing for persons with a lighter skin tone (Charles, 2010; Hickling, 2008).

We have introduced here an overview of psychological resources in Jamaica and hinted at some key areas of psychological need. In the rest of this chapter, we will present a fuller analysis of the situation. This involves examining what key needs we perceive exist and what resources are available and discussing challenges which may affect the meeting of these needs. We also include our recommendations for addressing those challenges.

Key Psychological Needs for Jamaica

In their launch of the *Caribbean Journal of Psychology*, editors Branche, Minor, and Ramkissoon (2004) wrote about the clear presence within the Caribbean of "significant psychological challenges at the individual, group and social structural/cultural levels" (p. 3). These challenges directly connect to the history of the region, so as for any client of psychological care, examining the history of this "client" (i.e. Jamaica) is imperative to understanding current psychological challenges.

Jamaica's history in relation to the rest of the world starts with European colonisation followed by a long period of European chattel enslavement of persons from Africa, a short period of a migration-based indentured labour system, and political rule by Britain until 1962. Although Jamaica's history is broader than its period of plantation life and colonial rule, no one can deny the far-reaching tangible and intangible effects, including psychological, of that period (Morgan & O'Garo, 2008). These effects are felt by descendants of all racial actors (i.e. European, African), but since nearly 92% of Jamaicans self-identify as black or black-mixed (Kelly, 2020), the focus here is on those of African ancestry.

The debilitating effects of being enslaved have been noted by researchers and cover all stages of the experience. There is the effect of capture and the journey to the ships which transported the captured to the West Indies; the horrors of the journey by sea; and then the impact of being held captive in a foreign land, forced to provide free labour under extremely harsh and violent conditions with seemingly little control over one's life and future (Hutton, 1996; Sawh & Scales, 2006; Shepherd & Reid, 2019; Thomas, 2020). Each aspect of this experience resulted in negative psychological effects for many of the enslaved such as general anxiety, depression, suicidal ideation and suicide itself, and post-traumatic slavery disorder, as well as personality disorders (Hickling et al., 2011). Longman-Mills et al. (2019) note that at the time of the end of legal slavery, the formerly enslaved who had experienced psychological, physical, and sexual trauma were "released" to determine their own survival with no provisions provided for "psychological or economic restoration" (p. 86). Without any resolution of these harms, researchers assert there is an intergenerational inheritance of this trauma through beliefs, attitudes, and values (Akbar, 2021; DeGruy, 2017).

It can be argued that this "inheritance" manifests today in both internal (i.e. towards, and within the self) and external (i.e. towards others in the society) experiences. Internal indicators include some Jamaicans grappling with issues of identity and low self-esteem (Morgan & O'Garo, 2008) and battling personality disorders (Charles, 2010; Hickling et al., 2011). Externally, Jamaica, as documented since its independence in 1962, has consistently had high rates of violent crimes and has often ranked among the top ten of the most violent countries in the world (Harriott & Jones, 2016; United Nations Development Programme [UNDP], 2009). InSight Crime's report indicates that for 2020, Jamaica had the highest homicide rate for the Latin America and Caribbean region at 46.5 per 100,000 people (Asmann & Jones, 2021).

But Jamaica's criminal activities are not limited to homicide. Bailey (1999) identified a connection between Jamaica's murder rate and the occurrence of other violent crimes (e.g. robbery, rape). In addition, there exists a legacy of violence within the context of harsh and shaming disciplinary approaches levied by parents and other caregivers, so a general atmosphere of interpersonal violence persists in the country (Brown & Johnson, 2008; Meeks Gardner et al., 2006; Pottinger, 2012). This wider atmosphere is demonstrated in recent research which shows that nearly 28% of Jamaican women report having experienced physical or sexual violence by a partner (Watson-Williams, 2018) and a situational analysis which found that 68 out of every 100,000 Jamaican children have been victims of violent crimes (Caribbean Policy Research Institute [CAPRI] & UNICEF, 2018). Therefore, irrespective of age or gender, Jamaican citizens exist within an atmosphere where violence and/or abuse is a real possibility, and for many citizens it is the reality. Work-from-home and school-at-home orders implemented since April 2020 due to the COVID-19 pandemic have served to make this reality even worse for some Jamaicans (CAPRI, 2021).

Of course, violence is not the only negative sequelae of the historical experience of chattel slavery and colonialism. Financial and racial inequities are other long-standing problems for Jamaica with some attributing a direct connection to the systems built and fostered during slavery (Patterson, 1969). Like the inequity that existed during the period of enslavement, there is still great financial inequity among Jamaicans. For instance, 60% of Jamaica's wealth is controlled by just 10% of the population (Kelly, 2020). The nature of racial inequity in the Jamaican society has transitioned over time. The original plantation system produced a structure which equated whiteness with power and blackness with servitude (Patterson, 1969), and over the centuries the intermingling of the races and the emergence of "mixed-races" led to a system where colour determined privileges to which a person was entitled (Kelly, 2020). In present-day Jamaica, although official entitlements based on racial composition may no longer exist, many perceive that unofficial privileges exist for persons with a lighter skin tone (Charles, 2010). Perceptions of this shadism or colourism system of privilege have been linked to some Jamaicans' negative sense of self and issues with colour and racial identity and their general self-esteem (Morgan & O'Garo, 2008). Researchers also examine whether these internal uncertainties contribute to behaviours such as skin bleaching (Charles, 2010).

Although presented above as separate issues, the complicated nature of these social systems means that the commingling of these financial- and racial/colour-based issues has produced Jamaica's complex class system which facilitates social mobility. For instance, Kelly (2020) found that participants' self-identified skin colour and their racial categorisation each predicted their access to household amenities (e.g. refrigerator, cars, indoor plumbing) and their years of schooling, with those of a darker hue having less of each type of commodity. This combination may further affect black Jamaicans' sense of racial identity as some may believe that their inability to improve economically is tied to their racial hue.

Another key issue for Jamaica concerns the physical health of its citizens, in particular the high prevalence of chronic non-communicable diseases (CNCD) (Samuels & Fraser, 2010). Amuleru-Marshall et al. (2013) name behaviour change in relation to physical health issues as a key area for Caribbean psychologists and note that effective interventions will need to consider the environmental context where citizens of African ancestry have spent most of the region's history with their "…physical and psychosocial health" (p. 217) under "…horrific and unrelenting assault" (p. 216).

One example of how our historical context is possibly related to our CNCD rates is the diet which was typically provided to enslaved persons. The protein content relied heavily on dried fish and meats which were low in protein and high in salt content (Wilson & Grim, 1991). Noting this, they theorised that the current prevalence of hypertension among those descended from enslaved persons is partially due to these types of diets (Wilson & Grim, 1991). A recent study has shown that mothers of undernourished children in Jamaica have poorer psychosocial functioning than mothers of adequately nourished children as they were more depressed and reported lower levels of parenting esteem and higher levels of economic stress (Baker-Henningham et al., 2003). This shows the direct connection between dietary practices and psychosocial performance and emphasises the need to address our nutritional practices. Part of the challenge is that the longevity of some of our eating habits makes them ingrained customary practices (e.g. dried salted fish is still a dietary staple for many Jamaicans and is part of our national dish). Having psychological interventions with the citizenry would increase the likelihood of shifting such traditions.

In addition to post-colonial legacies, Jamaica is not free from the other woes that can plague any society as it evolves. For instance, a recurring issue is how we interact with our physical environment, manage annual threats from hurricanes, and address our experience of the worldwide phenomenon of climate change; these are all pivotal to our continued survival and need to be addressed. Our education system, which has not changed significantly since we gained independence, also needs reformation to ensure that we produce not only graduates who are employable to improve the country's economic situation but also critical thinking citizens who can contribute to national development. Another key area directly connected to Jamaica's economic development is the need to maximise employees' capabilities and productivity levels and to ensure an appropriate fit between employees and their positions.

The variety of areas for development raised in this section indicates the need Jamaica has for psychologists of all types (e.g. clinical and counselling, community, health, industrial-organisational, environmental, experimental and research, political, and social psychology and psychometricians). But does Jamaica currently have the resources as listed here? Next, we describe the nature and scope of psychological resources available in Jamaica.

Psychological Resources in Jamaica

For this section we will cover three main areas, namely, educational opportunities, the professional associations, and available resource services. Before going into those areas, we thought it is important to look back and recognise the work of some pioneers in the field.

Pioneering Psychologists

Early contributions to psychology in the Jamaican landscape started in the 1960s and centre around the work of four influential women: Dr. Ruth Doorbar, Dr. Ilna Janice Evans who paved the way in the clinical/counselling field, and Professors Elsa Leo-Rhynie and Marlene Hamilton whose main contributions were educational development of the field. While Dr. Doorbar worked to build psychology in the public system, implementing clinics and advising government officials, Dr. Evans was improving statistical systems for tracking clients at a major hospital, implementing services at hospitals island-wide, and working to provide facilities for children needing special education. They were also both part of the team responsible for founding Jamaica's first psychological association. Professors Hamilton and Leo-Rhynie both trained in educational psychology; had long careers at the University of the West Indies (UWI), Mona Campus: and were involved in the shaping of psychology degree programmes there. These women, in combination with other trailblazers who supported them, laid a solid foundation for the fruit that have borne today.

Psychology Educational Opportunities

Like other places, Jamaica's psychological landscape is significantly painted by its educational offerings. The oldest university on the island is the UWI, which opened its Mona Campus in 1948, and is, not surprisingly, the first Jamaican institution to provide psychology training—a certificate programme in general psychology which was first offered in 1969 through its continuing education unit (Salter, 2000).

The first tertiary degree in psychology was a master's in clinical psychology out of the UWI (Mona) in the early 1980s. However, the programme was short-lived and had no graduates. A smattering of programmes developed in the 1980s and 1990s, but it was in the early 2000s that there was exponential growth with a slew of programmes being implemented. Today, there are approximately 15 degree programmes offered by 7 universities covering 5 bachelor's, 7 master's, and 2 doctoral (PhD) degrees. Four of the seven master's degree programmes are in the field of counselling psychology; the others are in general applied psychology, clinical psychology, and forensic psychology; the two doctoral degree programmes are in educational psychology and counselling psychology. This imbalance in offerings is, not surprisingly, also reflected in the types of psychologists present on the island, as we will illustrate later.

Associations and Advocacy

The first local association, the Jamaica Psychological Association, was formed in the 1980s by a small group of psychologists. Due to administrative shifts, the association changed its name in 2001 to the Jamaica Psychological Society (JamPsych). The Society has strengthened and today has 128 full members (persons with a master's degree or doctorate), 20 student members, 10 international affiliates, and 7 affiliate members (from professions such as social work and psychiatry).

A major game changer for the profession, which is the direct result of JamPsych's advocacy work, is policy development for the registration of practicing psychologists and counsellors. Through this work, psychologists and counsellors in 2014 were added to the roster of the Council of Professions Supplementary to Medicine (CPSM) which oversees professions viewed as allied to medicine (e.g. nutritionists, physiotherapists, speech pathologists), and in 2016 licensure for psychologists and counsellors became mandatory. Five classes of professionals under two levels (master's degree and doctoral) were included: clinical, counselling, applied-social, educational/school, and professional counselling. This single feat has impacted the growth of the profession in a number of ways. It has enhanced the credibility of the professional nature of the field and provided protection for the public. Additionally, it has opened the door for greater recognition of the field by, and collaboration with, government entities and allowed for increased insurance-related benefits for practicing psychologists.

JamPsych also contributes in the process to establish accreditation standards for tertiary educational institutions and has assisted with the development of national policies (e.g. tobacco control, media standards, and mental health). The Association has developed alliances with Government Ministries (e.g. Health and Wellness, Justice, Education, Youth, and Information), as well as strong regional and international organisational bonds (Caribbean Alliance of National Psychological Associations [CANPA], American Psychological Association). These various avenues of advocacy and networking provide opportunities for Jamaican psychologists to strengthen their skills and provide service at national, regional, and international levels.

Two final ongoing areas of advocacy should be mentioned as they directly relate to the public's access to psychological services. First, JamPsych liaises with Government Ministries to establish appropriate regulations for fair and equitable salary compensation for psychologists working in the public sector. Second, the Association is working with insurance companies to address matters related to insurance empanelling and coverage for psychology clients. These areas will be examined in more detail in subsequent sections.

Psychological Services Available

Jamaicans can access psychological services through either public or private means. Identifying the number of psychologists on the island is difficult as not all are registered. However, registration records indicate that there are 128 professionals with counselling psychologists being the largest subfield represented, followed by both clinical psychologists and professional counsellors; there are also a small number of registered applied-social, school, and educational psychologists.

An examination of a country's psychological services necessitates considering the wider mental health landscape. A recent analysis by UN agencies concluded that while "[H]historically mental health has not been a priority in Jamaica" (p. 5), there has been an increase in concern about this matter in recent times (UNITAF, PAHO & UNDP, 2019). Apart from our professional interest in having this shift in priority, it is also important economically to the country as based on the statistics, these agencies expect "the burden of mental illness" to "…cause US$ 2.76 billion in lost economic output from 2015-2030" (UNITAF, PAHO & UNDP, 2019, p. 2). In line with this reality, national committees have been formulated to address several areas of mental health.

In terms of psychiatric care in Jamaica, our facilities are largely centred in two locations. There is the Bellevue Hospital (BVH) which has been in existence since 1861 and is the largest psychiatric institution in the English-speaking Caribbean. Originally called the Jamaica Lunatic Asylum, it has 700 beds with 23 wards which are divided into acute, subacute, psycho-medical, mental subnormal, long stay, psycho-geriatric, and rehabilitative wards. In addition, the quasi-public University

Hospital of the West Indies has a 20-bed psychiatric ward for acute hospitalisations. All other psychiatric patients are treated on general medical wards.

Significant efforts have been made by the Ministry of Health over many administrations to shift psychiatric care from a long-stay, institutionally focused mental health approach to a community-based one, and there is greater focus on primary and secondary prevention strategies (Hickling, 1994; UNITAF, PAHO & UNDP, 2019). This move of deinstitutionalisation started from the 1960s, but the granting of autonomous functioning to BVH in 2010 should allow for a speeding up of this process (Hickling, 1994; UNITAF, PAHO & UNDP, 2019). Another encouraging move was the 2017 recommendation from the Mental Health and Homelessness Task Force to expand the mental health training of relevant health professionals (e.g. psychiatric nurse aides, social workers). This should help fill gaps in services and support the integration of mental health services into primary care (UNITAF, PAHO & UNDP, 2019).

With increased focus on mental health and psychological needs, more posts are being created in Government Ministries. It is currently difficult to map all the psychologists working in the Government as some operate in positions whose titles do not readily indicate their profession. Nevertheless, across the Ministries of Education, of Youth and Information, of Health and Wellness, and of Justice, there appear to be approximately 30 psychologists in counselling/clinical/educational positions, and there are other psychologists who are contractually employed for specific projects. Within the private sector, one is most likely to find psychologists working on a contractual basis on specific projects such as implementing wellness programmes, addressing employee engagement, and on-boarding exercises. Anecdotally, it is known that some of these services are being fulfilled by psychologists not domiciled on the island.

Summary of Resources

As outlined in this section, Jamaica provides a vibrant training ground for psychological training, has an active national association which has helped to formalise the recognition of the profession, and has psychologists trained to the doctoral level in a number of subfields. In general, this augurs well for the field's future and to the continued development of national services.

However, we note that most graduate programmes focus on counselling and/or clinical-type areas. Currently, there are no comparative programmes offering training in other psychology subfields such as health, occupational psychology, community psychology, sport, and industrial and organisational psychology, all of which are needed in Jamaica. Fortunately, there are psychologists trained in these subfields in Jamaica, and this allows some programmes to offer courses in some of these areas.

Jamaica has realised some benefits from the advent of mandatory registration for practicing psychologists and counsellors, but there is a need to have a system whereby all persons practicing psychology are identifiable. It is important that there is centralised documentation of all types of psychological services available on the island as this will help increase the visibility of the field.

Barriers to the Growth of Psychology

As outlined above, Jamaica has great need for psychological services to address a range of issues, and simultaneously it offers a fairly wide assortment of psychology-related resources, especially compared to other islands in the region. In this final section of the chapter, we present key challenges we believe affect both greater use of psychological services and the availability of services. These are (i) limited understanding of the field; (ii) citizens' attitude towards seeking help for mental health; and (iii) a need to develop training grounds which will produce effective professionals on a timelier basis. This is not an exhaustive list but are fundamental issues to tackle to improve the use of psychology in Jamaica.

As a preface to that discussion, we believe it is fundamental to the Jamaican people to understand the linkage between our colonial history and our current behavioural and social patterns and even our personality traits. Unfortunately, this connection is not apparent to many (if not most) Jamaicans, nor do many appear interested in examining this relationship. We believe that Jamaican psychologists have a role in promoting this level of understanding which is vital to the country's growth. To achieve these two things at least are needed: (1) for psychologists themselves to examine this issue and perform their own analyses and (2) for psychologists to advocate in political fora in order to convert individual work into community, social, and national approaches based on our cultural realities. Fortunately, the work has already begun as there is existing literature, interventions, and advocacy from Jamaican mental health professionals on this topic (e.g. Charles, 2010; Hickling et al., 2008; James et al., 2016). This is a goal to which psychologists from all subfields can contribute as it really speaks to the context in which we would practice our profession, the lens within which we would engage with our students and clients (whether they are individuals, groups, organisations, or communities). It is within this broadscale vision that we now discuss the key challenges.

Limited Understanding of the Field

From our vantage point, there is limited understanding of what psychologists do and what we can do which affects what potential clients (i.e. individuals, public, and private entities) expect of us. Overall, there are misunderstandings that almost anyone from any field can perform the role and functions of a psychologist and that a psychologist is an expert in all areas of psychology. The current situation for psychologists working in the public sector is one good demonstration of some of these issues.

The salary structure as managed by the government ministries is based on a biosocial/biomedical framework that does not fit well with the practice of psychology. This affects the demands placed on psychologists and their compensation packages. For example, while psychologists and counsellors usually maintain longer session times from other medical professionals, the expectations of the number of cases to be managed by each type of professional is not commensurately adjusted. Additionally, the differences in entry-level requirements for professionals in independent practice are typically higher for psychologists and counsellors (minimum of a master's degree) than for many medical professionals (minimum of a bachelor's degree), but this is not accounted for in the current governmental salary structure. Therefore, JamPsych has been making representation to correct these and other anomalies which result in psychologists being underpaid. We also note that non-psychology trained professionals serve in positions which really require adequate psychological training. This we recognise as a combination of a lack of understanding about the purpose and focus of our field, as well as the lack of personnel resources to meet the demand.

The misunderstanding of the field also results in poor insurance coverage for psychological services. Typically, either they are not covered or coverage is at a lower percentage of the cost than provided for other professional services. JamPsych is therefore advocating for better coverage through alignment with the registry for practitioners and to also help insurance companies better understand assessment as a diagnostic process, so clients may receive coverage for this service.

Jamaican psychologists will need to be the ones to lead the move for persons to better understand what the field of psychology entails and how it can contribute to the country's development. Being more visible on national matters and ensuring that when we share our voice, we consistently include theoretical positions and research findings from the field are some ways that this can be achieved. Recently, we had the positive sign, whereby the only social scientist appointed to a national oversight committee to address the management of the country's COVID-19 plan was a social psychologist. Hopefully, this will mean continued inclusion of psychologists on similar task forces. While we cannot deny that there has been some progress in the visibility of psychology on the national scene, more work is needed.

Societal Attitudes to Mental Health

Jamaica is not exempt from the impact of stigma towards mental health. Like many other nations, the very thought of a psychiatrist, psychologist, or any mental health professional brings forth visions of "madness", feelings of cognitive dissonance, and resistance for many Jamaicans. Spiritual factors are often understood as being the aetiology for mental illness, and the use of herbs and oils is not uncommon as part of the healing process for any ailment (Morgan, 2014). This practice is not limited to persons of any specific religious or spiritual practice and sometimes means that persons delay seeking mental health interventions until all other avenues have been exhausted. It is important to note that others also endorse a more integrated approach with the use of both traditional and conventional healing methods (Morgan, 2014).

Fortunately, there has been some positive change in attitudes towards psychology, and we note many efforts from different sectors to further reduce the levels of stigma of mental health. For instance, the Ministry of Health and Wellness regularly runs radio and television advertisements promoting their mental health services, and some advertisements directly tackle the issue of stigma. There has also been an increase in the number of non-governmental mental health advocacy groups on the island in the last decade, and many of them are very active on social media and use their platforms to share messages which encourage the act of seeking help for mental health issues. In a twist of fate, the stress produced for many Jamaicans in the advent of the COVID-19 pandemic has increased public discussion about mental health, and so has placed psychology in the forefront more than ever before. Jamaican psychologists should take the opportunity to capitalise on this and to broaden the discussion by illustrating other areas in which the field can be of use.

Shaping Educational Training to Match Country Needs

To advance the field in Jamaica, we need to ensure that our training grounds are structured to best support the overarching goal of national development. There have been numerous calls from psychologists across the region for the development of a Caribbean psychology (Amuleru-Marshall, 2013; Dudley-Grant, 2013; Bradshaw Maynard, 2013; Ramkissoon; 2010; Sutherland, 2011; Thompson, 2013, 2016), as well as the recognition that there will also likely be the need for country-specific psychology frameworks (Thompson, 2016). There are also examples of site-specific programmes and curricula (Thompson, 2013, 2016). These all provide a foundation for continued interrogation of our educational offerings to maximise their contribution to advancing a Jamaican and a regional psychology.

This requires, as has been expressed elsewhere, greater inclusion of regionally developed theory, research methods, and research in curricula and course content that examines our social issues and explores how graduates can practically work to tackle these issues (Amuleru-Marshall, 2013; Dudley-Grant, 2013; Bradshaw Maynard, 2013; Sutherland, 2011; Thompson, 2013, 2016). Greater culturally driven course content interrogating issues of self-, family, national, and regional identity and tackling areas such as the psychology of interpersonal violence and relationship-building in the workplace comes readily to mind.

The landscape in Jamaica is often a resource-depleted environment, and for us, as psychologists and mental health professionals in general, it calls for creative ways in which to prune and harvest. So, in addition to working on content at the course and programme level, we should examine the overall degree structure and requirements for graduates to be practice-ready. Our academic degree standards were developed to align with international, largely North American, standards (Dudley-Grant, 2013), but as a country and a region, we need to start examining whether other standards—ones suited for our context—can simultaneously exist (Amuleru-Marshall, 2013; Dudley-Grant, 2013). Those indigenously generated standards should produce "work-ready" graduates, with more real-life and supervised experiences and who are able to meet existing demands.

Currently, the degree offerings in Jamaica are between three and four years, but this structure could be broadened to include an additional period with focus strictly on students gaining practical experience based on the nation's needs. Some areas which could be included are cultural therapy (art, music, play), psychometrics, public health psychology, and community psychology; this could all help to enhance and create jobs and careers. We recognise such a major shift would require significant manoeuvrings on related fronts (e.g. the national registration system) but still believe it is possible.

A final possibility we raise to address the gap in accessible psychological resources is professionally linking psychology with related fields. This could mean working more alongside allied fields (e.g. counselling, psychiatry, social work), with each area contributing its unique strengths, and together developing more unified strategies to combat social ills. Additionally, building the psychology training of guidance counsellors and social workers whose numbers range into the thousands would benefit Jamaica.

The recommendations presented here are not to suggest that relevant work and advocacy are not currently happening within our educational and government institutions, but to encourage more of it to occur. We see great benefit from intra- and inter-institutional and interdisciplinary collaboration.

Conclusion

The field of psychology in Jamaica has grown exponentially in the last 20 years with several posts being provided at the national level, private and public facilities offering more services, and the development of psychology programmes resulting in increased number of graduates. The future looks bright but needs guidance and advocacy to reach its potential. Endeavours on the horizon for the field include the development of locally specific educational standards, the broadening of training to other psychology subfields, and increased understanding by the public about what the field can offer for national development. Hopefully, these will occur in the not-too-distant future. We see psychologists working together, and along with allied professionals, to create strategies that can be used to help fill the gaps we have identified. Jamaica will need the contribution of psychologists across the island to build the visibility and demonstrate the capability of this great profession. United we stand, divided we fall.

References

Akbar, N. (2021). *New visions for Black men*. Mind Productions & Associates.

Amuleru-Marshall, O. (2013). Capacity development of psychology in the Caribbean: Lessons from near and far. *Revista Interamericana de Psicología/Interamerican Journal of Psychology, 47*(2), 245–254.

Amuleru-Marshall, O., Gomez, A., & Neckles, K. O. (2013). Psychology, spirituality, and well-being in the Caribbean. In P. Sutherland, R. Moodley, & B. Chevannes (Eds.), *Caribbean healing traditions: Implications for health and mental health* (1st ed., pp. 215–226). Routledge.

Asmann, P., & Jones, K. (2021, January 29). *InSight Crime's 2020 homicide round-up*. InSight Crime. https://insightcrime.org/news/analysis/2020-homicide-round-up/

Bailey, B. (1999). *National report: Jamaica. Regional project: National reports on the situation of gender violence against women*. United Nations Development Programme.

Baker-Henningham, H., Powell, C., Walker, S., & Grantham-McGregor, S. (2003). Mothers of undernourished Jamaican children have poorer psychosocial functioning and this is associated with stimulation provided in the home. *European Journal of Clinical Nutrition, 57*(6), 786–792. https://doi.org/10.1038/sj.ejcn.1601611

Bradshaw Maynard, D. (2013). The history and current status of psychology in Barbados: Research and professional practice. *Revista Interamericana de Psicología/Interamerican Journal of Psychology, 47*(2), 227–238.

Branche, C., Minor, S., & Ramkissoon, M. (2004). Psychology in the Caribbean [Editorial]. *Caribbean Journal of Psychology, 1*(1), 3–4.

Brown, J., & Johnson, S. (2008). Child rearing and child participation in Jamaican families. *International Journal of Early Years Education, 16*, 31–41. https://doi.org/10.1080/09669760801892110

Caribbean Policy Research Institute. (2021). *Stress test: The impact of the pandemic on domestic and community violence*. Foreign, Commonwealth & Development Office of the United Kingdom. https://docs.google.com/viewerng/viewer?url=https://www. capricaribbean.org/sites/default/files/public/documents/report/stress_test_the_impact_of_the_pandemic_on_domestic_and_community_violence.pdf

Caribbean Policy Research Institute & United Nations Children's Fund. (2018). *Situational analysis of Jamaican children – 2018*. UNICEF. https://www.unicef.org/jamaica/media/546/file/Situation%20Analysis%20of%20Jamaican%20Children%20%E2%80%93%202018.pdf

Charles, C. A. D. (2010). Skin bleaching in Jamaica: Self-esteem, racial self-esteem, and Black identity transactions. *Caribbean Journal of Psychology, 3*(1), 25–39. https://www.researchgate.net/profile/Christopher-Charles-7/publication/259496152

Degruy, J. A. (2017). *Post traumatic slave syndrome: America's legacy of enduring injury and healing* (Revised ed.). Joy Degruy Publications.

Dudley-Grant, R. (2013). Capacity, collaboration, credentials: Challenges to psychology in the Caribbean. *Revista Interamericana de Psicología/Interamerican Journal of Psychology, 47*(2), 255–264. http://journals.fcla.edu/ijp

Harriott, A. D., & Jones, M. (2016). *Crime and violence in Jamaica* (IDB series on crime and violence in the Caribbean). http://thewgsg.com/wp-content/uploads/2018/05/Crime-and-Violence-in-Jamaica-IDB-Series-on-Crime-and-Violence-in-the-Caribbean-Copy.pdf

Hickling, F. W. (1994). Community psychiatry and deinstitutionalisation in Jamaica. *Hospital and Community Psychiatry, 45*(11), 1122–1126.

Hickling, F. W. (2008). Psychopathology of the Jamaican people. In F. W. Hickling, B. K. Matthies, K. Morgan, & R. C. Gibson (Eds.), *Perspectives in Caribbean psychology* (1st ed., pp. 32–69). Caribbean Institute of Mental Health and Substance Abuse.

Hickling, F. W., Matthies, B. K., Morgan, K., & Gibson, R. C. (2008). *Perspectives in Caribbean psychology* (In F. W. Hickling, B. K. Matthies, K. Morgan, & R. C. Gibson (Eds.), Caribbean Institute of Mental Health and Substance Abuse.

Hickling, F. W., Robertson-Hickling, H., & Paisley, V. (2011). Deinstitutionalization and attitudes toward mental illness in Jamaica: A qualitative study. *Revista Panamericana de Salud Pública/Pan American Journal of Public Health, 29*(2), 169–176. https://www.scielosp.org/pdf/rpsp/2011.v29n3/169-176/en

Hutton, C. (1996). *Manufacturing violence shaping social psychology: Aspects of the Columbian holocaust in the Americas*. Unpublished essay. Department of Government, University of the West Indies, Mona, Kingston, Jamaica.

James, C., Seixas, A. A., Harrison, A., Jean-Louis, G., Butler, M., Zizi, F., & Samuels, A. (2016). Childhood physical and sexual abuse in Caribbean young adults and its association with depression, post-traumatic stress, and skin bleaching. *Journal of Depression & Anxiety, 5*(1). https://doi.org/10.4172/2167-1044.1000214

Kelly, M. D. A. (2020). Examining race in Jamaica: How racial category and skin color structure social inequality. *Race and Social Problems, 12*, 300–312. https://doi.org/10.1007/s12552-020-09287-z

Longman-Mills, S., Mitchell, C., & Abel, W. (2019). The psychological trauma of slavery: The Jamaican case study. *Social and Economic Studies, 68*(3&4), 79–101.

Meeks Gardner, J., Henry-Lee, A., Chevannes, P., Thomas, J., Henningham, H., & Coore, C. (2006). Violence against children in the Caribbean: A desk review. In A. Henry-Lee & J. M. Gardner (Eds.), *Promoting child rights: Selected proceedings of the Caribbean Child Research Conference 2006* (pp. 25–54) http://www.unicef.org/jamaica/Promoting_Child_Rights_CD_version.pdf

Morgan, K. A. D. (2014). Rastafari: Cultural healing in the Caribbean. In P. Sutherland, R. Moodley, & B. Chevannes (Eds.), *Caribbean healing traditions: Implications for health and mental health* (1st ed., pp. 164–175). Routledge.

Morgan, K. A. D., & O'Garo, K. (2008). Caribbean identity issues. In F. W. Hickling, B. K. Matthies, K. Morgan, & R. C. Gibson (Eds.), *Perspectives in Caribbean psychology* (1st ed., pp. 3–31). Caribbean Institute of Mental Health and Substance Abuse.

Patterson, O. (1969). *The sociology of slavery: An analysis of the origins, development and structure of Negro slave society in Jamaica*. Fairleigh Dickinson University Press.

Pottinger, A. M. (2012). Children's exposure to violence in Jamaica: Over a decade of research and interventions. *West Indian Medical Journal, 61*(4), 369–371. http://caribbean.scielo.org/pdf/wimj/v61n4/14.pdf

Ramkissoon, M. (2010). Psychology in the Caribbean: Call for an assessment framework [Editorial]. *Caribbean Journal of Psychology, 3*(1), 1–3.

Rey, T. H. (1953). [Review of the book *Personality and conflict in Jamaica,* by Madeline Kerr]. *The International Journal of Psychoanalysis, 34,* 345. https://www.pep-web.org/document.php?id=ijp.034.0345a

Salter, V. (2000). The status of psychology in the commonwealth Caribbean: Emphasis on Jamaica. *Revista Interamericana de Psicología/Interamerican Journal of Psychology, 34*(2), 211–221.

Samuels, T. A., & Fraser, H. (2010). Caribbean Wellness Day: Mobilizing a region for chronic noncommunicable disease prevention and control. *Revista Panamericana de Salud Pública/Pan American Journal of Public Health, 28*(6), 472–479. https://scielosp.org/article/rpsp/2010.v28n6/472-479/

Sawh, R., & Scales, A. M. (2006). Middle passage in the triangular slave trade: The West Indies. *Negro Educational Review, 57*(3), 155–170. 266. https://search.proquest.com/scholarly-journals/middle-passage-triangular-slave-trade-west-indies/docview/219047417/se-2?accountid=42530

Shepherd, V. A., & Reid, A. (2019). Women, slavery and the reparation movement in the Caribbean. *Social and Economic Studies, 68*(3), 31–59. 254–255. https://search.proquest.com/scholarly-journals/women-slavery-reparation-movement-caribbean/docview/2471028518/se-2?accountid=42530

Statistical Institute of Jamaica. (2019). https://statinja.gov.jm/Demo_SocialStats/PopulationStats.aspx

Sutherland, M. E. (2011). Toward a Caribbean psychology: An African-centered approach. *Journal of Black Studies, 42*(8), 1175–1194. https://www.jstor.org/stable/41304580

Thomas, C. A. (2020). Psycho-resistance: Probing the historical discourse on madness amongst the enslaved Africans during British Caribbean chattel slavery. In G. Araoz (Ed.), *Madness in context: Historical, poetic and artistic narratives* (pp. 15–25). Inter-Disciplinary Press. https://doi.org/10.1163/9789004400290_003

Thompson, A. D. (2013). Fulfilling psychology's promise: A model of undergraduate psychology education. *Revista Interamericana de Psicología/Interamerican Journal of Psychology, 47*(2), 277–286.

Thompson, A. D. (2016). Toward a Caribbean psychology: Context, imperatives, and future directions. In J. L. Roopnarine & D. Chadee (Eds.), *Caribbean psychology: Indigenous contributions to a global discipline* (pp. 15–44). American Psychological Association.

United Nations Development Programme. (2009). *Mapping the global partnership for development Jamaica: Riding the waves of globalization.* http://content-ext.undp.org/aplaws_publications/3104085/Jamaica_MappingGlobalPartnership.pdf

United Nations Interagency Task Force on Noncommunicable Diseases, United Nations Development Programme, & Pan American Health Organization. (2019). *Care for mental health conditions in Jamaica: The case for investment. Evaluating the return on investment of scaling up treatment for depression, anxiety, and psychosis*. Pan American Health Organization.

Watson Williams, C. (2018). *Women's health survey 2016 Jamaica.* United Nations Women. https://doi.org/10.18235/0001170

Wilson, T. W., & Grim, C. E. (1991). Biohistory of slavery and blood pressure differences in blacks today. A hypothesis. *Hypertension, 17*(suppl. 1), 122–128. https://doi.org/10.1161/01.HYP.17.1_Suppl.I122

Chapter 13
Psychology in Barbados: Looking Back and Moving Forward

Donna-Maria B. Maynard, Mia Amour Jules, and Suriya Daya

Psychology in Barbados

Barbados is a small island (34 km in length and 23 km wide) located in the south-eastern Caribbean; it has an estimated population of 301,865 (65 years and over: 13.57%, 2020) and a life expectancy of 78.31 years. The population of Barbados is predominantly Black of African descent 92.4% (Central Intelligence Agency, 2021). The predominant religious affiliation is Protestant 66.4% (includes Anglican 23.9%, Pentecostal 19.5%, Adventist 5.9%, Methodist 4.2%, 2010 est.; Central Intelligence Agency, 2021). English is the official language spoken, and Bajan is the local dialect. Barbados is famous for its high literacy rate of 99.6% (UNESCO, 2021). As a former colony of the British Empire, Barbados gained independence from Britain in 1966 (Carter, 2016) and is a member of the British Commonwealth. The country is governed as a parliamentary democracy, with a house of representatives and a senate (Barrow-Giles, 2011). With regard to human resource development, the government heavily invests a large portion of its national budget on education and health. For example, in 2019, 10.8% of total government expenditure was allocated to education (UNESCO, 2021) and 6.56% in 2018 on health (World Health Organization [WHO], 2021).

As it relates to mental health specifically, there is an underdeveloped national mental health information system and no formal mechanism for the annual reporting of mental health data (Jintie, 2012). Furthermore, many reports on mental health exclude or do not represent the work of psychologists as demonstrated by the most recent Barbados Health Report (2019), which refers to a range of professional

D.-M. B. Maynard (✉) · M. A. Jules · S. Daya
The University of the West Indies, Cave Hill, Barbados
e-mail: donna-maria.maynard@cavehill.uwi.edu; Mia.Jules@cavehill.uwi.edu; Suriya.Daya@cavehill.uwi.edu

G. J. Rich, N. A. Ramkumar (eds.), *Psychology in Oceania and the Caribbean*, International and Cultural Psychology, https://doi.org/10.1007/978-3-030-87763-7_13

mental health practitioners (Human Resources for Health in Barbados) but does not include psychologists. The exclusion of the role of psychologists in the main body of the report is concerning given that psychologists are employed and provide services in the public health sector. Some of the critical mental health issues affecting the Barbadian population (as reported by PAHO/WHO, 2020) include conduct disorders, anxiety disorders (most found among children between 5 and 15 years), anxiety, depression, self-harm, somatic symptom, substance use, schizophrenia, and bipolar disorders (for those 20 years onwards) and Alzheimer's disease (for those 80 years and above; PAHO/WHO, 2020).

Furthermore, underlying maladaptive thought processes result in many Barbadians engaging in unhealthy lifestyle choices such as poor diets, physical inactivity, alcohol abuse, and tobacco use. Such choices among the populace have led to Barbados having a high prevalence of noncommunicable diseases (NCDs, i.e., cardiovascular disease, diabetes mellitus, cancer, and chronic pulmonary disease) and correspondingly high rates of NCD risk factors which have caused 83% of all deaths (PAHO/WHO, 2020). In light of the above, psychologists (as behavior change experts) clearly have a role to play in the health sector to address the national burden of disease.

The paragraphs to follow will first briefly outline the origins and development of the discipline of psychology in Barbados, followed by the research that has been conducted to examine national and psychosocial concerns and then the work that psychologists conduct in the sectors of health, education, and social care. We conclude with recommendations for the future.

The Practice of Psychology: Informal and Formal Origins

Questioning who we are and attempting to understand what it is to have a healthy mind, body, and soul have traditionally been sought through dialogue with respected figures in society (Downes, 2002; Griffith et al., 2008; e.g., priests, teachers, doctors) – figures in whom we have confidence and can trust with our innermost thoughts, especially in times of need. Inherent in mental well-being is the principle that there is a need for people to articulate their feelings and concerns through close interpersonal communication that is built on trust, respect, mutual concern, and confidentiality – fundamental principles of modern-day psychological practice (Rogers, 1951).

Some historical examples demonstrate the importance of seeking advice and counsel to resolve mental distress. For example, Barbados during colonial times adopted Christianity as the dominant religion (Jules & Maynard, 2016; Segal, 1995; Taylor & Case, 2013), and hence many leaders of the Christian faith served (and continue to serve) in the capacity of counsellor to those in need. Another example demonstrating a national understanding of the need for psychologically based interventions was the installation of the first psychologist at the sole Psychiatric Hospital in 1965 (Frey & Black, 2012; Maynard, 2013).

It is documented that psychology in Barbados became formally regulated in 1975 by the Government of Barbados as demonstrated by Section 2(1) of the Paramedical Professions Act 2008 (COB) CAP.372C. Implicitly, placing psychology within the Paramedical Professions Act, alongside professions such as physiotherapy, dietetics, and chiropody, suggests that the profession is perceived as being "supplementary to medicine." Hence, it is understandable that in the 1970s, clinical psychology was the sole subfield recognized under which qualified practitioners could register and practice legally using the nomenclature of "psychologist." Furthermore, the Ministry of Health has committed to a registered psychologist serving as a standing member on the Board of the Paramedical Professions Council to ensure representation and oversight of the validity of applications for registration as a psychologist in Barbados. Moreover, since 1997 the professional practice of psychology in Barbados has developed from an emphasis on clinical psychology and expanded to include counselling psychology and educational psychology (PAHO/WHO, 2008). Professionals trained within these three subfields served as the founders who formalized the professional association of psychologists that currently exists to this day, that is, the Barbados Society of Psychology (BSP).

Established in 2001, the BSP (formerly known as The Barbados Association of Psychologists) is charged with the responsibility to develop and maintain the professional standards of psychology as a discipline in Barbados. The BSP is an organization of psychologists and related mental health professionals (Barbados Society of Psychology, 2020a, 2020b). As of 2020, the BSP membership consisted of 46 members – a significant achievement for the society since 1999 when the first registered psychologists met informally, thereby serving as the founding members of the association (Barbados Association of Psychology, organizational communication, May 30, 2001). The Barbados Society of Psychology Code of Ethics (BSP-BCE) informs the practice of psychologists and psychological research by BSP members. The BSP-BCE was adapted from the Jamaican Psychological Society, which in turn was influenced by the American Psychological Association's Code of Ethics (Maynard, 2013).

Training in Psychology

The first members of the BSP were trained outside of the Caribbean; hence, the adoption of ethical principles for psychological practice within Barbados is guided by very similar practice and aspirational principles of extra-regional contexts. These extra-regionally trained psychologists worked throughout the1980s and 1990s to provide psychological services through the Ministries of Health and Education, for example, the psychology department in the psychiatric hospital, the student services department, the Child Care Board, Her Majesty's Prison, and Government Industrial Schools.

The importation of psychologists trained outside of the Caribbean highlighted a clear need for psychology graduate programs to be offered in the region at the time.

Furthermore, the increasing challenges of modern-day society (e.g., stress, learning disabilities, anxiety) and the need for culturally sensitive skillsets served as the impetus for the development of Caribbean-trained psychologists. Barbados was not left out of this movement, and hence, The University of the West Indies (The UWI) Cave Hill Campus established undergraduate psychology programs in the 2000s. The UWI sister campuses in Jamaica (in 2001; Hickling & Matthies, 2003) and the twin-island Republic of Trinidad and Tobago (in 2006; Hutchinson & Rose, 2011) developed Masters of Science (MSc.) degree programs in clinical psychology. In 2006, the MSc. degree programs in applied psychology and counselling psychology were launched at The UWI Cave Hill Campus. Subsequently, graduates from the clinical and counselling psychology programs were able to register as psychologists in Barbados; such that of the 27 registered psychologists in the BSP, 19 obtained their MSc. in psychology from The UWI. Furthermore, of those BSP members with doctorates (i.e., 13), the majority (i.e., 7) have doctorates in the field of educational psychology – of which five hold a PhD from The UWI Cave Hill Campus in education with a specialization in educational psychology and the remaining two obtained their doctorates in the United Kingdom (BSP Membership Directory, 2020b).

Research in Psychology

It should be noted that the Government of Barbados invests a great deal of its annual budget on education (Best, 2019), and hence, this national priority arguably resulted in a concentration of psychologists (researchers and practitioners) contributing to the education sector. Therefore, the body of empirical research conducted by academics in psychology in Barbados has primarily centered on education-related issues. Researched areas include teacher training (e.g., Maynard, 2018; Maynard & Jules, 2017), cultural validation of psychological measures (e.g., Campbell et al., 2012, 2018; Griffith et al., 2020; Maynard et al., 2010), and youth identity exploration and development (e.g., Jules et al., 2015, 2017, 2019; Marshall & Maynard, 2009; Maynard & Jules, 2020). In addition, research work focused on psychosocial factors (e.g., psychological resilience, emotional intelligence, parental involvement) which may contribute to or undermine academic achievement and school engagement among youth in Barbados (e.g., Fayombo, 2010, 2012, 2015; Jules et al., 2020; Marshall et al., 2015; Maynard, 2007; Maynard & Fayombo, 2015; Maynard & Springer-Proverbs, 2010; Maynard & Welch, 2009; Stubbs & Maynard, 2017).

Despite the research that heavily focused on education-related matters, there is still a lack of research to inform the practice of psychology. This may be due to there not yet being a PhD program in psychology in Barbados, which would help in building a more robust research base. Research that has been conducted that could be used to inform the practice of psychology in Barbados has largely concentrated on the exploration of the psychometric properties and validation of measures of mental well-being. Psychological instruments such as the Beck Depression Inventory, the Zung Self-Rating Depression Scale, the State-Trait Anxiety Inventory, and the

Perceived Stress Scale (e.g., Campbell et al., 2009, 2012; Maynard et al., 2010). Moreover, there are other researchers trained in industrial and organizational psychology (e.g., Cadogan-McClean, Devonish, Greenidge) in Barbados who have contributed to psychological research (e.g., Alleyne et al., 2010; Alleyne et al., 2013; Devonish, 2016, 2017; Greenidge & Coyne, 2014; Lorde et al., 2010; Ramsey et al., 2008). Research is shared in regional journals (e.g., *Caribbean Journal of Psychology*, *Journal of Eastern Caribbean Studies*, *West Indian Medical Journal*), as well as several international journals (e.g., *Journal of Black Psychology*, *The Journal of Clinical Child Psychology and Psychiatry*, *International Journal of School & Educational Psychology*, *Interamerican Journal of Psychology*).

Psychology's Contribution to the Sectors of Health, Education, and Social Care

Psychologists in Barbados practice as clinical, counselling, or educational psychologists, with only one of the clinical psychologists specialized in clinical neuropsychology. These practitioners operate throughout Barbados and in some cases provide services for clientele in the Eastern Caribbean. As well as providing individual, group, and systemic services for their private clientele, they also provide consultancy and contracted services for other entities such as the law courts, business organizations, and private schools.

In Barbados, the application of psychology within the labor force is conducted by four distinct categories of workers. They include (1) independent private-practicing registered psychologists; (2) registered psychologists that are in non-practitioner posts (e.g., academics, research assistants, teachers, guidance counsellors); (3) graduate-level qualified workers in subfields of psychology (e.g., forensic, music, behavioral), who are not eligible for registration as psychologists; and (4) non-registerable independent private practitioners with non-psychology graduate degrees who use psychological principles in their practice (e.g., counsellors, therapists, and life coaches). Workers in all four categories arguably contribute, in some way, to the mental health and well-being landscape of Barbados through psychological and psychoeducational assessment, diagnosis, treatment/intervention, care, research, policy, and practice. Psychologists also work with nonprofit, voluntary, and nongovernmental organizations (e.g., UNICEF, Rotary Barbados, Network Services Centre, Supreme Counselling for Personal Development) to provide services (e.g., individual and group therapy) and mentorship for those in the community who are experiencing psychosocial problems.

Hospitals and Development Centers

The public health system in Barbados primarily places psychiatry as the foundation of assessment, diagnosis, and treatment of mental illness. Despite the emphasis placed on the discipline of psychiatry in this sector, psychology (a relatively younger field by comparison) is slowly emerging as a discipline to address the needs of those requiring assistance with their mental health and well-being. As such public agencies (e.g., the general hospital, psychiatric hospital, polyclinics) and private organizations (e.g., Strong Hope, Network Services Centre) recognize the role that psychologists play in the field of mental health.

The Barbados Psychiatric Hospital is the largest public employer of psychologists in the country. A total of four psychologists are employed full-time to provide services through the Psychology Department (Maynard, 2013). The hospital has a Drug Rehabilitation Unit, which provides psychological and medical screening, assessment and counselling services for clients, and walk-in services for people with substance abuse issues (CBC News Barbados, 2017). Forensic patients can be hospitalized at Her Majesty's Pleasure in the hospital's security unit (WHO, 2009). The hospital is also home to the Child Guidance Clinic which has recently been expanded to take a holistic approach including parental education and family support; the Child and Adolescent Unit (officially opened in November 2018) is now known as the Thrive Family Centre. The Centre delivers in-patient mental healthcare services to children and adolescents (Barbados Health Report, 2019).

The Department of Psychiatry is housed in the premier general hospital in Barbados, The Queen Elizabeth Hospital (QEH), which serves a consultatory-liaison function that provides community-based mental health services. In 1993 the Psychiatric Unit was established to provide acute care and an outpatient clinic for children and adults (QEH, 2021a). Also, through the Pediatrics Department of the QEH, a pediatric psychologist is appointed to provide services for children facing many difficulties from birth to 16 years old. This involves working with children who present with concerns ranging from developmental challenges to behavioral and mental health-related difficulties resulting from issues such as child abuse and neglect (The QEH, 2021b).

The National Mental Health Policy of Barbados (2004) highlighted the importance of integrating mental healthcare with primary healthcare. As such Barbados has started with the provision of community-based services within the polyclinics and the general hospital. In keeping with this mandate, further support is provided by the public health system through the decentralization of services from the hospitals to community mental health via selected polyclinics located throughout Barbados. Units at two of the district hospitals operate as residential community service providers for persons with mental and developmental disorders (i.e., St. Lucy District Hospital–Elayne Scantlebury Centre and St. Philip District Hospital–Evalina Smith Ward). With regard to the Evalina Smith Ward, it houses both children and young adults. Many of the children who live there are referred from the QEH or the Albert Cecil Graham Development Centre (UNCRC, 2015).

The Albert Cecil Graham Development Centre (formerly known as the Child Development Centre), a unit of the Ministry of Health and Wellness, is mandated to protect the rights of children with disabilities (i.e., mental, developmental, physical, and sensory) by providing assessment, treatment, education, and rehabilitation services. Using a multidisciplinary approach, the Centre employs a clinical psychologist and other specialists (e.g., physiotherapist, occupational therapist, speech therapist; Barbados Health Report, 2019).

Psychology Within Private Health Entities

Many psychologists provide services within the private healthcare sector, for example, psychologists working with The Substance Abuse Foundation provide care to clients staying in residential rehabilitation centers (such as Verdun House and Marina House). Psychologists also work with organizations such as the Barbados Fertility Centre and the Barbados electric utility provider, as well as with nongovernmental agencies such as the Barbados Association of Endometriosis and Polycystic Ovary Syndrome and the Variety Club Barbados–the Children's Charity. In some cases, psychologists provide their services voluntarily, for example, in The Heart and Stroke Foundation's (nonprofit organization) childhood obesity program.

Psychological Support Services in Education

The Ministry of Education seeks to address problem behavior among primary and secondary school students (e.g., emotional, behavioral, learning problems, violence, victims of abuse, substance abusers) through their Student Support Services Unit (Est. in 1997). This Unit has a special education officer and a psychologist who provide support to parents/guardians, teachers, and guidance counsellors. Recognizing the need for more psychological assistance for students of Barbados, the Ministry in 2010 implemented the Psychological Assistance Programme (PAP) through which consultant psychologists are hired to conduct psychological evaluations and counselling for students (UNCRC, 2015). In recent times the Ministry has expanded the PAP to include provision for the support of teaching staff (Agard, 2021).

Psychological services are embedded within several tertiary institutions and private schools throughout Barbados. For example, the Barbados Community College has a counselling and placement center staffed by psychology graduates, the Samuel Jackman Prescod Institute of Technology has a guidance office run by a counselling psychologist, and The UWI through its Office of Student Services has two registered clinical psychologists (i.e., psychological counsellor and career counselling specialist). There are a few offshore universities that also employ registered psychologists to provide psychosocial support for their students.

Several private schools in Barbados serve children with special needs (e.g., The Sunshine Early Stimulation, The Schoolhouse for Special Needs, PAREDOS: Parent Education for Development in Barbados) and hire psychology graduates to work as counsellors and educators with infants and older children who have developmental and neurodevelopmental challenges. These professionals also work with the children's families and teaching staff. They offer a range of services including parent support groups, educational workshops, and individual and family counselling as well as home visits.

Rehabilitative Educational Programs and Facilities

An out-of-school suspension program is delivered by the Edna Nicholls Centre (Est. in 1998), which provides a two-week rehabilitative program for students who have been suspended from their secondary school for violent behavior. Students are tested for drug use and referred to a clinical psychologist and pediatric psychiatrist should the results be positive. The program also facilitates the students' successful reintegration into school (Bailey, 2016).

The New Horizons Academy is an educational facility that is designed to work with children experiencing behavioral challenges and low self-esteem in the formal school setting. The Academy was the brainchild of the psychologist posted at the Ministry of Education and was designed to remove those students from schools and expose them to behavior change interventions for a short period, followed by the children then returning to their original school.

Psychological Social Care Support Services

The child protection system in Barbados is administered by the Child Care Board (CCB). The CCB has a clinical psychologist who provides assessment (i.e., psychological, psychoeducational) and counselling services to children and their parents or guardians. The custodial institution for minors is the Government Industrial Schools (GIS) that also functions as a psychosocial and educational institution providing comprehensive psychological services to rehabilitate young people and return them to their family home (UNCRC, 2015). Recently, GIS appointed a clinical psychologist to their Advisory Board (King, 2021).

There is also a rehabilitative program for adults at The Barbados Prison Service (H.M. Dodds Prison) aimed at reducing recidivism (Bailey, 2016, Barbados Prison Service, 2012). The two psychologists working with this program conduct psychological assessment of offenders and provide psychological reports to the Courts. There is also an inmate drug rehabilitation counselling program through which ongoing assessments, evaluation treatment, relapse prevention, planning, and preparing statistical data are provided (Bailey, 2016).

Moreover, to address issues related to domestic violence, the Business and Professional Women's Club of Barbados (BPWC) runs programs that include a telephone crisis hotline. This organization also offers counselling and support services to victims of abuse and a shelter for battered women and their children. The victims of domestic violence have access to the services of trained psychological counsellors (Bailey, 2016).

Psychology in Barbados: The Way Forward

As it relates to addressing major health concerns of the nation, there is a dire need for psychologists to assist with the fight against NCDs, especially as the risk factors for these diseases are infused in unhealthy lifestyle practices. More psychological input and interventions for the elderly, their families, and care workers are essential going forward. Psychologists can play a role in policy development and proactive public health education. Psychologists can also assist in mental health promotion in schools via curriculum infusion and providing information about mental illnesses as well as protective mental health content as it pertains to self-care, resilience, coping, and other elements of wellness. Moreover, psychologists are needed to provide psychoeducational assessment for identification and intervention of learning challenges and disorders in children, in addition to providing support for teaching staff.

The medical model is no longer the sole umbrella under which psychologists are trained. Currently, there is a wide range of subfields, all of which require extensive professional training. Thus, it should be noted that some psychologists work independently, while others liaise directly with professionals in the medical field. Hence, the placement of the discipline in the Paramedical Professions Act arguably gives a narrow view of the scope of the work that psychologists perform. There is a need to establish a separate governing body for the psychological profession. This would allow for the legal practice and use of the professional title "psychologist" by those qualified in a subfield of psychology (other than clinical, counselling, and educational) and trained to work directly with individuals, groups, and families providing therapeutic and rehabilitative services.

Where does psychology in Barbados go from here? Although psychology's link to mental illness in Barbados is relatively young, it has steadily developed over the past 20 years during which time there has been a call for more psychologists (Maynard, 2013; Dennison, 2017, Moore, 2017). In spite of these strides, there continues to be a need to build a strong corpus of practitioners who engage in research to develop the field of psychology.

References

Agard, R. (2021, March 29). Stressed teachers seeking help. *Nation News*. https://www.nation-news.com/2021/03/29/stressed-teachers-seeking-help/

Alleyne, M., Alleyne, P., & Greenidge, D. (2010). Life satisfaction and perceived stress among university students in Barbados. *Journal of Psychology in Africa, 20*(2), 291–297.

Alleyne, P., Cadogan-McClean, C., & Harper, A. (2013). Examining personal values and ethical behaviour perceptions between accounting and non-accounting students in the Caribbean. *The Accounting Educators' Journal, 23*, 47–70.

Bailey, C. (2016). Crime and violence in Barbados: IDB series on crime and violence in the Caribbean. *Relatório Técnico*. https://publications.iadb.org/publications/english/document/Crime-and-Violence-in-Barbados-IDB-Series-on-Crime-and-Violence-in-the-Caribbean.pdf

Barbados Health Report, The. (2019). Retrieved April 10, 2021, from https://www.barbadosparliament.com/uploads/sittings/attachments/0c85813fd4d9746f1558af6c13239fca.pdf

Barbados Prison Service. (2012). *Annual Report 1st January to 31st December 2012*. https://www.barbadosparliament.com/htmlarea/uploaded/File/Prison%20Service%20Annual%20Report%202012.pdf

Barbados Society of Psychology, The. (2020a). *2020 Psychology week – Mental health for all, mental health today* [Brochure].

Barbados Society of Psychology, The. (2020b). *Membership Directory 2020*. Retrieved March 8, 2021, from https://www.facebook.com/TheBarbadosSocietyofPsychology/photos/2716043748506169

Barrow-Giles, C. (2011). Democracy at work: A comparative study of the Caribbean state. *The Round Table, 100*(414), 285–302.

Best, K. I. (2019). *Gauging stakeholders' perceptions on policy shifts in the financing of tertiary education at the University of the West Indies-Cave Hill Campus, Barbados*. Doctoral dissertation, University of Sheffield.

Campbell, M. H., Gromer, J., Maynard, D. B., & Emmanuel, M. K. (2018). Measuring stress in Caribbean university students: Validation of the PSS-10 in Barbados. *Caribbean Journal of Psychology, 10*(2), 65–88.

Campbell, M. H., Maynard, D., Roberti, J. W., & Emmanuel, M. K. (2012). A comparison of the psychometric strengths of the public-domain Zung Self-Rating Depression Scale with the proprietary Beck Depression Inventory-II in Barbados. *West Indian Medical Journal, 61*(5), 483–488. https://doi.org/10.7727/wimj.2010.145

Campbell, M. H., Roberti, J. W., Maynard, D., & Emmanuel, M. K. (2009). Factorial structure of depressive symptoms in an Anglophone Caribbean university student population: Psychometric properties of the Beck Depression Inventory-II. *Interamerican Journal of Psychology, 43*(3), 577–585. Corpus ID: 53454062.

Carter, H. (2016). Resisting hegemony: Black entrepreneurship in colonial Barbados, 1900–1966. In *History conference. Business and economic history on-line: Papers presented at the BHC annual meeting* (Vol. 14, pp. 1–18).

CBC News Barbados. (2017, January 3). By February, the Psychiatric Hospital should have an improved rehabilitation unit to cater to the needs of its clients. [Image attached] [Status update]. *Facebook*. https://www.facebook.com/CBCNews.bb/photos/by-february-the-psychiatric-hospital-should-have-an-improved-rehabilitation-unit/1844546199159415/

Central Intelligence Agency World Factbook. (2021, April 14). Barbados. In *The world factbook*. Retrieved April 16, 2021, from https://www.cia.gov/the-world-factbook/countries/barbados/

Dennison, A. (2017). *Using Interpretative Phenomenological Analysis and psychodynamic theory to explore teachers' experiences of what they perceive as negative pupil behaviour*. Doctoral dissertation, University of Leicester.

Devonish, D. (2016). Emotional intelligence and job performance: The role of psychological well-being. *International Journal of Workplace Health Management, 9*(4), 428–442.

Devonish, D. (2017). Managers' perceptions of mental illness in Barbadian workplaces: An exploratory study. *The Journal of Mental Health Training, Education, and Practice, 12*(3), 161–172. https://doi.org/10.1108/JMHTEP-09-2016-0047

Downes, A. D. (2002). Freemasonry in Barbados before 1914: The limits of brotherhood. *Journal of Caribbean History, 36*(2), 285–310.

Fayombo, G. (2010). The relationship between personality traits and psychological resilience among the Caribbean adolescents. *International Journal of Psychological Studies, 2*(2), 105–116.

Fayombo, G. (2015). Learning styles, teaching strategies and academic achievement among some psychology undergraduates in Barbados. *Caribbean Educational Research Journal, 3*(2), 46–61.

Fayombo, G. A. (2012). Emotional intelligence and gender as predictors of academic achievement among some university students in Barbados. *International Journal of Higher Education, 1*(1), 102–111.

Frey, R., & Black, J. (2012). The development and practice of psychology: Case studies from the Caribbean. In D. Baker (Ed.), *Oxford handbook of the history of psychology: Global perspectives*. Oxford University Press.

Greenidge, D., & Coyne, I. (2014). Job stressors and voluntary work behaviours: Mediating effect of emotion and moderating roles of personality and emotional intelligence. *Human Resource Management Journal, 24*(4), 479–495.

Griffith, E. E., Mahy, G. E., & Young, J. L. (2008). Barbados Spiritual Baptists: Social acceptance enhances opportunities for supporting public health. *Mental Health, Religion and Culture, 11*(7), 671–683.

Griffith, S., Maynard, D.-M. B., & Bagner, D. (2020). Barbadian teachers' identification of social-emotional, behavioral, and learning challenges in young children. *International Journal of School & Educational Psychology*, advanced online publication. https://doi.org/10.1080/21683603.2020.1802377

Hickling, F. W., & Matthies, B. (2003). The establishment of a clinical psychology post-graduate programme at the University of the West Indies. *Caribbean Journal of Education, 25*(1), 25–36.

Hutchinson, G., & Rose, J. (2011). The development of clinical psychology in Trinidad and Tobago. *Clinical Psychology, 215*, 40.

Jintie, H. A. (2012). *Analysis of the pathway of developing a national mental health plan for Suriname*. Doctoral dissertation, Faculdade de Ciências Médicas. Universidade Nova de Lisboa. Retrieved March 30, 2021, from https://run.unl.pt/bitstream/10362/8401/1/Jintie%20Herman%20TM%202012.pdf

Jules, M. A., & Maynard, D.-M. (2016). Contextualising the psychology of spiritual development among Caribbean emerging adults: Correlates with healthy family relationships, peer associations and drug use. *Journal of Eastern Caribbean Studies. Special Issue on Religions and Identities, 41*(1), 111–149.

Jules, M. A., Maynard, D.-M. B., & Coulson, N. (2015). The susceptibility to online peer influence – Sexual Risk Scale: Preliminary evidence of validity. *Caribbean Journal of Psychology, 7*(1), 64–82.

Jules, M. A., Maynard, D.-M. B., & Coulson, N. (2017). Emerging adults' susceptibility to sexting influences on Facebook: Dangerous or developmental? *International Psychology Bulletin, 21*(3), 45–53.

Jules, M. A., Maynard, D.-M. B., & Coulson, N. (2019). Youth drug use in Barbados and England: Correlates with online peer influences. *Journal of Adolescent Research*, advanced online publication. https://doi.org/10.1177/0743558419839226

Jules, M. A., Maynard, D.-M. B., Lowe, G., Lipps, G. A., & Gibson, R. C. (2020). Psycho-social analysis of depression, anxiety, and student engagement: Effects of parenting practices. *The Journal of Clinical Child Psychology and Psychiatry*. https://doi.org/10.1177/1359104520972447

King, K. (2021, April 2). Youth advocate Christa Soleyn joins GIS Advisory Board. *Loop News Barbados*. https://www.loopnewsbarbados.com/content/youth-advocate-christa-soleyn-joins-gis-advisory-board

Lorde, T., Devonish, D., & Beckles, A. (2010). Real pirates of the Caribbean: Socio-psychological traits, the environment, personal ethics and the propensity for digital piracy in Barbados. *Journal of Eastern Caribbean Studies, 35*(1), 1–35.

Marshall, A., & Maynard, D. (2009). Black female sexual identity: The self defined. *Souls: A Critical Journal of Black Politics, Culture, and Society, 11*(3), 327–336. https://doi.org/10.1080/10999940903088960

Marshall, J. E., Fayombo, G., & Marshall, R. (2015). I paid for it, so I deserve it! Examining psycho-educational variables and student consumerist attitudes to higher education. *International Journal of Higher Education, 4*(4), 73–80.

Maynard, D. (2013). The history and current status of psychology in Barbados: Research and professional practice. *Interamerican Journal of Psychology, 47*(2), 227–238.

Maynard, D., Campbell, M. H., Devonish, D., Leon, T., Roberti, J., & Emmanuel, M. K. (2010). Psychometric properties and factorial structure of the State Trait Anxiety Inventory-Trait Version (STAI-T) in Caribbean university students. *The Journal of Psychology in Africa, 20*(1), 7–12. https://doi.org/10.1080/14330237.2010.10820337

Maynard, D., & Jules, M. A. (2020). Exploring her roots: Black-Caribbean hair identity and going natural using social-media networks. *Journal of Black Psychology*. https://doi.org/10.1177/0095798420971892

Maynard, D., & Springer-Proverbs, R. (2010). An examination of gender differences in characteristics of Barbadian adolescents' same-sex friendships. *Caribbean Journal of Psychology, 3*(1), 40–53.

Maynard, D., & Welch, P. (2009). Coping strategies of Caribbean "Problem Students". *International Journal for the Advancement of Counselling & Development, 31*(1), 17–31. https://doi.org/10.1007/s10447-008-9065-x

Maynard, D. M. (2007). *An investigation into the relationships among certain psychosocial variables and learned helplessness among a sample of Barbadian adolescents: A longitudinal study*. Doctoral dissertation, The University of the West Indies, Cave Hill, Barbados.

Maynard, D.-M., & Jules, M. A. (2017). Promoting inclusive education in Barbados: Applications of the Pre-service Emerging Reflective Teacher Training (PERTT) Model. [Special Issue]. *Caribbean Curriculum, 25*, 19–37.

Maynard, D.-M. B. (2018). Research in educational psychology in the English-speaking Caribbean: A systematic literature review. *Caribbean Journal of Psychology, 10*(1), 18–53.

Maynard, D. M. B., & Fayombo, G. A. (2015). Influence of parental employment status on Caribbean adolescents' self-esteem. *International Journal of School and Cognitive Psychology, 2*(2), 123–129.

Moore, R. S. (2017, September 6). Call for more psychologists in schools. *Barbados Advocate*. https://www.barbadosadvocate.com/news/call-more-psychologists-schools

PAHO/WHO. (2008). *Health Systems Profile Barbados*. Retrieved March 30, 2021, from *https://www.paho.org/hq/dmdocuments/2010/Health_System_Profile-Barbados_2008.pdf*

PAHO/WHO. (2020). *Mental Health Country Profile – Barbados*. Retrieved March 30, 2021, from https://www.paho.org/en/node/73494

Paramedical Professions Act 2008 (COB) CAP.372C (Barbados).

QEH, The Queen Elizabeth Hospital. (2021a). *Psychiatry*. https://www.qehconnect.com/services/psychiatry/

QEH, The Queen Elizabeth Hospital. (2021b). *The Paediatrics Department*. https://www.qehconnect.com/services/paediatrics/

Ramsey, J., Punnett, B. J., & Greenidge, D. (2008). A social psychological account of absenteeism in Barbados. *Human Resource Management Journal, 18*(2), 97–117.

Rogers, C. R. (1951). *Client-centered therapy: Its current practice, implications, and theory, with chapters*. Houghton Mifflin.

Segal, R. (1995). *The black diaspora: Five centuries of the black experience outside Africa.* Macmillan.

Stubbs, N. S., & Maynard, D. M. B. (2017). Academic self-efficacy, school engagement and family functioning, among postsecondary students in the Caribbean. *Journal of Child and Family Studies, 26*(3), 792–799. https://doi.org/10.1007/s10826-016-0595

Taylor, P., & Case, F. I. (Eds.). (2013). *The encyclopedia of Caribbean religions: Volume 1: A-L; Volume 2: M-Z.* University of Illinois Press.

UNCRC, UN Convention on the Rights of the Child. (2015). *Consideration of reports submitted by States parties under article 44 of the Convention Second periodic reports of States parties due in 1997 Barbados.* https://www.refworld.org/pdfid/5853ffe34.pdf

UNESCO. (2021). *Barbados: Education and literacy.* Retrieved April 10, 2021, from http://uis.unesco.org/en/country/bb

World Health Organization. (2009). *WHO-AIMS Report on Mental Health System in Belize: A report of the assessment of the mental health system in Belize using the World Health Organization-Assessment Instrument for Mental Health Systems (WHO-AIMS).* https://www.who.int/mental_health/barbados_who_aims_report.pdf?ua=1

World Health Organization. (2018). *Noncommunicable Diseases (NCD) Country Profiles, 2018.* Retrieved April 1, 2021, from https://www.who.int/nmh/countries/brb_en.pdf

World Health Organization. (2021). *World Health Organization Global Health Expenditure database.* Retrieved April 10, 2021, from https://data.worldbank.org/indicator/SH.XPD.CHEX.GD.ZS?locations=BB

Chapter 14
Psychology and Mental Health in the Federation of Saint Kitts and Nevis

Krista L. Nelson

Mental illness has been called a "disease of pain and exclusion" that is often misunderstood and poorly treated (Theodore, 2017). Research statistics have identified that 60% of mental health patients within the Caribbean islands will not receive psychological assistance or mental health counseling for their mental health issues. Fear of being labelled or discriminated against has contributed to the lack of treatment for mental health issues. Thousands of Caribbean residents endure mental health ailments with no treatment options available. In 2017, the number of individuals having mental illness in the Caribbean was projected to increase by 50% before 2020. The projected increase in 2017 was based upon an increase in the aged population, stress of worry regarding climate change, political environments, and economic and social decline in some countries. The COVID-19 pandemic exacerbated the availability of mental health diagnosis and treatment options. Devastatingly, up to 80% of the individuals living in the Caribbean with mental illness have no access to mental health treatment. The Caribbean region overall is recognized as being understaffed for treating mental disorders and is in dismal need of mental health clinicians to treat the mentally ill (Theodore, 2017).

Mental illness is a significant concern for the population of Saint Kitts and Nevis. The government is presently working to better integrate mental health information and education into the primary health-care system. There are ongoing attempts to promote education about mental illness and the dangers of suicide by government officials (WIC News, 2019). More than 800,000 people die by suicide each year, which makes suicide the principal cause of death among 15–29-year-old individuals (World Health Organization, WHO, 2014).

K. L. Nelson, PhD (✉)
Southern Arkansas University, Magnolia, AR, USA
e-mail: KristaNelson@saumag.edu

G. J. Rich, N. A. Ramkumar (eds.), *Psychology in Oceania and the Caribbean*, International and Cultural Psychology,
https://doi.org/10.1007/978-3-030-87763-7_14

History and Background of Saint Kitts and Nevis

The Federation of Saint Christopher and Nevis, commonly known as Saint Kitts and Nevis (Freeman, 2021), is comprised of two islands of the Lesser Antilles (Momsen & Mills, 2021). The islands are located in the Leeward Islands chain within the eastern part of the Caribbean (Bailey, 2020) and are approximately two miles apart separated by a strait called The Narrows (Bailey, 2020; Momsen & Mills, 2021). The islands straddle the Caribbean Sea and the North Atlantic Ocean and are about 1200 miles southeast from Florida in the United States (Freeman, 2021). The land mass area of the two islands is approximately 104 square miles (Momsen & Mills, 2021). The two islands were once colonies of Great Britain, but gained their freedom from British rule on September 19, 1983 (Bailey, 2020). The Federation continues to remain as a member of the Commonwealth of Nations, while continuing to be heavily influenced by British ideals. The Federation is identified as a Parliamentary democracy and a Commonwealth realm with the legal system being based upon English common law (Bailey, 2020). The capital of the Federation is Basseterre, which is located in Saint Kitts and is the country's main urban center. Population in 2018 in Basseterre was about 14,000 residents. The only large town on the island of Nevis is Charlestown, which is the second-largest town on the two islands of the country (Bailey, 2020).

Saint Kitts and Nevis have a year-round tropical climate. The temperatures range between 24 and 32 degrees Celsius, 75 and 89 degrees Fahrenheit, respectively (Issitt, 2020). The humidity levels range between 70 and 80% most of each year, with frequent rainfall occurring that results in 50–80 rain inches per year. Hurricanes are a possibility for the islands, with the months between June and November being the greatest risk for storms (Issitt, 2020).

The majority of the population of both Saint Kitts and Nevis is descendants of enslaved Africans who were brought to the islands by early settling colonial Europeans. There are minority populations of Portuguese, Lebanese, British, and some individuals of mixed African and European ancestry (Bailey, 2020). In addition, there are some smaller groups of individuals who have origins from India and the United States. There is a very small population of South Asian residents (Momsen & Mills, 2021).

The official language of the Federation is English, which is spoken by most inhabitants (Bailey, 2020; Freeman, 2021; Momsen & Mills, 2021). One estimate is that over 99% of the population speaks English (Issitt, 2020). There is a creole dialect called Saint Kitts Creole, which is English-based, and spoken widely by Kittitians and Nevisians. A 2020 estimate of the population for the two islands is 53,821 with a 0.67% growth in population. More than two-thirds of the population live in rural areas (Momsen & Mills, 2021). Population on the islands is predominantly of African descent (90%), with Caucasian following next (2.7%). Those individuals of mixed race account for approximately 2.5% of the overall population. Life expectancy is identified at 73.1 years for men and 78.0 years for women. Senior adults, over the age of 65, represent 7.5% of the population (Pan American Health Organization, PAHO, 2021). The currency used in the Federation of Saint Kitts and Nevis is that of the East Caribbean dollar (Momsen & Mills, 2021; Bailey, 2020).

Religious involvement is a significant component in many Caribbean homes, specifically in Black Caribbean households. Research has recognized that participation in organized religion is positively related to self-esteem and coping and negatively correlated with depressive symptoms (Rose et al., 2017). Most residents of Saint Kitts and Nevis identify their religious orientation as Christian, with Anglicanism as the primary denomination (Bailey, 2020). Overall, Protestantism is practiced by over 80% of the population (Issitt, 2020). There are a significant number of residents who are Methodists as well (Momsen & Mills, 2021). Other Protestant denominations are practiced on both islands, with a significant population of Roman Catholics on both islands (Bailey, 2020). There are small populations of Rastafarian and Hindu religion practitioners, with both religions having worship centers available in Basseterre (Issitt, 2020).

Archaeologists have identified the earliest inhabitants of Saint Kitts and Nevis as a preagricultural society known as the Archaic people (Bailey, 2020). These early settlers migrated to the islands sometime between 3000 and 2000 BCE from the area that is now known as Florida. The Archaic people culture only remained for a few centuries before disappearing from the islands. The Saladoid people were the next known inhabitants who migrated north from Venezuela in around 100 BCE. The Saladoids were an agricultural society who became known for their unique ceramics. Archaeologists have identified that later groups, including the Igneris and the Carib, lived in Saint Kitts and Nevis. There have been over two dozen archaeological sites located on the islands that yielded artifacts of pottery, flint tools, shells, and, on occasion, human remains (Bailey, 2020).

In 1493, Christopher Columbus visited Saint Kitts and found it inhabited by Carib people. At that time, he named the island "Saint Christopher" for his patron saint (Bailey, 2020; Momsen & Mills, 2021). Columbus also sighted Nevis in 1493. He described the island as having clouds on top of Nevis Peak. He called it *las* nieves, or "the snows," which is how the name of Nevis originated.

Arriving in 1623, British settlers, under the leadership of Sir Thomas Warner, shortened the name to Saint Kitts. These settlers established the first successful English colony in the West Indies. Following the British settlers, French colonists arrived in 1625 and established their own colony in 1627 under the direction of Pierre Bélain, sieur d'Esnambuc (Momsen & Mills, 2021). This was the first French colony established in the Caribbean (Freeman, 2021). In Saint Kitts, in 1626, the last of the Carib peoples were massacred by British and French settlers on Bloody Point (Bailey, 2020).

The island of Nevis was settled in 1628 by British colonists arriving from Saint Kitts (Freeman, 2021). During the seventeenth century, Saint Kitts was divided between warring French and English colonists (Momsen & Mills, 2021). In April 1713, Saint Kitts was given to Great Britain by means of the Treaty of Utrecht and remained under British rule regardless of the capture of Brimstone Hill in 1782 by the French. The Peace of Paris treaty at Versailles restored Saint Kitts back to Great Britain in 1783 (Momsen & Mills, 2021).

Sugarcane plantations developed on the islands of Saint Kitts and Nevis during the seventeenth century. Prior to their growth, smaller plantations grew tobacco, cotton, and indigo (National Archives, 2021). Eventually, sugar plantations became the primary crop grown on the island and were often self-contained with their own labor force. In 1626, Europeans brought the first enslaved Africans to arrive in Saint Kitts island (National Archives, 2021). The majority of the current population of both islands is made up of descendants of the enslaved Africans that worked in sugarcane plantations (Bailey, 2020).

The economy of Saint Kitts and Nevis was based on the cultivation and refinement of sugar from early in the colonial period up through the mid-twentieth century (Issitt, 2020). During the 1960s and 1970s, the sugar industry began to decline. During that time, the government of the Federation began to diversify agricultural crops for production and export. Meat, fish, rice, and vegetables became primary agricultural products, with it accounting for 4% of the gross domestic product (GDP). In 2005, the previously state-sponsored sugarcane industry was discontinued; however, sugarcane is still grown on some farms on both islands and is one of the nation's best export products (Issitt, 2020).

The Federation of Saint Kitts and Nevis is categorized to be a high-income country. The islands had the highest per capita income within the Caribbean region back in 2013, reporting at US $13,330 (PAHO, 2017). Since the 1980s, tourism for the islands has been heavily promoted by the government. Basseterre's quickest growing industry is tourism, and it is also one of the city's largest employers. Alongside with the services industry, tourism accounts for over 70% of the GDP. There was a decline in tourism in the 1990s when the islands were damaged by hurricanes and also after the terrorist attacks on September 11, 2001 in the United States. However, even accounting for those slow periods in tourism, the Federation's economy has increased annually by approximately 4% since 2002 (Issitt, 2020).

Another significant portion of the GDP is created by the manufacturing industry. Saint Kitts and Nevis manufacture products that include cotton, textiles, and clothing. There are mines and refineries located near Basseterre that are exported out of the city. The United States receives approximately 60% of the nation's exports, including agricultural and industrial products. The unemployment rate for the Federation is reasonably low at around 4%. When in comparison to other West Indian and Caribbean countries, the poverty rate for Saint Kitts and Nevis is quite low (Issitt, 2020).

Nevis is the birthplace of the eighteenth-century American founding father, statesman, and politician Alexander Hamilton. Hamilton was born in Charlestown, Nevis, in either 1755 or 1757 out of wedlock. He lived in Charlestown during part of his childhood before moving to St. Croix with his mother and brother. There is debate over his actual birth year, but he was sent to New York to pursue his education as a teen. Hamilton was recognized as taking an early role in the American Revolutionary War, and he later became the first secretary of the treasury of the United States (McDonald, 1979).

Education

Literacy is abundant in Saint Kitts and Nevis with over 97% of the population being educated (Issitt, 2020). Women have a higher literacy rate (97.4%) than do the men (96.5%) in the 15–24-year age group (PAHO, 2017). School attendance is required for children between the ages of 5 and 16 on the islands (Bailey, 2020). The Ministry of Education oversees the schooling of children; educational classes are provided free to the island students (Freeman, 2021). Education is provided "through a countrywide system of free public schools as well as private church-affiliated schools" (Momsen & Mills, 2021). Compulsory attendance begins with primary school at age 5 that lasts for 7 years. Secondary school lasts for 5 years (Bailey, 2020). There are seven public high schools and several private high schools available for secondary school programs. Upon completion of secondary school, students must take the *Caribbean Examinations Council (CXC) Secondary Education Certificate* (Freeman, 2021). Available, if desired, are two additional years of preprimary schooling and two years of postsecondary schooling (Bailey, 2020).

Students can choose to continue their studies at Clarence Fitzroy Bryant College, which confers associate and some bachelor's degrees and is located on the island of Saint Kitts (Clarence Fitzroy Bryant College, 2021; Freeman, 2021). In addition, there is a University of West Indies Open Campus center located in Basseterre, Saint Kitts, where students can teleconference classes to receive bachelor and associate's degrees (The University of the West Indies, 2021). Also on the islands, there are several medical schools and a veterinary school available to entice students from the United States, Canada, and other countries to study (Bailey, 2020). In the Federation, psychology as a major is only available through the University of West Indies teleconference classes (University of West Indies, 2021). Psychology as a degree is not offered at Clarence Fitzroy Bryant College in Saint Kitts (Clarence Fitzroy Bryant College, 2021).

Universal Health-Care Availability

The Ministry of Health Department of the government is responsible for the health care in the Federation (Martin et al., 2011). The islands have government-funded access to health care for children and senior adults. Children under the age of 18 and senior adults over the age of 62 are exempt from public health charges for basic health care (PAHO, 2017). For those who are incapable of paying for health services, there is a "safety net" of social security that provides assistance benefits to ensure health care to citizens, even if they are unable to pay for services (PAHO, 2017).

Psychological Presence in Saint Kitts and Nevis

The psychological background for the islands of Saint Kitts and Nevis was significantly impacted by the late Dr. Arthur W. Lake (St. Kitts Observer, 2018). Dr. Lake was originally from Canada, receiving his medical degree from McGill University in Montreal. However, he received his training and certification as a druggist and dispenser in Antigua (ZIZ, 2018). Dr. Lake was a recipient of the Member of the British Empire (MBE) in 1960, and he was named a member of the Order of the British Empire in 1967. These honors were recognition for his years of service to the fields of psychiatry, medicine, surgery, and obstetrics (St. Kitts Observer, 2018).

Dr. Lake was responsible for establishing the first mental health clinics throughout the Federation of Saint Kitts and Nevis. His establishment of clinics occurred during a time in the community when mental illness was "very much frowned upon," with mentally ill and psychiatric patients often ostracized or hidden from society (ZIZ, 2018). Dr. Lake is also recognized as spearheading the establishment of the Saint Kitts Mental Health Association (ZIZ, 2018). On February 20, 2018, due to his "long and meritorious service" to pioneering mental health care in Saint Kitts, the island's first national mental health day treatment center was renamed to *Dr. Arthur Wilfred Lawson Lake Mental Health Day Treatment Centre*. The Prime Minister of the Federation, Timothy Sylvester Harris, remarked that the renaming of the treatment facility was a salute to the pioneering work of Dr. Arthur Lake (St. Kitts Observer, 2018). The Mental Health Day Treatment Centre originally opened in December 2016 in La Guerite, which is outside of Basseterre in Saint Kitts (St. Kitts Observer, 2016).

The Saint Kitts Mental Health Association was established in October 2007. The vision of the organization is to decrease the stigma and improve the mental health of the citizens of the twin-islands through "cooperation, acceptance research, education, and service" (St. Kitts Mental Health Association, 2021). Members of the mental health association are comprised of mental health professionals including psychiatrists, psychologists (PhD level and masters' level), social workers, and counselors who offer a diverse range of services to treat mental illness.

There is a more recent organization that has been established for the Federation, the St. Kitts and Nevis Mental Health and Psycho-social Committee (Nevis Ministry of Health, 2020). This committee was established with the Ministry of Health to provide mental health and psychosocial support to residents of the two islands. The committee recently embarked on a specific campaign to provide information to community members about the concerns of mental illness, specifically relating to life during the COVID-19 pandemic. The committee team provided short articles online to Federation residents to assist in educating about how to improve mental health and provide self-care during such a stressful life experience. The Mental Health and Psycho-social Committee also partnered with the Pan American Health Organization (PAHO) to provide support networks and mental health initiatives to reduce stress and improve education regarding mental health and coping (Nevis Ministry of Health, 2020).

Mental Illness in Saint Kitts and Nevis

Official records note that mental illness affects approximately 1% of adults on the islands of Saint Kitts and Nevis (Martin et al., 2011). However, actual records indicate that the true prevalence is likely closer to 5–10% of adults having mental disorders (PAHO, 2008). The most commonly seen mental health issue diagnosed is schizophrenia. Next diagnosed on the twin-islands are mood disorders, which include depression and bipolar disorders. The PAHO (2017) reports that between the years of 2011 and 2015, the following psychiatric disorders were diagnosed and treated: schizophrenia (793 cases), schizoaffective disorders (297), bipolar disorder (190), depression (120), and cannabis-induced psychosis (54).

Adolescents in the Federation have been shown to be susceptible to depression symptomology. In one study, students in grade 10 were identified as having diagnosable depression after taking the Beck Depression Inventory-II (BDI-II) at their high school. The results indicated that 62.1% reported some symptoms of depression. There were 14.8% reporting moderate to severe depressive symptoms, while 9.7% scored reporting severe symptoms of depression. Females reported significantly higher BDI-II scores, with 70% reporting some level of depressive symptoms. Only 52% of males disclosed depressive symptomology (Lowe et al., 2009). Another study found that 52.1% of surveyed adolescents in the Caribbean, including students from Saint Kitts and Nevis, reported mild to severe depressive symptoms (Lipps et al., 2010). Of the surveyed adolescents, 29.1% reported moderate to severe depressive symptoms (Lowe et al., 2014; Lipps et al., 2012).

The government of Saint Kitts and Nevis is cognizant that mental health needs require more education and funding for the country. The Ministry of Health is the governing body for mental illness identification and treatment for the islands of Saint Kitts and Nevis (Ministry of Health, 2021). It is also accountable for organizing and managing all health services and for formulating policies for health care (SKN Vibes, 2021). The World Health Organization (WHO) stated in their *Mental Health Atlas* (2005) "There is a paucity of epidemiological data on mental illnesses in Saint Kitts and Nevis in internationally accessible literature."

Nevis Island has one 50-bed hospital, the Alexandra Hospital. At the Alexandra Hospital, when necessary, individuals requiring inpatient mental health treatment are hospitalized. A Saint Kitts psychiatrist conducts outpatient biweekly psychiatric clinic appointments at the hospital. Additionally, there are two psychiatric nurses that see psychiatric patients for necessary triage, make necessary home visits, and are able to see patients in the community mental health clinics (Lamba & Aswani, 2012–2013). When there are psychiatric emergencies, urgent care is frequently provided by nonpsychiatric primary care providers. This urgent care can include visits and admission into the emergency department and the preliminary management of psychiatric symptoms for patients. The supervision of the psychiatric patients' symptoms and behaviors by nonpsychiatric providers typically lasts from one to four days before the patient is seen by a visiting psychiatrist (Lamba & Aswani, 2012–2013).

Both Saint Kitts and Nevis would benefit from additional staff in the mental health field. One research article (Lamba & Aswani, 2012–2013, p. 27) stated that there is a "paucity" of mental health workers on the island of Nevis. However, there are shortages in mental health-qualified staff in Saint Kitts as well. In 2017, a mental health center was delayed in opening because of the lack of mental health-certified nurses. Specifically, there were only four nurses with training in mental health available, and these nurses would have to coordinate their working schedules with the psychiatric units elsewhere on the islands (St. Kitts Observer, 2017).

In 2007, the World Health Organization Assessment Instrument for Mental Health (WHO/AIMS) was used to collect data regarding the mental health structures available in Saint Kitts and Nevis (WHO, 2009). According to the report, approximately 1% of current and non-recurrent expenditures was allotted for mental health services for the islands. The WHO reported in 2011 that the majority of primary health-care doctors and nurses in Nevis and Saint Kitts have not received official in-service trainings in the past five years for mental health treatment for disorders.

There are seven outpatient mental health facilities available on the two islands. There are 12 psychiatric beds available in general hospitals for inpatient stays for mental illness (WHO, 2011). There is only 1 psychiatric inpatient unit, having 14 beds, in the Federation that is located in Saint Kitts (Lamba & Aswani, 2012–2013). In 2011, there were 1172.47 individuals treated (per 100,000 population) in mental health outpatient facilities. Females comprised 41% of the total treated. There were approximately 2% of children under the age of 18 treated (WHO, 2011).

The primary delivery service for mental health care is the community-based approach for treatment. In the Federation, mental health treatment is provided through several options. The first opportunity is weekly-scheduled clinics in 3 of the 11 primary health-care centers. The second option is provided through bimonthly clinics provided at Her Majesty's Prison for mental health treatment. The third opportunity is at the counseling center. And the fourth option is treatment at the outpatient counseling clinic at the Joseph N. France Hospital. At specific nursing homes, CARDIN house in Saint Kitts and the Flamboyant Nursing Home in Nevis, inpatient care is provided to some mental health patients. Government mental health officers occasionally make home visits for treatment and are sometimes accompanied by psychiatrists (WHO, 2011).

There are potential cultural considerations that likely contribute to mental illness in Saint Kitts and Nevis. The first consideration is that marijuana is often not viewed as a drug on the islands. The Rastafarian religion incorporates the usage of marijuana into their religious rituals (Murrell, 1998). This usage of marijuana for religious purposes reduces the taboo factor of marijuana as a psychoactive drug (Lamba & Aswani, 2012–2013). The next concern that impacts mental health treatment is the lack of psychiatric medication available for patients. Specifically, occasional financial concerns at the Nevis hospital create inconsistent availability for treatment with modern antipsychotic medications (Lamba & Aswani, 2012–2013). According to the WHO, there is significant scarcity of psychotropic medications for neurological and mental health illness in the Federation (2011). If medication is available, it is provided for free through the government pharmacies from the Ministry of Health (Lamba & Aswani, 2012–2013). However, sometimes the medications which are available are expensive and are only available from private businesses (WHO, 2011). The third cultural consideration is the stigma of mental illness. In larger cities and urban environments, the stigma attached to mental illness is often buffered by larger populations and more options for treatment. In Nevis, one researcher noted that with only approximately 12,000 in population, it is more difficult to ensure anonymity because it is a smaller community (Lamba & Aswani, 2012–2013). Difficulties in retaining patient anonymity in small island populations, such as Saint Kitts and Nevis, can create ethical dilemmas similar to ones noted in rural communities (Roberts et al., 1999). The final cultural consideration is that of hurricane trauma and its impact on mental health (Lamba & Aswani, 2012–2013). The islands have significant hurricane activity, which can be traumatic and life-threatening. This should be a consideration in the diagnosis of such disorders as post-traumatic stress disorder or acute stress disorder. Researchers have suggested that local health-care providers should be competently trained for post-disaster mental health issues (Kutcher et al., 2005).

Conclusion

This brief synopsis of the psychological and mental health availability options within Saint Kitts and Nevis does show that there are concerns for the government to address. There are several opportunities for growth for the twin-islands to provide more mental health services and allocate more resources to the treatment of mental illness. However, this summary also illustrates the growing commitment to improve and expound mental health education and services to the residents of the Federation. The Ministry of Health has identified their need to improve education about mental health illness and is working to provide informative training to destigmatize the myths surrounding mental disorders. There is a significant need for more highly trained professionals in the field of psychology, psychiatry, social work, and counseling on the islands. These professionals would enhance the existing mental health network and would allow for more citizens to receive the necessary mental health treatment for their mental illness.

References

Bailey, E. (2020). *Our world: Saint Kitts and Nevis*. Great Neck Publishing.

Clarence Fitzroy Bryant College. (2021). *Academics*. Retrieved May 13, 2021, from www.cfbc.edu.kn

Freeman, K. (2021). Saint Kitts and Nevis. *AACRAO*. Retrieved May 11, 2021, from www.aacrao.org/edge/country/saint-kitts-and-nevis

Issitt, M. (2020). Basseterre. *Our world: Saint Kitts & Nevis*. Great Neck Publishing.

Kutcher, S., Chehil, S., & Roberts, T. (2005). An integrated program to train local health care providers to meet post-disaster mental health needs. *Revista Panamericana de Salud Pública, 18*(4), 338–345.

Lamba, G. S., & Aswani, V. (2012–2013, Winter). A case study of mental illness and psychiatric services on the Caribbean island of Nevis. *International Journal of Mental Health, 41*(4), 24–29.

Lipps, G., Lowe, G. A., Gibson, R. C., Halliday, S., Morris, A., Clarke, N., & Wilson, R. N. (2012). Parenting and depressive symptoms among adolescents in four Caribbean societies. *Child and Adolescent Psychiatry and Mental Health, 6*(31), 1–12.

Lipps, G., Lowe, G. A., Halliday, S., Morris-Patterson, A., Clarke, N., & Wilson, R. N. (2010). The association of academic tracking to depressive symptoms among adolescents in three Caribbean countries. *Child and Adolescent Psychiatry and Mental Health, 4*(16), 1–10.

Lowe, G. A., Lipps, G., Gibson, R. C., Halliday, S., Morris, A., Clarke, N., & Wilson, R. N. (2014). Neighbourhood factors and depression among adolescents in four Caribbean countries. *PLoS One, 9*(4), 1–14. https://doi.org/10.1371/journal.pone.0095538

Lowe, G. A., Lipps, G., Halliday, S., Morris, A., Clarke, N., & Wilson, R. N. (2009). Depressive symptoms among fourth form students in St. Kitts and Nevis high schools. *The Scientific World Journal, 9*. https://doi.org/10.1100/tsw.2009.16

Martin, P. A., Martin, M. L., & Faulkner, M. S. (2011). Overview of health care in St. Kitts and Nevis. *The Journal of Race & Policy, 7*(1), 15–21.

McDonald, F. (1979). *Alexander Hamilton, a biography*. W.W. Norton & Company.

Momsen, J. D., & Mills, G. E. M. (2021). Saint Kitts and Nevis. *Britannica*. Retrieved May 11, 2021, from www.britannica.com/place/Saint-Kitts-and-Nevis

Murrell, N. S. (1998). Introduction: The Rastafari phenomenon. In N. S. Murrell, W. D. Spencer, A. McFarlane, & C. Chisolm (Eds.), *Chanting down Babylon: The Rastafari reader* (pp. 1–22). Temple University Press.

National Archives, St. Kitts Nevis. (2021). *The sugar factory*. Retrieved May 10, 2021, from www.historicstkitts.kn

Nevis Ministry of Health. (2020, April 26). *St. Kitts-Nevis' Mental health team continues to provide support to citizens and residents during the COVID-19 Pandemic*. Retrieved May 10, 2021, from http://covid19.gov.kn/2020/04/26/st-kitts-nevis-mental-health-team-continues-to-provide support-to-citizens-and-residents-during-the-covid-19-pandemic/

Pan American Health Organization. (2008). *Health situation in the Americas: Basic indicators*.

Pan American Health Organization. (2017). Saint Kitts and Nevis. *Health in the Americas. Summary: Regional Outlook and Country Profiles* (pp. 205–208).

Pan American Health Organization. (2021). *Saint Kitts and Nevis*. Retrieved May 13, 2021, from www.paho.org/en/saint-kitts-and-nevis

Roberts, L. W., Battaglia, J., & Epstein, R. S. (1999). Frontier ethics: Mental health care needs and ethical dilemmas in rural communities. *Psychiatric Services, 50*(4), 497–503.

Rose, T., Finigan-Carr, N., & Joe, S. (2017). Organized religious involvement and mental health among Caribbean Black adolescents. *Child and Adolescent Social Work Journal, 34*, 147–157.

St. Kitts & Nevis Observer. (2016, December 6). *As Mental Health Day Treatment Centre opens, senior minister says no health without good mental health*. Retrieved May 9, 2021, from www.thestkittsnevisobserver.com/mental-health-day-treatment-centre-opens-senior minister-says-no-health-without-good-mental-health/

St. Kitts & Nevis Observer. (2017, August 4). *Opening of mental health center delayed*. Retrieved May 16, 2021, from www.thestkittsnevisobserver.com/opening-of-mental-health-center-delayed/

St. Kitts & Nevis Observer. (2018, February 20). *Prime minister commends work of the late Dr. Arthur Lake*. Retrieved May 2, 2021, from www.thestkittsnevisobserver.com/prime-minister-commendswork-late-drarthur-lake/

St. Kitts Mental Health Association. (2021). *About us*. Retrieved May 13, 2021, from www.skmha.wordpress.com/about-us/

The University of the West Indies. (2021). *The open campus in St. Kitts and Nevis*. Retrieved May 11, 2021, from www.open.uwi.edu/st_kitts_nevis

Theodore, R. (2017). Mental health in the Caribbean: The silent epidemic. *BahamasLocal.com.* Retrieved May 14, 2021, from www.bahamaslocal.com/newsitem/174028/Mental_health_in_the_Caribbean_The_silent_epidemic.html

WIC News. (2019, October 11). *St. Kitts-Nevis gov't holds activities to increase public awareness of mental health*. https://wicnews.com/caribbean/st-kitts-nevis-govt-holds-activities-increase-public awareness-mental-health-131022606/. Accessed 6 May 2021.

World Health Organization. (2005). Saint Kitts and Nevis. In *Mental Health Atlas*. www.who.int/mental_health/evidence/atlas/profiles_countries_s1.pdf. Accessed 6 May 2021.

World Health Organization. (2009). Mental health system in Saint Kitts and Nevis. *The World Health Organization Assessment Instrument for Mental Health Report.* Retrieved May 6, 2021, from www.who.int/mental_health/who_aims_report_st_kitt_nevis_english.pdf?ua=1

World Health Organization. (2011). Saint Kitts and Nevis. *Mental Health Atlas 2011*. Retrieved May 7, 2021, from www.who.int/mental_health/evidence/atlas/profiles/kna_mh_profile.pdf?ua=1&ua=1

World Health Organization. (2014). *Preventing suicide: A global imperative*. WHO Press.

ZIZ. (2018, February 20). *Mental Health Day Treatment Centre Renamed*. Retrieved May 2, 2021, from www.zizonline.com/mental-health-day-treatment-centre-renamed/

Chapter 15
Psychology in Haiti

Grant J. Rich and Wismick Jean-Charles

Haiti has a rich heritage. Originally inhabited by the Taínos/Arawak, the indigenous people, Christopher Columbus landed there on his first voyage in 1492, near the modern cities of Cap-Haïtien and Limonade. Spanish colonialism brought much devastation, including infectious diseases, smallpox epidemics, and maltreatment of the Taínos including the forced labor *encomienda* system and forced conversions to Catholicism. Within a generation, the indigenous population was almost completely eradicated. After Spanish rule, French rule dominated, and the western third of the island was renamed Saint Domingue (The Treaty of Ryswick in 1697 formally ended French-Spanish hostilities). The French enslaved thousands of Africans transporting them to St. Domingue to work in both sugarcane and coffee plantations. Rapidly, colonial whites became vastly outnumbered by enslaved Africans, over time resulting in the ethnogenesis of new social groups, such as free blacks and free coloreds (Cheney, 2017; Dubois, 2004; Geggus, 2014; Girard, 2010; James, 1963).

Ultimately the free coloreds, as well as enslaved and free blacks, advocated for freedom. Revolts beginning mostly in the 1790s, such as one led by Ogé and Chavannes, foreshadowed the coming of the full Haitian Revolution, which was led by Toussaint Louverture, a former slave (and notably a slave owner himself), and was in part inspired by the 1789 French Revolution. The Vodou religion also played a key role in the Haitian Revolution; in a famous event, Boukman, an enslaved Haitian who was also a Hougan (Vodou priest), convened a secret meeting at Bois Caïman in northern Haiti in 1791, which led to the ultimately successful revolution (Dubois, 2004). The extraordinary outcome of the Haitian Revolution was the end

G. J. Rich (✉)
Walden University, Juneau, AK, USA

W. Jean-Charles
Université Notre-Dame d'Haiti (UNDH), Port-au-Prince, Haiti

G. J. Rich, N. A. Ramkumar (eds.), *Psychology in Oceania and the Caribbean*, International and Cultural Psychology,
https://doi.org/10.1007/978-3-030-87763-7_15

of slavery and the defeat of Napoleon Bonaparte's army. In sum, by 1804, under the leadership of Jean-Jacques Dessalines, Haiti became not just the only nation in the world created from a successful slave revolt, it also became the first independent country in Latin America and the Caribbean and the second republic in the Americas (Dubois, 2004; Geggus, 2014; Girard, 2010; James, 1963). Nevertheless, the young nation was forced to pay an indemnity to France for over one hundred years (rather than France compensating the formerly enslaved people with reparations), and the new country was largely shunned by other nations, especially European powers. Even the Roman Catholic Church did not recognize Haiti in its early years (WHO, 2010).

Sadly, the decades that followed were tumultuous ones politically, socially, and economically for Haiti, with many leadership transitions, including an almost 20-year-long occupation by the USA and its forces from 1915 to 1934. The US Marines soon took control of Port-au-Prince and the banks, declared martial law, and censored journalists (Dash, 2010; Dubois, 2004, 2013; Farmer, 2005; Girard, 2010). After this period, Francois "Papa Doc" Duvalier and his son Jean-Claude "Baby Doc" Duvalier headed regimes infamous for their corruption and repression. During the Duvalier dynasty, among the many abuses and corruption under both Papa and Baby Doc Duvalier were the rulers' use of the *Tontons Macoutes* group, which kept order by terrorizing the public, notably political opponents. When, in 1986, Baby Doc was forced to leave the country, political instability continued, with several coups d'état in 1988, 1991, and 2004, followed by numerous crimes.

Without doubt, the most salient event of the past decade was the magnitude 7.0 earthquake in Haiti on January 12, 2010. Estimates of the death toll ranged from 100,000 to over 300,000, and thousands were more injured. Over 1.5 million were left homeless, and infrastructure was decimated, especially in Port-au-Prince, the national capital and largest city. Approximately 250,000 buildings collapsed (WHO, 2010). Among many impacts of the earthquake was a large cholera outbreak that followed, which added to and prolonged the devastation. Though many in the USA would not know it, 600 miles from the USA state of Florida is Haiti, a nation that is probably as poor as the USA is wealthy. Even before the earthquake, Haiti was the poorest nation in the Western hemisphere, and its institutions and recovery were further decimated by the earthquake. Haiti is ranked 163 of 183 nations in the 2016 UN Human Development Index (Jean-Charles & Rich, 2020). The real GDP per capita is estimated at $2905 (2019), with 60% of Haitians living under the national poverty line (Haiti World Factbook, 2021). As scholars, aid groups, and journalists have documented clearly, humanitarian aid from foreign governmental and nongovernmental groups was not always received, was not received in timely fashion, or was distributed in corrupt fashion, resulting in even more challenges for Haiti (Dubois, 2013; Farmer, 2011).

Haiti often ranks among the most corrupt countries in the world on the Corruption Perceptions Index, and crime, especially in Port-au-Prince, is a continuing concern, especially in areas such as Cité Soleil. Social science offers mountains of evidence to support the reality that poverty is often associated with social problems, and indeed even in modern Haiti, as a result of poverty and lack of social welfare supports, there are cases of modern-day slavery, in which poor, vulnerable children are sent to live and work with an adult, sometimes a distant relative, termed *restavèk* in Haitian Kreyòl, in what amounts in many cases to brutal servitude (Cadet, 1998; Patterson, 2019). Contributing factors to Haiti's poverty include corruption, the impact of natural disasters, and the overall comparative low level of education of the population. Many Haitians rely on remittances sent back to Haiti from family members who are working abroad such as in the USA. Given Haiti's political instability and often poor infrastructure (such as lack of reliable electricity in all places, most rural housing without indoor plumbing, and just 33% of population are Internet users), economic investment in the nation is often difficult to encourage. Its economy relies on agricultural products such as sugarcane and various tropical fruits and vegetables, as well as some industries such as textiles, sugar refining, flour milling, and cement (Haiti World Factbook, 2021; WHO, 2010).

Modern Haiti shares the island with the Dominican Republic and is approximately the size of the US state of Maryland. Its population is estimated to be approximately eleven million, and both French and Haitian Kreyòl are official languages. In terms of religion, about 55% are Roman Catholic, 28% Protestant, and about 2% Vodou, with 4% representing other religions and 10% reporting no religion (Haiti World Factbook, 2021). Notably many Haitians will practice some aspects of Vodou in conjunction with a Christian religion, and sometimes adherence to Vodou beliefs is kept private and not reported in interviews or surveys. The Haitian population is young, with a median age of 24.1 years, with a life expectancy of about 65 years, and a high infant mortality rate of approximately 41 deaths per 1000 live births (Haiti World Factbook, 2021). Estimates suggest that about 51% of the population is single and 44% married or cohabiting; indeed common law unions (*viv avek* or *plasaj*) are prevalent (WHO, 2010). Recent figures suggest a literacy rate of about 62% or, by gender, 65% for males and 58% for females. Some estimates suggest that in rural areas, approximately 80% of the population cannot read French. As of 2010, 72% of the population received only a primary school level education, with just 1% having a university education. About 58% of the population may be considered urbanized, with estimates of the population of the largest city, Port-au-Prince, at about 2.8 million (Haiti World Factbook, 2021; WHO, 2010). Racially, Haitians are about 95% black and 5% mixed/other; historically and to the present day, as a result of colonization as well as slavery, there remain social class/stratification issues and discrimination based on skin color (Trouillot, 1990). Indeed Haiti's income inequality is one of the highest in the entire world (e.g., in 2001 the Gini coefficient was 0.66, WHO, 2010).

In October 2016, Hurricane Matthew struck Haiti as a Category 4 storm. Death toll estimates range from the official figure of 546 to over 1000, and damage estimates approach two billion US dollars, with approximately 175,1000 left homeless (Ahmed, 2016; Stewart, 2017). Much of the worst of the hurricane was in southern Haiti, though gusts of 60 MPH reached Port-au-Prince. More recently the COVID-19 pandemic has wreaked havoc in Haiti. In July 2020, reports indicated 6948 cases and 145 deaths (Obert, 2020). By the writing of this chapter in April 2021, Haiti has documented 12,944 confirmed cases of COVID-19 with 251 deaths and a 5% test positivity rate (Haiti COVID-19, 2021). This number is likely underestimated due to incomplete testing of the population. The impact of the pandemic on the mental health of Haitians is especially pronounced, as Haiti has already suffered and endured so many challenges and traumas leading up to the pandemic, from the 2010 earthquake to hurricanes, floods, cholera, and coups, as well as unemployment, violence, and periodic civil unrest and political instability.

In fact, some research conducted shortly before the 2010 earthquake indicates that 40% of Haitian youth have experienced trauma linked to physical or sexual assault, kidnapping, death of a family member, or gang violence, with Haitian females already especially vulnerable to PTSD (Auguste & Rasmussen, 2019). An additional consideration is that lockdown measures in the pandemic have resulted in increases in family and gender-based violence, as when, for instance, an abuser resides in the same home as the abused. One program run by Médecins Sans Frontières (MSF) has operated a clinic in Port-au-Prince since 2015 that aims to serve survivors of gender-based violence. This program offers medical and psychological services and now also COVID-19 testing (Obert, 2020). While resilience is a "word often used to describe Haitians," according to Laetitita Dégraff, a Haitian psychologist (Nicolas, 2013; Obert, 2020; Rich et al., 2018), the combination of a behavioral health workforce shortage with a population that has endured chronic and multiple traumas is challenging indeed.

Despite the stigma regarding mental health, available indicators do demonstrate increasing utilization of mental health services during the pandemic. For instance, the United Nations via its migration agency IOM converted its human trafficking hotline to serve as a hotline offering psychological assistance and COVID-19 counseling; in the first week of April 2020, it received over 14,000 calls. In addition, the Center for Spirituality and Mental Health (or, CESSA, for its French acronym: Centre de Spiritualité et de Santé Mentale), in collaboration with Baylor University, for the training of its counselors, has also developed a telepsychology program which has served 701 people, including 167 frontline workers (Baylor University, Community Connection Magazine, 2020). Furthermore, the Haitian Psychology Association began operating its own hotline at the onset of the pandemic, with psychologists who volunteer their time to offer free mental health services; the volunteer nature of the services is especially notable and praiseworthy as there are perceptions and often realities that psychology in Haiti is for the wealthy elites as it is typically expensive (Obert, 2020).

Psychology in Haiti

To begin to understand psychology in Haiti, it was first necessary to provide the sociohistorical context described above. Haitian psychology, as a discipline, is a relatively recent development (Boursiquot, 2001; Jean-Charles & Griff, 2014). However, prior to the founding of formal psychology as an independent discipline, which some scholars date to the founding of Wilhelm Wundt's psychological laboratory in Leipzig in Europe in 1879 (Rich & Gielen, 2015), there was of course healing and medicine of various sorts in Haiti and its precursor St. Domingue. For instance, French colonials in St. Domingue were influenced by the work of Mesmer and others involved with hypnosis and related techniques in Paris, France, and Europe (McClellan, 1992). In addition, Weaver, a historian (2006), has detailed how enslaved healers including herbalists, diviners, nurses, and midwives were common in the eighteenth-century St. Domingue and in fact played a role, often as leaders, in ending slavery through the Haitian Revolution. Indeed, traditional healing remains a commonly utilized practice today, especially in rural Haiti. As medical anthropologist Brodwin (1996) documents, persons who are ill may simultaneously seek treatment both from Western doctors, when available, and also from herbalists and religious leaders.

Psychology's introduction in Haiti can be attributed to the return to the country of the first psychiatrists trained abroad, in Europe specifically. To mention a few, Louis Mars, Jeanne Philippe, and Legrand Bijoux aided significantly in founding the first Institute of Psychology in Haiti, in the 1970s, as part of the School of Ethnology. In 1975, the psychology department was created, and psychology's evolution in Haiti may be attributed to these psychiatrists' dedication. Furthermore, the pioneering work of eminent psychologists, including Chavannes Douyon, Ernst Myrville, and Jean-Claude Edmond, nurtured the discipline (Jean-Charles & Griff, 2014). In terms of mental hospitals, the American model was imported by the mid-twentieth century, with the opening of *Hospital Beudet* (120 beds) and the *Centre Psychiatrique Mars et Kline* (20 beds), both of which are located in or near the capital Port-au-Prince (Nicolas et al., 2012). As of 2012, there were three additional private centers and two psychological units in private hospitals in Port-au-Prince, and elsewhere in the nation were four more psychological units in public hospitals, offering basic services, serving the north (Cap-Haïtien and Gonaïves) and south (Les Cayes and Jérémie) (Nicolas et al., 2012). More broadly speaking, some analyses view Haiti's healthcare system in four sections: public institutions administered by the Ministry of Public Health and Population (MSPP), the private nonprofit sector (NGOs and religious organizations), the mixed nonprofit sector, and the private nonprofit sector (WHO, 2010), to which one may add the role of folk, traditional, and religious healers (Rich, 2013). Among the latter include several types, including *fanm saj* (midwives), *pikirist* (injectionists), *doktè zo* (bone setters) *doktè fey* (herbalists), and Vodou priests and priestesses (WHO, 2010).

Prior to the 2010 earthquake, there were less than 40 psychiatrists and psychiatric nurses for a national population of roughly 10 million persons, with 2 main psychiatric hospitals in Port-au-Prince, both of which received significant damage (St. Louis, 2014; WHO, 2010). At the time of the earthquake in 2010, just 500 students were enrolled in the 2 psychology schools that then existed to serve the entire nation, and at that time the bachelor's degree was the highest degree awarded (Jean-Charles & Griff, 2014; Jean-Charles & Rich, 2020). A State University assessment found only 100 Haitian psychologists were then on site to attempt to meet Haiti's mental health needs (Nicolas et al., 2012).

After the earthquake, the global humanitarian community responded by pledging funds and/or sending international psychologists. Many of these psychologists/humanitarians came on brief missions, leaving when the media was no longer there (Jean-Charles, 2011a, 2019). While the assistance was needed/valued, longer-term sustainability and local capacity regarding mental health services appropriate for Haiti were crucial (Farmer, 2011; Katz, 2013). While in 2010, before the earthquake, there were only two departments of psychology within the State University (Faculté d'Ethnologie and Faculté des Sciences Humaines), two years after the earthquake, there were three more. In 2011, the Université Franco-Haitienne du Cap-Haïtien (UFCH) opened a department of psychology. In September 2012, the Catholic Université Notre Dame d'Haiti (UNDH) created a new school of Letters of Human Sciences, known in French as the Faculté des Lettres et des Sciences Humaines, with the acronym (FLESH), with a psychology department. Finally, in 2012, the Henri Christophe Limonade campus of the State University in the northern region of the country has also opened a new school of Human and Social Sciences with a department of psychology.

As of 2020, ten years after the earthquake, five psychology schools with three master's programs exist in Haiti. In 2020, 1053 students are enrolled in psychology at both the bachelor and master's levels. The present status of Haiti's psychology indicates that the field's size is increasing. However, these initiatives do not automatically imply quality improvements (Jean-Charles & Rich, 2020). There continue to be workforce issues in other mental health professions as well; for instance, in 2015, though this figure is contested and is likely not completely accurate, one Haitian psychologist commented that there were only two public psychiatrists for a nation of ten million persons (Partners in Health (PIH), 2015). Notably, Haiti's Ministry of Health reports Haiti's investment in health actually declined from over 16 percent in 2004 to under 5 percent in 2017, after the 2010 earthquake (Obert, 2020).

In 2011, the Ministry of Public Health and Population created a mental health unit, and it published an official policy document on mental health in 2012 (MSPP, 2012). Despite the creation of the mental health unit in 2011, it has been underfunded, and as of 2020, the coordinator of the mental health unit, René Domersant, notes that Haiti only has 23 psychiatrists and 124 psychologists (Obert, 2020). Haiti has arguably the lowest rate of psychosocial support in Latin America and the Caribbean. For instance, some analyses show that while the Dominican Republic, which shares the island with Haiti, has a population roughly equal to Haiti, the Dominican Republic has about 2000 mental health professionals, compared to estimates ranging from 32 to 200 mental health professionals in Haiti in 2011 (Nicolas et al., 2012). One significant step towards capacity building in Haiti was the creation of *L'Association Haitienne de Psychologie* (AHPsy), which has made progress towards several of its aims, including work on a code of ethics and establishment of regulatory frameworks. Haiti has also been active and represented at CANPA (the Caribbean Alliance of National Psychology Associations), which was launched in 2013. Haiti's participation has included hosting in Haiti one of its biennial meetings, the Caribbean Regional Conference of Psychology (CRCP) in 2016, and service on the CANPA executive council (e.g., Guerda Nicolas as its Secretary-General).

In addition to the formal university course programs, there have been other relevant psychology initiatives in Haiti since the 2010 earthquake. For instance, the Teachers Mental Health Training (TMHT) program in Arcahaie, Haiti (about two hours from Port-au-Prince), was led by Haitian psychologist Guerda Nicolas, who is chair of University of Miami's psychology department (St. Louis, 2014). This program was implemented over six months with work towards aims of providing psycho-educational training to teachers regarding: (1) risks and signs of various mental illnesses; (2) improving teacher understanding of effect of mental health on students' academics and social development; and (3) providing teachers with knowledge on methods of better supporting students. TMHT also included a "train the trainer" component so that a subset of participants could provide training to others in their own communities. The program had a participatory, community empowerment focus, including community perspectives on cultural beliefs, and integration of historical components to the curriculum. The TMHT model acknowledges the impact of Haiti's history on present-day culture and well-being (St. Louis, 2014).

Another example of psychology in practice is exemplified by the *Centre de Spiritualité et de Santé Mentale* (CESSA) through the Global Kids Connect Project (Kuriansky & Jean-Charles, 2012) and the group therapy initiative within the schools (Nitza, 2018; Franck et al., 2019). On the 1-year anniversary of the earthquake, in 2011, Kuriansky, along with Jean-Charles, initiated in Port-au-Prince a program called Global Kids Connect Project (GKCP) which included modules that communicate to children that peers around the world are having similar experiences and that they care about each other, even from afar. The project consisted of two aspects:

(I) A workshop for children which involves four components: (1) exchange of an object with a message of hope among children affected by the earthquakes in Haiti and Japan (and other countries); (2) training about simple psychological techniques for stress reduction and recovery; (3) a geography lesson about the countries; and (4) cultural programming (e.g., music, song, dance, drawing, artwork) from the cultures

(II) A training workshop for youth volunteers to teach them how to give the workshop to children (Kuriansky, 2018)

Furthermore, through the group therapy initiative, trainings are offered to teachers, and therapy continues to be provided once a week to children from nine schools of the metropolitan region of Port-au-Prince.

In addition, another example of psychology in practice in Haiti is represented by Zanmi Lasante/Partners in Health's mental health program (Partners in Health (PIH), 2015). Eddy Eustache, known as Père Eddy, was hired in 2005, as PIH's first psychologist in Haiti. Since his hire he has grown the mental health team to include 50 social workers and 13 psychologists in 12 clinics serving some of the most intensely poverty-stricken communities in Haiti. Père Eddy embraced liberation theology as a student and served as a chaplain at a high school in Cap-Haïtien, in northern Haiti, prior to earning his master's degree in psychology in Ottawa, Canada. Approximately ten years after the 1994 Rwandan genocide, he served traumatized staff and women who had been raped and contracted HIV during the genocide. In Haiti, after the earthquake, Père Eddy noted many deceased were not provided a formal burial, and thus surviving loved ones lacked a mourning process. To meet this gap, Père Eddy developed memorial services for survivors, including PIH staff, that integrated religious and mental health messages in culturally meaningful and appropriate ways (Partners in Health (PIH), 2015).

Another perspective on integrating spirituality and mental health is represented by Wismick Jean-Charles, coauthor of this chapter. Jean-Charles, commonly known as Père Wismick, is a Haitian priest as well as a Fordham University educated psychology PhD. Since 2011, Père Wismick has directed the Annual Symposium of Spirituality and Psychotherapy in Haiti (Jean-Charles, 2011b, 2021) in Port-au-Prince. The event brings Haitian psychologists and mental health workers together with many visiting international psychologists and mental health workers, along with Haitian religious leaders, to share and discuss best practices and how to appropriately and effectively bring together religion with psychology to best serve the mental and spiritual health of Haitians in culturally sensitive ways. The topic of religion as it relates to mental health in Haiti merits many chapters and many books, but given space limitations, the following section provides an introduction to some of the ways religion and mental well-being intersect in the context of Haiti.

Role of Religion

As with the role of the family, the role of religion figures prominently in Haitian culture. As noted earlier in this chapter, about 55% of Haitians are Roman Catholic, 28% Protestant, and about 2% Vodou, with 4% representing other religions and 10% reporting no religion (Haiti World Factbook, 2021), though other estimates indicate about 80% of the population self-identifies as Roman Catholic and 20% as Protestant (Gopaul-McNicol et al., 1998). Research indicates persons from the lower classes are more likely to express beliefs in Vodou, though in challenging times, some persons from all social classes may cope through Vodou (Desrosiers & St. Fleurose, 2002). Many persons express that they are Christian while also practicing some elements of Vodou.

Historically, Catholicism was the religion that was officially recognized in Haiti, though in 2003, Vodou also became designated as an officially recognized religion (Nicolas et al., 2012). In fact, the Louis XIV's 1685 Code Noir made it mandatory that the enslaved Haitians convert to Roman Catholicism (WHO, 2010). At any rate, religion provides a significant means of coping for many of today's Haitians, especially given that many Haitians find it difficult to self-disclose mental health and other personal difficulties to nonfamily members and strangers such as mental health professionals (Nicolas et al., 2012). Some scholars argue that Catholic and Protestant priests, together with Vodou priests, known as hougans (male) and mambos (female), provide the majority of mental healthcare in Haiti (Auguste & Rasmussen, 2019).

Since Christianity is likely to be more familiar to most readers of this chapter than Vodou, a capsule description of Vodou is in order. In brief, Vodou is a religion that has its origins in Africa, and its Gods, the loas, typically are described as spirits of African ancestors, which serve as protective guardian angels (Desrosiers & St. Fleurose, 2002; Métraux, 1959). In addition to the *loas*, also known as *petit ange* (little angels), the Vodou system recognizes the highest entity as *Le Bon Dieu* (the good God) (Auguste & Rasmussen, 2019; Métraux, 1959). The Vodou system indicates that each person has a *ti bon anj* (*loa*) that is viewed as bonded to an individual person's body. Through a *crise de possession*, a Vodou adherent may have a spiritual experience in which a *loa* mounts the person for a short period of time (Bourguignon, 1976; Hurston, 1938; Métraux, 1959; Rich, 1999). Hougans and mambos serve as healers, after a training period of roughly five years, and offer diagnostic interviews to clients, and services including rituals to remove bad luck, and treatments such as cleansings with oils and potions, amulets, and incense. Ceremonies may also include sacrifices of animals or foods. Vodou priests and practitioners recognize that some ailments are physical and require referral to allopathic Western-style physicians; however, adherents of Vodou may express that "*tout maladi pa maladi doktè*" (all illnesses are not illnesses for doctors), and many such illnesses are what would be viewed as mental illnesses by Western psychologists (Auguste & Rasmussen, 2019).

Some scholars document local knowledge that distinguishes mental illness of the head (*tèt*), such as linked to anxiety, odd behavior, and difficulty concentrating, from mental illness of the heart (*kè*), such as linked to emotional/physical upset. Local Haitian understanding of mental condition categories suggests culture-bound syndromes, or at least culturally influenced conditions, such as *rèflechi twop* (too much thinking) and *santi m prale* (fear). As an additional example, some Haitians will distinguish *depression* and *depression mentale*, the first describing "general discouragement" and the second more closely aligning with what would be diagnosed as major depressive disorder in the DSM (Auguste & Rasmussen, 2019). Some evidence suggests that suicidal ideation is more likely to be reported to a Vodou healer than to a credentialed mental health professional or Catholic priest, given the stigma with the first and due to the religious proscription against suicide by the latter's religion (Auguste & Rasmussen, 2019). Though discussion of the full range of folk diagnoses and categories is beyond the scope of this chapter, suffice it to say that there are additional culture-bound syndromes and culturally influenced terms and lay diagnoses, including *sezisman* (a paralysis often linked to shock, anger, or sadness) and *endispozisyon* (an indisposition involving weakness or fainting and emotional upset) (WHO, 2010). In sum, generally speaking, Haitians, especially in lower classes and in rural areas, will not view a psychologist as the first option in considering mental health treatment and will first consult family for support. One study in fact found that three of four rural Haitians "preferred community care, which included Hougans, priests, community leaders, and herbal healers, to clinical care at hospitals" (Auguste & Rasmussen, 2019).

Thus, Vodou offers more than a religion and often includes advice and information on healing practices and illness prevention, as well as a worldview that offers devotees a way to make meaning in life. Though many Westerners have negative or inaccurate views of Vodou, some professionals are now recognizing that judicious use and integration of some select elements of Vodou, such as possession, may possibly "represent a tool for treatment" (Auguste & Rasmussen, 2019). While the precise nature and type of integration remain controversial and merit further research, it is clear that at the least, mental healthcare practitioners working with Haitian clients should understand the significance and relevance of Vodou for many clients so that a more culturally sensitive approach may be developed. More broadly, regardless of the specific religion or belief system of the particular Haitian, understanding that religion likely plays a central role in the person's life is critical to providing effective care for mental well-being, and research has demonstrated that most Haitians indicate that religion and spirituality has played an important role in coping and in resilience and posttraumatic growth post-2010 earthquake (Mercado et al., 2018; Rich et al., 2018).

Conclusion

While Haiti has made significant progress in the decade since the devastating 2010 earthquake, many challenges remain. Poverty, disease, corruption, crime, political instability, lack of access for many to quality healthcare and education, and natural disasters are just a few of the obstacles. Yet there is clear progress and indeed hope. The Haitian people are famously resilient, and notable gains have been accomplished regarding psychology and mental health services and education. The development of an infrastructure for psychology, such as a professional association and university-level educational programs, is especially encouraging. However, the precise implementation and impact of these improvements remain to be assessed. As Jean-Charles and Rich (2020) noted, "How can these [new] Master's programs provide tools, resources, and models to aid those Haitian students, tomorrow's leaders, to become locally/globally engaged for peace? Can what is learned from the earthquake response be applied elsewhere internationally? What is the appropriate role for foreign aid volunteers and workers, so that they are as helpful as possible, rather than ineffective or even damaging? What lessons are learned for promoting global peace and understanding between Haitians and the rest of the world?"

References

Ahmed, A. (2016). Hurricane Matthew makes old problems worse for Haitians. *The New York Times*. Retrieved from https://nyti.ms/2dI37LU

Auguste, E., & Rasmussen, A. (2019). Vodou's role in Haitian mental health. *Global Mental Health, 6*(e25), 1–6.

Baylor University. (2020, May 29). GSSW professor provides telepsychology program training in Haiti. *Community Connection Magazine, Diana R. Garland School of Social Work,* 1–3.
Bourguignon, E. (1976). *Possession*. Chandler & Sharp Publishers.
Boursiquot, M. U. (2001). *The history of psychology and associated disciplines in Haiti*. Doctoral dissertation (UMI No. 3040648). Carlos Albizu University, Miami.
Brodwin, P. (1996). *Medicine and morality in Haiti: The contest for healing power*. Cambridge University Press.
Cadet, J. R. (1998). *Restavec: From Haitian slave child to middle-class American*. University of Texas Press.
Cheney, P. (2017). *Cul de sac: Patrimony, capitalism, and slavery in French Saint-Domingue*. University of Chicago Press.
Dash, M. (2010). *Culture and customs of Haiti*. Greenport Press.
Desrosiers, A., & St. Fleurose, S. (2002). Treating Haitian patients: Key cultural aspects. *American Journal of Psychotherapy, 56*(4), 508–521.
Dubois, L. (2004). *Avengers of the New World: The story of the Haitian Revolution*. Harvard University Press.
Dubois, L. (2013). *Haiti: The Aftershocks of history*. Henry Holt and Company.
Farmer, P. (2005). *The uses of Haiti*. Common Courage Press.
Farmer, P. (2011). *Haiti after the earthquake*. Public Affairs.
Franck, S., Julien, R., Rouzier, D. G., Surinon, C., & Nitza, A. (2019). Thérapie de groupe avec les invisibles dans les périphéries de Port-au-Prince: de la blessure à la beauté. In W. Jean-Charles (Ed.), *Empathie en Haiti: De la recherche à la pratique, à la croisée de différents regards* (pp. 277–304). Educa Vision, Inc.
Geggus, D. (2014). *The Haitian Revolution: A documentary history*. Hackett Publishing Company.
Girard, P. (2010). *Haiti: The tumultuous history: From pearl of the Caribbean to broken nation*. Palgrave Macmillan
Gopaul-McNicol, S., Benjamin-Dartugye, D., & Francois, E. (1998). Working with Haitian Canadian families. *International Journal for the Advancement of Counselling, 20*(3), 231–242.
Haiti. (2021). *World Factbook*. Retrieved from https://www.cia.gov/the-world-factbook/countries/haiti/
Haiti COVID-19. (2021, January 5). Retrieved from https://ht.usembassy.gov/covid-19-information/
Hurston, Z. N. (1938). *Tell my horse*. Harper Perennial.
James, C. L. R. (1963). *The Black Jacobins: Toussaint L'Ouverture and the San Domingo Revolution*. Random House.
Jean-Charles, W. (2011a). Rebati: After the earthquake the IAAP UN team continues to remember Haiti. *IAAP Bulletin of the International Association of Applied Psychology, 23*, 33–35.
Jean-Charles, W. (2011b). First international conference on restoring life and maintaining hope in Port-au-Prince: Establishing a new "Center for Spirituality and Mental Health in Haiti". *International Psychology Bulletin, 15*, 39–41.
Jean-Charles, W. (2019). 2010 earthquake in Haiti. In J. Halpern, A. Nitza, & K. Vermeulen (Eds.), *Disaster mental health case studies: Lessons learned from counseling in chaos* (pp. 149–157). Routledge, Taylor Francis Group.
Jean-Charles, W. (2021). Traumatismes, spiritualité et gratitude: De la recherche scientifique à l'expérience haïtienne. In W. Jean-Charles (Ed.), *Prévention et promotion de la santé mentale en Haiti: La force de la gratitude et de l'espérance* (pp. 17–40). Educa Vision.
Jean-Charles, W., & Griff, K. P. (2014). The history of psychology in Haiti. In Symposium chaired by G. Rich & A. Consoli (Eds.), *Psychology in Latin American and the Caribbean.* Paper presented at the annual meeting of the American Psychological Association, Washington, DC.
Jean-Charles, W., & Rich, G. (2020). Ten years after the Haitian earthquake: Lessons for international psychology and global peace. In G. Rich & S. M. Fatemi (Eds.), *The role of international psychology in establishing global peace.* (D48 & D52). Paper presented at the annual meeting of the American Psychological Association, Washington, DC.

Jean-Jacques, R. (2011). *La psychologie en Haïti à partir des années 60.* Unpublished Manuscript.
Katz, J. M. (2013). *The big truck that went by: How a world came to save Haiti and left behind a disaster*. St. Martin's Press.
Kuriansky, J. (2018). Reconstruire la raison et l'esprit en Haiti: Contributions du Centre de Spiritualité et de Santé Mentale (CESSA). In W. Jean-Charles (Ed.), *Santé mentale et Psychothérapie en Haiti* (pp. 71–76). Educa Vision, Inc.
Kuriansky, J., & Jean-Charles, W. (2012, July/October). Haiti Rebati: Update on activities rebuilding Haiti through the global kids connect project. *Bulletin of the International Association of Applied Psychology, 24*, 2–3. Retrieved from http://www.iaapsy.org/uploads/file/newsletters/July2012.pdf
McClellan, J. E. (1992). *Colonialism and science: Saint Domingue and the old regime*. University of Chicago Press.
Mercado, M. A., Valsaint, M., Sirikantraporn, S., Rich, G., & Jean-Charles, W. (2018). Understanding posttraumatic growth in Haiti. *APA's Trauma Psychology News, 13*(3), 14–16.
Métraux, A. (1959). *Voodoo in Haiti.* Schocken Books.
Ministère de la Santé Publique et de la Population (MSPP). (2012). *Composante santé mentale de la politique nationale de santé*. Document officiel.
Nicolas, G. (2013). Haiti's "resilience" and mental health. *Caribbean Journal.* Retrieved from https://www.caribjournal.com/2013/05/10/haitis-resilience-and-mental-health/#
Nicolas, G., Jean-Jacques, R., & Wheatley, A. (2012). Mental health counseling in Haiti: Historical overview, current status, and plans for the future. *Journal of Black Psychology, 38*(4), 509–519.
Nitza, A. (2018). Construire des ponts de compassion: Utiliser la thérapie de groupe pour augmenter la compréhension interpersonnelle et promouvoir la guérison. In W. Jean-Charles (Ed.), *Santé mentale et Psychothérapie en Haiti* (pp. 71–76). Educa Vision.
Obert, J. (2020, July 17). Haitian mental health needs rise yet again with COVID-19 trauma. *The New Humanitarian.* Retrieved from https://www.thenewhumanitarian.org/news/2020/07/17/Haiti-coronavirus-mental-health-earthquake-depression-anxiety-trauma-GBV
Partners in Health (PIH). (2015, October 22). *Pere Eddy, Haiti's Patron Saint of Mental health.* Retrieved from https://www.pih.org/article/pere-eddy-haitis-patron-saint-of-mental-health
Patterson, O. (2019). *The confounding island: Jamaica and the postcolonial predicament*. Harvard University Press.
Rich, G. (1999). Erika Bourguignon: A portrait of the anthropology of consciousness. *Anthropology of Consciousness, 10*(2–3), 50–58.
Rich, G. (2013*). Bien-être psychologique et massothérapie: Résultats de recherche pour la pratique professionnelle. Psychological well-being and massage therapy.* La Troisième Conférence Internationale sur la Spiritualité et la Psychothérapie en Haiti.
Rich, G., & Gielen, U. (Eds.). (2015). *Pathfinders in international psychology*. IAP- Information Age Publishing. 278 pages. *(Foreword by Past APA President Florence Denmark).*
Rich, G., Sirikantraporn, S., & Jean-Charles, W. (2018). The concept of posttraumatic growth in an adult sample from Port-au-Prince, Haiti: A mixed methods study. In G. Rich & S. Sirikantraporn (Eds.), *Human strengths and resilience: Developmental, cross-cultural, and international perspectives* (pp. 21–38). Lexington Books.
St. Louis, G. (2014, March). Building mental health capacity in Haiti: The Teachers Mental Health Training Program. *Psychology International.* Retrieved from https://www.apa.org/international/pi/2014/03/haiti
Stewart, S. (2017). *National Hurricane Center Tropical Cyclone Report: Hurricane Matthew.* National Weather Service. Retrieved from http://www.nhc.noaa.gov/data/tcr/AL142016_Matthew.pdf
Trouillot, M.-R. (1990). *Haiti, state against nation: The origins and legacy of Duvalierism.* Monthly Review Press.
Weaver, K. K. (2006). *Medical revolutionaries: The enslaved healers of eighteenth century Saint Domingue*. University of Illinois Press.
WHO. (2010). Culture and mental health in Haiti: A literature review. WHO.

Chapter 16
Mental and Emotional Health in the Dominican Republic

Maysa (Duarte) Akbar

Psychology and the science behind mental health have continued to advance and progress over the years, so much so that many countries have begun to implement policies, campaigns, and programs to destigmatize the need for mental health treatment. For the many Caribbean islands, the West Indies, and Latin America, the implementation process has been challenging at best, while most times considered a herculean effort. The inability to implement successful mental health services is due to various factors such as colonization, economic inequality, corrupt government, and mistrust of psychological programming. Specifically, within the Caribbean territories, mental health has faced delays in widespread acceptance. Psychological needs are diminished in terms of importance as untreated mental illness increases daily.

To add further complexity, there are inconsistencies in terms of psychological services given the lack of trained mental health professionals, culturally appropriate resources, and inconsistent implementation. In order for there to be a successful development of psychology within Caribbean nations, there needs to be a better understanding of psychology and provision of services to the people of the region—preferably from people that look like them, speak their language or dialect, are able to implement a combination of mental health strategies, and can build trust within their patients.

Throughout this chapter, we will examine the history of psychology and mental health as it has been introduced to the Dominican Republic (DR) and its people. A historical lens will reveal the many challenges, hindrances, and societal factors that impact the awareness, utilization, and implementation of reliable psychology within the Dominican Republic. A path forward and recommendations will be included for consideration to increase awareness of mental health service delivery options.

M. (D). Akbar (✉)
American Psychological Association, New Haven, CT, USA
e-mail: makbar@integratedwellnessgroup.org

G. J. Rich, N. A. Ramkumar (eds.), *Psychology in Oceania and the Caribbean*, International and Cultural Psychology,
https://doi.org/10.1007/978-3-030-87763-7_16

Quisqueya*: La Republica Dominicana

Brief History

Once called La Española (Hispaniola), the first African enslaved were forcefully brought to the Dominican Republic in 1492, through the transatlantic expedition led by Christopher Columbus, a practice that continued until the sixteenth century. Spain and the Spanish monarch sanctioned for free individuals, indentured servants, and enslaved laborers to continue their voyage through both unauthorized smugglers and legal permits. By 1520, the indigenous Tainos were almost extinct due to the brutality of colonization (Alvarez-López et al., 1997). This population shift made the island-born Blacks and mixed-race people the majority demographic, marking Hispaniola the first Black colony in the western hemisphere, a racial demographic that prevails through today. From the very beginning, the African enslaved resisted slavery and engaged in a battle for freedom even if it cost them their lives. The entire land of Hispaniola remained under Spanish rule until 1697, when the Spanish rulers were forced to hand over the western third of the island to France following years of conflict and war for control of the island. Under French rule, thousands of Africans were enslaved to aid in the production of sugar, coffee, cacao, and cotton (Morfa, 2011).

By 1791, the region witnessed a slave rebellion which led to a brutal war of liberation and the beginning of the Haitian Revolution, led by the chief commander Toussaint L'Oventure and lasting over 12 years (Alvarez-López et al., 1997). A bloody war and hundreds of thousands of deaths led to the end of direct French rule over Haiti. From 1801 to 1844, Haiti began to expand their territory by fighting for and taking control of Santo Domingo (now the capital of the Dominican Republic). The inner conflict gave rise to a resentment of Haiti by Dominicans, a sentiment that has continued for over five centuries. Renewed fighting, due to newly arrived troops from France on the western side of the island, and the unstable rule of Santo Domingo, led to the deterioration of its economy, trade, and exports. Resistance occurred throughout the Haitian occupation, and on February 27, 1844, a rebel leader, Juan Pablo Duarte, removed Haitian troops from the capital to secure freedom and thus marked the birth of the newly independent island nation of the Dominican Republic. The leaders of this newly formed country called on US President James Polk for support and recognition of their independence (Aponte, 1999). This led to many negotiations as well as political and economic connections with the United States.

Today, the Dominican Republic is located in the eastern two thirds of the island of Hispaniola, which it shares with its neighbor Haiti. It's the second largest Caribbean nation after Cuba, and its capital, Santo Domingo, is considered the oldest and largest Caribbean city. Over the years, it has continued to have conflict with Haiti due to fear, mistrust, and economic hardship. This historical split was driven by colonization, greed, and a desire for power which generated anger, frustration, and envy between Haitians and Dominicans (Metz, 2001), so much so that Haitians who are living within the DR are often discriminated against. They have faced many challenges, including administrative and legal barriers to Dominican citizenship. The children of Haitian descendants endure systemic prejudice with birth registration practices and impediments to citizenship (Matibag & Downing-Matibag, 2011). In 2013, the Dominican Republic issued a ruling to revoke the citizenship of the children of "unauthorized" migrants born in the Dominican Republic since 1929. This verdict caused a political uproar as those individuals of Haitian descent had to figure out how to prove their citizenship. Even as recently as February of 2021, government officials discussed the possibility of building a border around Haiti to decrease trafficking, immigration, and criminal activity. Racial biases, systemic discrimination, and ethnic prejudices have been rooted in a history of conflict between the two countries and continue to plague Hispaniola with no clear path of peace and reconciliation (Matibag & Downing-Matibag, 2011).

Today's Dominican Society

Today the Dominican Republic is known for its beautiful scenery, tropical weather, rhythmic music, delicious cuisine, and warmhearted people. It is also my birthplace, and in my eyes the most beautiful island in this world. Whether I am walking on the white sandy beaches in *Las Terrenas* looking out into endless turquoise waters, breathing in mother nature in the mountains of *Jarabacoa*, or haggling in *el Mercado Modelo* in *Santo Domingo*—I am fascinated by every aspect of my beautiful island. Dominican society and culture largely reflect its mix of the indigenous peoples of the island, the Arawak/Taino, African, and Spanish colonial heritage (Caplan et al., 2018). The mixture of "*la cultura*" gives the Dominican Republic its vibrancy, yet it also haunts our people with centuries of colonizers' racism which took root during enslavement. Interestingly, for a land that struggles with colorism, it has a documented 7.8 million Black people in the Dominican Republic, ranking it the fourth country outside of Africa with the largest Black populations (Fernandez, 1999). More than four-fifths of Dominicans are adherents to the Roman Catholic Church, which exerts a marked influence on cultural, political, and economic life (Wiarda & González, 2021). It is known for its vivacious African-inspired music, including *merengue*, *bachata*, and *perico ripiao*, and astounding Afrocentric art and is one of the most visited countries for tourists all over the world.

Dominican Economy

The Dominican Republic has the ninth largest economy in Latin America and the second largest economy in the Caribbean with a gross domestic product (GDP) growth rate of 4.5% in 2011. It is also known for the strong economic development that occurred between 1990 and 2000. Despite its strong economic standing in Latin

America, mental health services reform in the DR has not been on par with that of other nations in the region. Present-day Dominican society has undergone rapid transformation leading to societal stressors that have eroded the mental health and well-being of its society. The recent economic expansion benefits a small minority of the population, due to high income inequality (the DR has a GINI index inequality ranking of 38, out of 144 countries; Central Intelligence Agency (CIA) Factbook, 2015) and a poverty rate of 41%. Migration to the United States, "the land of opportunity" for many Dominicans, was reserved for the elite and wealthy, perpetuating an even greater divide among the haves and have-nots—economically and mentally.

Mental Health Disparities

Mental health disparity in the Dominican Republic goes as far back as the Spanish colonization period. It is a known fact that many of the natives committed suicide, even with their children, as a way to avoid abusive conditions imposed by the Spaniards during enslavement. The only institutionalized care for the mentally ill that existed during this period of Dominican history took place in the capital city of Santo Domingo, where the military hospital had two cells devoted to the care of psychiatric patients. It is said that there was a dual role for the asylum: (1) to protect the mentally ill from mistreatment, neglect, and abuse suffered from wandering the streets and (2) to isolate these patients from high society (Rothe & Mella Mjias, 2013). As the DR democracy evolved, many of its citizens continued to struggle with serious mental health conditions that remained untreated, the result: increased homelessness, substance abuse, and/or incarceration (Moscoso Puello, 1945). It is estimated that 63% of patients with severe mental illness do not receive necessary care, and if care is provided, it is often of poor quality (Lora et al., 2012).

Motivation and Development of a Psychologist

In the early 1980s, during my preschool years, my parents made the tough decision to migrate to the United States. As a young child I was socialized in the high middle social class of Santo Domingo. My father was a successful business owner, having several wholesale food distribution centers and gas stations throughout the island. We lived comfortably, my mother was a stay-at-home mom, we had a nanny, and I attended a prestigious private school. Our entire quality of life quickly diminished once we migrated to the United States. Like many immigrants, my parents left in fear of governmental changes that were looming, but I am not sure that they would have anticipated the struggle of being an immigrant in America. Every summer when I went back to the DR, I vacillated from living in poverty in New York's inner city to great comfort as one of Santo Domingo's privileged. It was the strangest juxtaposition of extremes. However, this lens allowed me to see firsthand the difference in how people suffering from mental illness are treated in both places. As the family translator, in New York I witnessed the impact that poverty has on creating a host of accompanying challenges (poor education, housing, health, access), and despite the availability of government programs, nothing really changed. This was especially true living through both the crack and AIDS epidemic. Similarly, in the DR, mental illness and substance use were largely ignored. In either place, whether walking through the "concrete jungle" of NY or in the lush tropics of the DR, mental illness was completely neglected, disregarded, and overlooked. In many ways, being exposed to these two drastically different experiences engendered in me a curiosity around human behavior. My early upbringing, coupled with many lived experiences and childhood adversity, led me to pursue the profession of psychology. Writing this chapter is cathartic because it represents the intersection of my cultural and professional identity.

We will now unpack the state of mental health in the Dominican Republic. There are a host of psychosocial factors that play a role in the lack of proper mental healthcare. Many factors are similar to the United States, and some are not: they include stigma, mistrust, traditional healing methods, poverty, violence, abuse, exploitation, and the sequelae of substance misuse (Hernández et al., 2011).

Mental Illness: Unseen and Untreated

The DR has been known to overlook and even ignore mental illness. Unfortunately, mental illness directly correlates to poverty, ageism, and gender inequality. Most people with mental illness, developmental or learning delays, or substance abuse issues are considered "*loco*" and cast to the side as mostly nonfunctional. Inequality remains an issue within the country. Some regions are so impoverished that crime is heavily prevalent. For the general population, research within the census suggests that 40.4% of citizens live in poverty and 10.4% are in extreme poverty conditions, mostly prevalent with the "*campesinos*," those who live in the less developed parts of the island. Reasons for poverty vary from national disasters, governmental decisions, and poor living conditions (Taylor, 2009). There is a direct correlation in the DR between poverty, crime, and chronic mental health conditions. In 2019 alone, there were over 700 homicides reported, a majority of which were a result of theft or attempted theft. Poverty is a well-known factor that impacts other mental health conditions such as depression, anxiety and schizophrenia, intellectual disability, and epilepsy (up to 40% of the population needs mental healthcare). It is estimated that schizophrenia affects approximately 80,000 people (Hernández et al., 2011). Depression affects an estimated 13.8% of the population. Due to poverty and lack of proper resources, less than half of those living with the illness will receive some type of treatment (Caban-Martinez et al., 2012).

Stigma in Dominican Culture

Psychology has struggled to battle stigma since the introduction of mental health. While many *adolescents and young adults* struggled with significant mental health issues, they rarely have access to treatment. A common pattern that was noticed among college students was the low help-seeking rate due to internal and external stigma, as well as inadequate services including a lack of trained professionals to provide mental healthcare (Pacheco, 2017), so much so that there was an alarming rate of suicide and engagement in self-injurious behavior among Dominicans, which constituted a major public health issue (Pengpid & Peltzer, 2020). For *older adults*, dementia and mental health disorders, in general, are among the major causes of disability and dependency, representing one of the most serious medical and social issues confronted by Caribbean health systems. In terms of *men* within the Dominican culture, certain mental health symptoms are not considered a category of mental illness such as depression, anxiety, alcoholism, or abuse. Moreover, cultural belief systems that associate aggressive and assertive men to machismo minimize the implication of violence in domestic abuse situations. Toxic masculinity is often normalized and justified by traditional "defined gender roles" within the DR culture. Dominican men tend to not seek treatment for mental illnesses due to shameful feelings. During the *pandemic*, many Dominicans have been seeking out therapy given the worldwide increase in anxiety and psychological distress due to self-isolation and uncertainty around COVID-19. Cases of mental health problems in the Dominican Republic have surged, and research shows that, interestingly, men are impacted more than women (Caban-Martinez et al., 2012).

Lack of Mental Health Resources

The Dominican government's mindset and lack of funding for mental health programs have been hindrances to progress in this area. Less than 1% of the health budget administered by the Ministry of Public Health and Social Assistance (MISPAS) is allocated to mental health, and the public system is generally underfunded (Pan American Health Organization & World Health Organization, 2008). Lack of resources further attributes to insufficient care. In Latin America and the Caribbean, mental disorders have risen from 8.8% in 1990 to 22% in 2009 (WHO and Pan American Health Organization [PAHO], 2008). This is not just an issue of the past.

Lack of resources in the DR is a coalescence of insufficient budgets for mental health services, a lack of essential medications, a lack of treatment facilities, and a lack of human resource workers. Resources were put into economic development and not into mental health as the country evolved from its days of enslavement—an era to which the roots of some of the nation's mental health issues can be traced. Additionally, medical facilities are challenged in maintaining adequate supplies of essential psychiatric medicines all together. Therefore, medication management is a struggle due to the low quantity of antipsychotics and SSRIs (Caplan et al., 2018). Many of the treatment facilities are private, making it difficult for those individuals diagnosed with severe chronic mental illness to obtain required services if they do not have the financial ability to pay for this kind of treatment. Many patients with behavioral symptoms who are unable to be cared for by their families lack access to follow up care and psychiatric facilities; therefore, many end up homeless. The lack of coordinated healthcare facilities is the underlying reason for the observed health disparities between rural and urban communities in countries such as the Dominican Republic. As indicated previously, a shortage of adequately trained health professionals is also a huge barrier.

With such a high need of psychologists, psychiatrists, and psychotherapists, one would think that there would be more organizations seeking to hire people to fill those roles. Present psychologists and psychiatrists report feeling that they have limited knowledge in managing patients with mental illness. Poor health insurance does not provide coverage for psychiatric medications, creating a financial barrier for most patients, especially for long-term care.

Culturally Relevant Healing Practices to Promote Mental Wellness

Help-Seeking Behaviors

Help-seeking behaviors have been impacted by the public stigma to mental illness which led to a resistance in acknowledging or addressing the presentation of psychological symptoms. The stigma of mental health has been repeatedly found to account for negative attitudes and decreased intentions toward help-seeking (Chang, 2007; Masuda & Boone, 2011; Masuda et al., 2012; Mendoza et al., 2015; Tillman & Sell, 2013). There are proactive steps that can be taken to help reduce the stigma associated with mental health and lack of long-term care follow-up. First, a psychoeducational campaign can be key in creating a community that is willing to address mental health issues and improve the lives of many families.

Remedios Casero

It would be difficult to try and comprehend mental health treatment without properly understanding the cultural belief and value system concerning mental healthcare. Traditional diagnosing and healing extend not only to physical ailments but also to most psychological and interpersonal problems as well (Baez, 2005). These are the culturally accepted and anticipated methods of healing. Many Dominican women, especially mothers, believe in utilizing remedies derived from their folk beliefs—*remedios casero*—about health and illness rather than the use of prescribed medicines (Bearison et al., 2002). *Remedios casero* are remedies created with herbs and roots typically obtained through a healer or administered to cure sickness and illness (Hufford, 1997; Leininger & Reynolds, 1991). Other times, it is the use of candles and incense to purify the atmosphere of negative energy and to stabilize chaos. Small offerings are often left for deities to help accelerate the healing process. Many Dominican or Caribbean people do not particularly believe or trust in Western medicine to heal any physical or psychological needs. Ancestral practices and alternative medicine are used instead of, or in conjunction with, whatever the doctor prescribes. These types of healing practices have been found to be actively used in the Dominican culture. Dominicans truly value their cultural folk medicine, and folk healers' spiritual and mystical practices have been used as coping techniques to stabilize irrational moods and maintain overall well-being (Pacheco, 2017) and are often passed down from one generation to the next.

Despite being a trained psychologist with almost 20 years of clinical experience, I still use many of the traditional and homemade medicinal remedies my mother used with me, which were passed down from her mother and her mother before her. I have bundles of herbs and roots in my cabinets in reused containers for all kinds of ailments. It is second nature to make tea or to crush some herbs in a pilon**, which will likely cure almost any type of health concern, even "*los nervios*" in my family. An integration between the traditional medicinal approaches to building health in conjunction with Western psychological approaches may render the best results for the Dominican Republic in the evolution of mental health access in the country.

Family and the Therapeutic Process

In addition to Dominican cultural practices, research has found that family involvement leads to better mental health outcomes and greater success. Whether it be deemed clinically necessary or a requirement, for Dominican families it can be considered an essential part of the treatment plan and symptom amelioration. Policies have been issued by some public inpatient units for a patient to be admitted with a family member. This family member serves as the patient's advocate which leads to reduced long-term stays and decreases unnecessary idle time (Hernández et al., 2011). Furthermore, it ensures the patient's comfort as well as a timely discharge plan. Considering mental health services as part of a diverse interdisciplinary and family systems approach, inclusive of cultural traditions and holistic methods, would yield a more successful level of acceptance of mental health treatment in the DR.

Public Health Systems Approach

In general, the public health system is challenged by low-quality care, non-existent improvement initiatives, poor administrative policies, and crime (Rathe & Moliné, 2011). A shift is needed to yield more positive results. For instance, health service professionals can be placed where they are most needed, like "*en el campo*" the rural areas with less population density. Pop-up clinics placed in these communities would allow for patients to have access to resources without having to travel to reach public healthcare facilities or possibly even farther to reach private facilities (Caban-Martinez et al., 2012).

It wasn't until 1977 that a community mental health clinic was constructed in the Dominican Republic. In the late 1990s, mental health was declared a priority which led to the construction of services and implementation of programming to assist those in need. Research suggests that the quality of life would improve and mortality rates would decrease with the addition of early diagnosis and proper treatment of illnesses (Caplan et al., 2016, 2018). The Dominican Republic has been through significant hardships, challenges, and advances over the past decades. Sustained economic growth, structural change, and political advantages have impacted the strategy used to propel the DR to be the country that it is today. However, difficulties are still observed when we consider what it would take to improve mental health access, reduce racial tension with the citizens from the neighboring country of Haiti, and address severe poverty and crime. Inequality stands as the country's biggest obstacle, poor education and government inaction follow right behind it. The Dominican Republic needs to urgently figure out a strategy to overcome the serious obstacles which limit the population's access to sound and comprehensive mental healthcare. While roadblocks are expected along the way, there seems to be greater awareness for the need to better understand mental illness and the appropriate provision of mental health services throughout the country. This is a positive first step in the right direction.

References

Alvarez-López, L., Baver, S., Weisman, J., Hernández, R., & López, N. (1997). *Dominican studies: Resources and research questions*. CUNY Dominican Studies Institute.

Aponte, S. (1999). *Dominican migration to the United States, 1970–1997: An annotated bibliography*. CUNY Dominican Studies Institute.

Baez, A. (2005). Chapter 7. Mental health intervention with Dominican immigrants: A psychosocial perspective. *Journal of Immigrant & Refugee Services, 3*(1–2), 125–139.

Bearison, D. J., Minian, N., & Granowetter, L. (2002). Medical management of asthma and folk medicine in a Hispanic community. *Journal of Pediatric Psychology, 27*(4), 385–392.

C. I. A. Factbook (2015). *The world factbook: 2010*. Retrieved from http://www.ciagov/library/publications/the-world-factbook. Accessed 30 January.

Caban-Martinez, A. J., Halder, G. E., Tellechea, L., Fajardo, M., Kaltman, J., Anand, J., … Fleming, L. E. (2012). Health status and behaviors among adults residing in rural Dominican Republic. *Rural and Remote Health, 12*(2), 99.

Caplan, S., Little, T. V., & Garces-King, J. (2016). Stigma about mental illness among multidisciplinary health care providers in the Dominican Republic. *International Perspectives in Psychology: Research, Practice, Consultation, 5*(3), 192.

Caplan, S., Little, T. V., Reyna, P., Sosa Lovera, A., Garces-King, J., Queen, K., & Nahar, R. (2018). Mental health services in the Dominican Republic from the perspective of health care providers. *Global Public Health, 13*(7), 874–898.

Chang, H. (2007). Psychological distress and help-seeking among Taiwanese college students: Role of gender and student status. *British Journal of Guidance & Counselling, 35*(3), 347–355.

Fernandez, N. (1999). Women, race, and tourism in Cuba. In K. Kempadoo (Ed.), *Sun, sex, and gold: Tourism and sex work in the Caribbean* (pp. 81–89). Roman & Littlefield.

Hernández, M. R., Gibbs, T. A., & Gautreaux-Subervi, L. (2011). Mental health in the Dominican Republic. *International Psychiatry: Bulletin of the Board of International Affairs of the Royal College of Psychiatrists, 8*(1), 12–14.

Hufford, D. (1997). Cultural diversity, alternative medicine & folk medicine. *New Directions in Folklore, 1*.

Leininger, M., & Reynolds, C. (1991). *Culture care diversity and universality theory: A theory of nursing*. National League for Nursing.

Lora, A., Kohn, R., Levav, I., McBain, R., Morris, J., & Saxena, S. (2012). Service availability and utilization and treatment gap for schizophrenic disorders: a survey in 50 low-and middle-income countries. *Bulletin of the World Health Organization, 90*, 47–54B.

Masuda, A., Anderson, P. L., & Edmonds, J. (2012). Help-seeking attitudes, mental health stigma, and self-concealment among African American college students. *Journal of Black Studies, 43*(7), 773–786.

Masuda, A., & Boone, M. S. (2011). Mental health stigma, self-concealment, and help-seeking attitudes among Asian American and European American college students with no help-seeking experience. *International Journal for the Advancement of Counselling, 33*(4), 266–279.

Matibag, E., & Downing-Matibag, T. (2011). Sovereignty and social justice: The 'Haitian problem' in the Dominican Republic. *Caribbean Quarterly, 57*(2), 92–117.

Mendoza, H., Masuda, A., & Swartout, K. M. (2015). Mental health stigma and self-concealment as predictors of help-seeking attitudes among Latina/o college students in the United States. *International Journal for the Advancement of Counselling, 37*(3), 207–222.

Metz, H. C. (2001). *Dominican Republic and Haiti. Country studies. Research completed* (3rd ed.). Federal Research Division.

Morfa, W. (2011). *The difficult relationship between Haiti and the Dominican Republic*. CUNY City College of New York.

Moscoso Puello, R. M. (1945). *Palmas dominicanas*. Editora Montalvo.

Pacheco del Castillo, L. A. (2017). *Dominican college students' experiences of distress, help-seeking and stigma*. Unpublished Doctoral dissertation, Western Michigan University. Retrieved from https://scholarworks.wmich.edu/dissertations/3101

Pengpid, S., & Peltzer, K. (2020). Hand and oral hygiene practices among adolescents in Dominican Republic, Suriname and Trinidad and Tobago: Prevalence, health, risk behavior, mental health and protective factors. *International Journal of Environmental Research and Public Health, 17*(21), 7860. https://doi.org/10.3390/ijerph17217860

Rathe, M., & Moliné, A. (2011). The health system of Dominican Republic. *Salud pública de Mexico, 53*, s255–s264.

Rothe, E., & Mella Mejias, C. (2013). History of psychiatry in the Dominican Republic. *Adolescent Psychiatry, 3*(1), 18–25.

Taylor, E. B. (2009). Poverty as danger: Fear of crime in Santo Domingo. *International Journal of Cultural Studies, 12*(2), 131–148.

Tillman, K. S., & Sell, D. M. (2013). Help-seeking intentions in college students: An exploration of eating disorder specific help-seeking and general psychological help-seeking. *Eating Behaviors, 14*(2), 184–186.

Wiarda, H. J., & González, N. L. (2021, March 10). *Dominican Republic. Encyclopedia Britannica.* Retrieved from https://www.britannica.com/place/Dominican-Republic

World Health Organization. (2008). *The world health report 2008: Primary health care now more than ever: Introduction and overview* (No. WHO/IER/WHR/08.1). World Health Organization.

Chapter 17
Psychology in Puerto Rico

Irene López and Ethan Estrada

In this chapter, we review the psychological issues of relevance to Puerto Ricans, by first describing the history and political status of the island and reviewing the conditions that have shaped the lives of Puerto Ricans living in Puerto Rico and, by extension, the lives of Puerto Ricans living in the continental United States. Central to our review is the understanding that social suffering must always be understood in all of its complexity and context in order to avoid describing behavior using reductionistic models.

Conceptual Framework

Contradictory and often contested, the story of Puerto Rico is one which can leave the reader easily overwhelmed. In the face of such difficulties, social scientists, such as psychologists and anthropologists, have at times sought overly simplistic explanations for historically complex problems (e.g., emphasizing a culture of poverty instead of looking for more nuanced and structurally informed explanations to explain distress). To counteract this tendency, we deploy the tenets of liberation psychology to provide a more sophisticated and enlarged understanding of the present circumstances in Puerto Rico.

I. López
Kenyon College, Gambier, OH, USA
e-mail: lopezi@kenyon.edu

E. Estrada (✉)
Yale University, New Haven, CT, USA
e-mail: ethan.estrada@yale.edu

G. J. Rich, N. A. Ramkumar (eds.), *Psychology in Oceania and the Caribbean*, International and Cultural Psychology,
https://doi.org/10.1007/978-3-030-87763-7_17

Traditional psychological theories have often put forth models of functioning that are ahistorical (or decontextualized) and that often locate distress solely within the individual (Comas-Díaz & Torres Rivera, 2020). Liberation psychology, by contrast, (1) acknowledges the reality of oppression and that such oppression originates and is maintained through social, economic, and political subjugation; (2) recognizes that conditions are harmful for the majority of a population; (3) affirms that such conditions are antithetical to healthy functioning and, indeed, are the cause of human suffering; and (4) promotes the notion that healing requires a systemic and collective approach that advances liberation as opposed to adjustment (McNeill et al., 2017). Using such a liberatory framework allows us to understand the problems faced by Puerto Ricans in their "complex historical situatedness" (Comas-Díaz et al., 1998), without engaging in unjust and individualized oversimplifications. We also move away from categorizing distress based on a series of risk factors and move toward a more nuanced understanding of social suffering that sees functioning as the continual unfolding and response to a set of historically grounded and intertwined forces. In the following chapter, we thus consider the many complex and interconnected issues Puerto Rico faces using the framework of liberation psychology.

Demographics and History

An archipelago in the Caribbean Sea, Puerto Rico is the largest of all US territories. Approximately 100 miles long and 30 miles wide, the population of Puerto Rico is slightly over 3 million people (U.S. Census Bureau, 2019a), making it also one of the most densely populated territories in the Caribbean, Latin America, and the United States (Pasquali, 2018; Statista, 2021). In the continental United States, including Hawaii, currently there are over 5.5 million Puerto Ricans, making Puerto Ricans, in total, the second largest Latino group in the United States (U.S. Census Bureau, 2019b). Migration to the United States has occurred in three waves. The first two waves, from 1917 to 1944, and then from 1945 to 1965 (often called the Great Migration), consisted primarily of agricultural workers to New York, while the third wave consisted of a more diverse group who have settled in greater areas of the United States. This current wave is also most characterized by growing "revolving door" or circular migration (Duany, 2012). Most recently, following Hurricane Maria, there has also been a growing trend of more Puerto Ricans migrating to the US South, especially states such as Florida.

By birth, Puerto Ricans are American citizens, although all the rights afforded by the US Constitution are not, by default, extended to those living in Puerto Rico. For example, although birthright citizenship has guaranteed freedom of travel, Puerto Ricans cannot (nor can any other American) vote for president if they choose to live in Puerto Rico. Although the reasons for this are complex, and beyond the scope of this chapter, a brief review of the political status of Puerto Rico explains the "absolute and perpetual liminality" felt by many Puerto Ricans in regard to their association to the United States (Gene Locke, Jr., 2021). Specifically, since the beginning of the last century, island-born (or insular) Puerto Ricans have had, in total, three different types of citizenships, all of which have never quite given them full access to the benefits and protections established by the US Constitution (Venator-Santiago, 2013). First, following the 1898 annexation of the island by the United States from Spain, Puerto Ricans were given a local citizenship, which simultaneously revoked their Spanish citizenship but precluded American citizenship; then, in 1917, the Jones-Shafroth Act, extended a *jus sanguinis* (blood right) naturalized American citizenship, and finally, the National Act of 1940 gave Puerto Ricans *jus soli* (birthright) citizenship (Venator-Santiago, 2013).

Although each subsequent change has, in some respects, brought Puerto Ricans closer to the Union, they are not, in fact, part of the Union. As stipulated in the series of US Supreme Court decisions known as the insular cases, Puerto Rico remains to this day "*foreign to the United States in a domestic sense*" (Downes v Bidell, 1901). Hence, even though its residents are by birth US citizens, their citizenship is statutory and not constitutional (Valle, 2019). Psychologically foreign, in a domestic sense, is therefore how many Puerto Ricans feel they are perceived by other Americans. For example, a recent study with Puerto Ricans in Orlando, Florida indicated that a stunning 92% reported that despite having US citizenship, they did not feel that Puerto Ricans were accepted as full Americans (Valle, 2019). And indeed, a recent US national poll indicated that almost half of all Americans actually did not know that Puerto Ricans were American citizens (Morning Consult, 2017).

Although we may be tempted as psychologists to view such perceptions as the result of intrapsychic forces, liberation psychology demands that we recalibrate our lenses and see perceived discrimination as the direct result of objective political subjugation. Additionally, the corrosive effects of such oppression are robust and far-reaching. For example, in a large representative sample of both island and continental Puerto Rican children, perceived discrimination remained a consistent predictor of antisocial behaviors, above and beyond a host of risk factors (Rivera et al., 2011).

Economic Conditions

The unstable political status of Puerto Rico has also contributed to many of the economic worries currently afflicting the island. Currently, over 40% of the population lives below the US poverty line (43.5%, U.S. Census, 2019c), which is twice the poverty rate of the poorest state in the union, (i.e., Mississippi, which is approximately 20%) and significantly lower than the US national average of 10.5% (Semega et al., 2020). As the poorest of the poor, Puerto Ricans earn less money and pay more for housing, food, consumer goods, and electricity than other Americans

(Centro for Puerto Rican Studies, n.d.; U.S. Census, 2019a, 2019c; Puerto Rico Data Lab, 2017).

The reasons for such economic hardships are manifold, but such costs can, in part, be understood as a consequence of historical forces that have consistently prioritized the needs of the few over the many. For example, the reason that Puerto Ricans pay more for consumer goods than other Americans is because of protectionist policies, such as the Merchant Marine Act of 1920, which mandates that Puerto Ricans must only buy their goods from ships that are built, owned, staffed, and flagged in the United States. Yet, because US ships are far more expensive to purchase and operate than non-US ships, this results in overall higher costs for individuals in Puerto Rico—but a greater profit for the US marine industry (Gabrow, 2019).

Attempts to remedy these issues have often had unexpected consequences. For example, Operation Bootstrap was a development policy that transformed Puerto Rico's agricultural economy to one centered on manufacturing and tourism. While in the short run this policy led to a number of improvements in the lives of some on the island, such as higher wages and greater access to education; in the long run, it also paradoxically led to a mass outmigration of Puerto Ricans to the mainland United States, as the shift to industrialization led to a greater displacement of agricultural workers. The separation of families due to such migratory pressures, and the potential loss of familial and social support, has had an enduring impact on Puerto Rican families. Among US born Puerto Ricans, this has been hypothesized as a potential reason for their higher rates of psychopathology when compared to their peers in Puerto Rico and other Latinos. Such separation has also at times led to an estrangement between island and US Puerto Ricans, because despite feeling affiliated to their culture, these groups may speak different languages and have different life experiences.

In 2014, the situation in Puerto Rico took a particularly difficult turn when all three credit rating agencies in the United States downgraded Puerto Rico's bonds to junk status. Faced with a looming debt of $74 billion dollars, which almost overshadowed Puerto Rico's GDP, a fiscal oversight board was created which put in place austerity measures. These measures led to significant cuts in worker pensions, an increase in teacher layoffs, and school closures—which, unsurprisingly, led to a number of street protests. The continuing economic decline in Puerto Rico is therefore particularly worrisome, as research has consistently noted that poverty is often directly related to a host of negative psychological outcomes (Sareen et al., 2011).

With regard to Puerto Ricans, however, the measurement and impact of socioeconomic status has at times been difficult to establish, as there is not much variability in income. In such instances, researchers have recommended more expansive measurements of social class that are more specifically cued to targeted outcomes (Diemer et al., 2013). Thus, because so much of the island is poor, researchers have found it to be more useful to assess subjective social status or perception of poverty, rather than only rely on objective measures of poverty in Puerto Rico to assess the effect of economic and social marginalization on outcome (Canino et al., 2004). However, among US-born Latinos, including continental Puerto Ricans, it is still the case that objective measures, such as income and education, can, and do, have a more pronounced effect on self-rated health than subjective measures (Garza et al., 2017). Clearly, then, the experience of poverty and declining social capital are important markers of distress for both island and continental Puerto Ricans, although their impact and measurement varies by site.

Health Status

Despite the aforementioned differences in self-reported health, across a variety of conditions, it is island Puerto Ricans who typically have a more problematic health profile. For example, residents in Puerto Rico have the highest percentage of diabetes compared to all 50 US states and territories (Chowdhury et al., 2016); and with regard to asthma, Puerto Rican children have outstandingly high rates of asthma (e.g., 35%–41% for island and US-born children, respectively) as well as elevated rates of mortality when compared to other children worldwide (Busse et al., 2001; Vila et al. 2010).

In part, these health difficulties may stem from unequal access to care due to their colonial status. By virtue of living in an unincorporated territory, Puerto Ricans are either not eligible for specific types of aide and they receive less federal aid than other Americans—even though they pay federal taxes, such as social security and Medicare (Colón & Sánchez-Cesareo, 2016; Kovacs & Rodríguez-Vilá, 2020). For example, with regard to Medicaid, the federal and state program aimed to support low-income populations, this program "is not available to many people in Puerto Rico who would be eligible if they resided on the mainland" (Solomon, 2019). Additionally, when available, this aide does not cover the full range of services that are provided in other states, such as nursing home care, home health services care, and medical transport (Solomon, 2019). Furthermore, even though Medicaid is used by well over half of the population, it typically covers fewer prescription drugs than in the mainland United States (Solomon, 2019). It does not, for example, cover any drugs to treat hepatitis C and, in the case of asthma, only covers certain types of asthma medications, which is problematic given the extraordinarily high rates of asthma on the island.

With regard to Medicare, which is another federal health insurance program, and which provides aid for those 65 and older, the situation is not much better. Although Puerto Ricans are, on average, older than US citizens and have a significantly older population than the United States (U.S. Census, 2019a), Puerto Ricans typically receive the least amount of aid per resident when compared with their stateside peers, even though they contribute toward this program at the same rate as other Americans in the United States (Colón & Sánchez-Cesareo, 2016; Kovacs & Rodríguez-Vilá, 2020). In other words, despite being the oldest, most populous, and one of the poorest territories in the nation, Puerto Rico receives less funding to support its constituents than all other states in the union.

This situation becomes even more concerning when we consider that as recently as 2018, of those doctors who received their training in Puerto Rico, approximately 60% ended up leaving the island to practice medicine; and of those doctors who were trained in the continental United States, only *five* went on to practice on the island (Wilkinson et al., 2020). Simply put, despite the need, there are not enough doctors to service the island, and the doctors that are currently available are older than those in the United States, are not getting replaced at a sufficient rate, and, on average, are being reimbursed at substantially lower rates than doctors in the states (Park, 2021). This shortage in doctors is alarming in light of new research noting that, at least among mainland US Puerto Ricans, there is a positive relationship between allostatic load, defined as biological cumulative load of stressful life events, and lifetime perceived discrimination (Cuevas et al., 2019)—one would then only have to speculate what this relationship would be for island Puerto Ricans who, every day, have to navigate a health system that is chronically understaffed and underfunded (Perreira et al., 2017).

Mental Health

Given the issues discussed, it may surprise the reader to know that, overall, the psychiatric literature has not found that island Puerto Ricans are at greater risk for psychopathology than their continental peers; instead, it is continental Puerto Ricans who typically have had higher rates of disorders, especially when compared to other Latinos (Alegria et al., 2008). In fact, in the most recent study to date on this issue (Canino et al., 2019), island Puerto Ricans had, on average, *lower* adjusted rates of psychiatric disorders when compared to the mainland US Puerto Ricans. Additionally, even though continental Puerto Ricans had higher rates of adjusted anxiety and depression than island Puerto Ricans, these differences disappeared once social support was taken into account. The only notable exception to this pattern was for substance abuse, wherein island Puerto Ricans had almost twice the percent of substance abuse than their US peers and significantly greater use than their continental Puerto Rican peers.

How, then, can we explain the lowered expected rates of psychopathology among Puerto Ricans given the risk factors we have discussed? The research on this is still evolving. Some researchers claim that circular migration of Puerto Ricans contributes to their decreased distress because it allows families to reunite and thus support each other (Canino et al., 2019). However, we believe this needs to be further investigated because while circular migration can help families connect and can facilitate the transmission of cultural values, cultural migration can also be costly and disrupt familial bonds (Arévalo et al., 2014). Future research, thus, needs to unpack under what conditions circular migration protects or impairs social support and subsequent distress.

Cultural Idioms of Distress

The study of Puerto Rican mental health can also be enriched by studying cultural idioms of distress. Briefly, cultural idioms are ways of experiencing distress that, while not easily categorized using conventional classification systems, are expressions that have high saliency in a culture (López & Ho, 2013). In this regard, research has examined experiences such as *ataques de nervios* (or nervous attacks) and found that *ataques* are associated with an array of psychiatric disorders (see Lewis-Fernández & López, 2016 for a more extensive review). Specifically, among adults in Puerto Rico, compared to those without the cultural syndrome, *ataque* sufferers had over five times the odds of meeting criteria for a psychiatric diagnosis for depression or anxiety (Guarnaccia et al., 2009), while among island children, having an *ataque* was associated with four times the odds of any psychiatric disorder in the community and two times the odds in a clinical setting (Guarnaccia et al., 2005). Similar findings have been reported among Puerto Rican children in New York, indicating that across sites, *ataques* are a well understood marker of distress (López et al., 2009). Indeed, ataques are also associated with a host of psychological risk factors, such as traumatic exposure, dissociative capacity, anxiety sensitivity, and increased suicidality, making ataques a potent transdiagnostic risk factor for psychopathology (Cintrón et al., 2005; Guarnaccia et al., 2009; Hinton et al., 2008; Lewis-Fernandez et al., 2010).

Ethnic Risk and Protective Factors

Understanding behavior in context also means assessing functioning with reference to ethnically specific risk and protective factors that, of course, may vary by context. Among US Puerto Ricans, a lack of connection with their Puerto Rican culture can be related to a host of negative outcomes. For example, among a sample of continental Puerto Ricans, participants who reported partial marginalization (categorized as low endorsement of both Puerto Rican and American culture, but with some exploration of American culture) reported the highest distress, indicating that, at least for US participants, distress may be tied to feelings of racism, discrimination, relative lack of access to resources due to this group's comparatively lower socioeconomic status, and/or cultural homelessness (Capielo Rosario & Dillon, 2020).

Related to this, other research has found that endorsing a colonial mentality, defined as endorsing items that are reflective of cultural shame (e.g., *I would like to have a skin tone that is lighter than the skin tone that I have*), increased depressive symptomatology for Puerto Ricans when they experience acculturation stress (Capielo Rosario et al., 2019). Skin color is a topic that is complicated to study among Puerto Ricans given their multiracial background (López, 2008a), but at least, with regard to protective factors, among Puerto Rican women, the relationship between skin color and self-esteem was not direct, but, rather, moderated by ethnic identity (López, 2008b). The differences, and interconnections, between ethnic and racial identity, and their associations with mental health outcomes, remain an area that needs to be further explored in this multiracial population.

Gender-Based Violence

While ethnic specific factors are important in the study of Puerto Rican mental health, gender remains an important stratifying variable in the lives of many Puerto Ricans, and gender-based violence has unfortunately been on the rise in Puerto Rico. While the research in this area is still evolving, available data indicates that intimate partner violence, a form of gender-based violence, occurs at a greater rate in Puerto Rico than in the United States and that it appears through all sectors of the population, from the community to college students (Villafañe-Santiago et al., 2019). For women, the situation is particularly toxic as research with Puerto Rican samples has found that economic abuse was a unique predictor of depression for women, even after controlling for other forms of victimization (Stylianou, 2018). More specifically, intimate partner violence for women is deadly—as data from 2014 to 2017 indicated Puerto Rico had one of the highest rates of femicide in all the United States (Proyecto Matria, 2019). Gender-based violence can also manifest as violence against transgender and gender-nonconforming individuals (Transgender Law Center (n.d.)). In Puerto Rico, in particular, there has been an alarming rate of violence against trans women (Martinez-Velez et al., 2019). The situation has been so precarious that in 2021, the governor of Puerto Rico declared a state of emergency over gender-based violence (La Fortaleza, 2021).

While some research points to traditional gender roles, and patriarchy, as the roots of these different forms of gender violence (Morales Díaz & Rodríguez Del Toro, 2012), this needs to be further explored as older research has instead reified old tropes regarding *machismo* and *marianismo* and insufficiently explored other aspects of gender socialization, such as *caballerismo*. Future research should explore predictors of violence that are multifactorial, structural, and interconnected, and such work could help explain the reasons why, following disasters, such as Hurricane Maria, gender-based violence surged (APA Committee on Women in Psychology, 2020; Hurtado & Rivera-Vázquez, 2020).

Disasters in Puerto Rico

Disasters, themselves, are not random singular events but rather the result of long-standing structural violence (Rivera, 2020). In particular, ecological colonialism explains not only why disasters occur so frequently on the island but also why recovery has been so slow (Rivera Joseph et al., 2020). In Puerto Rico, during the past century, there have been over 10 hurricanes, over half of which have been at least either a category 4 or 5. Hurricane Maria, which struck in 2017, occurred only two weeks after Hurricane Irma and was one of the deadliest hurricanes in US history, and its effects are still felt on the island to this day.

Although estimates vary, death counts from Hurricane Maria have ranged from 4,645 (CI 793–8498) when based on household survey research (Kishore et al., 2018) to 2,975 (95% CI 2658–3290) when based on death certificates (Santos-Burgoa et al., 2018). For those who survived, life was difficult, as the disaster led to problems with drinking water (Lin et al., 2020), school and hospital closures, as well as a host of other difficulties. Immediately following the hurricane, people fled the island, and estimates are that the population of Puerto Rico experienced a 3.9% decline in growth, which is the largest year-to-year change in well over half a century (Flores & Krogstad, 2019). The effect of this net migration loss has been stunning, with the overall age in Puerto Rico increasing, accompanied by a decrease in the number of births. Indeed, from 2017 to 2019, Puerto Rico was estimated to have lost 14% of its population (Meléndez & Hinojosa, 2017). Psychologically, the effect of Hurricane Maria has also been profound. Following Hurricane Maria, the number of reported suicide attempts increased to almost 250% in the first three months following the disaster (Comisión Para la Prevención del Suicidio, 2017). The storm also elicited traumatic experiences in transnational communities in the United States, who reported higher anxiety symptoms and more stress following the natural disasters.

Most recently, like every other country in the world, Puerto Rico has been hit with COVID-19. While some of infrastructure and psychological issues existed prior to the pandemic, the ongoing pandemic, coming in the wake of Hurricane Maria, has magnified the aforementioned issues and, of course, created its own unique set of problems as well (Pérez-Pedrogo et al., 2020). For example, while unemployment has historically been an issue on the island, following the pandemic, Puerto Rico had an unemployment rate of 23%, the second highest in the United States (Rosa & Robles, 2020). Currently, trust in the US and the Puerto Rican government is at an all-time low, as residents remain skeptical of their effectiveness given the difficulties experienced by the austerity measures, the low access to personal protective equipment, and slow vaccination rates. In fact, one year after the pandemic began, in March 2021, only 12.5% of Puerto Ricans had received one dose, and only 11.2% had received two doses—the lowest of any state or territory in the entirety of the United States (see how the vaccine rollout is going in your state, 2021). Thankfully, the situation has improved, although recent waves in tourism have led to an increase in cases.

Training Opportunities in Psychology

As the reader can see, there is much to attend to in Puerto Rico. However, the practice of psychology in Puerto Rico has a long and active history trying to bring attention to these issues (Bernal, 2013). In Puerto Rico, there are a growing number of programs where students can receive training in a variety of areas, such as community, health, industrial, and school psychology. For those interested in the applied professions, such as counseling or clinical psychology, there are four APA-accredited programs: Carlos Albizu University, Ponce School of Medicine, the Universidad Ana G. Méndez, and the University of Puerto Rico, where students can get trained and become eligible for licensure in either Puerto Rico or the mainland United States. At the postdoctoral level, there is now a fellowship program at the VA in San Juan that has been APA-accredited since 2014. These opportunities are well needed as there is still more work to be done to scale up services in Puerto Rico and close the treatment gap (Kohn et al., 2018).

Future Directions

Despite the widespread tragedies Puerto Ricans have faced, both on and off the island, research also highlights the community resilience among people who have endured so much (Lybarger, 2018). Puerto Ricans have shown remarkable grittiness in the face of multiple calamities, and future research should investigate the protective aspects of Puerto Rican culture, such as *familismo*, parental warmth, and religiosity, that have helped them cope during difficult times (Macias et al., 2021). In keeping with the goals of liberation psychology, our hope is that clinicians and researchers not only focus on the reduction of personal suffering but also work toward acquiring a more advanced understanding of social suffering that centers on freedom for the oppressed.

References

Alegria, M., Canino, G., Shrout, P., Woo, M., Duan, N., Vila, D., Torres, M., Chen, C., & Meng, X.-L. (2008). Prevalence of mental illness in immigrant and non-immigrant U.S. Latino groups. *American Journal of Psychiatry, 165*, 359–369. https://doi.org/10.1176/appi.ajp.2007.07040704

APA Committee on Women in Psychology. (2020, October 13). *Intimate partner violence and natural disasters.* https://www.apa.org/topics/covid-19/partner-violence-disasters

Arévalo, S. P., Tucker, K. L., & Falcón, L. M. (2014). Life events trajectories, allostatic load, and the moderating role of age at arrival from Puerto Rico to the US mainland. *Social Science & Medicine, 120*, 301–310. https://doi.org/10.1016/j.socscimed.2014.09.040

Bernal, G. (2013). 60 years of clinical psychology in Puerto Rico. *Revista Interamericana De Psicologia [Interamerican Journal of Psychology], 47*(2), 211–226. https://doi.org/10.30849/rip/ijp.v47i2.216

Busse, W., Raphael, G. D., Galant, S., Kalberg, C., Goode-Sellers, S., Srebro, S., Edwards, L., & Rickard, K. (2001). Low-dose fluticasone propionate compared with montelukast for first-line treatment of persistent asthma: A randomized clinical trial. *Journal of Allergy Clinical Immunology, 107*(3), 461–468. https://doi.org/10.1067/mai.2001.114657

Canino, G., Shrout, P. E., NeMoyer, A., Vila, D., Santiago, K. M., Garcia, P., Quiñones, A., Cruz, V., & Alegria, M. (2019). A comparison of the prevalence of psychiatric disorders in Puerto Rico with the United States and the Puerto Rican population of the United States. *Social Psychiatry and Psychiatric Epidemiology, 54*(3), 369–378. https://doi.org/10.1007/s00127-019-01653-6

Canino, G., Shrout, P. E., Rubio-Stipec, M., Bird, H. R., Bravo, M., & Martize-Taboas, A. M. (2004). The DSM IV rates of child and adolescent disorders in Puerto Rico: Prevalence, correlates, service use, and effects of impairment. *Archives of General Psychiatry, 61*, 85–93. https://doi.org/10.1001/archpsyc.61.1.85

Capielo Rosario, C., & Dillon, F. (2020). *Ni de aquí, ni de allá* [Neither here, nor there]: Puerto Rican acculturation-acculturative stress profiles and depression. *Cultural Diversity and Ethnic Minority Psychology, 25*(1), 42–53. https://doi.org/10.1037/cdp0000272

Capielo Rosario, C., Schaefer, A., Ballesteros, J., Rentería, R., & David, E. (2019). *A caballo regalao no se le mira el colmillo*: Colonial mentality and Puerto Rican depression. *Journal of Counseling Psychology, 66*(4), 396–408. https://doi.org/10.1037/cou0000347

Centro for Puerto Rican studies. (n.d.). *Puerto Ricans in the U.S. earn less money and pay more for housing*. https://tinyurl.com/2yx2m924

Chowdhury, P. P., Mawokomatanda, T., Xu, F., Gamble, S., Flegel, D., Pierannunzi, C., Garvin, W., & Town, M. (2016). Surveillance for certain health behaviors, chronic diseases, and conditions, access to health care, and use of preventive health services among states and selected local areas- behavioral risk factor surveillance system. *The Morbidity and Mortality Weekly Report CDC Surveillance Summaries, 65*(4), 1–142. https://doi.org/10.15585/mmwr.ss6709a1

Cintrón, J. A., Carter, M. M., & Sbrocco, T. (2005). *Ataques de nervios* in relation to anxiety sensitivity among island Puerto Ricans. *Culture, Medicine & Psychiatry, 29*(4), 415–431. https://doi.org/10.1007/s11013-006-9001-7

Colón, H. M., & Sánchez-Cesareo, M. (2016). Disparities in health care in Puerto Rico compared with the United States. *Journal of the American Medical Association, 176*(6), 794–795. https://doi.org/10.1001/jamainternmed.2016.1144

Comas-Díaz, L., Lykes, M. B., & Alarcón, R. D. (1998). Ethnic conflict and the psychology of liberation in Guatemala, Peru, and Puerto Rico. *American Psychologist, 53*(7), 778–792. https://doi.org/10.1037/0003-066X.53.7.778

Comas-Díaz, L., & Torres Rivera, E. (Eds.). (2020). *Cultural, racial, and ethnic psychology book series. Liberation psychology: Theory, method, practice, and social justice.* American Psychological Association. https://doi.org/10.1037/0000198-000

Comisión Para la Prevención del Suicidio. (2017). *Estadísticas preliminares de casos de suicidio en PR, enero – diciembre 2017* [Commission for the prevention of suicide: Preliminary statistics of suicide cases, January-December 2017]. https://tinyurl.com/msuj4h83

Cuevas, A. G., Wang, K., Williams, D. R., Mattei, J., Tucker, K. L., & Falcon, L. M. (2019). The association between perceived discrimination and allostatic load in the Boston Puerto Rican Health Study. *Psychosomatic Medicine, 81*(7), 659–667. https://doi.org/10.1097/PSY.0000000000000715

Diemer, M. A., Mistry, R., Wadsworth, M. E., López, I., & Reimers, F. (2013). Best practices in conceptualizing and measuring social class in psychological research. *Analyses of Social Issues and Public Policy, 13*(1), 77–113. https://doi.org/10.1111/asap.12001

Downes v Bidell (182 U.S. 244). (1901). https://tinyurl.com/486duc2d

Duany, J. (2012). *The Puerto Rican diaspora to the United States: A postcolonial migration?* https://tinyurl.com/vb9tmk3r

Flores, A., & Krogstad, J. M. (2019, July 26). *Puerto Rico's population declined sharply after hurricanes Maria and Irma.* https://www.pewresearch.org/fact-tank/2019/07/26/puerto-rico-population-2018/

Gabrow, C. (2019, February 29). *New reports detail the Jones Act's cost to Puerto Rico.* https://tinyurl.com/2yuzv8wm

Garza, J. R., Glenn, B. A., Mistry, R. S., Ponce, N. A., & Zimmerman, F. J. (2017). Subjective social status and self-reported health among US-born and immigrant Latinos. *Journal of Immigrant Minority Health, 19*, 108–119. https://doi.org/10.1007/s10903-016-0346-x

Gene Locke, R. Jr. (2021). Absolute and perpetual liminality: The insular cases and Puerto Rico. *The Yale Historical Review.* https://www.yalehistoricalreview.org/absolute-and-perpetual-liminality/

Guarnaccia, P. J., Lewis-Fernández, R., Martinez Pincay, I., Shrout, P., Guo, J., Torres, M., Canino, G., & Alegría, M. (2009). *Ataque de nervios* as a marker of social and psychiatric vulnerability: Results from the NLAAS. *International Journal of Social Psychiatry, 56*(3), 298–309. https://doi.org/10.1177/0020764008101636

Guarnaccia, P. J., Martinez, I., Ramírez, R., & Canino, G. (2005). Are *ataques de nervios* in Puerto Rican children associated with psychiatric disorder? *Journal of the American Academy of Child & Adolescent Psychiatry, 44*(11), 1184–1192. https://doi.org/10.1097/01.chi.0000177059.34031.5d

Hinton, D. E., Chong, R., Pollack, M. H., Barlow, D. H., & McNally, R. J. (2008). *Ataque de nervios*: Relationship to anxiety sensitivity and dissociation predisposition. *Depression and Anxiety, 25*(6), 489–495. https://doi.org/10.1002/da.20309

Hurtado, R. & Rivera-Vázquez, O. (2020, Special Issue). *Denaturalizing surviving: Domestic violence, narrative, and social justice in the aftermath of Hurricane Maria. Label Me Latina/o, 1–16.* https://tinyurl.com/tm28cukh

Kishore, N., Marqúez, D., Mahmud, A., Kiang, M. V., Rodríguez, I., Fuller, A., Ebner, P., Sorenson, C., Racy, F., Lemery, J., Maas, L., Leaning, J., Irizarry, R. A., Balsari, S., & Buckee, C. O. (2018). Mortality in Puerto Rico after Hurricane Maria. *The New England Journal of Medicine, 379*(2), 162–170. https://doi.org/10.1056/NEJMsa1803972

Kohn, R., Ali, A., Puac-Polanco, V., Figueroa, C., López-Soto, V., Morgan, K., Saldivia, S., & Vicente, B. (2018). Mental health in the Americas: An overview of the treatment gap. *Pan American Journal of Public Health, 45*(165). https://doi.org/10.26633/RPSP.2018.165

Kovacs, R. J., & Rodríguez-Vilá, O. (2020). The challenges of inequitable care: A look at Puerto Rico versus U.S. States. *Journal of the American College of Cardiology, 75*(15), 1857–1859. https://doi.org/10.1016/j.jacc.2020.03.007

La Fortaleza. (2021, January 24). *Gobernador declara estado de emergencia por violencia de género* [Governor declares a state of emergency over gender based violence]. https://tinyurl.com/j3s7wwhp

Lewis-Fernández, R., Gorritz, M., Raggio, G. A., Peláez, C., Chen, H., & Guarnaccia, P. J. (2010). Association of trauma-related disorders and dissociation with four idioms of distress among Latino psychiatric outpatients. *Culture, Medicine and Psychiatry, 34*(2), 219–243. https://doi.org/10.1007/s11013-010-9177-8

Lewis-Fernández, R., & López, I. (2016). Ataques de Nervios. In B. A. Sharpless (Ed.), *Unusual and rare psychological disorders: A handout for clinical practice and research.* Oxford University Press.

Lin, Y., Sevillano-Rivera, M., Jiang, T., Guangyu, L., Cotto, I., Vosloo, S., Carpenter, C. M. G., Larese-Casanova, P., Giese, R. W., Helbling, D. E., Padilla, I. Y., Rosario-Pabón, Z., Vélez Vega, C., Cordero, J. F., Alshawabkeh, A. N., Pinto, A., & Gu, A. Z. (2020). Impact of Hurricane Maria on drinking water quality in Puerto Rico. *Environmental Science & Technology, 54*(15), 9495–9509. https://doi.org/10.1021/acs.est.0c01655

López, I. (2008a). Puerto Rican phenotype: Understanding its historical underpinnings and psychological associations. *Hispanic Journal of Behavioral Sciences, 30*(2), 161–180. https://doi.org/10.1177/0739986307313116

López, I. (2008b). "But you don't look Puerto Rican": The moderating effect of ethnic identity on the relation between skin color and self-esteem among Puerto Rican women. *Cultural Diversity and Ethnic Minority Psychology, 14*(2), 102–108. https://doi.org/10.1037/1099-9809.14.2.102

López, I., & Ho, A. (2013). Culture-bound (or culturally salient?): The role of culture in disorder. In K. D. Keith (Ed.), *The Encyclopedia of cross-cultural psychology*. Wiley. https://doi.org/10.1002/9781118339893

López, I., Rivera, F., Ramirez, R., Guarnaccia, P., Canino, G., & Bird, H. R. (2009). *Ataques de nervios* and their psychiatric correlates in Puerto Rican children from two different contexts.

The Journal of Nervous and Mental Disease, 3(12), 923–929. https://doi.org/10.1097/NMD.0b013e3181c2997d

Lybarger, J. (2018, May). Mental health in Puerto Rico. *49*(5). https://www.apa.org/monitor/2018/05/puerto-rico

Macias, L. R., Lebrón, A., Taylor, K., & Silva, M. (2021). Después de la tormenta [After the storm]: Collective trauma following Hurricane Maria in a northeastern Puerto Rican community in the United States. *Journal of Community Psychology, 49*, 118–132. https://doi.org/10.1002/jcop.22442

Martinez-Velez, J. J., Melin, K., & Rodriguez-Diaz, C. (2019). A preliminary assessment of selected social determinants of health in a sample of transgender and gender nonconforming individuals in Puerto Rico. *Transgender Health, 4*(1), 9–17. https://doi.org/10.1089/trgh.2018.0045

McNeill, B., McCubbin, L. L., & Sevedge, S. (2017). Mestiza/o, indigenous, and liberation perspectives on social issues. In A. W. Blume (Ed.), *Social issues in living color: Challenges and solutions from the perspective of ethnic minority psychology: Overview and interpersonal issues* (pp. 49–74). Praeger/ABC-CLIO.

Meléndez, E., & Hinojosa, J. (2017). *Estimates of post-Hurricane Maria exodus from Puerto Rico*. https://tinyurl.com/kz9sr7k

Morales Díaz, N. E., & Del Toro, R. (2012). Experiencias de violencia en el noviazgo de mujeres en Puerto Rico [Experiences of violence in dating of women in Puerto Rico]. *Revista Puertorriqueña de Psicología, 23*, 57–90.

Morning Consult. (2017, September 23–24). *National tracking poll ##170916*. https://tinyurl.com/6nxy4at8

Park, E. (2021). *How states would fare under Medicaid block grants or per capita caps: Lessons from Puerto Rico*. https://tinyurl.com/j2jhyhh7

Pasquali, M. (2018). *Population density in Latin America and the Caribbean in 2018, by country*. https://tinyurl.com/w56jduds

Pérez-Pedrogo, C., Francia-Martínez, M., & Martínez-Taboas, A. (2020). COVID-19 in Puerto Rico: Preliminary observations on social distancing and societal response toward a novel health stressor. *Psychological Trauma: Theory, Research, Practice, Policy, 12*(5), 515–517. https://doi.org/10.1037/tra0000664

Perreira, K., Peters, R., Lallemand, N., & Zuckerman, S. (2017). *Puerto Rico health care infrastructure assessment: A site visit report*. https://tinyurl.com/3s5jm6u2

Proyecto Matria. (2019). *La persistencia de la indolencia: feminicidios en Puerto Rico 2014–2018* [The persistence of indolence: Femicides in Puerto Rico 2014–2018]. https://tinyurl.com/dcjbapzk

Puerto Rico Data Lab. (2017, November 16). *Do Puerto Ricans pay the highest electricity rates in the United States?* https://tinyurl.com/f7t5jd6

Rivera, F., López, I., Ramirez, R., Guarnaccia, P., Canino, G., & Bird, H. (2011). Perceived discrimination and antisocial behaviors in Puerto Rican children. *Journal of Immigrant and Minority Health, 13*(3), 453–461. https://doi.org/10.1007/s10903-010-9421-x

Rivera Joseph, S., Voyles, C., Williams, K. D., Smith, E., & Chilton, M. (2020). Colonial neglect and the right to health in Puerto Rico after Hurricane Maria. *American Journal of Public Health, 110*(10), 1512–1518. https://doi.org/10.2105/AJPH.2020.305814

Rivera, R. Z. (2020). Disaster colonialism: A commentary on disasters beyond singular events to structural violence. *International Journal of Urban and Regional Research*, 1–10. https://doi.org/10.1111/1468-2427.1295

Rosa, A., & Robles, F. (2020, July 8). *Pandemic plunges Puerto Rico into yet another dire emergency*. https://tinyurl.com/2na6sszz

Santos-Burgoa, C., Sandberg, J., Suárez, E., Goldman-Hawes, A., Zeger, S., Garcia-Meza, A., Pérez, C. M., Estrada-Merly, N., Colón-Ramos, U., Nazario, C. M., Andrade, E., Roess, A., & Goldman, L. (2018). Differential and persistent risk of excess mortality from Hurricane Maria in Puerto Rico: A time-series analysis. *The Lancet. Planetary Health, 2*(11), 478–488. https://doi.org/10.1016/S2542-5196(18)30209-2

Sareen, J., Afifi, T. O., McMillan, K. A., Asmundson, J., & G. (2011). Relationship between household income and mental disorders: Findings from a population based longitudinal study. *Archives of General Psychiatry, 68*(4), 419–427. https://doi.org/10.1001/archgenpsychiatry.2011.15

See how the vaccine rollout is going in your state. (2021, March 8). *The New York Times*. https://www.nytimes.com/interactive/2020/us/covid-19-vaccine-doses.html

Semega, J., Kollar, M., Shrider, E. A., & Creamer J. F. (2020). *Income and Poverty in the United States: 2019* (Report No. P60-270). U.S. Census Bureau. https://tinyurl.com/z36t27dv

Solomon, J. (2019, April 22). *Puerto Rico's medicaid program needs an ongoing commitment of federal funds.* https://www.cbpp.org/sites/default/files/atoms/files/4-22-19health.pdf

Statista. (2021). *Population density in the U.S., by state 2020.* https://tinyurl.com/2x9tpkyh

Stylianou, A. M. (2018). Economic abuse experiences and depressive symptoms among victims of intimate partner violence. *Journal of Family Violence, 33*, 381–392. https://doi.org/10.1007/s10896-018-9973-4

Transgender Law Center. (n.d.). *The roots of anti-trans violence: Puerto Rico*. Transgender Law Center. https://transgenderlawcenter.org/regional-reports-puerto-rico

U.S. Census Bureau. (2019a). *Selected Population Profile in Puerto Rico, 2019 American Community Survey 1-year estimate.* https://tinyurl.com/9hway4xs

U.S. Census Bureau. (2019b). *Hispanic or Latino Origin by Specific Group, 2019 American Community Survey 1-year estimate*. https://tinyurl.com/z9sw66y3

U.S. Census Bureau. (2019c). *Quick facts: Puerto Rico.* https://www.census.gov/quickfacts/PR

Valle, A. J. (2019). Race and the empire-state: Puerto Ricans' unequal U.S. citizenship. *Sociology of Race and Ethnicity, 5*(1), 26–40. https://doi.org/10.1177/2332649218776031

Venator-Santiago, C. R. (2013). Extending citizenship to Puerto Rico: Three traditions of inclusive exclusion. *Centro Journal, 25*(1), 50–75.

Vila, D., Rand, C. S., Cabana, M. D., Quiñones, A., Otero, M., Gamache, C., Ramírez, R., García, P., & Canino, G. (2010). Disparities in asthma medication dispensing patterns: The case of pediatric asthma in Puerto Rico. *Journal of Asthma, 47*(10), 1136–1141. https://doi.org/10.3109/02770903.2010.517338

Villafañe-Santiago, A., Serra-Taylor, J., Jiménez-Chafey, M. I., & Irizarry-Robles, C. Y. (2019). Violencia familiar y de pareja en estudiantes universitarios Puertorriqueños [Family and Intimate Partner violence among Puerto Rican university students]. *Revista Puertorriqueña de Psicología, 30*(1), 70–81.

Wilkinson, E., Killeen, D., Pérez-López, G. J., & Jabbarpour, Y. (2020). A shrinking primary care workforce in Puerto Rico. *American Family Physician., 101*(1), 13–14. https://www.aafp.org/afp/2020/0101/p13.html

Chapter 18
Psychology in Guyana and Trinidad and Tobago

Jaipaul L. Roopnarine, Derek Chadee, and Mark A. Primus

Over the last 40 years, training in the psychological sciences has grown steadily in Barbados, Grenada, Jamaica, Suriname, and Trinidad and Tobago. Institutions of higher learning, such as the University of the West Indies in Trinidad and Tobago, went from offering a few courses in psychology to granting graduate degrees. Individual countries have also established national psychological organizations that partner with the Caribbean Alliance of National Psychological Associations (CANPA) to sponsor biannual conferences. At the other end of the spectrum are countries (e.g., Guyana) with fledging programs that are only now offering basic courses in psychology. In this brief chapter, an attempt is made to provide a glimpse into what we know about some aspects of psychology in the southernmost Caribbean countries of Guyana and Trinidad and Tobago. We begin with a discussion of socio-historical experiences, pertinent sociodemographic factors, family dynamics, and religious practices of different ethnic groups in the two countries, before turning our attention to key mental health challenges, human resources, training programs in psychology at tertiary institutions of learning, and psychological organizations.

J. L. Roopnarine (✉)
Syracuse University, Syracuse, NY, USA

Anton de Kom University of Suriname, Paramaribo, Suriname
e-mail: jroopnar@syr.edu

D. Chadee
The University of the West Indies, St. Augustine, Trinidad and Tobago
e-mail: Derek.Chadee@sta.uwi.edu

M. A. Primus
Nazareth College, Rochester, NY, USA
e-mail: mprimus4@naz.edu

G. J. Rich, N. A. Ramkumar (eds.), *Psychology in Oceania and the Caribbean*, International and Cultural Psychology,
https://doi.org/10.1007/978-3-030-87763-7_18

Conceptual Frameworks

In Guyana and Trinidad and Tobago, there has been a general tendency for research in the fields of psychology and sociology to focus on risk factors and human functioning (e.g., family organization patterns and nonresidential fatherhood, criminal behavior, delinquency, and harsh parenting). To promote a more balanced view of psychological issues in these two countries, this chapter draws on propositions within positive psychology and developmental psychopathology to frame the topics discussed herein. In the main, positive psychology focuses on factors that enhance the optimal functioning of human beings, different groups, and institutions (Gable & Haidt, 2005; Hendriks & Graafsma, 2019). Whether oriented toward collectivistic (interdependence, group harmony) or individualistic (cost-benefit of relationships, autonomy, personal fulfillment) social organization patterns and goals (Oyserman et al., 2002), there is increased awareness of the need to incorporate cultural practices to adequately assess and meet the personal and interpersonal needs of individuals across countries (Dudley-Grant, 2016; Dudley-Grant et al., 2018). Evidence of this can be seen in the worldwide push to train professionals who can provide sensitively attuned care that is calibrated to enhance the well-being of diverse groups of individuals in different cultural communities. At the same time, the developmental psychopathology framework stresses the importance of considering both risk and protective factors within families (e.g., sensitive parenting, intimate partner violence (IPV), spousal/partner support, ethnic socialization) and communities (e.g., neighborhood quality and collective efficacy, crime, and violence) that have direct or indirect influences on behavioral development (Masten, 2006; Rutter & Sroufe, 2000).

Both these frameworks are ideally suited for understanding intrapersonal and interpersonal factors at the individual, family, and community level that instigate and/or impede psychological functioning. As posited by Masten (2006), developmental psychopathology invites multidisciplinary investigations, mapping multilevel dynamics within and across systems, plasticity, and resilience and recovery among other salient factors in understanding human behavior. Far too often, researchers in Guyana and Trinidad and Tobago have ignored the resilient nature of human beings and such positive attributes as religious and ethnic socialization and support offered by multigeneration units.

Sociohistorical Experiences, Sociodemographic Characteristics, and Cultural Practices

Sociohistorical Experiences As is the case with other Caribbean countries, Guyana and Trinidad and Tobago are societies with long oppressive histories steeped in European colonization, maltreatment of indigenous groups, slavery, and indentured servitude. Following the horrendous treatment of indigenous peoples,

Africans were brought as slaves to Guyana and Trinidad and Tobago to work in agriculture (e.g., sugarcane plantations). After slavery was abolished, Indians and Chinese were brought as indentured servants to supplant the shortage of labor on the plantations. The degree of trauma experienced by different ethnic groups and the adaptive strategies they implemented to cope with the adverse experiences of conquest, enslavement, and cultural transplantation have been actively debated by researchers and clinicians in diverse disciplines within the Caribbean and the Caribbean diaspora (see Fanon, 1967; Roopnarine & Chadee, 2016).

Anticolonial theory (Escayg, 2014) and the retentionist and creolization theses (see Vertovec, 1991 for a discussion) variously point to the loss of ancestral languages and cultural practices, invasion of the cultural psyche, emergence of nonmarital unions and female-headed households, and cultural and psychological adjustment strategies associated with the harsh experiences imposed by the colonizers. It would be a mistake to underestimate the adaptive strategies that Caribbean peoples displayed to cope with their oppressive histories. For instance, African Caribbean women formed bonds with kinship and nonkinship members to rear children while incorporating ancestral cultural and spiritual practices in daily life (Barrow, 1998; Beckles, 1989), and Indo-Caribbean marriage ceremonies (e.g., Matikor), religious worship, and celebrations brought from India to the Caribbean have been maintained and successfully nurtured during and after indentureship ended in Guyana and Trinidad and Tobago (Bahadur, 2015; Dabydeen & Samroo, 1987). The same can be said for Indigenous (Amerindian) customs (use of magical charm plants for luck in hunting) and healing practices in hinterland communities in Guyana and Suriname (van Andel et al., 2015). There has also been a fair amount of borrowing and blending of cultural practices from adjacent ethnic groups in efforts to develop ethnic identity and effectively navigate a common cultural space particularly in Trinidad and Tobago (see Vertovec, 1991).

Sociodemographic Factors and Family Dynamics Both Guyana and Trinidad and Tobago are multiethnic nations. With a population of approximately 750,000, Guyana consists of Indo-Caribbeans, African Caribbeans, individuals of mixed-ethnic ancestry, Indigenous groups (Amerindians), and people of Portuguese and Chinese ancestry. A similar ethnic mosaic is evident in Trinidad and Tobago's 1.4 million people. This diversity is both a strength and challenge for these two emerging democracies. Cultural identity has largely fallen along ethnic lines in both countries, with individuals of mixed-ethnic (Dougla) ancestry straddling and integrating multiple cultural traditions to form bidimensional or multiple-dimensional identity (Franco et al., 2017). The overlap between ethnic identity and orientation toward other cultural values and practices is largely unknown.

Historically viewed in pathological terms, multi-partner fertility is not a new phenomenon across Caribbean countries (see Anderson & Daley, 2015). It has been argued that slavery separated males from their families which contributed to matriarchal family patterns wherein women formed economic, social, and emotional alliances with other women to execute family functions and rear children in the absence of men in the household (Brunod & Cook-Darzens, 2002). Today, poor economic conditions, hegemonic beliefs about men's roles in families and society, and migration within the Caribbean and to high-income countries for employment all contribute to what has been termed progressive mating or mate-shifting (Anderson & Daley, 2015; Chevannes, 2001). Marriage is not a prerequisite for entering a heterosexual relationship union or for having children. Nor is the nuclear family held as the prototypical norm for rearing children. Diverse structural living arrangements often contain multigenerational households or units with extended emotional ties to nonkinship members.

Because so much of child and adolescent development is shaped by experiences within the family system, it is necessary to describe the mating unions and residential patterns of men in Guyana and Trinidad and Tobago. Psychologists and anthropologists have examined reproductive strategies and pair-bond stability, somatic investment, and residential patterns of males (see Belsky et al., 1991; Hewlett, 1992; Marlowe, 2005). There is general agreement that pair-bond stability, men's economic support, and their residence within the family reduce psychological risks to offspring and improve the overall welfare of the family unit (Carlson & McLanahan, 2010). However, it should be cautioned that mere physical presence, in the absence of emotional and economic investment, does not automatically result in positive psychological and other benefits to family members. Most would agree that the sensitive aspect of caring for others, relationship commitment and support, good communication and constructive conflict resolution strategies between partners, modeling moral concern for others, and altruism are all essential to healthy well-being than mere physical presence (see Roopnarine & Dede Yildirim, 2019a).

With the above in mind, among African Caribbean and mixed-ethnic Caribbean men and women in Guyana and Trinidad and Tobago, a fair share of mating relationships begins in visiting unions where men and women live apart while having children. They then move on to other partners and form common-law unions where they share a residence and have more children. Subsequently, marriage may occur with better economic standing (Anderson, 2021; Anderson & Daley, 2015; Roopnarine & Jin, 2016). A national survey conducted in Trinidad and Tobago showed that 28% of African Caribbean families, 32.2% of mixed-ethnic families, and 23.3% of Indo-Caribbean families were in common-law relationships. Marriage rates were higher among Indo-Caribbean (69%) than in African Caribbean (21.7%) and mixed-ethnic (27.2%) families (Roopnarine et al., 2013a). Relationship instability and progressive mating often undermine contacts and alliances with previous mating partners and offspring due to jealousy, inadequate or no economic support offered to children and their mothers by men, and lack of residential propinquity (see Anderson & Daley, 2015).

Recent analyses of UNICEF Multiple Indicator Cluster Survey data suggest that there were cognitive risks to children associated with nonresidential fatherhood and instability in family living arrangements in families in Trinidad and Tobago (Roopnarine & Dede Yildirim, 2019b), a pattern observed in Jamaica (Samms-Vaughn, 2005), and the United States (Adamsons & Johnson, 2013). That said, paternal engagement in cognitive and social activities was not consistently associated with children's cognitive and social skills in Barbados, Belize, the Dominican Republic, Guyana, Jamaica, and Suriname (Dede Yildirim & Roopnarine, 2017). These latter findings bring to the fore questions about gender essentialism in the Caribbean and the role of men in childhood development.

Religious and Spiritual Practices Ethnic groups in Guyana and Trinidad and Tobago engage in a range of religious (e.g., Hinduism, Islam, different sects of Christianity, Orisha) and spiritual practices that were either imposed upon them during colonization, were brought with them during slavery and indentured servitude, or emerged overtime as result of cultural contact with other ethnic groups (Bahadur, 2015; Dabydeen & Samroo, 1987; Houk, 1995). Based on the influence of European colonization, most African Caribbean and mixed-ethnic Caribbean families in Trinidad and Tobago and Guyana believe and observe religious precepts in Christianity. The lives of most Indigenous groups in Guyana have been affected by Christian missionaries as well. Hinduism and Islam practiced by Indian indenture laborers post-slavery remain fully entrenched in communities across Guyana and Trinidad and Tobago (Dabydeen & Samroo, 1987).

Having a common conceptual base, religiosity and spirituality are connected to physical and behavioral health in Guyana and Trinidad and Tobago (Oser et al., 2006; Toussaint et al., 2015). As noted already, across the Caribbean, religion and spirituality have played a significant role in coping with oppression and the throes of poverty, guiding childrearing and community life (e.g., baptisms, head shaving, Naamkaran [naming ceremony], burial rites, healing, obeah), in shaping the internalization of moral principles, and in extending altruism to others (Dabydeen & Samroo, 1987). It may come as no surprise then that people in Guyana and Trinidad and Tobago turn to religion and spirituality for healing purposes and to ward off evil spirits. A good example is the use of Hindu religious practices to attend to the mentally ill at Kali temples.

Mental Health Issues

In general, comprehensive epidemiological data on mental health disorders are lacking in most Caribbean countries. Stigma attached to mental health disorders (violent, dangerous) and cultural beliefs (supernatural forces, spiritual invasion), underdeveloped mental health systems, and social and economic factors are hindrances to access and treatment of mental health disorders in the Caribbean and Latin America (Mayascano et al., 2016). The World Health Organization (WHO-AIMS, 2011) reported that schizophrenia is the most common diagnosis at outpatient clinics in the Caribbean, followed by mood disorder and substance use (see also Lacey et al., 2016). In this segment, we provide some statistics on the prevalence of the most pressing mental health challenges and their associated correlates in Guyana and Trinidad and Tobago: suicides, depression, family violence, and substance abuse.

From World Health Organization (WHO-AIMS, 2011) estimates, suicide rates in Guyana (all age groups 34.8 per 100,000, males 50.8, females 18.3, highest for those 50 years and above), Suriname (27.2 per 100,000, males 42.4, females 11.9, highest for those 50 years and higher), and Trinidad and Tobago (14.4 per 100,000, males 50.8, females 6.9, highest in 20–69 age group) are among the highest in the world. Between 2000 and 2016, the rate dropped in Trinidad and Tobago to 7.9/100,000, the average age being 39.5 years (Nobie & Hutchinson, 2018). Across these three countries, Indo-Caribbeans have higher suicide rates than other ethnic groups. Poisoning (47%) and hanging (41.8%) are the common methods of suicides in Trinidad and Tobago (Nobie & Hutchinson, 2018), and the same methods (use of agricultural pesticides among youth) are reported for Guyana (Quinlan-Davidson et al., 2014). Factors associated with suicides and attempted suicides include mental health difficulties, intrafamily conflicts, being bullied, religiousness, alcoholism, and rural residence (Nobie & Hutchinson, 2018; Toussaint et al., 2015).

As far as depression is concerned, prevalence rates vary quite a bit between the two countries and may be attributed, in part, to differences in economic standing and access to mental health services. Among 13–19-year-olds (53.6% Indo-Trinidadians) in Trinidad and Tobago, the prevalence of depression as assessed by the Beck Depression Inventory (BDI) was 25.3%, with females 1.7 times more likely to be depressed than males. Youth who did not live with both parents were 1.5 times more likely to be depressed than those who did, and those who were afraid of their parents or concerned about being injured by their parents were three times more likely to be depressed than those who did not have these worries (Maharaj et al., 2008, 2009). In another sample of 18–49-year-olds in Trinidad and Tobago, drawn from family medical practices, 12.8% of the participants were depressed as determined by a modified version of the Zung Scale. Depression decreased with age, and those who were not currently in a relationship were more likely to be depressed than those who were in one (Maharaj, 2007). Yet other studies show higher rates of depression (measured by the Center for Epidemiologic Studies of Depression Scale [CES-D]) among Indo-Guyanese (36.6%) and diverse ethnic groups of adults in Trinidad and Tobago (46%). Personal stress and family life satisfaction predicted depression, and family support moderated the association between life satisfaction and depression in both countries (Roopnarine et al., 2017). Surveys of children across Antigua, Bahamas, Barbados, British Virgin Islands, Dominica, Grenada, Guyana, Jamaica, and St. Lucia showed that physical and sexual abuse heightened depression (69.2%) (Blum et al., 2003).

Families and youth often celebrate different functions and festivals (e.g., carnivals, public holidays) with the use of alcohol, marijuana, and other substances in Trinidad and Tobago and Guyana. A survey of teenagers in Trinidad and Tobago revealed that 35.7% used alcohol (16.8% were heavy drinkers, defined as more than five drinks on one occasion) and 8.8% used cigarettes. Parental substance use, parental mental health problems, parental violence, being male, absence of religious engagement, lower academic performance in school, being from a professional family, and having a family member or friend who had attempted suicide were correlated with substance use in teenagers across age categories (Blum et al., 2003;

Maharaj et al., 2009). Alcohol use among adults in Trinidad and Tobago was pervasive with 64% of households reported using alcohol, and 57% engaged in heavy drinking at different times (Maharaj et al., 2017). Lower estimates were obtained for alcohol abuse (3.6%), drug abuse (1.4%), and (1.4%) substance abuse (4.7%) among Guyanese (Lacey et al., 2016).

Family violence (e.g., intimate partner violence) and harsh parental treatment in the form of physical punishment are chronic issues across the Caribbean. Recently Guyana and Trinidad and Tobago have witnessed a surge in the death of women and children linked to domestic violence. It is also the case that across Caribbean countries there is high endorsement and use of physical punishment. Practices such as beating children and adolescents with an object, pulling on body parts, dragging them, and slapping can be so severe that they constitute abuse. To make matters worse, it is not uncommon for the physical assaults to be accompanied by psychological aggression (Dede Yildirim & Roopnarine, 2017). In a comparative analysis of the use of different methods of discipline in Belize, Dominican Republic, Guyana, Jamaica, and Suriname, 71.7% of mothers or primary caregivers used explanations; 55.6% screamed, shouted, or yelled at children (7.5% called child dumb/lazy); 17.6% shook; and 17.4% slapped children (Dede Yildirim & Roopnarine, 2017). Studies on families in Trinidad and Tobago also indicate high rates of slapping (49.7% of mothers and 34.5% of fathers) and hitting children with an object (Primus, 2018).

It is well established that intimate partner violence has negative consequences on women's physical and mental health and birth outcomes and is linked to sexually transmitted infections, issues with contraception, unintended pregnancy, and poor pregnancy and birth outcomes in developing countries (Garcia-Moreno et al., 2006). The effects of intimate partner violence on children are equally concerning and include getting injured in attempts to protect a parent, becoming isolated due to the abuser's behavior, being the recipient of violent acts directly, constant experiences with stress and tension, internalizing (e.g., depressive symptoms) and externalizing behaviors (e.g., aggression), trauma symptoms, and child neglect (DeBoard-Lucas & Grych, 2011). These difficulties become exacerbated under poor economic conditions and in nonresidential/nonmarital relationships. Inadequate material resources and relationship instability are associated with intimate partner violence and child maltreatment (see Roopnarine & Dede Yildirim, 2019b). Violent discipline and psychological aggression are associated with lower literacy and social skills in children in Guyana and Trinidad and Tobago and across 25 African countries (Primus, 2018; Roopnarine et al., 2013b; Dede Yildirm et al., 2020).

Human Resources

Decades of mass outward migration of qualified personnel, due in large part to political oppression and poor economic conditions, and inadequate training facilities have all contributed to the underdeveloped state of the mental health system in

Guyana. Likewise, over the last decade, deteriorating economic conditions and family and community violence have placed heavy demands on the existing mental health systems in Trinidad and Tobago. According to a World Health Organization Report (WHO-AIMS, 2011), Guyana did not have a mental health policy plan, spent 1% of its health budget on mental health with 61% of the spending allocated to mental hospitals, and had one mental hospital and two outpatient mental health facilities, no day-treatment facilities, no community residential facilities, and one community-based inpatient psychiatric unit. Between 11% and 20% of Guyanese patients are restrained or secluded. Because of the shortage of personnel (0.5% of psychiatrist, no psychologist, and 0.4% of nurses per 100,000 people), referrals for mental health care are often made by primary care doctors. Most nurses and psychiatrists offer care in outpatient facilities. By comparison, Trinidad and Tobago has a mental health policy plan, 4% of its total health expenditure is devoted to mental health, 94% of which is spent in mental health hospitals. The country has 1 mental hospital, 31 outpatient facilities, 3 day-treatment facilities, 2 community-based psychiatric inpatient facilities, and 8 community residential facilities and has 1.7 psychiatrists, 0.3 psychologists, and 32.7 nurses per 100,000 individuals. Most psychiatrists and nurses (81%) offer care in mental health facilities. In short, although there have been improvements in the mental health systems in both countries since these figures were compiled (e.g., child and adolescent psychiatrists are now available in Guyana), the mentally ill in Guyana and Trinidad and Tobago are way underserved.

Training Programs

To put it bluntly, psychological training in Guyana is in its neonatal stages. Before 2017, there were no formal training programs in the psychological sciences at the University of Guyana campuses. Nor were there specific courses tied to degree programs. Poor economic resources and lack of faculty trained in the psychological sciences may have led to the present state of the discipline. In 2017, a team from the Caribbean Alliance of National Psychological Associations (CANPA) visited the University of Guyana at the Turkeyen campus to assist with the development of formal training programs in psychology. Currently, the University offers a few basic courses in psychology with the hope of developing formal degree programs soon. A far different scenario exists in Trinidad and Tobago where the discipline has grown noticeably from the 1970s and 1980s to the present. From the meagre offering of two courses in psychology (general psychology and social psychology) in the sociology department and the chance to obtain a master's degree in sociology with a specialization in social psychology, the University of the West Indies, St. Augustine, currently grants bachelor's, master's, and doctoral degrees in psychology (Ramdhanie, 1999). The B.Sc. Psychology program was first offered at St. Augustine Campus in 1995 and came to fruition from the visionary and sterling initiative of Professor Ramesh Deosaran. There is a master's level clinical psychology program at Mount Hope Medical School at the University of the West Indies, where medical training in psychiatry is also offered.

At the country level, Guyana and Trinidad and Tobago are members of the Caribbean Alliance of National Psychological Associations (CANPA). One of the past presidents, Dr. Omowale Amuleru-Marshall, is of Guyanese ancestry, and the current president, Dr. Katija Khan, is from Trinidad and Tobago. Psychologists from these two countries and those of Guyanese and Trinidadian and Tobagonian ancestry in the high-income countries have worked with CANPA to build an indigenous understanding of Caribbean psychology that has a global reach (see, e.g., Roopnarine & Chadee, 2016, *Caribbean Psychology: Indigenous Contributions to a Global Discipline*, American Psychological Association). The *Caribbean Journal of Psychology* published by the University of West Indies Press has been a major publication outlet for a wide range of social science scholarships from across the region.

Conclusion

This brief excursion into psychology in Guyana and Trinidad and Tobago underscores the uneven development of the discipline in two neighboring countries with similar ethnic makeup. Swifter action is warranted for the development of a viable psychology discipline in Guyana. With its newly found oil wealth, Guyana is beginning to pay more attention to access to mental health services and in the training of mental health professionals. To address the mental health and other needs of these multiethnic nations, government officials in both countries need to allocate more economic resources to training programs, collaborate across countries, and recruit the expertise of well-trained Caribbean immigrants in the diaspora to assist in strengthening existing programs via online education and research and grant collaborations.

References

Adamsons, K., & Johnson, S. K. (2013). An updated and expanded meta-analysis of nonresident fathering and child well-being. *Journal of Family Psychology, 27*(4), 589–599. https://doi.org/10.1037/a0033786

Anderson, P. (2021). *Masculinity and fathering in Jamaica*. The University of the West Indies Press.

Anderson, P., & Daley, C. (2015). African-Caribbean fathers: The conflict between masculinity and fathering. In J. L. Roopnarine (Ed.), *Fathers across cultures: The importance, roles, and diverse practices of dads* (pp. 13–62). Praeger/ABC-Clio.

Bahadur, G. (2015). *Coolie woman: The odyssey of indenture*. University of Chicago Pres.

Barrow, C. (1998). *Family in the Caribbean: Themes and perspectives*. Ian Randle.

Beckles, H. (1989). *Natural rebels: A social history of enslaved Black women in Barbados*. Zed Books.

Belsky, J., Steinberg, L., & Draper, P. (1991). Childhood experience, interpersonal development, and reproductive strategy: An evolutionary theory of socialization. *Child Development, 62*(4), 647–670. https://doi.org/10.1111/j.1467-8624.1991.tb01558.x. PMID: 1935336.

Blum, R. W., et al. (2003). Adolescent health in the Caribbean: Risk and protective factors. *American Journal of Public Health, 93*(3), 456–460.

Brunod, R., & Cook-Darzens, S. (2002). Men's role and fatherhood in French Caribbean families: A multi-systemic resource approach. *Clinical Child Psychology & Psychiatry, 7*, 559–569.

Carlson, M. J., & McLanahan, S. S. (2010). Fathers in fragile families. In M. E. Lamb (Ed.), *The role of the father in child development* (5th ed., pp. 241–269). Wiley.

Chevannes, B. (2001). *Learning to be a man: Culture, socialisation and gender identity in five Caribbean communities*. The University of the West Indies Press.

Dabydeen, D., & Samroo, B. (Eds.). (1987). *India in the Caribbean*. Hansib.

DeBoard-Lucas, R. L., & Grych, J. H. (2011). Children's perceptions of interpartner violence: Causes, consequences, and coping. *Journal of Family Violence, 26*, 343–354. https://doi.org/10.1007/s10896-011-9368-2

Dede Yildirim, E., & Roopnarine, J. L. (2017). Nonviolent discipline, physical assault, and psychological aggression in five Caribbean countries: Associations with preschoolers' early literacy and social skills. *International Journal of Psychology*.

Dede Yildirm, E., Roopnarine, J. L., & Abolhassani, A. (2020). Violent and non-violent forms of discipline and social and literacy skills in preschoolers: An analysis of 25 African countries. *Child Abuse & Neglect, 106*. https://doi.org/10.1016/j.chiabu.2020.104513

Dudley-Grant, G. R. (2016). Innovations in clinical psychology with Caribbean peoples. In J. L. Roopnarine & D. Chadee (Eds.), *Caribbean psychology: Indigenous contributions to a global discipline* (pp. 357–386). American Psychological Association.

Dudley-Grant, G. R., Hamilton, D., & Parilla, S. J. (2018). Mental health issues and therapy with Caribbean peoples: Reflections of seasoned psychologists. *Caribbean Journal of Psychology, 10*(1), 223–259.

Escayg, K. A. (2014). *Parenting and pedagogical practices: The racial socialization and racial identity of preschool Trinidadian children*, Unpublished doctoral dissertation, University of Toronto.

Fanon, F. (1967). *Black skin, white masks*. Grove Press.

Franco, M. G. F., Castilow, G., Jones, N. P. E., & Neil, J. K. (2017). The Doogla identity in Trinidad. *Caribbean Journal of Psychology, 9*(1), 46–71.

Gable, S. L., & Haidt, J. (2005). What (and why) is positive psychology? *Review of General Psychology, 9*(2), 103–110. https://doi.org/10.1037/1089-2680.9.2.103

Garcia-Moreno, C., Jansen, H. A., Ellsberg, M., Heise, L., & Watts, C. H. (2006). Prevalence of intimate partner violence: Findings from the WHO multi-country study on women's health and domestic violence. *The Lancet, 368*, 1260–1269.

Hendriks, T., & Graafsma, T. (2019). Guidelines for the cultural adaptations of positive psychology interventions. *Caribbean Journal of Psychology, 11*(1), 7–32.

Hewlett, B. (Ed.). (1992). *Father-child relations: Cultural and biosocial contexts*. Aldine de Gruyter.

Houk, J. T. (1995). *Spirits, blood, and drums: The Orisha religion in Trinidad*. Temple University Press.

Lacey, K. K., Karen Powell Sears, K. P., Crawford, T. V., Matusko, N., & Jackson, J. L. (2016). Relationship of social and economic factors to mental disorders among population-based samples of Jamaicans and Guyanese. *BMJ Open, 6*(12), e012870.

Maharaj, R., Motilal, M., Babwah, T., et al. (2017). National Alcohol Survey of households in Trinidad and Tobago (NASHTT): Alcohol use in households. *BMC Public Health, 17*, 347. https://doi.org/10.1186/s12889-017-4266-z

Maharaj, R. G. (2007). Depression and the nature of Trinidadian family practice: A cross-sectional study. *BMC Family Practice, 8*, 25. https://doi.org/10.1186/1471-2296-8-25

Maharaj, R. G., Nunes, P., & Renwick, S. (2009). Health risk behaviours among adolescents in the English-speaking Caribbean: A review. *Child and Adolescent Psychiatry and Mental Health, 3*(1), 3–10.

Maharaj, R. G., et al. (2008). Depression among adolescents, aged 13–19 years, attending secondary schools in Trinidad prevalence and associated factors. *West Indian Medical Journal, 57*(4), 352–359.

Marlowe, F. (2005). Who tends Hadza children? In B. S. Hewlett & M. E. Lamb (Eds.), *Hunter-gatherer childhoods: Evolutionary, developmental, and cultural perspectives* (pp. 175–213). Aldine Transaction Publishers.

Masten, A. S. (2006). Developmental psychopathology: Pathways to the future. *International Journal of Behavioral Development, 30*(1), 47–54.

Mayascano, T., Tapia, T., Schilling, S., Alvarado, R., Tapia, E., Lips, W., & Yang, L. H. (2016). Stigma toward mental illness in Latin America and the Caribbean: A systematic review. *Brazilian Journal of Psychiatry, 38*(1), 78–85. https://doi.org/10.1590/1516-4446-2015-1652

Nobie, M. J., & Hutchinson, G. (2018). Demographic factors associated with suicide in Trinidad and Tobago: Analysis of completed suicides, 2000–2016. *Caribbean Journal of Psychology, 10*(1), 120–137.

Oser, F. K., Scarlett, G., & Bucher, A. (2006). Religious and spiritual development throughout the life span. In W. Damon & R. M. Lerner (Eds.), *Handbook of child psychology: Vol. 1. Theoretical models of human development* (6th ed., pp. 942–998). Wiley.

Oyserman, D., Coon, H. M., & Kemmelmeier, M. (2002). Rethinking individualism and collectivism: Evaluations of theoretical assumptions and meta-analysis. *Psychological Bulletin, 128*, 3–72.

Primus, M. A. (2018). *Parental warmth and physical punishment and their associations with children's social and academic skills in Trinidad and Tobago*. Unpublished doctoral dissertation, Syracuse University, Syracuse, New York, USA

Quinlan-Davidson, M., Sanhueza, A., Espinosa, I., Escamilla-Cejudo, J. A., & Maddaleno, M. (2014). Suicide among young people in the Americas. *Journal of Adolescent Health, 54*(3), 262–268. https://doi.org/10.1016/j.jadohealth.2013.07.012

Ramdhanie, I. K. (1999). *The Ansa McAl psychological research Centre: The miracle of St. Augustine 1989–1999*. Ansa McAl Psychological Research Centre, The University of the West Indies.

Roopnarine, J. J., & Jin, B. (2016). Family socialization practices and childhood development in Caribbean cultural communities. In J. L. Roopnarine & D. Chadee (Eds.), *Developmental, health, social, and clinical psychology: Contributions from Caribbean psychology* (pp. 71–96). American Psychological Association.

Roopnarine, J. L., & Chadee, D. (Eds.). (2016). *Caribbean psychology: Indigenous contributions to a global discipline*. American Psychological Association.

Roopnarine, J. L., & Dede Yildirim, E. (2019a). *Fathering across cultures: Developmental and clinical issues*. Routledge.

Roopnarine, J. L., & Dede Yildirim, E. (2019b). Fathers' cognitive engagement and preschoolers' literacy skills in three ethnic groups in Trinidad and Tobago. *Journal of Black Psychology, 45*, 494–517.

Roopnarine, J. L., Jin, B., & Krishnakumar, A. (2013b). Do Guyanese mothers' levels of warmth moderate the association between harshness and justness of physical punishment and preschoolers' prosocial behaviours and anger? *International Journal of Psychology, 49*(4), 271–279. https://doi.org/10.1002/ijop.12029

Roopnarine, J. L., Krishnakumar, A., Narine, L., Logie, C., & Lape, M. (2013a). Relationships between parenting practices and preschoolers' social skills in African, Indo, and mixed-ethnic families in Trinidad and Tobago: The mediating role of ethnic socialization. *Journal of Cross-Cultural Psychology, 45*(3), 362–380. https://doi.org/10.1177/0022022113509894

Roopnarine, J. L., Yang, Y., & Krishankumar, A. (2017). Moderating role of social support on the associations between individual level factors and depressive symptoms in young adults in Guyana and Trinidad and Tobago. *West Indian Medical Journal, 66*, 294–298.

Rutter, M., & Sroufe, L. A. (2000). Developmental psychopathology: Concepts and challenges. *Development and Psychopathology, 12*(3), 265–296.

Samms-Vaughn, M. (2005). *The Jamaican pre-school child: The status of early childhood development in Jamaica*. Planning Institute of Jamaica.

Toussaint, L., Wilson, C., Wilson, L., & Williams, D. R. (2015). Religiousness and suicide in a nationally representative sample of Trinidad and Tobago adolescents and young adults. *Social Psychiatry and Psychiatric Epidemiology, 50*(9), 1441–1450. https://doi.org/10.1007/s00127-015-1045-y

van Andel, T., Ruysscharet, S., Boven, K., & Daley, L. (2015). The use of Amerindian charm plants in the Guianas. *Journal of Ethnobiology and Ethnomedicine, 11*(66), 1–2. https://doi.org/10.1186/s13002-015-0048-9

Vertovec, S. (1991). East Indians and anthropologists: Acritical review. *Social and Economic Studies, 40*(1), 133–169.

WHO-AIMS. (2011). *Report on mental health systems in the Caribbean Region: A report of the assessment of the mental health system in the Caribbean Region*. World Health Organization.

Chapter 19
Psychology in Suriname

Manon Sanches, Tobi Graafsma, and Glenn Leckie

Background Information: History and Demographics

Suriname is a tropical country located on the northeast coast of South America, sandwiched between Guyana on the west and French Guyana on the east, and bordering Brazil in the south. It is a multi-ethnic society consisting of Afro-Surinamese (Creole 16% and Maroon 22%), Hindustani (27%), Javanese (14%), Amerindians (4%), Chinese (2%), and other ethnic groups (3%) (Menke, 2016; World Factbook, 2020). The Amerindians are the indigenous and oldest community in the country. It is estimated that around the time the Dutch took over the country (sometimes called "Dutch Guyana"), some 70,000 indigenous people lived in what we call now Suriname. In 2020, their number was reduced to approximately 20,000.

The multi-ethnic composition of Suriname and the decline in the number of indigenous people is a direct result of colonization that started in the seventeenth century. After the Anglo-Dutch Wars between 1665 and 1674, the sovereignty of Suriname was transferred to the Dutch, in exchange for New Amsterdam (New York) (Hendriks et al., 2019). Between 1665 and 1823, the slave trade brought more than 300,000 people from Africa to Suriname. Thousands of enslaved people fled to the interior of Suriname where they established independent communities that even today have a certain autonomy that is respected by the national authorities. The descendants of the escaped enslaved are known as Maroons, whereas the

M. Sanches · G. Leckie
Department of Psychology, Anton de Kom University of Suriname, Paramaribo, Suriname
e-mail: manon.sanches@uvs.edu

T. Graafsma (✉)
Institute for Graduate Studies and Research, Anton de Kom University of Suriname, Paramaribo, Suriname
e-mail: tobigraafsma@sr.net

G. J. Rich, N. A. Ramkumar (eds.), *Psychology in Oceania and the Caribbean*, International and Cultural Psychology,
https://doi.org/10.1007/978-3-030-87763-7_19

descendants of the enslaved are referred to as Creoles. After the abolishment of slavery in 1863, the Dutch imported contract laborers from India and Java, Indonesia. In 1975, the country gained its independence as the Republic of Suriname. In cultural and historical respects, Suriname has much in common with the other Caribbean countries.

Mainly resulting from the system of slavery and contract labor, Suriname grew and currently has a multicultural population of some 580,000 inhabitants (population density: 3,5/km^2). Most of the population live on the coastal area in the north of the country. The official language is Dutch. However, outside official and formal situations, most people speak the lingua franca Sranan Tongo. Reflecting descent, the major religions are Christianity, Hinduism, and Islam. One might add to that the existence of the Winti religion, which basically stemmed from West Africa and was brought to Suriname by captured and enslaved people, kept alive, and practiced. Nowadays, it is intertwined with contemporary Christian religions, in particular in the interior of the country.

As a nation, Suriname is young, democratic, and a republic. In the 1980s, the country was, after a coup, governed by the military (1980–1987). In 1995, Suriname became a member of the Caribbean Community and Common Market (CARICOM). Formerly the economy of Suriname was dominated by exports from hundreds of plantations. The export products were sugar, cotton, and coffee. Since the 1940s, Suriname has benefited from a large aluminum reserve. Currently, the main products are gold and lumber and, to a lesser degree, rice and fish. In 2020, oil reserves were discovered in the sea area north of Suriname. The nation ranks 97th on the Human Development Index (value 0.736; mean years of schooling 9.3) (middle range; HDI report 2020) and in general is considered to be a collectivistic society (Hofstede, 2001).

Unlike many other Caribbean countries (Abel et al., 2012), Suriname has no high incidence of natural disasters such as hurricanes or earthquakes. The main dangers seem to be a risk of flooding of large rivers and rising sea level, as well as contamination of the interior by the gold and wood mining industries. The life expectancy is 71.5 years (World Bank, 2018).

In terms of years of life lost (YLLs) due to premature deaths, the main risk factors are HIV/AIDS (14%), stroke (8%), preterm birth complications (remote areas of the interior are especially vulnerable) (7.3%), ischemic heart disease (6.8%), self-harm (5.5%), and road injury (4%) (GBD profile Suriname, 2010; also see Narine, 2016). In a study focusing on the prevalence of psychological distress across ethnicities and regions of Suriname, Gunther et al. (2017) reported that the prevalence of severe mental distress was 4%; the figure for moderate distress prevalence was 5%, and for mild mental distress it was 11%. Overall, 20% of respondents (between 15 and 65 years old) reported mental distress as measured by an adapted version of the Kessler Psychological Distress screening instrument. Far more research is needed on mental distress using adapted instruments (see also Hendriks & Graafsma, 2019).

History of Psychology in Suriname

Psychology: An Emerging Discipline

In the 1970s, there was no clear understanding in Suriname of what psychology entailed. A psychologist was associated with schools and often looked at as an assistant of a psychiatrist. A psychologist might be seen as someone who could be of help with the diagnosis of children with learning problems and also as a person who assisted in diagnosing patients with conduct disorders, more so in the role as social worker. A psychologist was definitely not thought of as somebody trained as a therapist, involved in treatment intended to relieve or cure a patient's mental and psychosocial problems. The approach to psychopathology was mainly medical, and as such issues of mental health were seen as strictly medical.

First Organization

It was in the 1970s that three clinical psychologists, educated and trained in the Netherlands and (later) also in Cuba, became informally associated with psychological issues in Suriname on a regular basis. They discussed treatment issues, professional and ethical issues, and possibilities to promote mental health literacy. They were credited with starting the first association for psychologists. After working on positioning psychology and its approaches, the association became dormant until some other and younger colleagues in 2004 restarted the association, resulting in the formal institution of the Surinamese Association of Psychologists and Orthopedagogists (SVPO) in 2008. Since 2012, SVPO has been a member of the Caribbean Alliance of National Psychology Associations (CANPA) and was the host of the CANPA regional conference in 2013.

Recent Developments

Psychologists working in the health sector need permission to work from the Ministry of Health. Access to psychological services is hampered by the stigma associated with experiencing psychological difficulties and the need for help. Mental health literacy is on the rise (Illes, 2020), and recent initiatives, such as the Mental Health Platform maintained by psychology students ("Tak nanga mi"—"Talk with me") using social media and webinars, do a lot of good for the cause of psychology. In this regard, the existence of psychology education at the Anton de Kom University of Suriname is a blessing for psychology as a profession.

Unfortunately, an ongoing dispute exists with the insurance companies responsible for reimbursing services offered by psychologists. It has been suggested that this is caused by the precarious economic situation in the country and a failure to recognize the importance of mental health and mental health services. This situation is a continuous source of tension and a threat to the possibility of establishing a psychotherapeutic practice. The tension is palpable and often dominates the discourse at meetings on the profession.

Psychology Education at the University

The University

Suriname has one university, the Anton de Kom University of Suriname, located in the national capital, Paramaribo. The university was founded as the University of Suriname on November 1, 1968 as a sequel to the Medical School and the Surinamese School of Law. Medical scientific education has been provided in Suriname since 1882. The then Medical School of Paramaribo was converted into the Medical Faculty on September 26, 1969. The Faculty of Legal Sciences (1968) and the Medical Faculty (1969) were the first faculties in the initial phase of the university. The proclamation of the Social and Economic Faculty took place in 1975. The Natural Technical Faculty (1976) and the Technological Faculty (1977) were subsequently established after thorough preparatory work within the Natural Technical Institute.

The university was reorganized between 1980 and 1987. It was renamed the Anton de Kom University of Suriname (1983),[1] and the six (6) faculties were reduced to three (3). The Natural Technical and Technological Faculty were merged into the Faculty of Technological Sciences. The Faculty of Legal Sciences and the Socio-Economic Faculty were brought together to form the Faculty of Social Sciences. The Medical Faculty became the Faculty of Medical Sciences. As of January 1, 2017, the Faculty of Legal Sciences has again become an independent Faculty and is no longer a part of the Faculty of Social Sciences. The organization of academic education takes place within the faculties. There are currently six (6) faculties, namely: Social Sciences (FMijW); Medical Sciences (FMeW); Technological Sciences (FTeW); Humanities (FHum); Mathematics and Natural

[1] Anton de Kom, born in Paramaribo (1898), was a Surinamese writer, poet, activist, and fighter of slavery and colonialism. He resisted colonial (Dutch) oppression and racism. In 1933, he was imprisoned and then banned by the colonial authorities to the Netherlands. In 1934, he published *Wij slaven van Suriname* (*We Slaves of Suriname*), the first book about the history of Suriname written by a Surinamese author. During World War II, then living in the Netherlands, he joined the underground resistance against the German occupation of the Netherlands. He kept writing for (then) illegal newspapers, was arrested (1944), and sent to a concentration camp. There he died in april 1945—with the end of the war in sight. In the 1960s, Surinamese students in the Netherlands rediscovered his writings and found inspiration in them. After Suriname became independent from the Netherlands, gradually his openmindedness and his writings received broad recognition (see also Marshall, 2003, pp. 18–23).

Sciences (FWNW); and Legal Sciences (FJW). In addition to the Faculties, the Institute for Graduate Studies and Research was founded (2006), where capita selecta, new, short, and interfaculty courses and research are initiated.

Psychology as an Academic Science: A Dual Unit

Psychology as an academic science was introduced within the Faculty of Social Sciences in 2010. Psychology education started as a collaboration project together with Erasmus University, Rotterdam, the Netherlands. After 2 years of intensely working together (1 year for developing and starting up and 1 year for running the very first year of the bachelor's program), the Psychology Department developed independently. The department uses a Numerus Fixus of 30 students. The reason for this is that the main didactic form (Problem Guided Education, PBL) utilizes small groups, and the required teaching capacity and expertise are scarce in Suriname. Biannually, a new cohort of master's degree students starts the program. Currently (in 2021), a small team of ten full-time instructors, a direction-coordinator, and four part-time instructors constitute the department. A total of 104 bachelor's and 33 master's students enrolled in the 2020–2021 academic year. Ninety-four bachelor's and seventeen master's level students have graduated so far (March 2021). The first master's program started in November 2017. Enrollment in the master's program is possible every 2 years. A first evaluation of the bachelor's program took place in 2013, which resulted in some minor adaptations. One is obligated to complete the bachelor-master program to be considered a qualified psychologist in Suriname. The bachelor-master structure is considered on the whole as a dual unit. In the final part of the bachelor's degree program, students start with the specialization process (clinical psychology, child and youth psychology, and work and organization psychology). The clinical psychology program focuses on diagnosis and treatment of mental health problems and disorders and on (in part preventive) approaches to mental health care. The child and youth program focuses on working with children and adolescents and their caretakers in clinical and school settings as well as in family settings. The work and organizational psychology program focuses on mental health in profit and non-profit workplaces, as well as on consultancy in the field of recruitment, selection, training, coaching, conflict management, and career advice.

The final attainment levels of the bachelor's program correspond with internationally accepted requirements. We agree with the formulation of the European Federation of Psychologists Association (EFPA) on the character of the bachelor phase:

> The first phase is typically devoted to the orientation of students in the different sub-specialties in psychology, but it can also be opened to related disciplines. It offers basic education in all psychology specialties, and in the major theories and techniques in psychology. It offers a basic education for psychology skills, and a grounding for research in psychology. It does not lead to any occupational qualification in psychology and does not provide the necessary competence for independent practice in psychology. (EFPA, 2011, p.28)

With the master's degree, and in line with the vision and mission of the Anton de Kom University of Suriname, the psychology program aims to provide high-quality academic education in the discipline. The aim of the course of study is to provide psychologists to the Surinamese society who are well versed in science and who can apply science to the issues they encounter as a psychologist in Surinamese practice. The program explicitly strives for respect for and understanding of Surinamese culture and its diverse population and communities. This applies also, for example, to age, disability, ethnicity, gender, language, origin, religion, sexual orientation, and socioeconomic status.

In contrast to the first bachelor's program, the first master's program was developed completely by the psychology department itself. However, in formulating objectives and attainment targets, international domain-specific requirements and comparisons with other master's programs have been taken into account. For example, the domain-specific requirements as described by the Chamber of Psychology of the Netherlands and final qualifications of psychology programs in the Netherlands were examined. A comparison with the psychology training of the University of the West Indies, Trinidad and Tobago, was conducted as well. Students are encouraged to pursue a scientific career with a PhD program.

Professional Standards

The master's program of study follows the professional ethical guidelines as generally used in the region by the Caribbean Alliance of National Psychology Associations (CANPA) and the guidelines used in the European Federation of Psychologists' Associations (EFPA). Due to different legal systems (Surinamese legislation is based on the Dutch juridical system), professional ethical guidelines differ slightly from those in other countries. The master's degree at the Anton de Kom University of Suriname is of course in line with Surinamese legislation. The professional ethical code of the Surinamese Association of Psychologists and Orthopedagogists (SVPO) is our dominant code. Thus, the targets have to be concordant with international standards, as well as with the needs and requirements of Surinamese professional practice and Surinamese law. To achieve this, there has been, and there still is, contact and coordination with various essential actors, such as the SVPO, the Ministry of Health, and the Ministry of Education and Culture.

It is of note that most of the current groups of psychologists working and teaching in Suriname have been educated in the Netherlands. Also, the literature used is mainly from European and American authors from so-called WEIRD, individualistic, analytic countries (Henrich et al., 2010).[2] The challenge is of course to adjust to the situations, cultures, values, and standards of Suriname (see also Dudley-Grant, 2016). Strengthened by purpose of underlining historical and cultural factors, the

[2] WEIRD: Western, Educated, Industrialized, Rich, and Democratic (Henrich et al., 2010)

master's program has a strong focus on the Caribbean context. For instance, the development of such modules as Caribbean Psychology, Family Structures in a Caribbean context, and Narrative Research Methods attests to this aim. The belief is that narrativity fits well with the Surinamese oral tradition. Qualitative and narrative research methods are part of the curriculum. A module on Suicide and Suicide Prevention is mandatory for the clinical psychology students because, unfortunately, Suriname ranks high on suicide: almost twice the world average (Graafsma et al., 2016).

The premise is that with more Surinamese research, using strict scientific methods, a robust scientific Surinamese indigenous psychology will be developed. Regional international collaboration is actively sought. This interaction is developing already in several areas, such as research into young adult health practices; research on fatherhood; research on intergenerational transmission of parenting; and research in the area of preventing violence against women and children and suicide prevention. Some regional colleagues teach in the master's course. The students and staff of the psychology department make use of two special chairs at IGSR, one founded in 2010 (clinical child and adolescent psychology) and one in 2018 (developmental psychology). In 2020, the University Board appointed two psychology staff members as lector clinical psychology and lector magnus child and youth psychology, respectively.

Post-Master's Professional Standards

Entry Level into the Profession

A professional psychologist in Suriname has at least a master's degree. This level of training is strongly recommended to attain membership in the Surinaamse Vereniging van Psychologen en Orthopedagogen (SVPO, Surinamese Association of Psychologists and Orthopedagogists). The SVPO is currently working on establishing a procedure for registration in it. The following provisions are included in the development of a registration process:

- Members must endorse professional ethics, as established by the SVPO or by another recognized professional association, and carefully observe these in their professional practice.
- Members have to accede to continuing education and further training, being aware that a master's certificate just is a valid starting point to become a good scientist/practitioner. Thus, they participate in continuing education in the field of the profession.
- Members of the SVPO meet all the aforementioned requirements. They are therefore committed to further training.

All these requirements are communicated and secured with the Ministry of Health.

Licensure

Suriname has no legislation regarding essential qualifications for being a psychologist. Awaiting further legislation within health care in general, a solid and fruitful collaboration exists between the SVPO and the Ministry of Health. When a psychologist turns to the Ministry of Health with a request to work in the health sector, the Ministry asks the SVPO for advice. The board of the Association then gives the Ministry written advice. The advice states why an applicant meets or does not meet the standards and qualification the SVPO holds for a clinical psychologist, child and youth psychologist, or orthopedagogist. The Ministry of Health makes the final decision on this matter. This procedure applies for psychologists working in the health sector.

Quality Assurance

There is no legislation on Higher Education in Suriname, but in general there is a strong understanding that all courses in tertiary education should be accredited. Therefore, the Ministry of Education and Culture installed an independent organization called NOVA (Nationaal Orgaan voor Accreditatie; National Organization for Accreditation) to oversee this process. In 2018, bachelor and master's programs in psychology gained accreditation from NOVA. In November 2017, NOVA hosted the Caribbean Area Network for Quality Assurance in Tertiary Education, CANQATE.

From the aforementioned, it can be seen that psychology in Suriname is a discipline under construction. Legislation is needed, as well as post-master's training that keep the professional psychologist in synchrony with academic developments and innovative scientific methodology. But the psychologist in Suriname also meets less "modern" (sometimes called "Western") approaches to psychological processes that have to be accommodated.

Remarks on Traditional Medicine (TM)

In an earlier section, we referred already to Winti religious practices. Winti refers to a specific nature religion and also to trance-like states that occur during traditional cultural Winti sessions. As in other religions, Winti is used as an explanatory model for causes of illnesses and many kinds of problems. Furthermore, Winti guides individuals in developing a personal and collective cosmology referring to the origin and purpose of life and death. Last but not least, as in some other religions, Winti espouses a moral and ethical code—prescribing how to behave so as to sail safely and happily through life, with a set of sanctions and cleansing rituals included. Until the 1970s (and before Suriname became independent), practicing Winti was prohibited by law. The ban has been lifted, and Winti is now an official religion, practiced next to Hinduism, Christianity, and Islam. To be fair, other religions brought their spiritual healing practices to Suriname as well. But for many Surinamese people, in particular of course persons from the Maroon and Creole community, Winti is embraced as part of the post-colonial national identity, representing collective pride.

This brings us to some general notes on traditional medicine (TM), part of the heritage of indigenous and other traditional communities in the country. TM in Suriname ranges from spiritual healing and spiritual rituals on the one and more symbolic end to plant-based treatments and cures on the other and more rational end. Most health-care workers respect traditional Winti healers as they bring a vision on health, disease, and illness[3] that for many people in mental distress is acceptable and helpful.

All ethnic groups in Suriname know and honor their traditional healers. They do the same, and they may be called in for spiritual and practical guidance as well. Generally, their approaches touch on spiritual, somatic, and psychosocial problems, eventually interpreted in terms of supernational powers that in the treatment are manipulated and hopefully brought to rest. Most psychologists respect such guidance, well aware that understanding the local "idiom of distress" is crucial in any healing process (see also De Jong & Reis, 2010).

This is concordant with the general respect for traditional medicine (TM) that exists in Suriname. That said, it is our impression, however, that psychologists do not seek active cooperation with traditional healers. In part that may be explained by the fact that Suriname knows no formal regulation of TM in terms of quality standards, control, and an ethical code. In order to protect their clients, psychologists refer reluctantly to TM, unless they sense that a client strongly tends to explain his or her complaints in traditional terms (for more on this, see Kleinman, 1988).

Turning to the traditional use of herbs and plants, Mans et al. (2020) state that in Suriname the use of plants and plant-based preparations is deeply rooted in society, despite the nationwide availability of affordable and accessible allopathic forms of medicine. Many traditional preparations are also used to promote general health, to fight stress, and to obtain health benefits (Mans et al., 2017). Worldwide, the extent of the use of TM to address psychological distress is not known. A WHO-SAGE study in five middle-income countries reported large differences in percentages in the use of TM, with the highest percentages found in India (Oyebode et al., 2016). It is our suspicion that TM use is probably less frequent than commonly reported. Of course the question remains as to what is considered as belonging to the field of traditional medicine. In the context of this discussion, should TM be discussed in an academic psychology curriculum? We believe that it should, if the subject is addressed in an academic and evidence-based manner. This applies also to "alternative practices." These practices have many followers in Suriname and are often misunderstood as derivatives of psychological science. They are not, but they deserve to be subjects of psychological research.

---

[3] In the sense as described and used by Kleinman (1988). Disease primarily refers to the perspective on the condition by the clinician; illness primarily refers to the client's perspective and explanation.

Closing Remarks

Psychology in Suriname is relatively young. With psychologists first educated abroad, mainly in the Netherlands and Cuba, since 2010 the Anton de Kom University of Suriname has taken the profession to different heights. As in the 1970s, values and norms are central components of psychology training still "under construction." We expect that the research conducted by Surinamese psychologists, concerning and directed at mental health issues in diverse situations and stages of life, will result in an indigenous, Surinamese psychology. Other than in the 1970s and using modern technology, scientific and professional standards profit from intense cooperation with regional and international relations and institutions.

References

Abel, W., Baboolal, E., & Gibson, R. (2012). The epidemiology of mental health issues in the Caribbean. In Pan American Health Organization (Ed.), *Mental health and psychosocial support in disaster situations in the Caribbean* (pp. 39–44). PAHO.

De Jong, J., & Reis, R. (2010). Kiyang-yang, a West African post war idiom of distress. *Culture, Medicine and Psychiatry, 34*, 301–324.

Dudley-Grant, R. (2016). Innovations in clinical psychology with Caribbean peoples. In J. Roopnarine & D. Chadee (Eds.), *Caribbean psychology: Indigenous contributions to a global discipline* (pp. 357–386). American Psychological Association.

European Federation of Psychologists Associations. (2011). Europsy Regulations. Brussels: EFPA.

Graafsma, T., Westra, K., & Kerkhof, A. (2016). Suicide and attempted suicide in Suriname: The case of Nickerie. Epidemiology and intent. *Academic Journal of Suriname, 7*, 628–642.

Gunther, P., Sanches, M., Smits, S., & Krishnadath, I. (2017, August). Prevalence of psychological distress in Suriname in urban and rural areas: The Suriname health study. *Journal of Human Psychology, 1*(1), 8–17.

Hendriks, T., & Graafsma, T. (2019). Guidelines for the cultural adaptation of positive psychology interventions. *Caribbean Journal of Psychology, 11*(1), 7–32.

Hendriks, T., Schotanus-Dijkstra, M., Hassankhan, A., Sardjo, W., Graafsma, T., Bohlmeijer, E., & Jong, D. (2019). Resilience and well-being in the Caribbean: Findings from a randomized controlled trial of a culturally adapted multi-component positive psychology intervention. *Journal of Positive Psychology, 15*(2), 238–253. https://doi.org/10.1080/17439760.2019.1590624

Henrich, J., Heine, S., & Norenzayan, A. (2010). The weirdest people in the world? *Behavioral and Brain Sciences, 33*(2–3), 61–83. https://doi.org/10.1017/S0140525X0999152X

Hofstede, G. (2001). *Culture's consequences: Values, behaviors, institutions, and organizations across nations*. Sage.

Illes, K. (2020). *Mental health literacy and mental well-being* [Bachelor's thesis]. Paramaribo: Anton de Kom University of Suriname.

Kleinman, A. (1988). *The illness narratives: Suffering, healing and the human condition*. Basic Books.

Mans, D., Friperson, P., Pawirodihardjo, J., & Djotaroeno, M. (2020). Antioxidant activity and totala phenolic contents of adaptogenic plants. *Journal of Antioxidant Activity, 2*(1), 1–11.

Mans, D., Ganga, D., & Kartopawiro, J. (2017). Meeting of the minds: Traditional herbal medicine in multi-ethnic Suriname (Chapter 6). In H. El-Shemy (Ed.), *Aromatic and medicinal plants – Back to nature* (pp. 111–132). InTech. https://doi.org/10.5772/66509

Marshall, E. K. (2003). *Ontstaan en ontwikkeling van het Surinaams nationalism. Natievorming als opgave. (Origin and development of nationalism in Suriname)*. Eburon.
Menke, J.. (Red.) (2016). *Mozaiek van het Surinaamse volk (Mosaic of the Surinamese people)*. ABS en IGSR.
Narine, L. (2016). Current state of health and health outcomes. In J. Roopnarine & D. Chadee (Eds.), *Caribbean psychology: Indigenous contributions to a global discipline* (pp. 149–169). American Psychological Association.
Oyebode, O., Kandala, N., Chilton, P., & Lilford, R. (2016). Use of traditional medicine in middle-income countries: A WHO-SAGE study. *Health Policy and Planning, 311*, 984–991.
World Bank. (2018). *World development indicators: Suriname*. Retrieved from databank.worldbank.org on March 24, 2021.
World Factbook. (2020). *Suriname*.

Chapter 20
Psychology in Belize

Grant J. Rich, Carolyn Gentle-Genitty, and Collin Estrada

Belize has a rich history. Thousands of years ago, its first inhabitants were the ancient Maya (Coe & Houston, 2015). Multiple attempts at colonization by the Spanish followed in the mid-sixteenth century (Campbell, 2011). Ultimately, after several centuries of settlement by British loggers (Bulmer-Thomas & Bulmer-Thomas, 2012), Belize became an official British colony in the nineteenth century, changed its name from British Honduras, and became independent in 1981 (Shoman, 2011). Belize is in Central America's east coast with the Caribbean Sea to the east, Mexico to the north, and Guatemala to the west and south. Despite unusual fluctuation, under the 2020–2021 COVID-19 pandemic, tourism is typically Belize's major foreign exchange earner. Belize is special and indeed unique in several ways; it remains the least densely populated Central American nation, the only one with English as the official language, and a relative pillar of political stability over the last 40 years, in a region filled with much violence, civil war, and turbulence in governance and economics. Its history and location, and its diverse people and environments, have led scholars frequently to refer to Belize as a "Caribbean nation in Central America."

G. J. Rich (✉)
Walden University, Juneau, AK, USA

C. Gentle-Genitty
Indiana University, Indianapolis, IN, USA
e-mail: cgentleg@iu.edu

C. Estrada
Principal All Saints Primary School, Member Belize Counseling Association, Belize, Belize

G. J. Rich, N. A. Ramkumar (eds.), *Psychology in Oceania and the Caribbean*, International and Cultural Psychology,
https://doi.org/10.1007/978-3-030-87763-7_20

Belize has an estimated population in 2021 of approximately 405,633 (Belize World Factbook, 2021), with great diversity represented in its ethnic and racial groups: Mestizo (52.9%), Creole (25.9%), three groups of indigenous Maya (Yucatec, Mopan, and Q'eqchi') (11/3%), an Afro-Indigenous Garifuna population (6.1%), East Indian (3.9%), Mennonite (3.6%), Caucasian (1.2%), Asian (1%), and other/unknown (1.5%). Likewise there is great religious diversity as well, in the following proportions: Roman Catholic (40.1%), Protestant (31.5%, which includes Pentecostal, Seventh-Day Adventists, Anglican, Mennonite, Baptist, Methodist, Nazarene), Jehovah's Witness (1.7%), others (10.5%, including Buddhist, Hindu, Mormon, Muslim, and Rastafarian), and none (15.5%) (Belize World Factbook, 2021). The racial, ethnic, and religious diversity also is reflected in Belize's languages. English is the official language and is spoken by 62.9% of the population, while Spanish is the primary language of 56.6% of the population, Kriol 44.6%, a Maya language 10.5%, Mennonite German 3.2%, Garifuna 2.9%, and others 2.1% (Belize World Factbook, 2021). Despite English as the official language, Kriol may be considered the lingua franca, and we may consider some Belizeans Kriol monolinguals (Udz, 2014). Some of the spoken Spanish, such as is utilized in northern communities, sometimes referred to as "kitchen Spanish," may utilize Kriol and English words and grammar in a unique blend (Gómez Menjívar & Salmon, 2018; Udz, 2014). Although English and Spanish may be afforded a certain prestige in some circles and settings, the use of Kriol has increased, even though stigmatized among some, while attenuation of Mopan Mayan and Garifuna have been documented by scholars (Gómez Menjívar & Salmon, 2018).

The racial, ethnic, and religious diversity of Belize reflects its history.

The Maya have been a consistent presence, though there has been variation in numbers and in specific Maya groups; for instance, the Caste Wars of the Yucatán, from 1847 to 1901, involved migrations and intermingling of nuanced complexity, as various Maya groups fell into and out of favor with the Mexican government, the British government, the settlers, and each other, blurring many racial and ethnic lines, with alliances frequently changing and moving across racial and ethnic lines of division, including intermarriage over many years with Hispanic groups (Dutt, 2020). Indeed, in the nineteenth century, one result of the decades-long Caste War of the Yucatán was the return of the Roman Catholic Church by refugees from the north of Belize. Many Mestizos and Garifuna, as well as Maya, are today members of this faith. The Garifuna, an Afro-Indigenous people created from the mixture of Africans and Caribs on St. Vincent, appeared in coastal Belize in the early nineteenth century, likely first arriving in 1802, and others several decades later, after exile to Central America (Gonzalez, 1969; Palacio, 2005). English colonialism resulted in its Protestant legacy, with many modern Belizeans identifying as Anglican or Methodist. Yet, as slavery neared its end, an 1835 census of Belize (then known as the Bay Settlement) reported 1184 enslaved persons, almost half (47%) of the entire population; the ethnogenesis of the Belizean Creole and its modern incarnations and variations are detailed by several scholars (Bolland, 1988; Johnson, 2019). Recent years have brought missionary work leading to increasing numbers of Pentecostal and Adventist converts. Traditional spiritual beliefs are also practiced today, often in a syncretic fashion, with more organized faith traditions (Rich, 2010; Waldram, 2020). Some Creoles (and others) maintain beliefs in obeah, and some Maya maintain traditional ways (e.g., Arvigo, 1994; Arvigo & Balick, 1998; Waldram, 2020; Waight, 2020). Traditional Garifuna spiritual practice, with its focus on honoring the ancestors, is well represented, typically in syncretic fashion with Catholicism (Palacio, 2005). Perhaps most recently of major groups, in 1958, at Belize's invitation, Mennonites arrived via Mexico and Canada (Sawatzky, 1971).

Belize's population is young, with 33% aged 0–4 and another 19% aged 15–24 (Belize World Factbook, 2021). Much of the population—25%–33%—is centered in Belize's largest city, Belize City, though about half of Belize's population may be considered rural. Politically Belize's government is a parliamentary democracy under a constitutional monarchy with universal suffrage for those 18 years of age or older. Economically, Belize's real GDP (purchasing power parity) is ranked 193 of the world's approximately 200 nations, and its real GDP per capita is estimated at $7005 (2019), making it ranked 158 of the world's approximately 200 nations. We estimated the unemployment rate in Belize at 9% (2017), with 41% of the population living below the poverty line (2013 estimate) (Belize World Factbook, 2021).

According to the 2020 Human Development Index (HDI) of the United Nations, which measures life expectancy, education, and income, Belize ranked 110th out of 189 ranked nations in the world, placing it the HDI category of high, though not very high development. This ranking places Belize behind such nations as Barbados (58), Trinidad and Tobago (67), Grenada (74), St. Kitts and Nevis (74), Cuba (70), Mexico (74), and Jamaica (101), but ahead of other Central American nations such as Guatemala (127) and Honduras (132). The HDI position for Belize reflects a decrease from the 2006 HDI, when Belize was ranked 88th of 179 ranked nations. Per the 2020 HDI, the life expectancy at birth in Belize is 74.6 years (an increase from the 2006 HDI figures), with 13.1 expected years of schooling and 9.9 mean years of schooling. (HDI, 2021).

Post-colonial Belize remains a nation in transition, as both tradition and modernity continue to coexist in Belize, as the nation's identity matures. Twenty-five years ago, introducing television to Belize, Wilk (1994) highlighted differences between "colonial time" and "TV time." Even then, as Wilk (1994) commented, in the 1950s, Belize City fashions lagged four or five years behind New York, whereas with television, perceived needs and fashions changed, as viewers instantly saw what was advertised to wealthy Americans. The extent to which Belizeans will embrace traditional values, and to what extent "TV time" will dominate, remains an ongoing debate. More recently, anthropologist Andrew Gordon (2017), in his examination of Bullet Tree Falls, explored how a Belizean village responded to influences of globalization, unpacking the impact, both pro and con, of changes such as tourism, including the "romance tourism" of young foreign backpackers, as well as a changing religious landscape, which made room for Pentecostals and Adventists, as well as a version of Rastafarianism, all of which combined in complex ways to reflect both change and stasis. How globalization, migration, and technological advances, such as social media and smartphones, on the one hand, as well as revitalization of old ways as evidenced by organizations such as the Maya Healers' Association or the Belize National Institute for Culture and History (NICH), will affect Belize, and Belizeans, remains an open question.

Social Issues in Belize

Several significant social and economic issues impact Belize. Among the challenges we can include a high crime rate, unemployment, a heavy foreign debt burden, a majority youth population, low-tax country, drug trading on the black market (especially cocaine and money laundering) with Mexico and Central and South American nations, a high HIV rate, gender discrimination and gender inequity, and frequent natural disasters, especially hurricane season every June through September and flooding (Belize World Fact Book, 2021).

In terms of crime, Belize has been described as the world's murder capital by the *Economist Magazine's* 2009 *Pocket World in Figures*, with a murder rate of 32.7 per 100,000 persons (Economist's pocket book says Belize is world murder capital, 2009). An article in 2014, from the *Guardian*, confirmed the assessment, listing Belize City as the city with the fourth highest murder rate in the world, and that the nation of Belize had the third highest murder rate in the world (Van Mead & Blason, 2014). Many of the homicides occur on the south side of Belize City, and many of the murders are gang- and drug-related. In 2018, they documented 143 murders in Belize, which calculates to a national homicide rate of 36 murders per 100,000 inhabitants, one of the highest in the world, though somewhat lower than the neighboring countries of Honduras and El Salvador. Again, data show that in 2018, Belize District (which includes Belize City, the nation's largest city) had the most homicides nationally. Indeed 66% of all the homicides occurred in Belize District (Belize Crime and Safety Report, 2018). Recent research by Gayle et al. (2016) was started after the infamous Mayflower Street grenade attack on May 21, 2008, and involved interviews with 2210 persons, including school children, community members, police officers, and government officials, as well as members of gangs including the Crips, the Bloods, and MS13 to best assess the nature of the social violence and potential paths towards peace. The authors note a range of factors and social and cultural variables that impact the violence, including the reality that 50% of children and 43% of youth live below the poverty line, resulting in violent competition for scarce resources. Other authors have also noted the impact of drugs and poverty on the violence, and Muhammad (2015) argues that competition for scarce resources and a decline and decay of moral values and of family structure also add to the increased violence.

Corporal punishment of children remains controversial in Belize. A recent study of positive discipline, physical discipline, and psychological aggression in five Caribbean countries and associations with preschoolers' early literacy found that Belizean parents/caregivers were more likely to use positive discipline than parents/caregivers in the Dominican Republic. There was a tendency for harsh physical punishment to be negatively associated with children's literacy skills in Belize. The child's age, household wealth, and preschool enrollment were positively associated with the child's literacy skills (Yildirim & Roopnarine, 2019). Education and social discipline in school and out of school is a continuing topic for dialogue to ascertain severity of youth violence.

Belize remains a source, destination, and transit nation for men, women, and children in forced labor (such as in restaurants, agriculture, and fishing) and in sex trafficking, with Belize listed as a Tier Three nation that is not fully complying with international standards to eliminate human trafficking (Belize World Fact Book, 2021). Scholars have noted that the prostitution not only involves internationally trafficked individuals and tourists paying for sexual activity but also includes some Belizean prostitutes and Belizean males paying for sex, which is an issue that naturally causes some discomfort for Belize and makes it more challenging to discuss openly (Ragsdale & Anders, 1999; Ragsdale et al., 2007; Rich, 2017). One result of the prostitution is an elevated HIV/AIDS in Belize, which has one of the highest rates in the region with approximately 2% HIV-positive infection rate (estimated 2018 figure; Belize World Fact Book, 2021).

Social issues regarding women remain significant in Belize (Rich, 2017). It's worth noting the World Economic Forum placed Belize at 101st of 135 ranked nations in its Global Gender Gap Report and noted that of all nations in Latin America and the Caribbean, Belize ranked 3rd from the bottom and had the lowest female-to-male ratio for primary school enrollment (Hausmann et al., 2012). Though women in Belize have made critical gains over the past century, from universal suffrage in 1954 to broader representation in political office, to increased participation in the paid workforce in a greater range of occupations (e.g., by law it is a criminal offense to not offer women equal pay for equal work [Rich, 2017]), to introducing legislation protecting against domestic abuse and trafficking, many challenges remain. While legislation aims to curb domestic violence, sexual harassment, and trafficking, such laws are not always successfully and fully implemented. In particular, domestic violence continues to be ubiquitous (Beske, 2016; McClusky, 2001). Additional challenges revolve around preventing school attrition, especially among rural and poor girls. There are very few women in the highest positions in politics (MacPherson, 2007). Nevertheless, there are many historical examples of women's activism and participation, from Vivian Seay and the Garveyite Black Cross nurses of the early twentieth century to leaders such as Elfreda Reyes, to other more recent icons including Dorothy Menzies, known for her social work, and Leela Vernon, the Queen of Brukdong music and Kriol culture, as well as the late Carrie Fairweather-Belgrave, an entrepreneur, writer, actress, and poet. Finally, one must mention the many modern Creole *bembe* and Garifuna *suber* women, exemplars of strength, resilience, and persistence (Rich, 2017).

Psychology in Belize

The history of modern, formal psychology and psychiatry in Belize may be said to begin with the arrival in 1964 of a chief medical officer who was also a psychiatrist to then British Honduras (Bullard, 1973). Within 30 years, the 70-bed Rockview Psychiatric Hospital had a medical staff of 28, with 2 psychiatrists, 6 psychiatric nurses, and 20 trained medical attendants (NCFC, 1995). In Belize, psychiatric disorders are especially unlikely to be treated by allopathic ("Western") practitioners, both because of stigma surrounding mental health and because of a lack of credentialed behavioral health professionals, as well as lack of access for persons who are not in Belize City or other larger communities. Classic research (on allopathic approaches) based on prevalence rates of psychological disorders (including anxiety, mood and thought disorders) in Puerto Rico, judged to be a more apt comparison than to the mainland USA, estimated 97% of all such disorders were untreated in Belize, including 63% of schizophrenia cases, 89% of affective disorders (such as depression), and 99% of anxiety disorders (including post-traumatic stress disorder) (Bonander et al., 2000). In 2005, 12,318 patients were reported to have been evaluated and/or treated for psychological disorders in Belize (Killion & Cayetano, 2009). Approximately one fourth of the patients were seen for schizophrenia/psychosis, 19.5% for mood disorders such as depression, 6.7% for anxiety disorders, 6.8% for relational issues, and 3.5% for substance misuse.

Belize today remains alarmingly underserved by behavioral health professionals (Rich et al., 2014; Rich et al., 2016). The Belizean government spends less than 3% of its health budget on mental health/illness (Killion & Cayetano, 2009). As Rich (2010) noted, "The 1995 telephone directory yellow pages listed no psychologists, no social workers, no therapists, ten social service agencies, and two pages of physicians (but no psychiatrists)." Thirteen years later, the 2008 telephone directory yellow pages show little change in terms of advertised services. That directory lists no psychologists, therapists, or social workers and several pages of physicians (but no psychiatrists); however, 12 social service agencies are listed, and some of these agencies, such as the Salvation Army and Dorothy Menzies Home, offer some relevant services. The physician density is just 1.12 physicians per 1000 population in Belize (Belize World Fact Book, 2021).

The WHO (2009) reported that only two psychiatrists served the entire nation of Belize and that the total number of persons "working in mental health facilities or private practice per 100,000 is 18," with a breakdown of 0.6 psychiatrists, 7.9 nurses, 0.3 psychologists, 0.3 social workers, 0.6 occupational therapists, and 7.9 other health/mental health workers (p. 18). Furthermore, the WHO (2009) found that except for "one psychologist who has a private practice, all social workers, nurses, and occupational therapists work only for the government administered mental health facilities. None of these professionals work with NGPs, for profit mental health facilities or private practice" (p. 18). Notably, the WHO (2009) report emphasizes that the distribution of the mental health workforce is highly unequal between urban and rural areas, with mental health services very centralized in the largest city, Belize City, and the national capitol, Belmopan, with 12 of 24 nurses working in or near Belize City.

The most notable service provision in behavioral health has been the Ministry of Health's initiative starting in 1991, to train 18 psychiatric nurses in a 3-year program with the help of Memorial University in Canada, the Bliss School of Nursing in Belize, and PAHO/WHO (Killion & Cayetano, 2009; Rich, 2010). A second cohort of PNPs was trained in 2004, and requirements included graduation from an accredited nursing program, at least 3 years or experience in nursing, and a six-month community psychiatric nursing course. Notably, Belize is one of just a handful of nations to permit PNPs to have extended mental health responsibilities, including an independent assessment of patients, prescription of psychotropic medications, and psychotherapy (Killion & Cayetano, 2009). Belizean PNPs also work in clinics, travel to rural regions, consult law enforcement on incarcerated individuals' psychiatric condition, and routinely make home visits. Belize's nursing and medical workforce is supplemented with ample support from staff from abroad, notably from Cuba and Nigeria. To increase efficiency and effectiveness of this workforce, steps towards increased quality assurance were taken recently, including development, and analysis, of a chart audit tool to monitor mental healthcare delivery non-compliance for initial psychiatric assessment notes (in BHIS [Belize Health Information System], an electronic health record system). Rather than use the tool punitively, presently it is used to educate staff as to best practices and areas for improved compliance from collecting data on chief complaint to medication lists, diagnosis, and family history as well as plan of care (Winer et al., 2014). Belize's PNP program has received attention from the WHO as a "best practices model for integrating mental health into a decentralized, primary care setting" (WHO, 2005; Winer et al., 2014, p. 377).

Formal advanced education for many behavioral health professions is lacking in Belize; historically, some Belizeans interested in pursuing careers in health and in behavioral health would seek education abroad, such as in the USA, in Canada, in Mexico, or at the University of the West Indies in Jamaica. Some of these persons would not return to Belize, and so there is a desire to create educational opportunities in Belize for Belizeans. Presently, the University of Belize offers associate and bachelor's degrees in social work, as well as a bachelor's degree in nNursing, including a certificate for psychiatric nurse practitioners (CPNP). Typically, the offerings in psychology are limited to an introductory course in psychology, as well as some courses in education and child development (University of Belize, 2021), but more is needed.

More broadly viewing the mental healthcare systems, Belize offers mental health services in district hospitals in all six regions of Belize, including Belize City's polyclinics and Karl Heusner Memorial Hospital (Killion & Cayetano, 2009). Rockview remains the nation's one inpatient facility. The WHO (2009) reports eight outpatient mental health facilities nationwide, no day-treatment facilities, one community-based psychiatric inpatient unit (with four beds), no community residential facilities, no specialty forensic beds in the mental hospital, and no inpatient unit or other residential facilities; patients who are incarcerated criminals are housed in the general prison where a psychiatric team visits monthly. The inclusion of the Community Rehabilitation Department in the Ministry of Human Development now offers therapy sessions for those mandated by the courts. Secondary schools now have at least one counselor at the secondary level—though they must carry out other duties. Lower school levels have a shared staff, but still there is no national response system.

For patient advocacy, the community activist group Belize Mental Health Association plays a prominent role (Killion & Cayetano, 2009). One example of the MHA's activism was successful efforts to decriminalize suicide and to work to see that survivors received psychological help instead of facing criminal prosecution (Killion & Cayetano, 2009). MHA and its members also provide commentary and public service announcements on Belizean media, including television, offering information about signs, symptoms, and treatment of psychological disorders and also working to reduce stigma concerning mental illness. The Mental Health Association and the Welcome Resource Center also offer informative websites, with information and referral resources on mental illness, homelessness, and related topics (Mental Health Association (MHA), 2021; Welcome Resource Center, 2021). Advocacy by the MHA is likely linked to some positive gains, such as a reduction in suicide attempts; for instance, in 2016 Belize reported 150 suicide attempts going to public health clinics, but in 2019, only 100 (BBN, 2020). Besides work by the MHA, Belize's PNPs also take part in some outreach and advocacy, such as teaching students and teachers in schools about signs, symptoms, and treatments for mental disorders and also serving as "liaisons between indigenous healers, patients, and the formal health care system" (Killion & Cayetano, 2009).

Traditional Healing

Given the paucity of allopathic behavioral health professionals, such as psychiatrists and psychologists, as well as their comparatively high cost, and the reality that they are often difficult for rural communities to access (Rich, 2010; Killion & Cayetano, 2009), many Belizeans rely fully or in part on traditional healers for their behavioral healthcare. There are points of contact between traditional healers and Western allopathic professionals; for instance, some Maya healers will refer out to a physician if their assessment shows it is warranted (Waldram, 2020), and some PNPs will serve as liaisons between native healers and the Westernized formal medical system (Killion & Cayetano, 2009). Likewise, some Belizeans will seek traditional healing for some types of ailments but may seek an allopathic "Western" professional for others (Rich, 2010; Waldram, 2020). In southern Belize, Hatala et al. (2015) find that, "most rural Belizeans first seek medical help from one of several types of local herbalists or traditional healers before going to a government sponsored biomedical practitioner" (pp. 454–455).

While space prevents a detailed description of indigenous and traditional healing systems, in Belize, and in all of its ethnic groups (such as Creole and Garifuna), an overview of some salient features of Maya healing can illustrate the importance of understanding Belizeans' worldviews both to provide the best care possible and to know when a particular practice or belief may be harmful. Several scholars have investigated Maya healing practices and note a range of types of healers. For instance, Arvigo and Balick (1998) have developed a classification system. They note some overlap between their categories, but they argue that at the top of the hierarchy is the shaman/h'men category, which is viewed as the most powerful and most connected to the divine. In contrast, a "village healer" is a person (man or woman) who has experience in caring for many family members and may be the primary healthcare provider in a village. Arvigo and Balick also describe a "grannie healer" category as a healer who not only cares for family members, but who may also offer home remedies for less serious, common ailments such as diarrhea. Another healer is the midwife, a traditional birth attendant, who also may provide herbal remedies and perhaps baths and teas. The "massage therapist/*sobadera*" may be a man or woman; we often consider their healing abilities divinely gifted and may be passed on to future generations. The "bonesetter/folk chiropractor" focuses on sprains and broken bones and may use a form of traditional Mayan acupuncture. Finally, the "snake doctor" healer category focuses on bites from snakes, scorpions, bats, rats, dogs, etc. In an intriguing development, the Maya Healers' Association has taken to issuing certificates of competency for each healer (*aj ilonel*), a fascinating compromise between traditional and modern expectations (Hatala et al., 2015).

Beyond the categories of healing are categories of mental illness described and understood by Maya healers and their clients (Hatala et al., 2015; Waldram, 2020). Though there are three Maya groups presently in Belize, Hatala et al. (2015) focus on the Q'eqchi' of Southern Belize. Their research over 9 months, including 94 interviews with 5 different Q'eqchi' healers, found a consistent pattern of agreement and diagnostic categories, including distinct conceptions of mental disorders that partially align and sometimes differ from psychological disorders as described in the APA's DSM-5. Taking a narrative approach to analysis, and using the healers' nosological system of mental disorders (including spiritual, cultural, social, historical, cosmological, and other factors), the authors found that the healers identified 17 recognizable illnesses of the mind grouped in four broad narrative genres. The four broad Q'eqchi' narrative genres were (1) thinking too much, (2) fright, (3) *Maatan* (days of birth), and (4) spirit attacks. Notably some of these themes relate in part to Western disorders as in the DSM-5, such as fright relating to DSM-5 anxiety disorders (or to *susto*), or *xiw* relating to GAD (DSM-5 generalized anxiety disorder), or *rahil ch'ool* and *po'ol k'a'uxl* to major depressive disorder, and *wax ru* and *waxk'ay* to schizophrenia, but others relate less well or not at all to the DSM-5, such as fated days of birth or spirit attacks.

Treatment for the ailments may align in some ways with the treatment from psychiatrists and psychologists, but often not at all; for instance, among the common treatments noted by Waldram (2020) and Hatala et al. (2015) were prayer, medicinal plants, ceremonies, smoking, blood-letting, flower remedies, and *awas* (sacrifices, including animal sacrifice). Notably, among the Q'eqchi' healers, the talk therapy favored by most modern Western psychotherapists is used rarely (Waldram, 2020);

instead psychosocial ailments are most often medicalized by Q'eqchi' healers and typically treated with prayers and herbal remedies. Hatala et al. (2015) conclude their research by noting the symptoms and prognoses of some of the Maya healers' categorization and comparing them with those of the DSM-5 (such as for depression and anxiety), arguing that, "some mental illness conditions may occur in cross-cultural contexts, with local variations and idioms, and that therefore some traditional, empirically based, localized, and culturally grounded approaches to treating them may remain salient and effective" (p. 482). Notably, the authors suggest that accepting such observations would lend itself to productive exchanges between the MHA and Belize's Ministry of Health towards a more collaborative approach for mental health services.

In sum, a message from this brief illustration of cross-cultural conceptions of mental illness is that a challenge for effective behavioral health service provision in Belize is the diversity of its many cultures. Understanding the worldview of one's clients, and potential clients, can be an essential starting point for effective treatment, and thus Belizean mental health professionals would be advised to immerse themselves in settings and situations leading to increased cultural competence.

Conclusion

Though it is a young nation, Belize has mushroomed its capacity for behavioral health service delivery, most notably through leveraging an enhanced psychiatric nurse practitioner workforce, which functions with an extended scope of practice to best serve Belize. That said, many challenges remain; there are few opportunities in Belize to pursue advanced graduate education in many behavioral health professions or in psychiatry. Rural populations continue to be underserved. While there have been impressive efforts to reduce stigma regarding mental illness, discrimination and misunderstanding continue to challenge those suffering psychological disorders. In addition, the sociocultural milieu of present-day Belize features high levels of poverty, violence, drug addiction, gangs, and crime. Still, there is reason for cautious optimism regarding mental health in Belize; effective practices and services that are appropriate for Belize are being identified and implemented, intercultural understanding is on the rise, and a healthy and respectful balance of tradition and modernity is in sight.

References

Arvigo, R. (1994). *Sastun: My apprenticeship with a Maya healer*. Harper.
Arvigo, R., & Balick, M. (1998). *Rainforest remedies*. Lotus Press.

BBN. (2020, September 8). *Mental health association: Suicides and attempted suicides are decreasing in Belize*. Retrieved from https://www.breakingbelizenews.com/2020/09/08/mental-health-association-suicides-and-attempted-suicides-are-decreasing-in-belize/

Belize. (2021). *World Factbook*. Retrieved from https://www.cia.gov/the-world-factbook/countries/belize/

Belize Crime and Safety Report. (2018). Retrieved from https://www.osac.gov/Content/Report/953a51e9-6582-49d7-88ca-15f4ae4a6921

Beske, M. A. (2016). *Intimate partner violence and advocate response: Redefining love in western Belize*. Lexington Books.

Bolland, O. N. (1988). *Colonialism and resistance in Belize: Essays in historical sociology*. Cubola Productions.

Bonander, J., Kohn, R., Arana, B., & Levav, I. (2000). An anthropological and epidemiological overview of mental health in Belize. *Transcultural Psychiatry, 37*(1), 57–72.

Bullard, M. (1973). *The recognition of psychiatric disorders in British Hondu ras*. Unpublished dissertation. Eugene: University of Oregon.

Bulmer-Thomas, B., & Bulmer-Thomas, V. (2012). *The economic history of Belize: From the 17t century to post-Independence*. Cubola Productions.

Campbell, M. C. (2011). *Becoming Belize: A history of an outpost of empire searching for identity, 1528–1823*. University of the West Indies Press.

Coe, M., & Houston, S. D. (2015). *The Maya* (9th ed.). Thames & Hudson.

Dutt, R. (2020). *Empire on edge: The British struggle for order in Belize during Yucatán's Caste War, 1847–1901*. Cambridge University Press.

Economist's pocket book says Belize is world murder capital. (2009, September 7). Retrieved from https://edition.channel5belize.com/archives/607

Gayle, H., Hampton, V., & Mortis, N. (2016). *Like bush fire: Male social participation and violence in urban Belize*. Cubola Productions.

Gómez Menjívar, J. C., & Salmon, W. N. (2018). *Tropical tongues: Language ideologies, endangerment, and minority languages in Belize*. Institute for the Study of the Americas.

Gonzalez, N. (1969). *Black Carib household structure*. University of Washington Press.

Gordon, A. J. (2017). *Agents of change in bullet tree falls: How a village in Belize responded to influences of globalization*. Cengage.

Hatala, A. R., Waldram, J. B., & Caal, T. (2015). Narrative structures of Maya mental disorders. *Culture Medicine and Psychiatry, 39*, 449–486.

Hausmann, R., Tyson, L. D., & Zahidi, S. (2012). *The global gender gap report*. World Economic Forum.

Human Development Index (HDI). (2021). Retrieved from http://hdr.undp.org/en/content/human-development-index-hdi

Johnson, M. A. (2019). *Becoming creole: Nature and race in Belize*. Rutgers University Press.

Killion, C., & Cayetano, C. (2009). Making mental health a priority in Belize. *Archives of Psychiatric Nursing, 23*(2), 157–165.

MacPherson, A. S. (2007). *From colony to nation: Women activists and the gendering of politics in Belize, 1912–1982*. University of Nebraska Press.

McClusky, L. J. (2001). *"Here our culture is hard": Stories of domestic violence from a Mayan community in Belize*. University of Texas Press.

Mental Health Association (MHA). (2021). Retrieved from https://www.mentalhealthassociation.bz/

Muhammad, N. (2015). *Insights into gang culture in Belize*. Reynolds Desktop Publishing.

Palacio, J. (Ed.). (2005). *The Garifuna: A nation across borders*. Benque Viejo del Carmen.

Ragsdale, A. H., & Anders, J. T. (1999). The *muchachas* of Orange Walk Town, Belize. In K. Kempadoo (Ed.), *Sun, sex, and gold* (pp. 217–236). Rowman & Littlefield.

Ragsdale, K., Anders, J. T., & Philippakos, E. (2007). Migrant Latinas and brothel sex work in Belize: Sexual agency and sexual risk. *Journal of Cultural Diversity, 14*(1), 26–34.

Rich, G. (2010). Integrating contemporary and traditional healing practices in Belize. *Shaman, 18*(1–2), 109–130.
Rich, G. (2017). Women in Belize. In C. Brown, U. Gielen, J. Gibbons, & J. Kuriansky (Eds.), *Women's evolving lives: Global and psychosocial perspectives* (pp. 239–256). Springer.
Rich, G., Gentle-Genitty, C., Simplis, K., & Karikari, I. (2014). *Psychology and the helping professions in Belize: Historical past and present realities*. Paper presented at the annual meeting of the American Psychological Association, Washington, DC
Rich, G., Simplis, K., & Simmons, J. (2016). *Current status of psychology and mental health services in Belize*. Paper presented at the Annual meeting of the American Psychological Association, Denver
Sawatzky, H. L. (1971). *They sought a country: Mennonite colonization in Mexico*. University of California Press.
Shoman, A. (2011). *A history of Belize in thirteen chapters* (2nd ed.). The Angelus Press.
The National Committee for Families and Children (NCFC). (1995). *The right to a future: A situation analysis of children in Belize*. UNICEF BELIZE.
Udz, S. (2014). Improving Kriol language attitude and English accuracy. In P. R. Cook (Ed.), *Educational trends: A symposium in Belize, Central America* (pp. 50–79). Cambridge Scholars Publishing (CSP).
University of Belize. (2021). Retrieved from https://www.ub.edu.bz/academics/academic-faculties/
Van Mead, N., & Blason, J. (2014, June 24). *The 10 world cities with the highest murder rates – in pictures*. Retrieved from https://www.theguardian.com/cities/gallery/2014/jun/24/10-world-cities-highest-murder-rates-homicides-in-pictures
Waight, B. T. (2020). *Fire heart: The life and teachings of a traditional Maya healer of Belize*. Zena Adalie Waight.
Waldram, J. B. (2020). *An imperative to cure: Principles of Q'eqchi' Maya medicine in Belize*. University of New Mexico Press.
Welcome Resource Center. (2021). Retrieved from https://www.welcomeresourcecenter.bz/
WHO. (2005). *Belize mental health atlas*. World Health Organization.
WHO. (2009). *WHO-AIMS report on mental health system in Belize*. WHO and Ministry of Health.
Wilk, R. (1994). Colonial time and TV time: Television and temporality in Belize. *Visual Anthropology Review, 10*, 94–102.
Winer, R. A., Bennett, E., Murillo, I., Schuetz-Mueller, J., & Katz, C. L. (2014). Monitoring compliance to promote quality assurance: Development of a mental health clinical chart audit tool in Belize, 2013. *Psychiatric Quarterly, 86*, 373–379.
Yildirim, E. D., & Roopnarine, J. L. (2019). Positive discipline, hash physical discipline, and psychological aggression in five Caribbean countries: Associations preschoolers' early literacy skills. *International Journal of Psychology, 54*(3), 342–350.

Part III
Conclusion

Chapter 21
Past, Present, and Future of Psychology in Oceania and the Caribbean: A Conclusion Chapter

Neeta A. Ramkumar and Grant J. Rich

The future for psychology in the Caribbean and Oceania is exciting to consider. There are ample opportunities to apply psychological knowledge in island contexts. There is much to discover about mental health and traditional ways of healing. Although the map for avoiding Amero-centric perspectives, colonial agendas, and top-down relationships is still being written, the field of psychology depends on it. Psychologists are not only needed to support island societies, they will also contribute to—and perhaps challenge—global understandings of the human mind and human behavior. In this chapter we hope to offer a brief integration and summary of some key themes that have emerged over the course of this special book project as they relate to the further development of psychology in the Caribbean and Oceania. We shall succinctly delineate some common challenges and concerns expressed across these mostly archipelago nations, as well as note some of the nuances between both Oceania and the Caribbean as distinct regions, as well as differences within at the island/national level. Finally, we shall conclude with a list of website links of resources to psychology and mental health organizations, behavioral health associations, journals, and publications of relevance to scholars and practitioners working with these regions, nations, and islands.

One indicator of the significance of our book's topic is that most of the authors struggled to keep their chapters within word limits, as there is much to say, and often few publication outlets receptive to the topic. The editors of the book also struggled with the word counts to keep publishing expenses manageable. Thus, this final chapter is by necessity brief, but we hope readers find it a relevant starting point for continued dialogue within and between our regions and islands.

N. A. Ramkumar
Psychology Across Borders, Austin, TX, USA

G. J. Rich (✉)
Walden University, Juneau, AK, USA

G. J. Rich, N. A. Ramkumar (eds.), *Psychology in Oceania and the Caribbean*, International and Cultural Psychology,
https://doi.org/10.1007/978-3-030-87763-7_21

As noted in our introductory chapter, and as mentioned by authors of most of the chapters in this book, nations and islands in both the Caribbean and Oceania share common environmental and climate adaptation challenges and concerns. Both regions are plagued by regularly occurring natural disasters, including hurricanes/cyclones, earthquakes, flooding, landslides, tsunamis, and volcanic eruptions. A major disaster can decimate the local and national economy for years, and even decades, disrupting agriculture and food supplies, housing, businesses, and educational institutions and displacing families and sometimes entire communities. Climate change as well has led to painful realities regarding decisions to remain or to leave traditional lands, as well as the economic, social, political, educational, community, family, and personal impacts that accompany such decision-making. The repeated effect of many events over time impacts a country's ability to develop and places island communities at increased psychological vulnerability. Psychologists can support climate resilience by being part of multidisciplinary teams planning for disaster preparation/risk reduction and addressing community needs holistically.

Both Oceania and the Caribbean also typically share post-colonial and neo-colonial realities and concerns in terms of implications for reducing health, educational, and economic disparities, and for creating community and national identities that are acceptable and meaningful to all, and ensuring service delivery is accessible and appropriate for all. Indiscriminate application of Western psychological constructs and principles to islander communities may inadvertently promote colonial agendas (McNamara & Naepi, 2018). The Caribbean and Pacific Islands are made up of multicultural, multiracial societies with distinct demographic, economic, and sociocultural contexts. Definitions of mental/emotional normality and cultural norms must be formulated by members of the specific cultural group as baseline data on mental health conditions is gathered. As an example, suicide rates vary dramatically across Oceania. For instance, suicide rates in Fiji have at times been reported as the highest in the entire world (e.g., Leckie, 2019; Prasad, 2010). In contrast, Samoa's suicide rate has at times, such as in the mid-1960s, been rated as the lowest in the world, and it continues to be at an extremely low rate today (0.7/100,000), especially when compared to recent estimates of global average rates of 9.30 suicides per 100,000 people (Pal & Pal, this volume). Thus, making sweeping generalizations about all dimensions relevant to mental health and to social organization and daily life is typically ill-advised, without also noting existing variation.

Another commonality is challenges and opportunities in higher education which notably impact mental health capacity, indigenous psychologies, and culturally responsive treatment options. Smaller population nations by definition have smaller numbers of potential workforce members from which to draw, and this is especially true when considering specialized professional needs, such as in healthcare, and in the behavioral health work force. In all of the countries surveyed in this book, there is a scarcity of MD psychiatrists, PhD psychologists, and MSW social workers. Many islands/nations do not have a large enough population to support full educational programs in those disciplines. Likewise, ensuring existing care is available outside of capital cities and large urban areas, in rural villages and more remote islands, is a huge logistical challenge. Isolation due to geographic distance, both within and between, islands are unique from mainland regions in that education and services are disrupted as much as supply chains. Some have adopted regularly scheduled traveling healthcare teams to meet this need. As Internet connectivity in these regions improves, appropriate use and implementation of distance education and telehealth technologies are critical solutions for bridging gaps in access—a fact that became evident worldwide in the COVID-19 pandemic.

Of course, there are also differences between the two regions. For instance, Oceania's islands/nations are generally more remote than are most islands/nations in the Caribbean, as much of the Caribbean is within a brief plane ride in distance from the mainland USA or Mexico, Central or South America, or even a boat ride to neighboring countries. In addition, the island/nation populations of Oceania tend to be smaller than those in the Caribbean, but still vary within the region. For instance, Papua New Guinea has a population estimated at about 8.5 million, and Aotearoa New Zealand has a population of about 4.7 million, while Federated States of Micronesia have a population of 103,000, and American Samoa has a population of 56,700 to name several of the nations/territories covered in this book's Oceania section (List of Oceanian Countries by Population, 2021). Similarly, island populations vary tremendously in the Caribbean, from the largest, such as Cuba, Haiti, and the Dominican Republic, each with over ten million in population, to the smallest such as Dominica (71,000), St. Kitts and Nevis (46,000), and Montserrat (5000) (List of Caribbean Countries by Population, 2021). Economic differences within the region are also notable. Within the Caribbean, the Gross Domestic Product per capita ranges widely in the Caribbean from relatively high, such as Puerto Rico ($41,198), Trinidad and Tobago ($33,026), and St. Kitts and Nevis ($29,098), to very low, such as Jamaica ($9726), Belize ($8467), and Haiti ($1940) (List of Caribbean Countries by GDP (PPP), 2021). Population size and distance from larger population centers have significant implications for economies and for availability of services such as provision of higher education and behavioral health care.

In terms of shared strengths, a reader of this volume will note that many of the islands/nations in both Oceania and the Caribbean found innovative methods to utilize existing workforce and educational infrastructures to leverage more specialized behavioral health scope of practice and expertise. For instance, several nations (e.g., Belize and Fiji) have utilized additional mental health certification and training of nurses, to diagnose and potentially treat psychiatric disorders, sometimes by dispensing psychotropic medications. Some universities are arranged as hubs for the region and may provide some opportunities and sensitivity to regional differences in development, culture, and situations. The University of West Indies in Mona, Jamaica, often trains students from around the Caribbean, and the University of the South Pacific in Suva, Fiji, was formed by 14 Oceanic countries and accepts Caribbean students in exchange programs. A number of smaller nations/islands also utilize work or educational exchange programs, which may be particularly effective when islanders are trained abroad and motivated to return to serve in their nation of birth. Seeking education abroad may be more expensive and less culturally relevant than local opportunities, but may offer a greater depth and range of study opportunities. Governments must work towards retaining local mental health expertise in an era of mass migration from island regions.

Another shared development and strength of many nations and islands in Oceania and the Caribbean is the renaissance on indigenous activism and advocacy and a movement in many cases from simply cultural survival beyond to cultural thriving. In many of the regions, the descendants of the first peoples continue to live and to work, whether one notes the Maya of Belize (Coe & Houston, 2015; Sharer & Traxler, 2005), the descendants of the Arawak/Taíno in the Caribbean (e.g., Hill & Santos-Granero, 2010; Rouse, 1993), or the descendants of groups such as the Lapita in Oceania (e.g., Kirch, 1997). In some places the post-colonial process has been peaceful, whereas in others there has been violence, including coups, civil war, and genocide, as examples such as in modern Fiji (e.g., Prasad, 2010; Thomson, 2008), and among the Maya of modernity (e.g., Kistler, 2018) demonstrate. A number of the chapters in this book have indicated the vital roles played in contemporary behavioral health services and treatment of careful, selective implementation and integration of some traditional healing practices with allopathic practice (see chapters on Belize, Suriname, and New Caledonia in this book); several other chapters in this book have noted the significant role played in behavioral health service and treatment of both Christianity and other faith traditions, including traditional religions, such as described in the chapters on Belize, Haiti, and Samoa. Other traditional supports for behavioral health issues were also noted in most chapters, such as the role of the family and village/community in assisting persons and families in psychological or social distress. Professional counseling may need to involve traditional healers and use of an alternative traditional etiology to frame mental illness experiences (Te Pou o Te Whakaaro Nui, 2010) and transform existing stigma.

If you, the reader, are interested in, or perhaps are currently involved in, contributing to the psychology education and research in Pacific and/or Caribbean regions without being from these communities, we offer some considerations for positive cross-cultural exchange. Indeed, global mental health requires an exchange of human capital to support growth of the profession (Fricchione et al., 2012). It is paramount that relationships with institutions and practitioners in higher-income countries remain collaborative. There is danger of exporting dominant standards and infrastructure in both research and practice that may not be appropriate for island contexts. Clarification of roles and agreement on how to maintain bidirectional inputs should occur at early stages of such partnerships. In terms of psychology education and training, supervisors and instructors from other countries must acknowledge that they may be expert in content, but not in context. Cross-cultural supervisory relationships necessitate enlightened collaborative processes (Pettifor et al., 2014). Since scholarly material is dominated by Western knowledge, discourse, and practice, decolonizing methodologies to indigenize learning and teaching must be intentionally engaged (McNamara & Naepi, 2018). Those in positions of power must navigate how to be in evaluative roles without imposing their world views. The context and learning environment created for developing psychologists are actually political acts in learning, teaching, research, and practice.

We hope that you, the reader, as we, the editors, found that this book's descriptions of the transformation of behavioral health systems in Oceania and the Caribbean are truly extraordinary while dispelling romanticized notions of life in paradisical regions. It is a story not either of simple stasis or of only linear change, but of one that continues to be written, and that encompasses hundreds and often thousands of years, reflecting strong personalities and sociocultural forces, including both tradition and change, integrating culturally nuanced innovations that aim for best practices for time and place. We someday hope to meet you all, if not in person or in community, through a revised edition of the present volume showcasing the forthcoming advances of psychology in the Caribbean and Oceania.

Websites for Select Psychological Organizations and Journals: Oceania and the Caribbean

Oceania
Oceania Society for Mental Health Professionals
 https://www.facebook.com/OSMHPacificMindsMatter/
 Pacific Behavioral Health Collaboration Council
 https://www.pbhcc.com

Federated States of Micronesia
SAMHSA: Directory of State Mental Health Authorities
 Mrs. Magdalena A. Walter
 Commissioner
 FSM Behavioral Health & Wellness Program
 Department of Health & Social Affairs
 P.O. Box PS-70,
 Palikir, Pohnpei, Federated States of Micronesia 96941
 Phone: 691-320-2619
 Fax: 691-320-5524
 Email: mwalter@fsmhealth.fm
 FSM Department of Health and Social Affairs
 https://hsa.gov.fm
 Behavioral Health and Wellness Program
 FSM Department of Health and Social Affairs
 https://hsa.gov.fm

Guam
Guam Psychological Association
 PO Box 12061
 Tamuning, 96931 Guam
 https://guampsychologicalassociation.org
 Guam Behavioral Health and Wellness Center

790 Gov. Carlos Camacho Road
Tamuning, Guam 96913
https://gbhwc.guam.gov/
SAMHSA: Directory of State Mental Health Authorities
Theresa C. Arriola
Director, Guam Behavioral Health and Wellness Center
Government of Guam
theresa.arriola@gbhwc.guam.gov
Phone: (671) 647-1901
Fax: (671) 649-6948

CNMI (Commonwealth of the Northern Mariana Islands)
Brabu Behavioral Health Services, CNMI
http://chcc.cnmi.mp/index.php/community-guidance-center/substance-abuse-prevention-services/project-brabu
James Edward H. Arriola
Brabu Behavioral Health Services
P.O. Box 7521 SVRB
Saipan, MP 96950
Email: jamesharriol@gmail.com
Community Guidance Center, CNMI Commonwealth Healthcare Corporation
http://chcc.cnmi.mp/index.php/community-guidance-center

Marshall Islands
RMI Ministry of Health and Human Services
https://rmihealth.org/
https://business.facebook.com/rmimoh/

Palau
Division of Behavioral Health, Palau Ministry of Health
http://www.palauhealth.org/

Fiji
Fiji Psychological Society
https://www.facebook.com/fijipsychologicalsociety/
fjpsychsociety@gmail.com

Vanuatu
Mental Health Vanuatu community
https://www.facebook.com/mentalhealthvanuatu/

American Samoa
SAMHSA: Directory of State Mental Health Authorities
Muavaefa'atashi John E. Suisala
Director American Samoa Government Department of Human and Social Services P.O. Box 997534, Centennial Building Suite 301 Pago Pago, American Samoa 96799 Phone: (684) 633-7506 Fax: Email: jsuisala@dhss.as

(Western) Samoa

Fa'ataua Le Ola – Samoa Lifeline
https://m.facebook.com/FLOsamoalife/

Hawai'i

Hawaii Psychological Association
(808) 521-8995
1188 Bishop Street, Suite 912
Honolulu, HI 96813
https://hawaiipsychology.org/
SAMHSA: Directory of State Mental Health Authorities
Edward Mersereau, L.C.S.W., C.S.A.C.
Deputy Director Behavioral Health Administration
State of Hawaii Department of Health
1250 Punchbowl Street, Room 325 Honolulu, Hawaii 96813
Email: edward.mersereau@doh.hawaii

Papua New Guinea

Mental Health Awareness for the People of Papua New Guinea
https://www.facebook.com/mentalhealthawaressforthepeopleofpng/
mentalhealthpng@gmail.com

Aotearoa/New Zealand

New Zealand Psychological Society
Wakefield House
Level 5, 90 The Terrace
Wellington 6011
https://www.psychology.org.nz/
office@psychology.org.nz
New Zealand Association of Counsellors
http://nzap.org.nz/
New Zealand Association of Psychotherapists
http://nzap.org.nz/

New Caledonia

CPNC Collège des Psychologues de Nouvelle Calédonie
https://www.facebook.com/CPNC-Coll%C3%A8ge-des-Psychologues-de-Nouvelle-Cal%C3%A9donie-773354332722702/?ref=page_internal

Australia

Australian Psychological Society
PO Box 38, Flinders Lane
Melbourne, Victoria 8009, Australia
https://www.psychology.org.au
contactus@psychology.org.au

Caribbean

CANPA: Caribbean Alliance of National Psychology Associations

https://canpanet.org/
Caribbean Journal of Psychology
http://ojs.mona.uwi.edu/index.php/cjpsy
Interamerican Journal of Psychology
http://www.psicorip.org/
APA: American Psychological Association
https://www.apa.org/
APA Division 52 (D52: International Psychology)
https://div52.net/

Barbados
Psychological Association of Barbados
P.O. Box 5069
Warrens, St. Michaels, Barbados
https://www.facebook.com/TheBarbadosSocietyofPsychology/
psychologistsbarbados@gmail.com

Bahamas
Bahamas Psychological Association
PO Box CB-13015
Nassau, Bahamas
https://bahamaspsych.org/
bahamaspsychassociation@gmail.com

Belize
Belize's Mental Health Association (MHA)
https://www.mentalhealthassociation.bz/

Bermuda
Bermuda Psychology Association (BPA)
P.O. Box HM 954
Hamilton, Bermuda HMDX
https://www.gov.bm/psychology
bermudapsychology@gmail.com
Bermuda Psychologists Council
P.O. Box HM 954
Hamilton, Bermuda HMDX
https://www.gov.bm/psychology
bdapsychcouncil@gov.bm

Cuba
Cuban Journal of Psychology
http://www.psicocuba.uh.cu/index.php/PsicoCuba
Cuban Society of Health Psychology/Sociedad Cubana de Psicologia de la Salud
Calle 27 No. 110 between M and N. Vedado, Plaza de la Revolution
Havana, Cuba
https://instituciones.sld.cu/psicosaludhabana/

mtabreu@infomed.sld.cu
Cuban Society of Psychology/Sociedad Cubana de Psicología
Calle Mazon No. 1168, E/c Baserrate y San Miguel
Vedado. Municipio Plaza
Provincia La Habana, Cuba 10400
mtabreu@infomed.sld.cu

Dominica
Dominica Psychological Society
c/o Social Services Department
Princess Margaret Hospital
Goodwill, Dominica
dominicapsychologicalsociety@gmail.com

Dominican Republic
Dominican Association of Psychology/Colegio Dominicano de Psicologos
CODOPSI
Av. Bolivar No. 809
Local 104
Primer Nivel, La Esperilla
Santo Domingo, Dominican Republic
https://codopsi.com.do/
codopsi@hotmail.com
FUNDEPSIC/La Fundación para el Desarrollo de la Psicología en el Caribe
Calle Uruguay No. 5
Edificio Profesional Don Cerame Apartamento 108
Gazcue, Santo Domingo, Dominican Republic
contact@fundepsic.com

French Guiana
Association of the Psychologists of French Guiana/Association Guyanaise des Psychologues
19 Rue Léonce PORRE a REMIRRE – BP 70
Rémire-Montjoly, French Guiana 97354
http://www.agp973.com/
psychologuesdeguyane@yahoo.fr

Guadeloupe
Association of the Psychologists of Guadeloupe/Association des Psychologues de la Guadeloupe
B.P. 123 Messagerie de Bergevin
97 110 Pointe-a-Pitre
Guadeloupe
aapsyg@yahoo.com

Guyana
Guyana Psychological Association

132 Noble's Lane, N/A North Melanie Damishana ECD
French Guyana
https://www.facebook.com/guypsychassociate/
guypsychassociate@gmail.com
WHO Caribbean Mental Health Systems
https://www.who.int/mental_health/evidence/mh_systems_caribbeans_en.pdf

Jamaica
The Jamaican Psychological Society
68 Lady Musgrave Road,
Kingston 10, Jamaica
https://www.jampsych.com/
info@jampsych.com

Haiti
Haiti Psychological Association/L'Association Haitienne de Psychologie
29 Rue du travail
Port au Prince, Haiti
https://ahpsy.org.ht/
info@ahpsy.org.ht

Puerto Rico
Puerto Rico Psychological Association/Asociacion de Psicologia de Puerto Rico
500 Ave. Muñoz Rivera
Condominio El Centro II, Suite 230-231
P.O. Box 363435
San Juan, Puerto Rico 00936-3435
http://www.asppr.net/
info@asppr.net
SAMHSA: Directory of State Mental Health Authorities
Suzanne Roig-Fuertes
Administrator
Mental Health and Anti-Addiction Services Administration
P.O. Box 607087,
Bayamon, Puerto Rico 00960-7087
Phone: 787-764-3670
Fax: 787-995-5164
Email: sroig@assmca.pr.gov

St. Kitts and Nevis
St. Kitts Mental Health Association
www.skmha.wordpress.com/about-us

Suriname

Suriname Society of Psychologists and Special Educators/Surinaamse Vereniging van Psychologen en Orthopedagogen
https://www.facebook.com/svpo80/
svposecretariat@gmail.com

Trinidad and Tobago

Trinidad and Tobago Association of Psychologists
P.O. Box 887, 92 Wrightson Road
Port of Spain, Trinidad and Tobago
https://psychologytt.org
secretary@ttpsych.org

US Virgin Islands

Association of Virgin Island Psychologists
PO Box 302037
St Thomas, VI 00803
http://www.vipsychologists.org/index.html

References

Coe, M., & Houston, S. D. (2015). *The maya* (9th ed.). Thames & Hudson.

Fricchione, G. L., Borba, C., Alem, A., Shibre, T., Carney, J., & Henderson, D. (2012). Capacity building in global mental health: Professional training. *Harvard Review of Psychiatry, 20*(1), 47–57. https://doi.org/10.3109/10673229.2012.655211

Hill, J. D., & Santos-Granero, F. (Eds.). (2010). *Comparative Arawakan histories*. University of Illinois Press.

Kirch, P. V. (1997). *The Lapita peoples: Ancestors of the oceanic world*. Blackwell.

Kistler, S. A. (Ed.). (2018). *Faces of resistance: Maya heroes, power, and identity*. University of Alabama Press.

Leckie, J. (2019). *Colonizing madness: Asylum and community in Fiji*. University of Hawai'i Press.

List of Caribbean Countries by GDP (PPP). (2021). Retrieved from https://en.wikipedia.org/wiki/List_of_Latin_American_and_Caribbean_countries_by_GDP_(PPP)

List of Caribbean Countries by Population. (2021). Retrieved from https://en.wikipedia.org/wiki/List_of_Caribbean_countries_by_population

List of Oceanian Countries by Population. (2021). Retrieved from https://en.wikipedia.org/wiki/List_of_Oceanian_countries_by_population

McNamara, R. A., & Naepi, S. (2018). Decolonizing community psychology by supporting indigenous knowledge, projects, and students: Lessons from Aotearoa New Zealand and Canada. *American Journal of Community Psychology, 62*(3–4), 340–349. https://doi.org/10.1002/ajcp.12296

Pal, S., & Pal, S. (this volume). Melanesian mental health and psychiatric services: Perspectives from Papua New Guinea. In G. Rich & N. A. Ramkumar (Eds.), *Psychology in Oceania and the Caribbean*. Springer.

Pettifor, J., Sinclair, C., & Falender, C. A. (2014). Ethical supervision: Harmonizing rules and ideals in a globalizing world. *Training and Education in Professional Psychology, 8*(4), 201–210. https://doi.org/10.1037/tep0000046

Prasad, R. (2010). *Tears in paradise: Suffering and struggles in Indians in Fiji 1879–2004* (Revised ed.). Glade Publishers.

Rouse, I. (1993). *The Tainos: Rise and decline of the people who greeted Columbus*. Yale University Press.

Sharer, R., & Traxler, L. P. (2005). *The ancient Maya* (6th ed.). Stanford University Press.

Te Pou o Te Whakaaro Nui. (2010). *Talking therapies for Pasifika peoples: Best and promising practice guide for mental health and addiction services*. Retrieved from: https://www.tepou.co.nz/resources/talking-therapies-for-pasifika-peoples/152

Thomson, P. (2008). *Kava in the blood* (Revised ed.). Booksurge Publishing.

Index

G. J. Rich, N. A. Ramkumar (eds.), *Psychology in Oceania and the Caribbean*, International and Cultural Psychology, https://doi.org/10.1007/978-3-030-87763-7